ONE WEEK IN JUNE
THE
U.S. OPEN

ONE WEEK IN JUNE
THE
U.S. OPEN

*Stories and Insights About Playing on the Nation's Finest Fairways
from Phil Mickelson, Arnold Palmer, Lee Trevino, Grantland Rice,
Jack Nicklaus, Dave Anderson, and Many More*

INTRODUCTION BY
Tom Kite, World Golf Hall of Fame inductee

FOREWORD BY
Don Wade, former senior editor at *Golf Digest*®

STERLING
New York

STERLING
New York

An Imprint of Sterling Publishing
387 Park Avenue South
New York, NY 10016

ISBN 978-1-4027-6629-9 (hardcover)
ISBN 978-1-4027-8398-2 (ebook)
ISBN 978-1-4027-9754-5 (paperback)

Distributed in Canada by Sterling Publishing
c/o Canadian Manda Group, 165 Dufferin Street
Toronto, Ontario, Canada M6K 3H6
Distributed in the United Kingdom by GMC Distribution Services
Castle Place, 166 High Street, Lewes, East Sussex, England BN7 1XU
Distributed in Australia by Capricorn Link (Australia) Pty. Ltd.
P.O. Box 704, Windsor, NSW 2756, Australia

For information about custom editions, special sales, and premium and corporate purchases, please contact Sterling Special Sales at 800-805-5489 or specialsales@sterlingpublishing.com.

Manufactured in the United States of America

2 4 6 8 10 9 7 5 3 1

www.sterlingpublishing.com

TABLE OF CONTENTS

THE PREWAR ERA 27

FOREWORD

My introduction to the U.S. Open actually began at the Concord Country Club in Concord, Massachusetts, which never came close to hosting the Open.

I began caddying there in 1963, became caddie master a few years later, and then worked for many years as an assistant to the longtime club professional, Harold Cahoon. Harold became friends with Bobby Jones, who was studying at Harvard following the end of his competitive golf career in 1930, the year he completed the unprecedented Grand Slam by winning the U.S. and British Opens and Amateurs. Jones was never particularly comfortable with his celebrity and liked to come out and play Concord because no one ever bothered him. Through Harold's stories, I came to appreciate Jones both as a competitor and as a person of uncommon grace and character.

Harold was also a close friend of Francis Ouimet, who, as a nineteen-year-old amateur, beat Harry Vardon and Ted Ray—the great British professionals of the day—in an eighteen-hole playoff for the 1913 U.S. Open at the Country Club in Brookline, Massachusetts, where he had learned the game as a caddie. He was also the winner of two U.S. Amateurs (the first player to win both an Open and an Amateur), played on eight Walker Cup teams, captained two others, and was the first American to serve as captain of the Royal and Ancient Golf Club of St. Andrews.

One blazingly hot and humid summer day in 1964, Harold telephoned me at home and asked me to come right over to the club. He said he had a doubles loop for me with Mr. George K. Whitney and a guest. Now, you should understand that Mr. Whitney was the ideal person to caddie for. Generally, he'd show up at 1 p.m. with his wife, Una, and they'd go out. They raced around the course—typically it would take them under three hours depending on how many groups they played through—and he always gave his caddie a crisp ten-dollar bill, this at a time when an "A" caddie got three dollars a bag.

I arrived at the pro shop and was introduced to none other than Francis Ouimet, a dear friend of Mr. Whitney and still very much a hero in the

Boston area. I remember vividly that Mr. Ouimet had a small leather golf bag—a blessing given the heat and humidity—and he had a set of Spalding Elite irons that had been given to him a year earlier to commemorate his victory in the Open fifty years before. They were beautiful clubs that had his signature engraved on each one. On the soles of the irons, instead of numbers, they had old-fashioned names like *niblick*, *mashie niblick*, and so on.

Mr. Ouimet was seventy-one at the time, but he still played beautifully. What I remember was his interest in me and his kindness. He asked about my golf game (mediocre) and how I was doing in school (ditto). When we finished, he shook my hand, apologized for not playing better, and thanked me. The pleasure was all mine.

It is said that there is no such thing as a bad Open, and I suppose that's true. But having said that, I must add that there are some Opens that are better than others. Certainly Harry Vardon's victory in 1900 would count, since he was arguably the best player in the world at the time. Ouimet's win in 1913 was one for the ages since he was the first native-born American to win the national championship and was a person of both modesty and grace. Walter Hagen's wins in 1914 and 1919 make the list because he was Walter Hagen. The same goes for Gene Sarazen in 1922. Any Open Bobby Jones won is likely to be on everyone's list, but his playoff win over Al Espinosa at Winged Foot in 1929 is almost certainly a lock because he sank an impossible putt on the seventy-second hole to get into a playoff. In the years since, thousands of players have concluded their rounds on the West Course by trying to replicate Jones's feat. Few have. His victory at Interlachen in 1930 was crucial since that was the year he completed the Grand Slam.

Moving into the modern era, you'd have to count Byron Nelson's victory in 1939, since it was his only win in the Open. The Bobby Jones Rule absolutely applies to Ben Hogan, who won his first of four Opens in 1948 at Riviera. By his own admission, his most emotional Open victory came in a playoff at Merion (most people's sentimental favorite among Open courses), since it marked his comeback from a near-fatal automobile accident, but his greatest Open win may have come in 1953—the year he won the Masters, the Open, and the British Open—because it came on a brutally difficult Oakland Hills course.

You will notice one name that is glaringly absent from discussions of great Opens: Sam Snead, who never won the Open but finished second three times. That the Slammer never won the Open is one of the game's saddest asterisks and most enduring mysteries. He often compared the Open to "the girl that got away," and his failures haunted him.

Tommy Bolt's win in 1958 was immensely popular among the writers because he was always good for a quote. Witness this gem: After the first round, Bolt confronted Tom Lobaugh, who was covering the Open for the local *TulsaWorld*, and complained because Lobaugh's story had given Bolt's age as 49 instead of 39.

"Sorry, Tommy," said Lobaugh. "It was a typo."

"Typo my ass," said Bolt. "It was a perfect four and a perfect nine."

Tommy Bolt was beautiful.

If writers liked Tommy Bolt for his quotes and all the great anecdotes associated with his name, they absolutely loved Arnold Palmer for simply being Arnold Palmer.

Arnold Palmer won just one U.S. Open, but it was a thing of beauty. The year was 1960 and the place was Cherry Hills Country Club near Denver. All Palmer did was go out and shoot a 30 on the front nine of the final round and then outduel an aging Hogan and a nineteen-year-old amateur of promise named Jack Nicklaus on the inward nine. The betting here is that Palmer's victory would make anyone's top five list of the greatest U.S. Opens.

In true Palmer fashion, his losses were often as dramatic as his wins. He finished second four times, with three of those coming in playoffs, one of them to Nicklaus in 1962 at Oakmont Country Club near Pittsburgh, Palmer's backyard.

Like Hogan, Nicklaus was the perfect Open player. He won four Opens and was runner-up in four others. There were many reasons for Nicklaus's success in the Open, but the biggest might be that he loved the pressure. He always said that he had an advantage in the Open because once the USGA ran up its flag, he felt two-thirds of the field choked themselves out of contention. The record suggests he was probably right.

Two other players who enjoyed being in the cauldron that is the U.S. Open were also two of Nicklaus's greatest rivals, Lee Trevino and Tom Watson. Trevino won two Opens, one at Merion, where he beat Nicklaus in a playoff, and the other at Oak Hill, where he was the first player to shoot four rounds in the 60s. Watson won the 1982 Open at Pebble Beach in dramatic fashion, chipping in from the rough on the seventy-first hole to edge Nicklaus by two strokes.

No listing of great Opens would be complete without Tiger Woods's victory at Pebble Beach in 2000, where he won by an almost unbelievable fifteen strokes. It was his first of three Open victories, the most unlikely being in 2008, when he beat Rocco Mediate in a playoff. It was unlikely because as a general rule, people aren't supposed to win the Open playing five rounds on a broken leg.

As a writer who has been covering golf since 1978, I have some personal favorites among the Opens, mostly because I have some personal favorites among the players.

I took great pleasure in watching Curtis Strange win back-to-back Opens in 1988 and '89, but especially his playoff victory over Nick Faldo in 1988 because it came at the Country Club, one of my favorite places in golf. He played beautiful golf in each round but especially in the playoff against a man who had a game that was ideally suited to the Open. Like Snead's, Faldo's failure to win an Open is surprising.

I was also delighted when Tom Kite won in 1992 at Pebble Beach. We had collaborated on many pieces for *Golf Digest* and I knew how much the Open meant to him, his wife, Christy, their three kids, and his beloved friend and teacher, Harvey Penick.

Having said all that, my favorite Open was Ken Venturi's dramatic win at Congressional Country Club in 1964. His game, which once held so much promise, had fallen victim to injuries and self-doubt. A man of considerable pride, he had been reduced to asking for sponsor's exemptions. But on the eve of the Open, his game had begun to turn around, and if he didn't exactly arrive at Congressional brimming with confidence, at least he had cause for hope.

On the final day of the Open (the last year thirty-six holes were played on the final day) the weather was brutally hot and humid. By the end of the first round, Venturi was hallucinating. A local physician, John Knowles, talked to Venturi between rounds, essentially begging him to withdraw, citing his well-grounded fears that the conditions could literally kill Venturi.

"Doc," Venturi said, "I'm already dead. I've got no place else to go."

Bobby Jones once said that there is no courage in golf because there is no physical danger, but on that day, in that place, Venturi showed enormous courage because there was considerable danger.

Playing the final hole, Venturi struggled to simply walk toward the green. Joe Dey, the executive director of the USGA, who had walked with the final group, offered his support to Venturi on the final hole.

"Ken, it's all downhill to the green, so how about holding your chin up, so that when you come in as a champion you'll look like one," Dye told him.

That's precisely what Venturi did, and when he sank the final putt, he dropped his putter, raised his arms, and collapsed in tears.

"My God, I've won the Open," he said.

And not just any Open, but perhaps the most dramatic Open in history.

In the pages that follow, we've tried to gather a collection of wonderful pieces by outstanding writers that capture the special flavor of the Open. To the extent that we have, then we've been successful and we hope you enjoy this book.

—Don Wade

INTRODUCTION

My Memories of the U.S. Open

The U.S. Open has always meant an awful lot to me because I regard it, our national championship, as the number one major championship in the world, more important than the Masters Tournament, the British Open, the PGA Championship, the Players Championship, or any other event.

I played in my first Open when I was a nineteen-year-old junior at the University of Texas. The 1970 U.S. Open was played outside Minneapolis at Hazeltine National Golf Club, at that time a relatively new course. Unfortunately, it became a very controversial championship, as the Robert Trent Jones design was criticized by many of the players, most famously Dave Hill, who said they ruined a good farm when they built the course.

But Hazeltine was my first U.S. Open, so I have many fond memories of that tournament. One of those was the drive from Texas to Minnesota with my mother and father. It was a long, two-and-a-half-day trip, but it was a wonderful experience, with lots of excitement and anticipation for all three of us. I did have a little experience playing in national championships, having competed in the U.S. Junior Amateur in 1966 and 1967 and the U.S. Amateur in 1968 and 1969. But this was my first Open, and I was unbelievably pumped about playing in the tournament I had watched on TV for so many years.

Ben Crenshaw, whom I played a lot of junior golf with as a kid in Austin and as a teammate at Texas, also qualified for that Open, and we had the opportunity to play some practice rounds with fellow Texans Lee Trevino and Charlie Coody, which was special. They gave us some great tips that somewhat prepared us for what we could expect during the tournament. But truth be known, nothing could have prepared me for the conditions I encountered at Hazeltine. The winds were strong, the fairways narrow, the rough deep, and the greens firmer and faster than any I had ever seen. I played poorly, shooting 81–74, missing the cut by a bunch. But even with all that, it was a wonderful trip and I gained some good experience.

I was not able to qualify for the 1971 Open at Merion because we were returning from the Walker Cup matches at St. Andrews, but from 1972 on I played every year through 2003, then gained a return trip in 2005. Now, that is a lot of U.S. Opens!

I always believed that the conditions at the U.S. Open fit my game better than those at any of the other majors. Unlike the Masters or the British Open, you must hit a lot of fairways and greens, and that was right up my alley. Playing from the rough all day at a U.S. Open will earn you quick trip home. Obviously, one also has to putt well, scramble well, and manage his game intelligently and patiently, and traditionally, those are all my strengths. But surprisingly, until I won in 1992, I had very few top-ten finishes and really had not contended in any U.S. Open.

The Open is without a doubt the most physically, psychologically, and emotionally exhausting event we play. I am always amused when a reporter asks the second- or third-round leader whether he will sleep well that night. After battling a U.S. Open course all day, I can assure you that getting to sleep was never a problem for me.

So what finally clicked for me at Pebble Beach in 1992, enabling me to win my first major after going almost twenty years without one? That week I did an excellent job of staying in the present—maybe the best job I've ever done.

My friend and teacher, the late Harvey Penick, used to tell me to "take dead aim." This was his mantra, which all of his students took with them when they went to play a tournament. What I took from this saying was that you have to concentrate on every single shot as though it is the absolute most important thing in the world to you. For that time frame when you are playing the shot, it has to be more important than your family, your health, your bank account, or anything else that could divert your concentration. Harvey said that it is crucial that you stay in the moment, be as committed as possible to playing a great shot, and not worry about what happened before or what might happen in the future. This is so easy to say and so difficult to do, and Harvey understood that. He warned me about writing my acceptance speech or thinking about how my name would look engraved on the trophy while there was still work to be done. As important as staying in the present is each and every week on tour, it is especially true at the Open because the conditions are so demanding that you can let a round get away from you in an instant. But "taking dead aim" is exactly what I was able to do at Pebble in 1992.

What was interesting about Pebble Beach that year is that the course conditioning got away from the United States Golf Association. What most people who watched the final round of that Open on television remember was how no one could hold a green with any approach shots and how the greens had turned a dirty brown color from lack of water. But in reality, early in the week the course was probably a bit too easy. Prior to the start on Thursday, the players were talking about how "fair" the course was and how much they were looking forward to a "reasonable Open setup." Anytime you hear a golf professional talk about how fair a course is, you can usually assume he thinks he can shoot a low score. Well, the weather was benign and the course soft leading up to Thursday's start, and those conditions continued into the first couple of rounds. The scoring reflected it, too. Dr. Gil Morgan got to twelve under par on Saturday, the first time a player ever got to double digits under par in a U.S. Open. But it was a completely different story come Sunday's final round. The USGA, expecting another day of relatively calm conditions, let the course dry out, and they set the course up to combat the low scores. The problem was that the winds unexpectedly increased throughout the day, actually gusting well over forty miles per hour for much of the afternoon. What had been "reasonable" quickly became "unfair."

Can anyone who has played Pebble Beach believe that not one player in the last fifteen groups, thirty players in all, could hit even the short par-3 seventh in regulation? The hole is only 105 yards and plays downhill, and most days a sand wedge is the preferred club. But on that Sunday many were choosing way more club than a wedge, trying somehow to keep the ball out of the wind. I chose a knockdown six iron, and the wind still turned the ball inside out, blowing it well left of the green. Faced with a daunting pitch shot over the back bunker to a rock-hard green, I played the pitch of my life, landed the ball perfectly, and watched in pure amazement as it slammed into the flagstick and dropped into the hole—a much-needed birdie on a hole where fours, fives, and even some sixes were recorded that day.

The course continued to play much more difficult than anyone expected, and when Colin Montgomerie finished early with a score of an even-par 288, Jack Nicklaus, who was commenting for ABC, congratulated him on winning his first major championship. I was on only the eleventh hole when that occurred and was not aware of his comments. But what Jack did not realize was that I was able to stay in the moment and "take dead aim" for the rest of the day. I shot an even-par 72 on Sunday to finish at three under, 285, for a two-stroke victory over Jeff Sluman. Finally, the monkey was off my back.

By and large, I think the USGA does an excellent job of selecting and setting up courses for our national championship. The Open is supposed to be a complete examination of a player's game, and I think that is usually true. The list of players who have won the Open verifies that most times the USGA gets it right.

But if I have any criticisms of the USGA, these are the two:

First, the USGA has a tendency to return to pretty much the same courses over and over. It's not exactly a rota like the British Open, but its pretty darn close. My criticism is not that these are not deserving courses. Who could honestly say that Winged Foot, Bethpage, Baltusrol, Shinnecock, and Oak Hill are not deserving? It just that the U.S. Open is our national championship, not just the Northeast's championship. Oh, sure, occasionally the USGA will head out to California to play Pebble Beach or Olympic and might even make a rare trip to Oklahoma to play Southern Hills. But most of the selections are close to the USGA's headquarters in New Jersey, rarely visiting other areas of the country. The U.S. Open is our national championship and the course selections need to reflect that. Also, there are some wonderful courses that have been built in the last twenty years by some fabulous architects. They should not be excluded just because they do not have a pedigree. My point is that there are so many great golf courses in areas of the country that have never hosted a major championship that I think the USGA ought to expand its horizons and bring the Open to some of them.

Second, as I said earlier about Pebble Beach, sometimes in their desire to challenge the golfers and possibly protect par, the officials of the USGA let a course get away from them. There have been multiple instances where the green speeds were not compatible with the slopes or hole locations. The seventh hole at Shinnecock Hills in 1995 or the eighteenth hole at the Olympic Club in 1998 are just two examples of greens that were never designed to putt at U.S. Open speeds and firmness. The result is usually a bunch of angry golfers having a difficult time even finishing the round and some slightly embarrassed USGA officials that meekly apologize for the over-the-top situation. I endorse difficult and demanding, but when the officials go right to the edge, sometimes they go a bit too far.

Still, those two complaints are minor in the grand scheme of things. The U.S. Open remains my favorite tournament, the one that means the most to me, and again, it is my national championship. Being able to compete in a U.S. Open is special to anyone, but especially to any American that has that opportunity. Having your name engraved on the U.S. Open trophy is just a dream come true.

—Tom Kite

OPENING THE OPEN

Open-Minded Geniuses

The Peculiarities of the Course Setup Have Identified a Select Group of Conquerors

by Frank Hannigan, *Golf Digest*, June 1995

The U.S. Open Championship, bolstered by a century's worth of history, exemplifies a particular form of golf: grim and merciless. These qualities are a consequence of the meticulous preparation of the courses—what has come to be known as the "U.S. Open setup."

The U.S. Golf Association philosophy presents the good people as those who drive accurately, if not for great distance, who hit a high percentage of greens in regulation figures, and whose nerve endings can deal with abnormally fast and firm greens. The bad people spray the ball off the tee, attempt to make amends with a variety of garbage shots around the greens, and get out of sorts after suffering a double bogey.

Open courses, once prepared for the championship, are not fun. The USGA says a 10-handicap golfer should expect to shoot 91 on its creations. But that is only a mechanical estimate not taking into account the dejection that goes with endless searches for balls in high rough, not to mention the shock of stroking a 25-foot putt 15 feet past the hole. I make the novice 10-handicapper's Open score nearer 100.

The Open setup can be expressed numerically. Fairways will average just over 30 yards wide at Shinnecock Hills. They will be bordered by a six-foot-wide layer of two-inch "intermediate" rough. Beyond that is the real stuff, about five inches and lush from the rains of spring. The USGA calls it "primary" rough.

The greens, starved and on a life-support system for the week, will never reveal a ball mark. In Stimpmeter terms, they are an honest 11. They may be juiced up to 12 at Shinnecock, where the greens are relatively flat. Historically, the primary rough has been brought in menacingly close to the greens.

Originally there was no such thing as a U.S. Open setup. Between 1895 and World War I the courses were whatever the host clubs had in mind. Fairways were much wider than now; the greens were slow by our standards. But the primary rough may not have been mowed for a full season and was therefore brutal.

The USGA began to make fitful attempts to influence course conditioning during the 1920s. By the '30s, clubs were receiving written instructions from USGA headquarters. The instructions were sometimes ignored by the locals, whose members equated high scores with manhood. Oakmont, in particular, gave the USGA fits in an attempt to come up with a course on which nobody could break 300 over 72 holes.

Open courses were also prepared inconsistently after World War II. Riviera was too easy in 1948 and yielded record scores. But the USGA was more dismayed with the celebrated renovation of Oakland Hills in 1951 by architect Robert Trent Jones. There were only two scores under 70. One was Ben Hogan's epic 67 in the final round.

There was a similar aberration in 1955 at the Olympic Club, where the rough was absurd—the equivalent of the one-shot penalty for driving into a lateral water hazard.

The components for a definitive U.S. Open arrangement were then settled upon permanently by Richard Tufts, the most effective of USGA presidents, and Joe Dey, the USGA executive director and therefore head of its staff.

Tufts and Dey called for rough that would be the equivalent of a half-stroke penalty, one that would allow the player to advance the ball purposefully but without being able to stop it on the greens.

Today the USGA tracks what it calls "cost of rough" with an index calculated from breaking down all the scores on the 14 non-par-3 holes into those made from the fairways and from outside the fairway.

Last year the USGA got just about what it wanted at Oakmont with a "cost of rough" index of .47 per hole. Indeed, the USGA purred when it was learned that its champion, Ernie Els, hit five more greens over 72 holes (54 of 72) than anyone else in the field.

By 1960, with an improved financial situation, the USGA was able to exercise complete control over Open courses by assigning staff members to take up residence months in advance to make sure the host clubs did not do anything bizarre.

The challenge of the Open then has been remarkably static over the past 35 years. Shinnecock Hills, aside from vagaries of weather, will be much as it was for the 1986 Open, just as the Oakmont of 1994 was recognizable as the Oakmont of the 1983, 1973 and 1962 Opens.

The length of Open courses crept up gradually from little more than 5,000 yards in the gutta-percha-ball 1890s to more than 6,500 yards in the '20s. It settled in at about 7,000 yards in the 1960s.

There has been no appreciable change in distance in more than 30 years. The average score declines because of a general improvement in the breed; that is, there are many more excellent players today than there were in the '60s.

There is one notable recent innovation in the Open setup: "Chipping areas" have been installed to the rear and sides of some greens. These are zones 12 to 15 feet long, cut at fairway height. Essentially, they enlarge the size of the targets.

The number of "chipping areas" has been expanded to nine for this year's Open. The USGA says this innovation is an appropriate reaction to the common criticism that chipping, a vital part of the game, was eliminated at the Opens.

Personally, I find the USGA misguided in its attempt to be all things to all people. The "chipping areas" are as out of place at an Open as occasional patches of five-inch rough would be near some greens at the Masters.

Course preparation is a matter of personal preference reflecting the facets of the game the organizers want to emphasize. The Masters rewards power and exquisite work around the greens. Its fairways are some 15 yards wider than those at an Open, and the Masters rough is hardly worthy of the name. In 1994 the top-24 finishers in the Masters hit, on average, 47 fairways out of 56. By comparison, the top 24 in the 1994 Open at Oakmont hit only 35 fairways.

It's no accident then that Curtis Strange has won two Opens while Seve Ballesteros has prevailed twice in the Masters.

But course preparation, no matter how calculated, can only tilt to favor varied styles of play. It is not necessarily decisive. Nick Faldo, the most precise of modern players, seemed more likely to win two U.S. Opens than two Masters. Meanwhile Andy North, by any standard a wild driver, won two Opens. (I attribute North's Open record to a rare capacity for final-round resolution that far exceeded his ball-striking abilities.)

Over the years and under these conditions, a select group of players emerged who consistently excelled in the national championship. Since we live in the age of quantification and this is the Open's 100th anniversary, it is fitting to reflect on the most successful U.S. Open players and to confect a list of the best.

A list of the Open's best follows, but with two quirks. It consists of 11 players, rather than the customary 10, and they are divided into three clusters presented alphabetically, with no attempt to separate them internally, on the grounds that a genius is a genius.

The methodology is necessarily subjective and reflects the following credos:

- Winning, if not the only thing, matters more than any other factor.

- Credit must be given for finishing near the top consistently.

- Longevity matters. No consideration is given to anyone who played in fewer than 10 Opens.

- Even though no man can do better than beat his contemporaries, I am influenced by the knowledge that it's harder to win now than it used to be.

Here then are the U.S. Open all-time best, and why they are the best:

GROUP A

The Three All-Time Conquerors

Ben Hogan won four Opens in five attempts between 1948 and 1953. He missed 1949 while convalescing from an automobile accident in which his car was hit by a bus. He finished in the top 10 on 15 consecutive occasions; was a late bloomer who did not win his first Open until age 35. He was held in such reverence by the USGA that they modeled their setup, dating from the 1950s, on the way Hogan played the game—fairways and greens. Because of World War II, Hogan missed out on four other Opens as he was reaching his prime.

Hoganophiles insist their man won a fifth U.S. Open, the fifth being an event titled the Hale America National Open, played in 1942. They point to the USGA gold medal Hogan received as its winner. Once and for all, that was *not* a U.S. Open Championship. The USGA announced suspension of its championships for the duration of the war immediately after Pearl Harbor. The USGA did lend its name as a co-sponsor (along with the PGA of America and the Chicago District Golf Association) to the Hale America event run for war-related charities. And the USGA threw in a medal. It was played on the short and easy Ridgemoor Country Club in Chicago, where Hogan shot 271, a score still not achieved in real U.S. Opens. The week was jazzed up with non–U.S. Open sideshows such as a long-driving contest.

Bobby Jones played in his first Open in 1920, as an 18-year-old prodigy, when he tied for eighth. He played in only 10 more before he gave up competitive golf after his Grand Slam of 1930. Between 1923 and 1930, Jones won four Opens and was second three times—twice in playoffs. He put more space between himself and his contemporaries than any golfer ever: Walter Hagen and Gene Sarazen were without argument great players, but they were miles behind Jones, who finished ahead of them during his 11 Open years 18 of 22 times. His Open scoring average of 73.1 was a shot and a half better per round than Sarazen's and Hagen's. Tommy Armour, himself winner of both the U.S. and British Opens, said unashamedly that in casual rounds of golf he received a handicap from Jones of one hole (not one stroke) per nine. Suppose Jones did not pull back from golf at age 28, but went on playing through his 30s, the prime decade for most golfers: He would probably have won at least two more Opens during the 1930s and settled forever any discussion as to who was the best Open golfer.

Jack Nicklaus is unique in that he stayed at the peak of the game longer than any other golfer, which is to say he could stand the heat better. He had his first chance to win as a 20-year-old amateur in 1960, when he finished second to Arnold Palmer. His four wins were spread over 19 years between 1962 and 1980 and he might have won an unprecedented fifth but for Tom Watson's miraculous birdie-birdie finish in 1982 at Pebble Beach. While Nicklaus has continued to play, and his nature is such that he always imagines he has a chance, the reality is that he has not been a presence in any fourth round of an Open since 1982.

Group B

More Multiple Winners

Willie Anderson won four Opens between 1901 and 1905, three of them in succession, but he still had to depend on club jobs to earn a living. A troubled man who held 10 different club jobs between 1894 and 1910, Anderson died at the age of 32—alcohol was likely a factor. I have relegated Anderson in the group below the top, despite his four victories, because his competition was not the equivalent of what was to come. In Anderson's years, there were never more than 91 entries for the Open.

Julius Boros had the primary Open attributes. He was imperturbable and a magnificent driver. He was unique in his capacity to get the ball close to the hole from the snarly greenside rough, something he accomplished with a long and languid swing. From 1950 to 1965, he had 10 top-10 finishes in the event, including victories in 1952 and 1963. At 53, in 1973, Boros was still very much in the Open until the final holes.

Walter Hagen was second only to Nicklaus in number of top-10 finishes, with 16 to Jack's 18. He is the only one of the elite 11 who was not a straight driver. He coined the classic put-down of freak winners by saying, "Anybody can win the Open—once." (He waited to say that until he'd won it a second time in 1919.)

Hale Irwin is the only three-time U.S. Open champion. The Open plays right to his strong suits—driving accuracy and a tough mental approach to the game. Irwin has conquered the Open's famously long, hard par-4 holes with a series of magnificent long-iron shots. His first victory, at Winged Foot in 1974, came on the harshest Open course of modern times. He won with seven over par.

Gene Sarazen comes closest to Nicklaus in terms of longevity. He entered the scene with a victory in 1922 at Skokie (the first year tickets were sold, mostly to a gallery dying to see Jones) and he was still at the top in 1940 when he lost a playoff to Lawson Little. Happily, he has prevailed as well in mortal longevity as the Open's oldest living champion. He is now 93. *(Editor's note: Sarazen died four years later in 1999.)*

Group C

Exceptions to the Rules

Arnold Palmer is the only one in the hierarchy of 11 who did not win at least two Opens. He had the misfortune to lose three Open playoffs in a five-year span between 1962 and 1966. A superb driver of the ball in the sense of being both straight and long, Arnold continued to be a threat to win the Open years after he was no longer a factor in the other majors. He was near the lead in the final round of every Open from 1972 to 1975.

Alex Smith was one of the five brothers from Carnoustie who emigrated to the United States. His younger brother Willie won the 1899 Open by the record margin of 11 strokes; Macdonald Smith appears on all lists of the best players who did not win an Open. One of Alex Smith's two Open wins came in a three-man playoff with brother Mac and Johnnie McDermott. Alex was a constant threat with a total of eight finishes in the top three starting in 1898. He won despite his celebrated putting woes, which inspired his classic advice: "Miss 'em quick."

Lee Trevino was an obscure Texas player when he qualified for the 1967 Open. Trevino finished fifth and, with his Open prize of $6,000 as a stake, joined the tour. A year later he won at Oak Hill. He won a classic Open at Merion in 1971 by beating Nicklaus in a playoff. He derided the common criticism that the Open "takes the driver out of their hands" by pointing out that the narrow fairways didn't scare *him* out of using his driver.

This list illustrates just how influential the Open has been. Only one American, Sam Snead, did not win the Open but still managed to meet everyone's historical definition of greatness. Snead was undoubtedly poisoned for the Open by making an 8 on its 72nd hole in 1939 when 5 would have won him the title.

Snead's Open honors reveal that the Open, like all of golf, has to be dealt with on two levels. The mechanics are useless if the emotions run amok. And while there might be something like the ideal way to grip a club, there is no state of mind guaranteed to survive an Open fourth round. The mental states of the Open's three great conquerors could not have been more diverse.

Jones had a fierce battle internally. He wrote that, prior to a round, he "had that hollow feeling in the pit of my stomach, and my concern was to get the agony over, rather than to have the conflict started." He had a terrible time retaining big leads. Later, two other supreme players would leave the game early. They were Byron Nelson and Mickey Wright, both of whom said that golf had become intolerable.

For Nicklaus, the Open's final day was what he lived for. He actually used the words "relish" and "pleasure" to describe the prospect. Nicklaus concocted a strategic approach based on the notion that if he could just stay anywhere near the lead for three rounds, the fourth was his.

Hogan set out, and apparently succeeded, in making the Open nothing more than the most important of his rituals. He was paired with the amateur Bill Campbell in the first two rounds of the 1954 Open at Baltusrol. On the 16th hole of the second round, within a shot of the lead, Hogan told Campbell he was ready to go home. He said he had put so much effort into preparing and planning that he found the championship itself an anticlimax. Hogan's exact words, according to Campbell: "I am bored."

The Men of the USGA

from *The Majors* by John Feinstein

In all, 580 players advanced from the ninety locals to the twelve sectionals. They were joined by 170 players who were exempt from local qualifying, meaning that there were 750 players left to compete for the eighty-nine nonexempt spots available at Olympic.

On the Thursday before the sectionals would be held, exactly two weeks before the Open would begin, David B. Fay sat down at his desk at USGA Headquarters in Far Hills, New Jersey, with the names of the sixty-seven exempt players. His job on that morning was to begin making the pairings for the ninety-eighth U.S. Open.

Fay is the executive director of the USGA, a job he has held since Frank Hannigan stepped down from the job in 1989 to become a full-time journalist and TV commentator, working then for *Golf Magazine* (now for *Golf Digest*) and ABC. Although he does wear the occasional bow tie, Fay is hardly what you would expect in a man who runs the day-to-day operations of an organization that has long had an image of being both patrician and conservative.

Fay is forty-eight, a cancer survivor, and the father of two teenage girls who readily admits his favorite sport is baseball. "You don't have a soul if you don't love baseball," he often says. Fay grew up in the tiny New York City suburb of Tuxedo, New York, but he was a long way from being a rich kid. Fay was introduced to golf working as a caddy at the tony Tuxedo Club. He started playing golf there on Mondays, the one day of the week caddies were allowed to play, teaching himself the game. His parents knew nothing about golf even though his father had been a very good athlete growing up in New Jersey, excelling as a pitcher in high school.

"My dad was a renaissance man in his own way," Fay said. "He played baseball and he boxed and he never went to college. But he was also a pretty good actor. One year in summer stock he was in a show opposite Mae West."

Fay went to Colgate, where he joined the golf team as a walk-on, grew his hair long, and went to Woodstock in the summer of '69. "I wasn't your typical concertgoer though," he said. "I went to the concert one afternoon, to the races that night at Monticello, and played golf at the Concorde the next day." Another renaissance man.

One summer his father, a steamship captain, got him a job working on the SS *United States*, which at the time was the largest passenger ship in the world with accommodations for 1,900 people. Fay had what may be the worst summer job in the history of college students: "When someone got seasick, I went and cleaned up after them."

One particularly busy night, Fay was called to one of the larger staterooms on the ship. When the door opened, he immediately recognized the face, even though it was somewhat green. "The Duke of Windsor," Fay said. "He always traveled the Atlantic by ship and he always went on American ships after his abdication. I guess he wasn't comfortable on Cunard under the circumstances."

He wasn't comfortable that night either. Fay did what he had to do and left. When the ship got back to New York he told his father that he appreciated the help finding a job, but enough was enough. He went back to the

Tuxedo Club, where he worked in the pro shop taking care of carts and clubs. About a month after he had returned, one of the members, Stanley Mortimer, showed up with a special guest: the Duke of Windsor. As Fay was putting the Duke's clubs on his cart, the Duke kept staring at him.

"You have seen me before," Fay finally said. "It was on the SS *United States*."

The Duke stared for another moment and then his eyes widened in recognition. "Oh yes," he said without a hint of a smile. "I *do* remember you."

After college, Fay worked as an investment counselor in a New York bank, a job he found very dull. When his roommate at the time, a man named George Peper, quit his job as communications director for the Metropolitan Golf Association, Fay thought, I can do that job, and applied. He was hired, and two years later the USGA offered him a job across the river. By 1979, he was the advance man on site for most USGA events.

In fact, he spent his honeymoon in Toledo, advancing the 1979 U.S. Open. "I got married, had one day with [new wife] Joan, and then went to Toledo," he said. "Back then part of my job was to set up the ropes around the golf course. If nothing else, it got you in shape."

That U.S. Open was the year the famous "Hinkle Tree" was planted. Several USGA officials became very upset when Lon Hinkle, one of the longest hitters on tour, decided the best way to play the par-five eighth hole was to aim way left and hit his ball down the 15th fairway. Hinkle was a prominent player at the time—he would win twice that year and finish third on the money list—and some of the USGA muck-a-mucks thought his strategy was making a mockery of the golf course. So, after Hinkle had made his second straight birdie on Friday, they ordered Inverness officials to go out and buy a tree and plant it to the left of the tee so Hinkle couldn't hit the ball in that direction.

The officials returned with a black spruce tree and a bill for $120, which they dropped on Fay's desk. "I thought they were joking," Fay said. They weren't. It was the USGA that wanted the tree, and the USGA that paid for the tree.

Fay became the starter for the Open when Hannigan became executive director in 1982. Since ABC televised all 18 holes of the Open on Saturday and Sunday, the network wanted to give the viewers an idea of what it was like on the first tee of a major championship. Fay figured this would be his fifteen minutes of fame. He would be on camera as he introduced the players in the last several groups and also introduced the walking officials with the groups.

"It was almost as if they wanted it to be like boxing with a microphone being lowered from the ceiling," Fay said. "It wasn't really a big deal, but I had never been on national TV before. I didn't want to take a chance on ending up standing there doing a Ralph Kramden, you know, humana . . . humana . . . humana."

Fay brought little note cards with him to the tee and smoothly introduced all the players and officials. That night he called his father to see if he had watched.

"I watched," Don Fay said. "Can I ask you a question?"

"Sure."

"Why is it that a reasonably intelligent college graduate needs note cards to read a total of ten lines?"

"Well, Dad, I didn't want to make a mistake and . . ."

"Can I ask another question?" Don Fay said.

"Sure."

"Did I really pay all that money for college so you could be a starter?"

Fay never used notes again.

Late in 1985, Fay began experiencing stomach pains. His doctors ran a number of tests and came back with a frightening diagnosis: cancer, a form known as Burkitt's lymphoma. Burkitt's lymphoma is a very aggressive form of stomach cancer that is found most often in children and, for some reason, very often on the coast of West Africa. "Gee," Fay said when his oncologist explained all this to him, "this would certainly be a strange way to find out I had ancestors from the Ivory Coast."

There weren't a lot more laughs during the next six months. The doctors told him that because the lymphoma had been discovered early, there was a good chance he could beat it but only with very aggressive chemotherapy. Fay was in the hospital, most of the time in isolation, for the next six months. "After a while I was convinced that if the cancer didn't kill me, the chemo would," he said. "I looked at it like a poker hand I had been dealt. One way or the other, I had to play it."

Fay's major concern during those six months was his family. His daughters, Katie and Molly, were four and two. "My thought was, okay this is tough on me, but what if they have to deal with my not being around. That was what worried me most."

The chemo worked. Fay had made it his goal to get out of the hospital in time for the U.S. Open at Shinnecock. He did—leaving the day the championship began—but landed right back there with a fever. A month later, he left for good. He was completely bald and had lost forty-five pounds. A week later, he ran the girls' U.S. Junior Championship in Marysville, California. "I bulked up on Mexican food and ice cream," he said. "I gained sixteen pounds in nine days."

Three years later, completely cancer free, he replaced Hannigan. Like Hannigan, Fay approaches his job of putting the pairings together with both a sense of history and a sense of humor. Before he sat down to start his work, he always looked up the pairings from the last time the tournament had been played at that site. The Open had been played at Olympic in 1987 with Scott Simpson beating Tom Watson by one shot to win his only major title. Fay noticed that Simpson had played the first two days that year with Nick Price and Don Pooley. So he made an "if" pairing. Simpson and Price were both exempt. Pooley was in the sectional in Rockville, Maryland. If Pooley qualified, he would be reunited with Simpson and Price at Olympic.

Fay did that for one other pairing. In 1987, Hannigan had paired three U.S. Amateur champions: John Cook (1978), Mark O'Meara (1979), and Scott Verplank (1984). O'Meara and Cook were exempt; Verplank was also in Rockville. If Verplank made it, he would play with O'Meara and Cook again.

One pairing was automatic: Ernie Els, Justin Leonard, and Matt Kuchar—the defending champion, the British Open champion, and the U.S. Amateur champion. After that, Fay could get creative. Each year Fay put together his version of the BPNTHWAM threesome. In 1997 at Congressional the group had consisted of Davis Love III, Phil Mickelson, and Colin Montgomerie. Love had made himself ineligible for the pairing with his victory at the PGA. That left Mickelson and Montgomerie. Fay put Montgomerie in the group and then added David Duval, who had won at Houston three weeks earlier, his fifth victory in eight months, not to mention his near miss at the Masters. But he left Mickelson out, replacing him with Jim Furyk.

"I did it because I honestly thought on this particular golf course, right now, based on recent play, Furyk had a better chance to win," Fay said. "In fact, I wouldn't have been surprised if the winner had come from that threesome."

What's more, Fay doesn't like to be predictable. He then put together a couple of groups for fun: the "three-Ws" pairing—Tiger Woods, Lee Westwood, and Tom Watson. This was actually a wonderful threesome: the old Stanford man (Watson) and the young Stanford man (Woods), and the hottest young player in the U.S. (Woods) playing with the hottest young player in Europe (Westwood). He also came up with a "God Squad" pairing: Steve Jones, Bernhard Langer, and Tom Lehman, all born-again Christians, the first two very vocal about it. Fay then created his "old men" pairing: Senior Open champion Graham Marsh, Jack Nicklaus (limping on a bad hip), and Ben Crenshaw (limping after foot surgery). "They can push each other along," Fay said.

Years ago, Hannigan had taken an opposite tack with a threesome that involved Crenshaw. He had been convinced for years that Tom Shaw, a very solid player during the 1970s, was fibbing about his age, making himself a couple of years younger than he really was. So, in 1971, Hannigan paired him for the first two rounds with nineteen-year-old Crenshaw and twenty-four-year-old Johnny Miller, both very good and very fast getting around the golf course. The weather was hot and Hannigan couldn't resist sneaking out Friday afternoon to watch Shaw come up 18. "He looked as if he had played 36 that day," Hannigan said. "He was the portrait of Dorian Gray."

It turned out Hannigan was right about Shaw. For years, he listed his birth date in the PGA Tour media guide as December 13, 1942. But in 1988, he produced a birth certificate listing his DOB as December 13, 1938. The reason: being fifty meant he was eligible for the Senior Tour.

Fay had followed in the Hannigan tradition of trying to be imaginative in making pairings. But he had toned down in recent years. "I decided I had gone too far one year at the Women's Open when I put three players together because they were all in therapy," he said.

He had not, however, given up one of Hannigan's more hallowed traditions: the prick pairing. Hannigan swears he did not give the pairing its name, but he admits that each year he would put three players together he didn't like or who were generally disliked in the golf world. Insiders loved guessing the prick pairing each year, although more often than not it wasn't that difficult.

For 1998 Fay's prick pairing was Mark Brooks, Scott Hoch, and Andrew Magee. Brooks and Hoch were easy to figure: both were known as complainers, although to be fair, Hoch always softened what he was saying with a tangy sense of humor. He just had a way of saying the wrong thing at the wrong time. Brooks wasn't the least bit mean, he just seemed perennially unhappy, even after winning the PGA Championship in 1996. Neither was likely to be voted man of the year in the locker room.

By contrast, Magee was well liked in the locker room. The only real complaint about him from other players was that he tended to be very slow on the golf course. Fay's complaint was different. Sometime after President Clinton had taken his fall in Greg Norman's house in 1997, he had seen

Magee quoted as saying that if Clinton had been at his house, he might have kicked him down the stairs himself.

Like his predecessor Hannigan, Fay is a liberal Democrat, someone who readily admits that his politics are well left of most people in golf and certainly far to the left of almost everyone who plays on tour. But he says he would have been just as offended by the comment if a liberal Democrat had made it about a right-wing Republican. Thus Magee would join Brooks and Hoch.

Once he had finished placing all sixty-seven exempt players into threesomes, Fay forwarded copies of his work to Mike Butz, his assistant executive director; to Larry Adamson, the man in charge of tournament entries; and to Tom Meeks, the director of rules and competition. It would fall to Meeks to make any changes and fill in the remaining players after qualifying was over. Fay had assigned a specific starting time to two groups: the three Ws at 9:02 Pacific Time on Thursday and the group of Nick Faldo, Tom Kite, and Corey Pavin at the same time Friday. The reason: television. NBC, which had wrested the Open's TV rights from ABC beginning in 1995 at a price of $13 million a year, had asked that Woods be on the golf course during the time they were on the air on Thursday (3 to 5 p.m. Eastern time) and the same for Faldo on Friday.

Fay was surprised by the Faldo request. "The only thing I can think is that's prime time in Europe," he said. "But the way he's playing you would think Montgomerie or Westwood would be a higher priority." Nonetheless, if TV wanted Faldo in Euro prime time, TV would get Faldo in Euro prime time.

As soon as he saw Fay's pairings, Meeks had two problems: there were four groups that included two foreign players. Meeks believes that at the U.S. Open there should be at least two American players in every group—especially among the exempt players—unless it is impossible to do so. Second, he thought Fay hadn't left enough exempt players unassigned. He didn't want the pairings to look as if they were tiered: exempt players together and qualifiers together. Fay agreed on both points. Meeks was the detail guy. He would have the job of filling in the entire bracket on the morning of June 10 after all the qualifiers had been completed.

"David gets to have the fun," Meeks said, laughing. "I get to do the work."

Meeks was a perfect alter ego for Fay. He was fifty-five and had worked for the USGA for twenty-three years. Although he was a devout St. Louis Cardinal fan and, being from Indiana, a basketball junkie, there was no doubting the fact that his first love was golf. He was a good player—his handicap fluctuated between six and eight—who liked to say that he was one year away from being a very good player. "And next year," he would add, "I'll be two years away."

Meeks is the point man for the USGA at every Open. It is his job to finalize the pairings and, more important, work with the staff to get the golf course into as close to perfect shape—USGA style—as possible. He had already made several trips to Olympic and would arrive in San Francisco on the Friday before the tournament began to see what kind of shape it was in. Then, on Sunday, the day before most of the players arrived, he would tour the golf course and select the pin positions for the week.

"Hole locations," he corrected. "There's no such thing as a pin, it's a flag-stick. That means there's no such thing as a pin position. You pick a spot to locate the hole—a hole location."

The Masters had its patrons and its first nine and second nine; the USGA had hole locations. No one on NBC would be caught dead uttering the dreaded words "pin position."

But there would be an awful lot of talk about hole locations before Tom Meeks's week at the Olympic club was over.

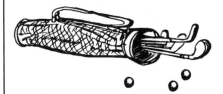

"Massacre at Winged Foot" Vivid 32 Years Later

by Art Spander, *Oakland Tribune*, June 11, 2006

This is what Tom Watson remembers: "After the second round I was eating lunch, and through the window we were watching them bring in the standards, 29 over par, 34 over par. I had never seen scores that high, ever."

This is what Sandy Tatum remembers: "When the scores came in, the perception was we were trying to humiliate the players. My precise response was we're not trying to humiliate the best players in the world. We're simply trying to identify who they are."

This is what the rest of us remember, a U.S. Open where Watson shot a 9-over 79 the last day, where Tatum was blamed for setting up a golf course that was seemingly impossible and where the late Dick Schaap and his army of correspondents compiled enough embarrassing moments and gallows humor to produce an account titled, "Massacre at Winged Foot."

The 106th Open will be held this week at Winged Foot, and while we're supposed to contemplate the future, it is the past that proves more enticing.

Winged Foot, in Mamaroneck, N.Y., maybe 20 miles from Manhattan on Long Island Sound. A course that opened in 1923 when the Roaring '20s were in full throttle.

Named for the symbol of the New York Athletic Club, Winged Foot was designed by Albert Warren Tillinghast, also creator of San Francisco Golf Club.

"Tillie," Schaap wrote, "was an heroic drinker, an habitual gambler, a dapper dresser, a golfer skilled enough to finish 25th in the 1910 U.S. Open, a phrasemaker clever enough to invent the term birdie. . . . He was also one of the great architects of American golf."

It was at Winged Foot where member David Mulligan couldn't start a round without getting a ball on the fairway, often hit a second shot, and the word "Mulligan" entered the golfing lexicon in 1937.

At Winged Foot, in the first Open there, 1929, the legendary Bobby Jones struggled to break 300 but did win.

At Winged Foot before the next Open, 1959, eventually taken by Billy Casper, Ben Hogan referred to the par-3 10th hole as "a 3- iron into some guy's bedroom."

At Winged Foot in the 1984 Open Fuzzy Zoeller beat Greg Norman by eight shots in an 18-hole playoff after they had tied at 4-under 276.

Watson, 55, a Stanford grad, who has won eight majors, now plays the Champions Tour. Tatum, in his 80s, is a Stanford grad, a Rhodes Scholar, an attorney, the 1942 NCAA golf champion, the former president of the U.S. Golf Association and in 1974 was chairman of the championship.

Tom and Sandy are friends, former partners in the AT&T Pro-Am. They probably weren't friends Open week in 1974.

The previous Open, 1973, Johnny Miller, the San Francisco native, shot a record 63 in the final round at Oakmont to win. That wasn't supposed to happen. Winged Foot, then, was the makeup tournament. Or was it?

"It would have been ridiculous for me," Tatum said this week, "to set up a golf course in retribution for one of the great rounds of golf."

The word "ridiculous" was heard frequently during the '74 Open, if in a different context.

The first hole the first day, Jack Nicklaus had a 28-foot birdie putt that went 25 feet past the hole. He opened with four straight bogeys and shot 75, 5-over-par. Playing partner Hubert Green, who would win the Open in '77, shot 81.

"I'd hate to see our best-ball," Green sighed. Nicklaus responded, "I'd hate to see our worst ball."

Watson led for 54 holes. Hale Irwin led after 72 holes. With a 7-over par 287, the highest winning total in an Open since 1963.

"They blamed me, correctly, for the setup," Tatum recalls, "but it was a combination of factors. There was tension between the touring pros and USGA, the tour courses being benign in those days, and the pros were distracted by the rough and very slick greens."

Watson said, "The greens were brutal."

Tatum, up early to set the pins, returned to his hotel before the second round and, weary, yawned as he passed two pros in the lobby, leading to one of the memorable quotes of all time.

"One of them told me, 'You look tired,'" Tatum recalled. "The other guy told us, 'You'd be tired if you had been out there all night on your hands and knees waxing greens.'"

In the end, Winged Foot waxed the whole lot of them.

"I thought it was a simply wonderful course," Tatum said.

It still is. As we'll find out once again.

THE
PREWAR
ERA

Horace Rawlins Champion

Defeated Old Golf Players on the Links at Newport

from *The New York Times*, October 6, 1895

Newport, R. I., Oct. 5—The first tournament of the National Golf Association closed yesterday with the open meeting. The wind blew half a gale over the links, and the air was cold. Fine play, therefore, was quite impossible. But, under the circumstances, the scores were remarkably good, and had the professionals played under the conditions of Thursday big records would have been made.

L. B. Stoddart of St. Andrew's, Charles B. MacDonald of Chicago, the amateur champion, and Winthrop Rutherfurd of Newport withdrew, which, except for A. W. Smith of Toronto, narrowed the meeting down to professionals, and all now in this country were engaged. The champion proved to be a dark horse—Horace Rawlins of the Newport Club, whom Davis brought over last January. He is a mere lad, but put up a great game of golf, especially in his two rounds this afternoon, each of which he made in 41.

The tournament was for strokes, called medal play. Eighteen holes were played this morning and eighteen this afternoon. The players went around in pairs, with some amateur refereeing and scoring for them. Rawlins's play, on the whole, was a remarkable exhibition. His was a well-balanced game, strong in all its elements, yet brilliant in none. He is a good heady player, with a happy faculty of not getting discouraged when in difficulties. Then he goes at his work with an ease and fearlessness that is most interesting. His putting is stronger than his driving, but the latter is good. These were the characteristics of his play to-day, that put him ahead of his older and more experienced competitors. Lawrence Curtis, the Vice President of the National Association, who refereed for Rawlins, told the young man as he congratulated him that his golf this afternoon was the best he had ever seen.

Dunn and Davis, old rivals, went around together, the former beating his old competitor, who slipped up badly on his morning play, taking nine to hole out of five hole in the second round. This one hole, where Davis found all the bunkers and pits on the green, pulled him away down, but otherwise his play was up to the mark. Both Dunn and Campbell were badly out of form, and both seemed too eager to win. The latter made a very brilliant start, holeing out of one and two in three each, but he soon got into a bad way, his play through the green to six hole being very poor. Then, in Round 4 he had a nine hole, driving first over into the road and then into the wall, each costing him two strokes. Campbell's play was singularly uneven, for it was the most brilliant of the day as well as the most careless.

Dunn's golf was steady, but hardly good. He had no bad holes and only two good ones. Lots of money was lost on him. The strongest element of his play was his putting. His driving was not up to his form. He came out with second money.

James Foulis of Chicago gave the finest exhibition of driving ever seen in this country. He has the knack of putting great power behind his ball. On the green, however, he was deficient, though he held out once on the longest putt of the day.

Tucker, the St. Andrew's professional, played pretty golf, starting in with two threes and two fours, but one took ten strokes to get through the long green to six hole on the first round, which put him out of the race. Willie Norton of Lakewood made a poor showing in the morning and withdrew. For an amateur A. W. Smith of Toronto made a fine record. Were he a professional he would have divided third money with Foulis.

Rawlins receives $200, $50 of which is to be expended for a gold medal. The Newport Golf Club has the custody of a silver cup for a year. Second money, $100, goes to Dunn; third money, $50, goes to Foulis; Davis and Campbell divide fourth, $25, and Patrick and Harland divide fifth, $10.

Horace Rawlins, to-day's winner of the open championship, was born at Benbridge, Isle of Wight, nineteen years ago. While a caddie there he learned to play golf. He played some on the famous links at Stanmore, in Middlesex, near London. He came to the United States less than a year ago, and has only played in one tournament here, which was at Shinnecock a few weeks ago. There he failed to get a place. His father is a famous player at Benbridge.

Charles B. McDonald of Chicago, who won the amateur championship yesterday, was on hand to-day, and watched the professional players with considerable interest. He was warmly congratulated on his victory by all present.

Following are the summaries:

WILLIE DUNN. SHINNECOCK HILLS CLUB.

Out	3	5	5	4	6	5	5	5	5—43
In		5	4	7	4	5	6	5	5	5—46
Out	5	5	4	4	6	7	4	5	4—44
In		4	5	3	5	4	6	6	5	4—42

Total   175

W. F. DAVIS, NEWPORT GOLF CLUB.

Out	3	4	5	4	6	7	5	6	5—45
In	5	5	5	5	9	6	6	4	4—49
Out	4	5	3	5	4	6	6	5	4—42
In	6	5	3	4	5	6	4	4	5—42

Total   178

WILLIE CAMPBELL, COUNTRY CLUB OF BROOKLINE.

Out	3	3	4	4	7	6	5	5	4—41
In	5	5	5	5	6	6	4	6	6—48
Out	3	4	4	4	5	6	6	5	5—42
In	5	5	9	4	5	7	4	5	4—48

Total   179

JAMES FOULIS, CHICAGO GOLF CLUB.

Out	6	4	4	5	5	6	5	5	6—46
In	5	4	4	3	5	8	5	4	5—43
Out	5	4	4	4	5	8	4	5	5—44
In	4	5	4	4	6	7	4	4	5—43

Total   176

JOHN REID, PHILADELPHIA COUNTRY CLUB.

Out	3	4	6	5	6	7	7	6	5—49
In	5	6	4	5	6	8	6	6	5—51
Out	5	6	4	4	6	12	6	5	7—55
In	5	6	5	5	5	8	6	6	5—51

Total   206

W. SMITH, TORONTO GOLF CLUB.

Out	3	5	8	4	6	7	6	4	4—47
In	5	6	3	4	5	6	5	5	4—43
Out	4	5	3	4	7	7	5	5	4—44
In	4	4	4	5	4	6	6	6	3—42

Total   176

SAMUEL TUCKER, ST. ANDREW'S GOLF CLUB.

Out	3	4	3	4	7	10	6	5	7—49
In	6	4	5	4	6	8	7	4	4—48
Out	4	5	3	5	6	7	7	4	4—45
In	3	6	4	6	6	6	4	4	4—43

Total   185

WILLIE NORTON, LAKEWOOD GOLF CLUB.

Out	3	7	6	5	6	7	6	5	6—51
In	5	7	6	5	7	8	6	7	7—58

Withdraws.

Total   109

JOHN HARLAND, WESTON GOLF CLUB.

Out	4	4	4	3	7	8	6	5	4—45
In	5	6	5	4	7	8	5	4	4—48
Out	4	5	3	4	5	7	4	7	4—43
In	5	6	4	5	5	6	5	5	6—47

Total   183

JOHN PATRICK, TUXEDO GOLF CLUB.

Out	4	5	5	4	6	7	5	5	5—46
In	5	6	5	5	6	7	4	5	5—48
Out	3	6	4	4	4	6	9	5	5—46
In	5	4	4	4	5	6	4	6	5—43

Total   183

H. RAWLINS. NEWPORT GOLF CLUB.

Out	4	5	4	4	6	5	7	5	5—45
In	6	5	3	4	5	7	5	6	5—46
Out	3	5	4	4	6	7	4	3	5—41
In	3	5	4	3	5	6	5	5	5—41

Total   173

Tie for Golf Honors

Anderson and Brown Finish Even in Open Championship

Douglas Does the Best of the Amateurs, Getting Eighth Place—Leaders Will Play Off To-morrow

from *The New York Times*, June 28, 1903

Willie Anderson, the Apawamis Club professional, of Rye, N. Y., and David Brown, the golf professional of the Wollaston Country Club, near Boston, tied for the open championship of the United States yesterday in the final play on the links of the Baltusrol Golf Club, near Short Hills, N. J. Their scores were 307 strokes for the 72 holes, including the two days' play. They will play off at 18 holes for the championship and the purse of $200 which goes to the winner to-morrow on the same club links.

Anderson was the open champion two years ago, and, singularly enough, he then tied for the honors with Alec Smith, now of Nassau County. The tournament was then held at the Myopia Club, near Boston, and Anderson won in the play-off by one stroke. A hot finish is looked for to-morrow, for Brown is playing remarkably steady golf. The latter really furnished the surprise of the event, for while he has always been acknowledged as an expert player, it had been taken for granted that his championship form had departed. Brown held the open championship of Great Britain in 1886. He came to America about two years ago, but has been playing very little in competitions.

Brown made the better score yesterday, as indeed he had to in order to tie Anderson, who led the field in the first day with 149 for the thirty-six holes. Yesterday Anderson needed 158, while Brown did the double round in 151 strokes. Anderson played up to his ability in the morning, when he did the course in 76 strokes, while Brown did 75. In the afternoon Anderson fell down badly on the ninth hole, taking 8 strokes. He drove into the edge of the woods, and on the stroke to get out his ball hit a tree, rebounding for forty yards. Another stroke was then lost in getting out. On the home green Anderson had a chance to get the hole, but he missed by less than an inch, and took four. A stroke saved at either of these places would have made Anderson the undisputed champion without the uncertainty of a play-off round.

Stewart Gardner, who was second last year, tieing with Travis, got third place and the $125 purse, his total being 315. Alec Smith of Nassau Country won fourth place, with 316 strokes, and the purse of $100. Donald J. Ross of the Oakley Club got the fifth purse, $80, with a score of 318. Jack Campbell, a young golfer and assistant professional of the Brookline Country Club, near Boston, got sixth and the purse of $70, his total being 319 strokes. Next came Laurence Auchterlonie, the former open champion from the Glenview Club, Chicago, with 321 strokes, and won the purse of $50. The only amateur to get a place among the ten money places was Findlay S. Douglas of the Nassau Country Club. He got eighth place, with 322 strokes, and will receive the value of the $40 purse in plate. Three men tied for the ninth and tenth places at 323, Willie Smith, a former champion, of

Midlothian, Alex Ross of Wilmington, and John Hobens of the Yountakah Country Club. They decided to divide the small purses for the two places, $30 and $25, respectively, among the three.

With the exception of Douglas, the amateurs did not figure prominently with the professional golfers of the country. F. O. Reinhart, the young Princeton player, finished with 325 and so led Travis, as the latter had 326. He played the 36 holes in ten strokes better than on the preceding day, but his golf was not of notable quality. The other amateurs to finish were George T. Brokaw, Frank H. Croker, W. C. Carnegie, J. S. Gillespie, Charles L. Tappin, R. C. Watson, Jr., L. L. Kellogg, John M. Ward, and H. G. Macdonald. In all, fifty-eight finished the tournament.

The scores of the players are, the complete cards of Anderson and Brown being given in full:

WILL ANDERSON, APAWAMLS—

Out	5	4	3	5	4	4	5	5	2—37	
In	3	4	4	4	4	4	5	4	4—36—73	
Out	5	5	3	6	3	4	5	4	3—38	
In	5	3	3	5	4	5	5	4	4—38— 76—149	
Out	5	4	5	5	5	3	4	3	3—37	
In	5	4	4	4	4	4	6	4	4—39—76	
Out	5	4	4	5	4	4	5	5	8—44	
In	3	4	5	4	4	5	5	4	4—38—82—158—307	

DAVID BROWN, WOLLASTON—

Out	7	5	3	6	4	4	6	5	3—48	
In	3	4	4	4	4	4	5	4	4—36—79	
Out	5	5	4	6	4	4	5	4	3—40	
In	3	4	3	4	3	5	5	5	5—37—77—156	
Out	5	3	4	5	4	4	4	4	3—36	
In	4	4	5	4	4	5	5	4	4—39—75	

```
Out    5   4   4   6   3   5   4   4   5—40
In         3   4   4   5   3   4   6   4   3—36—76—151—307
```

	1ST DAY	2ND DAY	TOTAL
Stewart Gardner, Garden City	154	161	315
Alex Smith, Nassau Country	154	102	316
Donald J. Ross, Oakley	160	158	318
Jack Campbell, Brookline	159	160	319
Laurence Auchterlonie, Glenview	154	167	321
Findlay S. Douglas, Nassau Country	156	166	322
Willie Smith, Midlothian	161	162	323
Alec Ross, Wilmington, Del	165	158	323
John Hobens, Yountakah	157	166	323
Horace T. Rawlins, Waumbek	159	165	324
F. O. Reinhart, Morris County	156	169	325
Isaac Mackie, Fox Hills	163	162	325
Gilbert Nicholls, St. Louis	168	158	326
Walter J. Travis, Garden City	163	163	326
Alec. Campbell, Brookline	163	163	326
Bernard Nicholls, Hollywood	163	165	328
David Ogilvie, Baltimore	167	162	329
Will Norton, Deal	159	170	329
George Cumming, Toronto	169	161	330
Henry Turpie, Auburn, Ill	168	168	331
John Reid, Philadelphia	164	168	332
Joe Lloyd, Boston	164	168	332
T. G. Campbell, Philadelphia	160	173	333
Frederick McLeod, Rockford, Ill	163	170	333
Arthur Smith, Philadelphia	165	168	333

George T. Brokaw, Deal		160	173	333
A. H. Fenn, Poland Springs	165	169	334	
David S. Hunter, Essex County	170	165	335	
John T. Dingwall, Alleghany	171	165	336	
R. C. Murray, Quebec	167	169	336	
William Braid, St. Louis	161	176	337	
A. H. Findlay, Boston	173	166	339	
Robert Thompson, Huntington	165	173	338	
Ernest Way, Detroit		173	167	340
Thomas L. McNamara, Boston	170	173	343	
Joseph Mitchell, Cleveland	169	176	345	
David Patrick, Bay Shore	172	173	345	
John Harland, Brooklawn	164	175	339	
Jack Tolly, Arlington	176	171	347	
Thomas Clark, Agawam	176	171	347	
Frank H. Croker, Deal	176	172	348	
Alexander Patrick, New York	180	169	349	
John S. Pearson, Richmond County	174	175	349	
W. C. Carnegie, St. Andrew's	170	183	353	
P. P. Burns, Morristown		177	175	352
John Brett, Tuxedo	180	173	353	
L. L. Kellogg, Fox Hills		186	176	356
Robert Dow, Knollwood	177	179	356	
J. S. Gillespie, Quebec	179	178	357	
Charles L. Tappin, Westbrook	177	182	359	
R. C. Watson, Jr., Westbrook	179	181	360	
John M. Ward, Fox Hills	184	179	363	
Robert Shiels, New Haven	186	179	365	
J. C. Davidson, Washington	185	182	367	
P. S. Honeyman, Champlain	185	185	370	
H. G. Macdonald, Florida	191	181	372	

Three Tie Scores in National Golf

McDermott, Simpson, and Brady Finish on Even Terms in Open Championship

from *The New York Times*, June 25, 1911

CHICAGO, June 24.—J. J. McDermott of Atlantic City, N. J.; George A. Simpson of Wheaton, Ill., runner-up to "Chick" Evans in the Western open championship last year, and M. J. Brady of Boston finished in a triple tie for the National open golf championship in the final thirty-six holes of the tournament at the Chicago Golf Club links to-day. Each had a score of 307 for seventy-two holes. The play-off to determine the champion will be played Monday afternoon.

Soon after the first pair teed off at 9 o'clock on the morning round, a rainstorm started and continued throughout the day. Although the rain fell in torrents while McDermott and McLeod were playing their final eighteen holes, a crowd of 100 or more enthusiasts followed the players. Fred

McLeod of St. Louis and Alex Ross of New Rochelle, who led at the close of the first day's play, fell down today, McLeod drawing 83 on his last round after getting a 76 in the morning. His total was 308, one stroke behind the leaders, which gives him fourth place. Ross's total was boosted to 312 by an 81 and 82, dropping him into ninth place, barely within the money.

Jack Hutchinson of Pittsburg tied with Gilbert Nichols of Wilmington, Del., at 309 for fifth place, and H. H. Barker of Rumson, N. J., tied with George Sargent of Washington for seventh, with 311.

Peter Robertson of Pittsburg tied with Alec Ross at 312 for tenth place, the prize limit. Albert Seckel of Chicago, the Princeton champion, made the most creditable showing of the amateurs, finishing with 313, just outside the money.

The downfall of National Champion Alex Smith of Boston, who scored 82 and 85 for a total of 167 to-day, boosting his grand total to 321, came as the surprise of the tournament. Smith complained of the intense heat yesterday, and said his work to-day was seriously hampered by its effects.

Following are the cards of the players who are tied and the leading scores:

PLAYER AND CLUB.	SCORE.
George A. Simpson, Wheaton	307
J. J. McDermott, Atlantic City	307
M. J. Brady, Boston	307
Fred McLeod, St. Louis	308
J. Hutchinson. Pittsburg	309
Gilbert Nichols, Wilmington	309
George Sargent, Washington	411
H. H. Barker, Rumson, N. J.	311
Peter Robertson, Pittsburg	312
Alec Ross, New Rochelle, N. Y	312
A. Seckel, Chicago	313

Alec Campbell, Boston	314
Harry Turpie, Chicago	314
O. P. Nelson, Battle Creek	315
George Low, Boston	316
P. S. Simpson, Kenosha	317
G. Donaldson, Chicago	316
D. E. Sawyer Wheaton	319
John Burke, Des Moines	319
George Cummings, Toronto	320
Grange Alvers, French Lick	320
*M. E. Phelps, Chicago	320
R. C. Watson, Westbrook	321
*H. C. Egan, Chicago	321
*R. A. Gardner, Hinsdale, Ill	321
Alex Smith, New Rochelle, N. Y.	321
W. G. Foyargue, Chicago	322
J. B. Simpson, Milwaukee	322
Tom McNamara, Boston	324
*R. G. McDonald, Cleveland	324

*Amateurs

DEAL GOLFERS TIED.

In three instances the club rule that scores of 76 or less shall count as 76 caused ties in the events at the Deal Golf and Country Club yesterday. There were two events run off, each in two classes. T. W. Kemball and S. D. Lounsberry led Class A in the eighteen-hole club handicap, finishing 78, 4—74, and 85, 10—75, respectively. In class B of the same event Macintosh Kellogg, with 98, 24— 74, and John T. Hettrick, with 94, 18—76, were thrown into a tie. In Class A of the ball sweepstakes W. H. Yawger and William V. Conover finished even, with 83, 9—74 and 79, 5—74, respectively. W. W. Peabody, Jr., led the B division in the sweepstakes with 100, 24—76. The scores follow:

Club Handicap.—Class A—T. W. Kemball, 78, 4—74; S. D. Lounsberry, 85, 10—75; J. F. Shanley, Jr., 80, 3—77; J. T. Gillespie, 95, 14—81; W. R. Delehanty, 95, 13—82; John F. Shanley, 96, 13—83; T. H. Moore, 96, 12—84; George A. Hagerty, 103, 17—86; John E. Kelly, 100, 14—86; J. H. Haggerty, 104, 17—87; John H. Hawley, 103, 13—90.

Class B.—Macintosh Kellogg, 98, 24—74: John T. Hettrick, 94, 18—76; R. Underhill, 101, 24—77: J. G. Newcombe, 103, 21—82; E. H. Raynolds, 120, 28—92.

Ball Sweepstakes.—Class A—W. H. Yawger, 83, 9—74; W. V. Conover, 79, 5—74; S. D. Loundsberry, 85, 10—75; George A. Hagerty, 96, 17—79: J. T. Gillesple, 95, 14—81; H. R. MacKenzie, 101, 16—85.

Class B.—W. W. Peabody, Jr., 100, 24—76; J. G. Newcombe, 101, 21—80; R. H. Higgins, 100, 20—80; S. J. Arend, 111, 26—85; S. J. Gubelman, 114, 24—90; Patrick Moore, 118, 27—91.

McDermott's Golf Title

Former Caddie First American-Born Player to Win Open Championship

from *The New York Times*, June 27, 1911

CHICAGO, June 26.—J. J. McDermott, 21 years old,* of Atlantic City, N. J., who began his golf career in Philadelphia as a caddie, to-day won the open golf championship of the United States at the Chicago Golf Club, outplaying his two opponents, with whom he tied last week.

McDermott is the first American-born player to win the open championship in the history of golf in America. Scotchmen have always won in the sixteen previous tournaments, but McDermott was runner-up last year. M. J. Brady of Boston was runner-up to McDermott this year, while George A. Simpson of the Chicago Golf Club, former amateur champion of Scotland, was third. The scores for the eighteen holes to-day were not good, because of heat, wet greens, and wind.

---

*Editor's note: McDermott was nineteen years old when he won the 1911 Open.

Nearly 400 enthusiasts followed the players around the course, expecting to see stellar golf, but each player was off his game in some respect. McDermott was the steadiest of the three, although his putting was poor. He made the course in 80, which is 4 above par. He frequently was on the green a stroke ahead of his opponents, but failed to run down several short puts. Brady, however, could not do better than 82, while Simpson took 85, which is bogey for the 6,636-yard course.

The Open Championship of 1913

from *A Game of Golf* by Francis Ouimet

Nineteen-thirteen was a big year, and the state championship played no small part. To begin with, I had a nineteen-hole match with Brice Evans. Then I was three down and five to play against Ray Gorton. Playing the eighteenth hole I was one down. We both reached the green on our seconds to the last hole at Wollaston, where the event was played. I got down in two putts and was on the point of conceding an eighteen-inch putt to Ray, which meant the match, when something prompted me to refrain from doing so. I stepped aside ready to grasp his hand the moment he holed the putt. To my amazement he missed, and the match was even. It taught me a good lesson—that is, never to concede the putt that is to defeat you. I beat Ray on the nineteenth.

The semi-final came, and this time I was opposed to John G. Anderson who was playing the finest golf of his life. John, possibly remembering our school-day clash when I caught him off form, was bent on squaring the account. At the twelfth hole he was two up. I proceeded then to go wild. I made a two on the short thirteenth and played the next four holes in three each. It gave me the match by three up and one to play. The approach to the seventeenth hole was blind, and John stood off to one side near the green to watch my ball. I knew I had hit a fine shot and looked over to where John was standing. John, with both hands in the air, said, 'Your ball is stone dead.' It was just twelve inches from the cup.

Even though beaten, John was thrilled, and asked me to play out the last hole. I made that in three also. My finish of 2-3-3-3-3-3 was six under par. My opponent in the final was Frank Hoyt, and I beat him ten up and nine to play. An interesting thing happened in Hoyt's semi-final match with Buck Whittemore. Hoyt knew Wollaston, and its many tricky approach shots, like a book. Playing the fifteenth, they stood even. Buck had driven to the right of the hole, expecting the contour of the ground to throw his ball down toward the green. He did not have quite enough length, and his ball stopped above the green, leaving him a difficult short approach to lay it dead. Hoyt was on with a long tee shot. Golf tournaments in 1913 were anything but serious affairs, and everyone played the game for the sport there was in it. Buck said, 'This is a tough shot.' Hoyt agreed. Buck failed to get his ball anywhere near the hole, and Hoyt won it.

'Buck, I will bet you a dollar I can lay a ball dead from where you just played,' said Hoyt, whom we called 'Stealthy Steve.'

'You're on,' said Buck.

Hoyt dropped a ball, played far up to the right. It seemed to stop for a fraction of a second and then, rolling ever so gently, came to rest about six inches from the hole. He collected the dollar.

The next feature was the national amateur championship. Jerry Travers was defending his title at Garden City, Long Island. The usual big field gathered for the qualifying round and there was plenty of talent. I played a very steady game in the first round and finished with a score of 75, one stroke better than the next man, Walter J. Travis. I was thrilled to death because it was the first time in the amateur championship that I had played consistently. The next day I scored a 76 and my thirty-six-hole total was one better than Travis's.

Friends in the locker room congratulated me and said that I was bound to win the medal for the qualifying round. I told them I was more than satisfied to qualify and was not worrying over winning the medal. It was just as well. Chick Evans had a 77 his first round. He was 39 out and needed a 34 on the last nine to beat me for low-score honors. A 34 today is a hard assignment at Garden City, and in 1913 it seemed almost impossible. All Chick did was to breeze home in 32, and the medal was his beyond any doubt.

I won one match and was then called upon to play the champion, Jerome D. Travers. Jerry had a terrible time on the last hole, a short one, over the pond, and the resultant seven he took on his second qualifying round almost knocked him out. As it was, he had to play off for a position in the match play rounds and I drew him after we had each won a match. To say I was overawed would be expressing it mildly: I was scared to death. Here was an opponent who had won three national championships and was conceded to be the greatest match-play exponent of the game. But there was nothing to do but to put on a bold front, and away we went.

The match was very close all morning. Holes were hard to win. Jerry seemed cold as ice. He accepted good shots with the same attitude as he did poor ones. I complimented him on his fine shots. My good ones seemed to pass unnoticed. After a time I thought, this fellow is determined to do just one thing and that is to win the golf game. I made up my mind to do the same. It was a thirty-six-hole match. Playing the eighteenth—the short one—we were even. Both reached the green with Jerry inside. I placed my putt from thirty feet on the edge of the cup. Jerry took one look at me and then proceeded to sink a twenty-footer, to become one up. I have always felt he did that to impress me, and it certainly did.

When we appeared on the first tee for the last half of the match a tremendous gallery awaited. Travers increased his lead by winning the first hole.

Off and on in the morning round he drove with a driver, and he missed many tee shots, although his recoveries and putting were positively amazing. I took the second and third holes and won the seventh to become one up. The golf was almost perfect—nothing given away. Playing the eighth or twenty-sixth hole, I hit a fine tee shot. Jerry was out in front with his black driving iron. I hit a fine iron of at least a hundred and eighty yards eight feet from the cup. I was proud of that shot, and looked at Jerry as much as to say, 'There, let's see you beat that one.' He took a bit more time than usual, made his swing, met the ball, and when it stopped, it was ten inches from the cup. That took the starch out of me, and I was beaten from then on.

That match with Jerome Travers did more toward getting me into the proper frame of mind than any I had ever had. I had been inclined to look upon golf lightly. A contest meant nothing more than a trip around the course. If my golf was good enough, I should win, and if not, then there was nothing to do but congratulate the winner. I learned that one must keep his thoughts focused entirely on the shot at hand, and in a hard match it is silly to be too passive. Jerry came to me in the locker room afterward and we went over our match hole by hole. I saw in Jerry Travers a great sportsman, one who put his heart and soul into the golf game, and when it was finished, he had time to reflect and express himself whole-heartedly on the simplest things.

In that same championship a funny thing happened in the match between Eben Byers and Chick Evans. Chick held a commanding lead for the better part of twenty-seven holes; then Byers began pecking away, winning a hole here and there, until they reached the home one. Evans was one up. Both got on the green. Chick was putting poorly as usual, but when he coasted an approach putt up to within three feet of the hole, it looked like a certain victory. Byers putted, got just inside Evans's ball and stymied him. Chick tried to jump the stymie, but failed, and his ball ran two feet beyond the cup. Byers putted again, missed, and again stymied Chick. Once more Chick missed and lost the hole. He was hard put to it to win on the thirty-ninth green.

Chick figured in another distressing situation. Against John Anderson in the semi-final round, he had been having a dreadful time of it on the greens. His tee shots were perfect and his irons sparkled with effectiveness, but his putting was woeful. He carried four putters in his bag and after so many sad experiences each had plenty to do. He never got acquainted with any one of them because he was shifting from one to another on every green. Finally, left with a three-foot putt to keep the match alive, he was at a loss to know which putter to use. He picked one out of his bag. He put it back and handled another. He tried them all, and the one he eventually selected was the wrong one.

The President of the United States Golf Association in 1913 was none other than Robert Watson, the man I had played with in my second qualifying round four years previously at the Country Club. The open championship was to be played at the Country Club, and Watson was seeking a good amateur entry. He thought I should enter. I argued with him about the folly of such a thing, and he won the argument. I was through school and employed by Wright and Ditson in the sporting goods business. I had taken my vacation by going to Garden City for the national amateur championship and I did not have the courage to ask for more time off to play in the Open.

Returning to Boston, I settled down to work. Vardon and Ray had come to this country to give golf exhibitions and also to play in the Open. One morning the papers carried the pairings for the open championship, and my chief came to me and said, 'Well, I see you are now going to play in the open championship.' John Morrill was an executive in Wright and Ditson's and a kindlier or more lovable character never lived. I might say the same about George Wright, who did as much toward developing the game of golf in this country as any man.

I was embarrassed. I told Mr. Morrill I had no intention of playing, but if he would be good enough to let me wander out to Brookline and see Vardon and Ray perform, I should be ever grateful to him. With a gleam in his eye, he said, 'As long as you have entered, you had better plan to play.' This was an order. I needed no further instructions.

The Sunday before the open tournament, I played at the Wellesley Country Club with friends. I bring this up merely to show you that one's form in golf is a mercurial affair. With the open championship two days away, I made two scores of 88 on a short and rather easy nine-hole course, the 88's being just twenty-two strokes higher than a record score I had established on one of my earlier rounds over the layout. The friend who invited me to play with himself and friends was broken-hearted, and thought he had ruined my game. I told him not to worry; that I had probably got all the bad golf out of my system—and, believe me, there must have been plenty of it in there. There was such a huge entry the field was divided into three qualifying sections and I was in the same group with Harry Vardon. With a 74 in my morning round, I finished a stroke ahead of Vardon. That was an accomplishment. In the afternoon I was playing quite as well until I reached the long fourteenth, and bumping into much trouble, I made a seven. At that I scored a 78 which ranked me next to Vardon, the leader in our section.

There is little to be said about the championship itself. After the first three rounds, I was tied with both Vardon and Ray at 225. Ray was finishing his final round as I walked to the first tee. I watched him hole out and learned he had made a 79. It was raining, but, even so, a 79 did not seem very low. It made his seventy-two-hole total 304. Playing the fifth hole, I was told that Vardon had tied Ray. The rumors in championship play, particularly if you happen to be in the running, come thick and fast. I was next told Barnes had the championship in the hollow of his hand. Then word came to me that Barnes had blown up.

I was having my own troubles out in that rain and nothing would go right. Out in 43, all hope seemed gone. Then someone said, 'Tellier will win in a walk.' The tenth hole was a par three. Owing to the sodden condition of the putting green, a high pitch was dangerous, because the ball would become embedded in the soft turf. I elected to use a jigger, intending to hit a low shot to the green. I forgot to look at the ball and hit it about fifteen feet. I put my next on the green eight feet from the hole and then took three putts for an inglorious five. Then I learned that Tellier had got into trouble and had finished behind both Vardon and Ray, who were still leading.

After that wretched five, walking to the eleventh tee between a lane of spectators, I heard one man say, 'It's too bad, he has blown up.' I knew he meant me, and it made me angry. It put me in the proper frame of mind to carry on. There was still a chance, I thought. People lined the fairway as I drove. A par four was helpful on the eleventh. A hard five on the twelfth helped not at all, because here was a hole where one might be expected to save a stroke, although it was a difficult four. Standing on the thirteenth tee, I realized I must play those last six holes in two under par to tie. There were two holes on the course where I thought I might save a stroke: the thirteenth, the one I had to play next, which was a drive and a short pitch, and the sixteenth, a short hole. I selected these two holes for reasons. I had been quite successful on the thirteenth and had scored threes there regularly. I had not made a two all the week, and I had a hunch I should get one at the sixteenth. It was just a hunch.

My drive to the thirteenth was satisfactory. With a simple pitch to the green, I mishit the ball and barely escaped a trap. My ball lay off the green thirty feet from the hole I had selected as one upon which to beat par. Instead of having a reasonably short putt, I was stuck with a chip shot. In any event, I chipped my ball right into the hole for my three and was still in the hunt. A routine five came on the long fourteenth. I missed my second to the fifteenth badly, so badly, I missed every trap. I pitched on and got my par four.

Then came the sixteenth, the hole I had been expecting to make in two. I not only did not get my two there, but actually had to hole a nine-footer for the three. One of the last two holes had to be made in three, the other in four. They were both testing holes. As I splashed along in the mud and rain, I had no further hunches. I just wanted an opportunity to putt for one of those threes. I got it on the seventeenth. A drive and second shot, played with a jigger placed my ball on the green fifteen feet from the cup. It was now or never. As I looked the line of putt over, I thought of one thing, giving the ball a chance—that is, getting it to the hole. I struck that putt as firmly as any putt I ever hit, saw it take the roll, bang smack against the back of the hole, and fall in for the three.

Now to get the four. A drive split the fairway to the last hole and was out far enough so that a long iron could reach the green. Eddie Lowery, my ten-year-old caddie, handed me an iron and said, 'Keep your eye on the ball and hit it.' I did. I lifted my head just in time to see the ball sail toward the pin, saw it land and, as I thought, kick forward, and I can then remember saying to Eddie, 'I have a putt to win this championship.' I was certain I had seen my ball clear the embankment and hop forward. As a matter of fact, the ball struck the top of the bank, and stopped instantly just off the cut surface of the putting green. A chip shot left me a four-foot putt which I popped in. I had ended that seventy-two-hole stretch in a tie with Vardon and Ray for the championship I had been most reluctant to enter.

Friends hustled me into the locker room building and the excitement was tremendous. One individual came to me and asked this question, 'Were you bothered while putting on the seventeenth green?' 'Not a bit,' was my reply. 'Why?' He went on to say that the highway directly in back of the green was littered with automobiles, so much so that it was impossible for machines to move in either direction. Just then a motor came along, and the driver, seeing his path blocked completely, kept up a constant tooting of his horn, as I was preparing to putt. I never heard a single sound, so thoroughly was my mind centered on the business of holing the putt.

After taking a bath, I walked home and turned in early for a real night's rest. I slept from nine-thirty until eight the next morning, and after a light breakfast, hustled over to the Country Club for my play-off with Vardon and Ray. I did not feel nervous or unduly excited. I slipped on my golf shoes, got hold of Eddie Lowery and went out to the Polo Field to hit a few practice shots. There was nobody around. The shots I hit felt fine. Soon some people came along and watched me. After perhaps a half-hour's practice, I was told that Vardon and Ray were on the first tee waiting for the match to begin.

Johnny McDermott took my arm and said, 'You are hitting the ball well; now go out and pay no attention whatsoever to Vardon or Ray. Play your own game.' It was excellent advice and I promised Johnny I would do my best.

On the way to the tee my good friend Frank Hoyt ('Stealthy Steve') asked me if I would not permit him to carry my clubs. I had played much golf with Steve and he was a master in the finer points of the game. I told him he must see Eddie Lowery. He made one or two offers of money, but they did not tempt Eddie in the least. It was interesting to see the reaction of Eddie as he definitely and positively refused to be bought off. Finally, Hoyt appealed to me. I looked at the ten-year-old Eddie, his eyes filled, and I think he was fearful that I would turn him down. In any event, he seemed so sincere I did not have the heart to take the clubs away from him, and my final gesture was to tell Steve, Eddie was going to caddie for me.

It was raining, and the three of us were ushered into the tent near the tee to draw lots for the honor. I drew the longest straw and had to drive first. As I walked over to the sand box, and realized what I was up against and saw the crowd, I was terribly excited. If I could only get my tee shot away! Eddie stepped up as he handed me a driver and said, 'Be sure and keep your eye on the ball.' The opening salute was a drive well down the middle of the fairway and for good length. Vardon and Ray followed suit. Ray was the only one who was long enough to reach the green on his second, but he sliced a brassie to the right.

We all got on in three and took fives on the hole. I was left with a four-foot putt for my five, and I worried not a little over it. I tapped it in, and then almost instantly any feeling of awe and excitement left me completely. I seemed to go into a coma. Eddie kept telling me to keep my eye on the ball. He cautioned me to take my time. He encouraged me in any number of different ways. My first mistake was on the fifth hole where the slimy grip turned in my hand and my second shot went out of bounds. But Vardon and Ray both erred on the same hole, and I was safe for the time being. Ray had taken a five on the third to our fours, and that was the only difference in the scores up to that point.

Vardon made the sixth in three and went into the lead. Ray was now trailing Vardon by two strokes and me by one. The seventh hole at Brookline is a hard par three. Vardon was to the right of the green with his iron and needed four. I failed to lay a long approach putt dead, and took four. Ray was the only one to get a three and he pulled up on even terms with me.

The eighth hole was sensational. This hole measures three hundred and eighty yards and the view of the green is more or less restricted by a hill. You can see the flag, but no part of the green. We all had fine drives. A tremendous crowd had gathered around the green to see the balls come up. I played my second with a mashie straight for the pin. In a few seconds a mighty roar went up. As I handed the club to Eddie, he said, 'Your ball is stone dead.' I wanted to think it was, but I wished also to prepare myself in case it was not. Therefore I said to Eddie, 'It is not stone dead, but I believe I shall have a putt for my three.' You see I did not wish to be disappointed.

As we walked toward the green and came to the top of the hill, I saw a ball twelve inches from the hole. It was mine. Ray was forty feet away with a sidehill putt and he tapped his ball as delicately as possible. It took the necessary turns and rolled right into the hole. Vardon had a four, and I got my three, which put us all even at the end of eight holes.

The next highlight was the short tenth. This green was so soggy that both Vardon and Ray, after pitching on, had to chip over the holes made by their balls as they bit into the soft turf and hopped back. I was fairly close in one. My opponents failed to make their threes, and I stepped into the lead by a stroke.

I added another stroke on the twelfth, where I got my four to their fives. Vardon dropped a nice putt for a three on the thirteenth, one under par, which brought him within a stroke of me. The long fourteenth was important. Ray might reach the green in two, but it was beyond the range of Vardon and myself. Ray drove last, and I saw him hurl himself at his ball to get just a little added length. When he played his second from the fairway, he put every bit of power into the shot, but his timing was poor and he hit the ball far to the right into a grove of chestnut trees. He recovered beautifully, and the hole was made in five by all.

I was paying as little attention as possible to the strokes of the others, because I did not wish to be unduly influenced by anything they did, I was simply carrying out McDermott's instructions and playing my own game. I could not help but notice, however, that Ray was struggling somewhat. I noticed, too, that Vardon, who seemed to be a master in mashie work, pulled his pitch to the green, which was not his natural way of playing such a stroke. Vardon normally played his pitches with a slight fade from left to right.

Ray got into all sorts of trouble on the fifteenth and he seemed out of the running. I never gave it a thought as he holed out in six. I still clung to my one stroke lead over Vardon through the sixteenth. Ray was now five strokes behind. Vardon had the honor on the seventeenth tee. This hole is a semi-dog-leg, and by driving to the right you eliminate all risk. On the other hand, if the player chooses to risk a trap on the left and gets away with it, he has a short pitch to the green. Vardon drove to the left. I saw his ball start, and that is all. I drove to the right. Ray tried to cut the trees on the left and hit a prodigious wallop that cleared everything, but his ball was in the long grass.

As we walked toward our balls, I saw that Vardon had caught the trap and his ball was so close to the bank he had no chance at all of reaching the green. He could just play out to the fairway. I knocked a jigger shot to the green, my ball stopping fifteen feet above the hole. Ray and Vardon took fives. As I studied my putt, I decided to take no liberties with the skiddy surface and simply tried to lay the ball dead for a sure four. I putted carefully and watched my ball roll quietly toward the hole. It went in for a three. With one hole left, I was now in the lead by three strokes over Vardon and seven over Ray.

The eighteenth hole was a hard two-shotter. The rains had turned the race-track in front of the green into a bog, and my one thought was to get over the mud. All hit fine tee shots. I placed my second on the green. It did not enter my head that I was about to become the open champion until I stroked my first putt to within eight or nine inches of the hole. Then, as I stepped up to make that short putt, I became very nervous. A veil of something that seemed to have covered me dropped from around my head and shoulders. I was in full control of my faculties for the first time since the match started, but terribly excited. I dropped the putt. Nothing but the most intense concentration brought me victory.

I was fearful at the beginning that I should blow up, and I fought against this for all I was worth. The thought of winning never entered my head, and for that reason I was immune to emotions of any sort. My objective was to play eighteen holes as well as I could and let the score stand for good or bad. I accomplished a feat that seemed so far beyond anything I ever hoped to do that, while I got a real thrill out of it, I felt I had been mighty lucky. Had I harbored the desire to win that championship or an open title of any kind, I might have been tickled beyond words. In sport one has to have the ambition to do things and that ambition in my case was to win the national amateur championship. Therefore, I honestly think I never got the 'kick' out of winning the open title that I might have done if I had thought I could win it.

Champion, 1914

from *The Walter Hagen Story* by Walter Hagen

Golf is a game which can start a mental flurry in a second, but Hagen has won so many championships because in addition to fine physical skill . . . he has built up a philosophy which Fate can't overthrow. . . . It takes an avalanche of accidents to make him sore. An earthquake would hardly leave him grouchy. He seems to be happiest when there's a hard battle ahead and he must come from behind to win.

—Grantland Rice, *Collier's* [1925]

Fate has a strange way of stepping in and taking over just when a fellow thinks he's pretty well lined up with life. In my case Fate and newspaper men have sort of teamed together to give me splendid publicity or a push in the right direction at the opportune time. And it happened first in July of 1914.

Dutch Leonard and I were sitting in the pro shop at the Country Club of Rochester and I was bragging how I'd murder big-league pitching when

I made good in the tryout with the Phillies. When winter training started I intended to be right there and ready.

While we were talking I saw Mr. Ernest Willard, editor of the Rochester *Democrat and Chronicle*, get out of his "glass house" electric and head for the shop. I knew he'd come to pick up his golf clubs for his vacation at Loon Lake, so I walked across the shop to get them for him.

"Aren't you going to enter the National Open at Chicago?" Dutch called to me.

"I'm not thinking of it," I said. "I'm going to work harder in baseball and let up on golf."

Mr. Willard overheard me and he repeated Dutch's question. I explained that I believed I could make the grade with the Phillies' team if I tried hard enough.

"Haven't you plenty of time for the Open and baseball?" he asked. "You did so well at Brookline last year, I think you should try again this year."

I told him I was sort of discouraged, that I'd begun to believe that golf was not my game.

"Rochester was mighty proud of you, Walter. You're the first pro we've ever had who has been able to qualify for the Open, let alone finish in a tie for second like you did. I'd like you to go to Chicago and win it."

He waited a few seconds, then said, "If you'll go, Walter, I'll pay all your expenses." He turned to Dutch. "And you, young fellow, if you can make the trip with Walter, I'll pay your expenses, too. Well, what do you say, boys?"

"I appreciate your offer, Mr. Willard, and I'll send in my entry to the National Open right away," I told him.

Yes, that did it. I thought I'd put all future golf competition out of my mind. I thought I was headed straight for the major leagues and baseball's Hall of Fame. But let a man express confidence in my ability as a golfer and I was right back in competition again. Then I remembered I'd told those fellows at Brookline I'd be back next year. Next year was here . . . and I had just three weeks to get ready for the Open in Chicago.

I worked harder than I'd ever worked in my life during the time which was left me, trying to perfect my game for another shot at the "big boys." I got my fancy golf outfit cleaned and ready with only one change, the white buckskin shoes with the red rubber soles. I'd slid all over the course at Brookline in the wet weather. Funny thing was that I'd only played golf in good, sunny weather until I went to Brookline. Now I bought a pair of hobnailed shoes for the 1914 Open. And I played in hobnailed shoes from that time on.

Dutch and I took the day coach to Chicago. We stopped at the old Great Northern Hotel. I'd never been out of the East before so just making the trip was quite an adventure. The night before the tournament started we blew ourselves to dinner at the best restaurant we could find. I forget the name, but the display window housed a huge red lobster. I'd never tasted lobster, so that's what we ordered, lobster and oysters. We ate plenty of lobster and oysters. Then we took in a movie. Before the picture was over my stomach pains began. By the time we reached the hotel I was howling in agony.

Dutch called the house physician about midnight and he gave me some pills. I continued to hold my head, rub my stomach and howl. He called the doctor again in the early morning and still I had no relief. I continued to be nauseated and retching with stomach pains. By dawn I was so weak I could scarcely stand. I told Dutch I didn't see how I was going to play a round of golf for a week, much less compete in a Championship tournament that day. He finally persuaded me to ride out to the club and see how I felt by starting time.

"For after all, Walter," he said, "Mr. Willard and your friends back home might have a little difficulty believing that lobster story."

The hotel doctor came once more, gave me some milk toast and aspirin and told me to take two more aspirin before I began to play . . . *if* I felt well enough to start.

Dutch and I rode the old South Shore Railroad out to Blue Island to the

Midlothian Country Club. The day was sweltering hot and the heat plus the coal soot and cinders blowing in on me from the wide open screenless windows added to my discomfort. I felt terrible and kept wondering if I had the strength even to walk around the course.

In the locker room I changed to my fancy outfit and staggered out to the practice field to hit some shots. It hurt me to take a full swing. Both my head and my stomach were throbbing with pain and my body was sore all over. I hit a hundred or more balls and took two more aspirin. Funny thing, but my headache was gone. I told Dutch.

"Then you can start," he said cheerfully.

"I can start," I told him, "but I'm so sore I can scarcely swing a club."

I've never been famous as a golfer who was always down the middle of the fairway with his drives. But that day I was wilder than ever before or since. I was all over the course. After every drive I was in the rough. Yet on the recovery shots I was deadlier than the ptomaine from which I was suffering.

The first hole is over a pond. I took a painful full swing knowing I must carry this pond. I carried it all right. I carried it so far the pond was never in my line of flight. I was in the rough, but my recovery was on the green and two putts gave me a par 4. After that I rarely took more than one putt. The rest of the round gave me lots of practice where my day was spent . . . in the rough. But I finished in an unbelievable 68 and the gallery was buzzing with excitement because I had set a new course record. That round was a miraculous cure for my illness. I even decided against returning to that lobster restaurant to tell the proprietor what I thought of his joint.

I changed to street clothes and went out in front of the club house to look at the scoreboard. Listening to the gallery, hearing them talk about my breaking the course record, led me to believe I was strokes ahead of anyone else. I was sure my 68 would stick up like a mountain peak over all the others. I just wanted to give myself the satisfaction of seeing how far ahead I was. I felt wonderful. At least I did until I looked at the scoreboard. For breathing down my neck with a 69 was Francis Ouimet, defending champion since his sensational victory over Vardon and Ray at Brookline. And he was getting most of the attention from the gallery at Midlothian. And I stood looking at the scoreboard and thinking, "I haven't done anything." One stroke is nothing at the start of a National Championship.

I stuck to regular food like steak and potatoes for the rest of the tournament. And my game stayed hot. I was never headed; I led all the way. Ouimet kept the pressure on, but after my final round I had posted a score of 290. That 290 equaled the lowest score ever made up to that year in the United States Open history. George Sargent, a wonderful golfer, had shot that score in 1909, playing the Open at the Englewood Country Club.

But I needed that 290. For after I had completed my final round news came into the locker room that Chick Evans had a chance. When he reached the seventy-second hole, I joined the crowd watching him on the green. He needed to hole a chip shot to tie me. And just one half hour earlier I had been in the rough to the left of that green short of a trap and had exploded out on the green twenty feet from the hole. I sank the curving putt. Now, as Chick was trying to hole his chip shot I thought how lucky I had been to get that putt down. He made a gallant effort but missed by fifteen inches. I beat him out of the championship by that one putt. It hadn't appeared too important at the time, but now it was the biggest and best shot I'd made.

The morning after my record-breaking 68, the sports pages of the Chicago dailies carried a boxed announcement headlining my name: *W. C. Hagen*! My first taste of publicity and how I loved it! The papers spelled my name correctly that year and ever afterwards. In Boston the year before I had been mentioned briefly as *W. C. Hagin*.

Bob MacDonald, the great old-time Scottish pro from Dornoch, Scotland, and then pro at Buffalo, joined Dutch and me on our journey back to New York State via the day coach. All the trip home I held the championship medal clutched tightly in my hand. It was the greatest thing in my life. I hadn't thought to notify anyone when we were arriving in Rochester, so nobody met us. But back at the club house the pro shop was gaily decorated with flags, the club sported holiday bunting and a huge American flag was set up on the eighteenth green.

Considering my win at Midlothian in relation to the showing I had made at Brookline the year before, one fact impressed me. My mind had been so occupied with the pains in my stomach and head I had had no thought of worry about each shot I made. Even after that first day, I was so spent from physical weakness that I concerned myself chiefly with getting around the course and just taking my strokes, good or bad, as they came. I decided then that mental and physical relaxation during competition was the most valuable asset any golfer could possess. Concentrate on playing the best you can on each shot . . . if it's a good one, that's fine. If it's bad, forget it. I expected to make so many bad ones anyway. I had to recognize that fact and aim to get the good ones where they counted most.

I wouldn't recommend a dose of ptomaine poisoning as a method of forgetting to worry about a golf score, but it taught me to look at each round as a unit and to take individual bad shots in my stride.

I went back to my job as pro at the Country Club of Rochester. Back to keeping the golf shop, giving lessons and making golf clubs. But what a difference in my outlook. Here I was, twenty-one years old and Open Champion of the United States. I notified Pat Moran of the Phillies that I would *not* be in Florida for a tryout with the team. After all, I'd hit the big time in golf, so why bother with baseball?

Almost immediately the winning of the Open began to widen the horizons for me. I was invited to give exhibitions and to play in tournaments arranged by the various clubs. I even endorsed a few products, and this more than anything else made me realize the importance and the potentials of the title. I was fully aware of the weaknesses in my game. I began right then to study golf. I learned the rules forward and backward. Through the years that knowledge has rewarded me many times over. I also began to improve my form. I believed the public had a right to expect the best I could give. In those early exhibitions I was more nervous than a wagering spectator.

I had never been much concerned with form. I had concentrated on getting the ball where I wanted it. Imitating Vardon's stance and swing at Brookline had made me aware of the value of perfect posture and body rhythm such as he had developed. Also I had something of a sway and a very noticeable movement of my hips and knees . . . first forward, then backward. One writer at the time said I "started my drive with a sway and ended with a lunge." And I guess he was about right.

In modifying movement in my swing I tried first to eliminate the exaggerated swaying as much as possible. I found that if I began the backswing by taking the club away from the ball my hip action and pivot would take care of themselves. In doing this I was getting a semi-sway but at all times keeping my left eye focused on the ball, thus keeping my head still. Then my pivot became automatic. The larger arc I got with this swing enabled me to keep the head of the club on the ball longer during the follow-through.

During those months of practice, also, I tried to pave my swing with guards. What is a guard? Well, a guard is the method of controlling the power a golfer gets from the combined use of arms, hip action and the placement of the hands. Keeping the arms together and pinching the knees together in unison, with complete hand control of the club, allows the player to fade or slice intentionally by letting the left hand be the master. In drawing or hooking a shot the right hand becomes master. Movement plays a very important part throughout the swing. With a fade the hips go forward with the arms, while with a hook one must pivot sooner. Don't exaggerate this action for it's wise to retain enough energy for extra-curricular activity—perhaps for some night work on a fancy tango or a few lively steps of the Charleston.

Guards are necessary throughout the game of golf, particularly when the prevailing wind is on one side or the other—or when trees block the way. This last, over a period of years, was my biggest problem, for I found myself in the woods so continuously I began carrying a hunting license. So

I practiced using guards by placing two newspapers at given distances on the fairway, and spent long hours learning to control my hooks and slices.

Needless to say, I did not acquire the rhythm and ease and smoothness I desired within the next few months or even the next few years. But I continued to work on it, polishing, practicing and perfecting . . . gaining in some small measure as the time passed.

Through the years I've been accused of dramatizing shots—of knowing just which club I intended to use, just how I intended to make the shot—then holding up the game or the match by carefully scrutinizing the turf, the sky, my opponent or even the caddie. Of making the difficult shots look easy and the easy shots look difficult. Only that last came naturally, believe me. Well, I always figured the gallery had a show coming to them. I deny I ever held up a game by any such shenanigans, but I don't deny playing for the gallery. I don't deny trying to make my game as interesting and as thrilling to the spectators as it was possible for me to make it.

I had the same feeling for the spectator in those early years, but I will admit my ability to put on a good performance increased through time and experience. I loved the excitement of the tournaments, the admiration of the gallery, the words—complimentary or otherwise—tossed my way by the sports writers and radio commentators. All these helped to build me into the international sports figure I became and to hold me there for thirty years of competitive golf.

Competition was always important to me. I played better golf under pressure, whether from an opponent or the elements or lack of money. When I was short of cash I could always win. When I needed a title to enhance my value in exhibitions, I went out and got it. The healthier my economic situation, the lousier I played. But give me some good stiff competition or a lack of the green stuff and I could usually shoot a winning score.

Back in 1914, with the championship medal from the USGA Open clutched in my fist, I was just starting for the top as a professional golfer. Even in those early days, I was brash enough to wonder where else there was for me to go. Too late now for me to go back to school! The many hours I spent studying myself and my game, learning the fine points of golf, perfecting my swing—those were wonderful and purposeful hours for me. And the amounts of cash dribbling in from endorsements and exhibitions were sauce for my first big thick steaks.

I was twenty-one and the world was my oyster. Only my dad could see no future ahead for me. He considered knocking the little white ball around a pasture a silly way to make a living. Although I always thought the British tough people to convince—you had to win their Open more than once before they acknowledged your game was championship caliber—my dad was tougher. He was seventy years young before he ever saw me play in a Championship.

Long Thoughts About Inverness and Vardon

from *Following Through* by Herbert Warren Wind

Inverness, one of Donald Ross's best-known courses, has been the venue of the U.S. Open in 1920, 1931, 1957, and 1979. The 1979 championship, which was won by Hale Irwin, did not quite come to life, but the first three were exciting, each in a different way. This is the part of the article that deals with them, and especially with Harry Vardon, the first really modern golfer and a thoroughly fine man. Vardon, who had won the first of his six British Opens way back in 1896, seemed to have the 1920 U.S. Open well under control with only nine holes to play, but a storm blew up off Lake Erie, and it proved to be too much for the old boy.

The most prolific golf-course architect of all time was Donald Ross, a pleasant, methodical Scot from Dornoch, in Sutherland, who became the professional at Pinehurst, North Carolina, in 1900, shortly after his arrival in this country, and remained there until his death, at seventy-five, in 1948. Ross, who quickly demonstrated his gift for building good golf holes when he remodelled Pinehurst's original eighteen-hole layout, later constructed three more courses there, making Pinehurst, shortly after the First World War, the first resort in America to offer its clientele seventy-two holes of golf. Because they enjoyed and admired Ross's work, a good many of the people who annually vacationed at Pinehurst approached him to do courses in their home towns, and he is credited with having built no fewer than six hundred in all parts of the country. This is a flabbergasting number, and one must assume that it includes not only the courses he himself worked on during his summers away from Pinehurst and those he looked in on from time to time to check on how his construction superintendents were faring but also those he merely laid out on paper. Apparently, it was not uncommon for Pinehurst regulars to bring with them topographical maps of property back home on which they and their friends intended to build a course, and for Ross to take these maps home with him in the evening and rough out nine or eighteen good, sound holes—a few of which inevitably possessed such Ross specialties as crown greens (formed by levelling the top of a hill) and small, slightly raised greens that were hard to hit because of the adroit positioning of the bunkers and hollows that set them off.

In 1918, the Inverness Club in Toledo, Ohio, which had been making do with nine holes since its formation, in 1903, felt that the time was ripe to build a modern eighteen-hole course. They got in touch with Ross, whose name had become an assurance of superior design. Giving the job his personal attention, he revamped the old nine and created a second nine. When the Ohio State Open was held over the new Inverness in the autumn of 1919, both the players and the spectators were enthusiastic about the course, and, as a result, the United States Golf Association selected it as the venue of the 1920 United States Open Championship. From the old golf hands who attended this Open, I gather that while Inverness proved to be a fairly testing layout, spread over nice rolling terrain, it struck no one as a truly great course. For one thing, its routing was uninspired: No fewer than eight holes (the second, the eleventh, the twelfth, the fourteenth, the fifteenth, the sixteenth, the seventeenth, and the sixth) ran more or less parallel to each other. Certainly it was not at all in the same class as the two courses that are today considered Ross's masterpieces—Seminole, in North Palm Beach, which was completed in 1929, and his wonderful wholesale revision of Pinehurst No. 2, done in the mid-thirties, when advances in agronomy made it possible to replace the old flat sand greens with subtly contoured grass greens. In any event, what made a newly golf-conscious America very much aware of Inverness was not the attributes of Ross's course but, rather, the exciting dénouement of the 1920 Open. It was won by Ted Ray, a burly Englishman with a soup-strainer mustache who always wore a felt or straw hat on the course and played with a pipe in his mouth. Harry Vardon, Leo Diegel, Jack Burke, Sr., and Jock Hutchison finished a shot behind him. Ray was then forty-three, and he remains the oldest golfer ever to win our national championship.[*]

Since 1920, Inverness has held the Open three more times—in 1931, in 1957, and this past June, when Hale Irwin carried the day—and each time an interesting Open took place. Before dealing with the recent championship, it would be worthwhile, I think, to touch on the high points of the earlier ones. Their scenarios differed considerably in some ways, but in other ways they were oddly similar—such as in the crucial role that the eighteenth hole, a par 4 that is only a drive and short pitch, nearly always played in the winning and the losing of the championship. In the 1957 Open, it looked as if Jimmy Demaret, who was then forty-seven, had at last won his first Open when, on the climactic double round on Saturday, he posted a par 70 and then a 72, for a total of 283. (He finished with a great burst: birdie, par, birdie, par.) Half an hour later, though, Dick Mayer holed a sliding nine-foot putt to birdie the eighteenth and nip him by a stroke. Half an hour after that, Cary Middlecoff, having taken several prolonged azimuth readings on the nine-footer he had to sink to birdie the last hole and tie with Mayer, finally got hunched over his ball and stroked it dead into the center of the cup. An exceedingly high-strung athlete, Middlecoff had expended all his energy on Saturday's double round (he had put together a pair of superb 68s), and he had nothing left the next day in the playoff, which Mayer won by seven shots.

---

[*] Editor's note: In 1990, Hale Irwin became the oldest golfer to win the U.S. Open. He was forty-five years fifteen days old.

The 1931 Open was also decided by a playoff—the longest playoff ever in a major championship. George Von Elm, who had turned professional the previous year, after a distinguished career as an amateur, made a playoff necessary when he holed for a birdie from twelve feet on the seventy-second green to match Billy Burke's four-round total of 292. The next day, Von Elm, a rather dashing type, and Burke, a steady, placid one, met in a thirty-six-hole playoff. Burke had a 73 in the morning and a 76 in the afternoon. Von Elm had a 75 in the morning, and on his second round he again cooly holed a birdie putt of twelve feet on the last green, for a 74 and a matching total of 149. So the two weary golfers set out once more the next morning on yet another double round to see who would be king. Von Elm had a 76 and a 73, Burke a 77 and a beautifully played afternoon round of 71. On the second nine that afternoon, he had eight straight 4s and could have easily made it nine straight, since he was on in two, thirty feet from the cup, on the home green. However, knowing that all he had to do to win was to get down in three putts, he made sure he did: He lagged his approach putt four feet from the hole, cozied the ball to the rim of the cup, and then tapped it in.

For all this, neither the 1957 nor the 1931 Open was as stirring or as significant as the 1920 Open. That was in many respects a watershed Open. To start with, it marked a changing of the guard; it was the last big championship in which Vardon and Ray, who had come to the fore in Britain in the distant days of the guttapercha ball, played a prominent part, and it was the first appearance in our Open of a clutch of young men, among them Bobby Jones, Gene Sarazen, Johnny Farrell, Tommy Armour, and Diegel, who went on to become outstanding golfers. It was also the first national championship, here or in Britain, in which the entire clubhouse was opened to the professional entrants. The men running Inverness simply made up their minds that it no longer made sense, if it ever had, to regard professional golfers as low-class workingmen who were the social inferiors of the club members and the amateur contestants. Inverness treated the professionals as its guests, and once it had shown the way, the long-standing barriers against the professionals began to disintegrate rapidly. With Walter Hagen, as usual, acting as their leader, the professionals did not fail to let Inverness know how deeply they appreciated "the Toledo spirit." They took up a collection at the close of the tournament and presented the club with a handsome cathedral-chime clock about eight feet high—a clock that still stands in the clubhouse foyer. On a brass plaque attached to the clock at that time is a short verse (no one has any idea who wrote it) that is quite moving:

> God measures men by what they are
> Not what in wealth possess.
> This vibrant message chimes afar
> The voice of Inverness.

Primarily, though, the 1920 Open was the story of Harry Vardon. People are forever debating about who is the greatest golfer who has ever lived. Today, the consensus would probably favor Jack Nicklaus. His credentials *are* awesome. He has won seventeen major championships—four more than the next man, Jones—and has done it over a period of twenty years: from 1959, when he won his first United States Amateur Championship, through 1978, when he won his third British Open. Longevity, no doubt about it, is a significant consideration in any evaluation of the relative merits of athletic heroes. However, in my opinion the best and fairest way to describe his position in the game's long history is to say that there has never been a better golfer than Nicklaus, just as there has never been a better golfer than Ben Hogan or a better golfer than Bobby Jones. As has been said so often that it is beginning to acquire a patina of triteness, all that one can ask of an athlete is that he be the finest performer in his field in his own age. Jones, Hogan, and Nicklaus have all been that. It is only natural that today's sports fans should be less well informed about the deeds of earlier champions than about the contemporary paragons, but sports experts are another matter, and most of today's experts know far too little about the exploits of Jones and Hogan. As for Vardon, his name hardly rings a bell at all, and yet, on the basis of his record, his marvellous technique, and his overall contribution to golf, he deserves a place on the same level as Nicklaus, Hogan, and Jones.

There has surely never been a better golfer than Harry Vardon. A native of the island of Jersey, he won his first British Open in 1896, at the age of twenty-six. In that era, when the British Open was *the* championship, he won it a record six times, his last victory coming in 1914. In 1900, when he made the first of his three visits to this country, he won our Open, at the Chicago Golf Club, and sold golf everywhere he went by the grace of his style and the astonishing accuracy of his shots. No one had had any idea that a player could control the golf ball in the masterly fashion that Vardon did. A medium-sized man with a strong, athletic frame and extraordinarily large hands, he was undoubtedly the most brilliant fairway-wood player ever; it was nothing unusual for him to rip a full brassie shot right at the flagstick and have the ball flutter down like a leaf ten or fifteen feet from his target. On Vardon's second American tour, in 1913, on which he teamed up with Ray, a fellow-native of Jersey, the two invaders, as fate would have it, tied for first with Francis Ouimet, a twenty-year-old amateur, at The Country Club, in Brookline, Massachusetts, and were subsequently defeated by Ouimet in the playoff—possibly the most momentous round of golf of all time. When the war was over, Vardon and Ray returned to this country for another tour. Vardon was then fifty years old, which in terms of athletic vigor would be roughly the equivalent of being sixty years old nowadays. He had stayed at the top of his profession for a quarter of a century, and that is a rare achievement in sports. At Inverness, he qualified handily. At the end of the first thirty-six holes of the championship, which was played in mid-August, he was in an excellent position: rounds of 74 and 73, for a halfway total of 147, placed him two shots behind the pacemaker, Hutchison, one shot behind Diegel, and in a tie with Hagen and Ray. (The weather was broiling hot in Toledo that week, but Vardon and Ray were used to playing in loose-fitting jackets, and they did so on this occasion. They also wore shirts and ties—as did the whole field.) Despite Vardon's precise golf on the opening day, no one expected too much from the old boy from there on, because the final thirty-six holes were set to be played the following day, and this would work to the advantage of the young and hardy. Thereupon Vardon, in top form, stepped out in front of the pack with a splendid 71 on the morning of the third round. At two o'clock, when he started his afternoon round, he carried most of the spectators with him; they realized that even Vardon couldn't go on forever, and they wanted to cheer him home in what well might be his last crack at winning another big championship.

On the first nine, continuing to split the fairways and hit the greens, Vardon was out in 36. He added a par and then a birdie, and, with only seven holes to go, had a margin over the closest man of a full five strokes. He seemed to have the championship wrapped up. When he was standing on the tee of the twelfth hole, then a 522-yard par 5, the skies suddenly grew dark and a wind of almost gale force swept off Lake Erie and across Inverness. Playing into the fierce wind, Vardon required four shots to reach the twelfth green, and lost a stroke to par there. He lost another stroke to par on the short thirteenth, when he jabbed a two-foot putt wide of the cup. (Near the end of his career, Vardon's play from tee to green was as impressive as ever, but he could be skittish on the greens when he was faced with short putts. As he prepared to tap the ball, a small muscle in his right forearm would sometimes jump visibly, and when it didn't his anxiety that it might ruined his ease and concentration.) By the time Vardon moved to the fourteenth, the extra effort of coping with the wind was beginning to wear him down, and missing that short putt completed his undoing. He took three putts on the fourteenth, three on the fifteenth, and three more on the sixteenth, losing a stroke to par on each of them. He lost two more strokes to par on the seventeenth, a 430-yard par 4. He was plain unlucky here: his second shot just caught the far edge of the brook guarding the green. On the eighteenth, he made his par 4, but apparently he did not have any chance for a birdie, since no account of his round which I have seen mentions how far from the pin he put his pitch or describes his putt.

It was all quite tragic, Vardon's collapse. After starting with a double bogey on the first hole on his morning round, he had played the next twenty-eight holes in four under par—a terrific pace in the circumstances—only to go seven over par on the last seven holes of the championship. He had taken forty-two strokes on the second nine in the afternoon. His 78 on the last round gave him a four-round total of 296 and tied him with Burke, an earlier finisher. Now the question was whether Ray, Hutchison, or Diegel, still out on the course, would be able to beat that figure. (Hagen had fallen away.) Ray finished soon after Vardon did. He brought in a rather loose 75, but it was good enough: 74–73–73–75—295. He had played erratic stuff on the last nine, bogeying the eleventh, twelfth, fifteenth, and seventeenth, but when he was confronted with the opportunity to win the Open he seized it, and that always takes some doing. Both Hutchison and Diegel eventually had to settle for 296. Hutchison's bid was over when his three-foot putt for a par on the fifteenth rimmed out of the cup. Diegel was in trouble after a double bogey on the fourteenth, but he pulled himself together and barely missed from eight feet on the seventeenth for the birdie he needed, and on the home green he failed to get down a longer but makable birdie putt. Had Diegel managed to win at Inverness, he might have gone on to win our Open several times, but, as it was, he never quite made it, and his two victories at match play in our P.G.A. Championship stand as the high point of his career.

The evening after the storm off Lake Erie prevented Vardon from achieving what had looked to be the perfect storybook climax to his long and illustrious career, he was his usual stoic self as he met with the press and went over his final round. "Even as tired as I was, I can't see yet how I broke so badly," he said. "Why, I am sure I could go out now and do better by kicking the ball around with my boot." It was easy to become fond of Vardon, for modesty and gentleness were deeply ingrained in his nature. His colleagues esteemed him highly, and the esteem was reciprocated. He thought the world of J. H. Taylor and James Braid, his chief rivals (each of them won the

British Open five times), who, along with Vardon, formed what was called the Triumvirate, and his regard for them is not difficult to understand. Both were of humble background—Taylor started out as a mason's laborer, Braid as an apprentice joiner—and they typified the old yeoman virtues of strong fibre and generosity of spirit. In Vardon's mind, golf was an ennobling game, and he believed that Braid's and Taylor's closeness to it had a lot to do with their exemplary character. When one considers Vardon's own mild, pleasant manner, with its undertone of shyness, it is odd, and amusing, that the two best-known anecdotes about him present him as a very abrupt person. The first is set in 1900, the year of his first American tour. In one of his appearances in Chicago, his foursome included a left-handed player who on that particular afternoon could do no wrong. After the round, probing for praise, he asked Vardon who was the best left-hander he had ever played with. Vardon took a moment to clear his throat and then said, "Never saw one who was worth a damn." The second anecdote involves Bobby Jones. Some astute member of the championship committee for the 1920 Open thought that it might be an interesting idea to pair Vardon in the qualifying round with Jones, who was then only eighteen but already had the look of a champion. On the seventh, a drive-and-pitch par 4, Vardon hit his second, a little run-up shot, fairly close to the stick. Jones decided he would play a steep niblick pitch, which he intended to strike so crisply that the backspin on the ball would cause it to brake itself quickly on the green and draw back dramatically toward the pin. He looked up on the shot, however, and skulled the ball yards over the green. He did well to make a 5. Still smarting with embarrassment as the two men walked off the green, Jones turned and asked, "Mr. Vardon, did you ever see a worse shot than that?" "No," Vardon said.

Vardon was born in Grouville, on the eastern end of Jersey, which is an island about the size of Nantucket, and which, like the other Channel Islands, belongs to Great Britain, although it lies much closer to France—only fifteen miles or so off the Cotentin Peninsula. Harry was one of eight children of a gardener, and the fourth of six sons. What proved to be the pivotal event of his youth took place in 1877, when he was seven. That summer, some English visitors received permission from the constable of the parish of Grouville to lay out a golf course on part of the common land. This became the Royal Jersey Golf Club, and, like most of the local boys, Harry caddied at the club and picked up the game. A surprisingly large number of those Jersey caddies—among them the Gaudins, the Boomers, the Renoufs, the Becks, and, of course, Ted Ray—became very successful professionals. As a boy, Vardon developed into a proficient golfer in no time. This was more or less expected of him, because he was an exceptional all-around athlete—a fast sprinter and a standout at both cricket and soccer. His boyhood ambition was "to excel at cricket," but any idea he might have had about possibly becoming a professional cricketer was hardly more than a daydream, and when his schooling was completed he was apprenticed to a gardener. Had it not been for his brother Tom, who was a couple of years younger but far more enterprising and confident, Harry might never have left Jersey. Hoping to make a career in golf, Tom went to England and got a job as an assistant professional. He proved to be not only an able player but a talented instructor. When he had things under control, he lined up a job for Harry as the professional at Studley Royal, a nine-hole course in the North of England. Harry moved on from Studley Royal to Bury and then, in 1896, to Ganton, an inland course in Yorkshire with some of the characteristics of a seaside links. He was affiliated with Ganton until 1903, when he left to become the professional at the South Herts Golf Club, in Totteridge, north of London, and there he stayed until his death, in 1937. During his first season at Ganton, Vardon came into his own, winning the British Open, at Muirfield, by defeating Taylor in a playoff. He won the championship again in 1898, at Prestwick, and in 1899, at Sandwich. He had by then established himself as the premier golfer in the world, and what a delight it is to picture him during these years returning to Ganton after some signal triumph in a tournament or a challenge match and playing center forward on the town soccer team, which he had organized. Later, when he had slowed down a little, he shifted to goaltender. Tom Vardon, incidentally, never won the British Open but came close three times, finishing second, in a tie for third, and fourth. When he was in his late thirties, he emigrated to this country and became the popular and much-admired professional at Onwentsia, one of the oldest and best clubs in the Chicago area.

If Harry Vardon remains very much alive for a number of people both here and in Britain who are deep into golf, it is not so much because of the many championships he won as because he revolutionized the golf swing. In fact, he might be regarded as the first modern golfer. It is true that before he appeared on the scene several of the top British players had cultivated individual methods of hitting the ball. Taylor, for instance, had a wide, somewhat flatfooted stance and spanked his shots forcefully with his powerful arms. As a general rule, though, the leading players felt that the golf swing called for unconcealed muscular effort, like tossing the caber. They believed that the fundamentals of the swing included a long, low take-away followed by a strenuous lifting of the elbows and winding of the shoulders as the backswing progressed. Then came an emphatic forward lurch on the downswing, so that the weight and strength of the body could be poured into the shot at impact, after which the player followed through with whatever vigor he had not expended. Just why Vardon, isolated in Grouville, happened on a totally different and much more advanced technique is as much a mystery as how it was that Addison and Steele hit upon and developed the personal essay, Chopin utilized the full melodic range of the piano, or Manet and the other early Impressionists evolved a new approach to the depiction of light. A genius, it appears, can pop up anywhere, and there is no accounting for his special gift. In any event, Vardon had some very definite ideas about the difficult game of golf, in which a stationary ball is hit from a stationary stance. To begin with, he believed that the two keys to a good swing were a steady head position and a sound grip. Because he had large palms and long fingers, the grip that he found gave him the most control was one in which the little finger of the right hand overlapped the index finger of the left hand. Speaking of this grip, he once said, "It did not come naturally to me, but it was well worth the trouble of acquiring. It seems to create just the right fusion between the hands, and voluntarily induces each to do its proper work." He was convinced that there was no master hand in the golf swing—that the two hands contributed equally. Other golfers had happened on the overlapping grip before Vardon did—J. E. Laidlay, a Scot who won the British Amateur in 1889 and 1891, was perhaps the first player of prominence to use it—but the grip has always been referred to as the Vardon grip since the last years of the nineteenth century, when he popularized it by making the British Open practically his private property. The swing he gradually evolved included many other departures from orthodoxy. Instead of employing a closed stance, he opened the toe of his right foot slightly and the toe of his left foot to about a thirty-degree angle (anticipating Hogan in the latter respect, though Hogan's left foot was a little less open—to about twenty-two degrees). He took the club back from the ball in a much more upright and less flat arc than any golfer before him. This was a critical innovation. Besides facilitating a correct hip turn and a full shoulder turn on his backswing, it enabled him to execute his downswing and his release through the ball with an unimpeded flow and rhythm that, in the opinion of the best authorities, only two other golfers, Bobby Jones and Sam Snead, have matched. Vardon's upright arc also made it much simpler for him to pick a ball cleanly from almost any type of lie, even with a club like a brassie, which has a face with comparatively little loft, and to sweep it away in a high trajectory. With his irons, he did not take a large or a deep divot but merely brushed across the turf. He differed from the great stylists who came after him in that his left arm was not straight but bent slightly at the elbow when he took the club back, but, interestingly, at the start of the downswing he straightened the arm. He was, by the way, the first golfer who hit the ball so that in its flight it moved from left to right in a controlled fade, and since a left-to-right shot tends to come down much more softly than a shot that moves from right to left, this, combined with the precision with which he struck the ball, put him in a class by himself when it came to playing full fairway shots and having the ball drop softly on the green and expire almost instantly. Many golfers have tried to copy Vardon's fade, but none of them have made the hitting action seem as natural as he did. He was an incredibly straight player; he once strung together seven consecutive tournament rounds without ever hitting the ball into the rough or into a hazard. The refined tempo and the synchronization of his movements disguised his power, but Vardon hit the ball a long, long way.

In a word, Vardon, as noted earlier, was a genius. It was fortunate that he was, for in 1903, not long after he won his fourth British Open, he came down with tuberculosis, and during the next half-dozen years he had to take things rather easy. An illness of this seriousness would have ended the career of most athletes. Vardon, in truth, was never quite the same again, but he managed to play in the British Open each year, and often managed to finish in the top five. The simplicity and correctness of his grooved swing permitted him to do this, although the game of golf underwent a substantial change during this period when the rubber-cored ball—the modern ball—replaced the old solid guttapercha ball that Vardon had grown up with and greatly preferred. In 1911, in much better health than he had been for some time, he amazed the golf world by emerging from the shadows and winning his fifth British Open, at forty-one. In 1914, he won the championship for the sixth and last time. He was not yet ready to pack it in, however. At the conclusion of the First World War, he felt strong enough to undertake his third American tour—the one that took him to Inverness. As I write, I am studying a splendid action photograph that shows Vardon following through on a drive off the fourteenth tee during the championship. In certain respects, the picture looks as if it were taken when it was—sixty years ago. Vardon is wearing knickers, a straw hat, and a two-buttoned, ventless jacket, which the force of his swing has sent billowing out at the bottom. The hat is probably an authentic panama, the jacket most likely pongee. On the other hand, as

Vardon nears the finish of his swing, with the heel of his right foot high off the ground, he is as beautifully on balance as Hogan was in his prime. His hitting action on that drive was obviously as free as Tom Watson's is today. In short, he looks absolutely contemporary.

Golf's Greatest Putt

**Time: 1929 U.S. Open. Place: 18th hole.
The Man: Bobby Jones**

by Grantland Rice, *Sports Illustrated*, August 16, 1954

GRANTLAND RICE

BORN: 1880

DIED: 1954

One of the last articles written by Grantland Rice, who died suddenly July 13, was a piece for SPORTS ILLUSTRATED. It is as typical of Grantland Rice as any article could be. It is about golf, the game he loved the best. Its central figure is Bob Jones, whom he esteemed above all the other champions he knew and admired as his ranking hero. Its setting is the '20s, the age when sports first became an important part of the American scene, assisted by Granny's incomparable ability to convey to his readers his genuine love of sport and the excitement that seized him at certain major moments—such as Jones's dramatic finish in the 1929 National Open. For these reasons, and others more personal, I think this story by Grantland Rice is the perfect one with which to inaugurate our regular golf column.
—Herbert Warren Wind

On a late June afternoon in 1929, some 10,000 tense spectators crowded up to the 18th green at the Winged Foot Golf Course in Westchester County, New York. As they came running up to the green, crowding as close as they could get, you heard every type of sound from a whisper to a shriek blended into one vast babble of excited human voices. The startling news was passed from person to person—Bob Jones was on the verge of the worst catastrophe any U.S. Open had ever known.

As Jones broke through the crowd and came upon the green, the babble suddenly was stilled. This was the silence of suppressed nerves. Since the first Scottish herdsman addressed an early golf ball with a shepherd's crook, I doubt if any golfer had ever faced a moment so packed with tension.

It was one of the great moments I have ever known in sports. The silence was complete. Only a few short minutes before, Jones had been six strokes up with only six holes to go. Now he had one putt left, for a tie. Bobby Jones had faced crucial putts before—more of them than any other golfer I have ever known—where important championships were at stake. But this putt meant more to Bob Jones than merely winning an Open. It meant the recapture of his golfing soul. It meant removing a dark stain from his pride, certain nationwide ridicule that was to follow failure.

Let's go back a minute. The real drama of this, the 33rd Open, and of Bob Jones's career, started at the long 12th hole.

Here Al Espinosa, the only challenger, took a destructive 8. When Espinosa took this 8, he felt he had no chance. With the tension off, he finished with four 4's and two 3's for a 75 and a total of 294.

Even with this spurt on Espinosa's part, Jones could drop three strokes to par over the last six holes and still win. There never was a surer thing in golf.

Bob lost one stroke at the short 13, and then at the 15th he had a heartbreaking 7, three over par. Now he needed three pars to tie Espinosa. Here was undoubtedly the finest golfer in the world . . . yet no duffer had ever blown so bad.

Jones got his pars on 16 and 17 and came to the final hole needing a par 4 to tie his Mexican-American rival. Bob's drive was good. His second shot hit the hard, keen green and ran down a grassy bank. He chipped from below, but the chip stopped 12 to 14 feet short. He stopped as he came up on the green and saw how far short he was—the putt he had to hole to even get a draw.

This wasn't the first 10- or 12-foot putt Bob had had to sink in his brilliant career . . . I could name any number of 10-footers he had holed to keep from being beaten on some closing green. I might add here that over a long period of years I have seen five great putters—Walter Travis, Jerry Travers, Walter Hagen, Horton Smith and Bobby Jones. I believe Jones was the greatest for the simple reason that he saved himself more times by holing the important ones—the 8- and 10-footers against George Voigt, against Cyril Tolley, against Maurice McCarthy, to beat out Gene Sarazen and Hagen in so many championships here and abroad.

But this occasion at Winged Foot was different. Jones's competitive career, by his own choice, was nearing its end. He had been working seriously at the game since he was 7 years old. He was now 27. The 1929 title meant his third U.S. Open. He had finished 1-2 in this Open since 1922, eight years with only one exception—1927. Later O. B. Keeler, Jones's Boswell and the best golf writer this country ever produced, told me that if Bob had missed this putt he would never have gone abroad the next year to make his Grand Slam.

On the green, Bobby Jones crouched partly on one knee studying the slanting line of the treacherous putt. There was a dip or a break in the green of at least a foot-and-a-half that had to be judged. Bob was usually a fast putter. This time he took a few seconds longer than usual, for in addition to the speed of the fast green he had to decide how big the break was.

I was with Mike Brady, the club pro, when the putt was made. I was on the ground, peering between legs. Mike had a step ladder and was above the mob.

"He's short," Mike shouted. "He's missed it. He's short." I lost the ball en route. I picked it up again near the cup. Suddenly the ball hesitated, stopped—and then turned over once more and disappeared.

That's the way Bob always putted—to get the ball just up to the cup where it has 4 inches to fall.

I have heard in my time a sudden roar—a great crash of noise, many, many times at many different games. I never heard before, or since, the vocal cataclysm that rocked the oaks of Westchester.

Jones beat Espinosa in the play-off by more than 20 strokes. The next year he won the Grand Slam. In the wake of that putt he went on his way to one record that may never be equaled. For, as George Trevor put it, "he stormed the impregnable quadrilateral of golf."

Bobby Jones, Interlachen

from *Triumphant Journey: The Saga of Bobby Jones and the Grand Slam of Golf* by Richard Miller

On Wednesday, July 2, 1930, Bobby Jones, the only American golfer ever to capture the British Amateur and Open championships in one year, arrived in New York City aboard the S.S. *Europa*. He was given the hero's welcome: the traditional ticker-tape parade.

At 4:00 P.M. that afternoon—a hot, humid day in the city, the kind when you can see heat shimmering off the pavement—the parade began from the Battery up Broadway. Beneath a blizzard of swirling ticker tape, preceded by seventy mounted policemen, and with a band playing "Valencia," the motorcade slowly wound its way up the narrow street. Thousands of spectators packed the sidewalks, as they had in 1926 for Gertrude Ederle, the first woman to swim the English Channel, and in 1927 for Charles Lindbergh. Jones wore the chaplet of a peaceful conquest. The channel he had crossed had been the Atlantic Ocean, and his plane had been a steep pitch to a small patch of green.

That day had been an unusually quiet one in the financial district. The brokers and traders were now working only five-hour days, and July 2 had been the slowest trading day in more than two years, with a mere 1.3 million shares of stocks being traded. One broker who didn't know about the parade approached a massive policeman, worrying and sweating profusely, and asked, "What's the parade for?" The policeman replied disgustedly, "Oh, for some God damn golf player!"

The shy and modest Jones was suffering and sweating just about as much as the policeman. Behind his broad, thankful smile was a grimace.

At 5:00 P.M. the motorcade reached City Hall Plaza, and Mayor Jimmy Walker greeted Jones. "Here you are, the greatest golfer in the world being introduced by the worst one."

Two hundred and fifty Atlantans who had taken a train called the "Bobby Jones Special" to New York City yelled in unison, "Atta boy, Jimmy."

That evening there was a dinner honoring Jones given by 400 of his closest friends at the Vanderbilt Hotel. The next day, Jones, his father and mother, and scores of friends left for Minneapolis aboard the Twentieth Century. The U.S. Open at the Interlachen Country Club, eight miles west of Minneapolis, would begin in seven days. Jones's wife, Mary, was returning to Atlanta to take care of their two children—Clara, age five, and Robert Tyre Jones III, age three. The boy had sent up a very important message to his father: "Tell Daddy I can whistle now."

Jones had only a few days to prepare for the U.S. Open, and this was during a scorching heat wave then gripping the Midwest. Jones worked on his timing. He was trying to coalesce those hundreds of elements that made up his beautiful and graceful long swing. The 6,672-yard course was set over rolling terrain with five lakes, smallish greens, and an almost knee-high rough which would be the mightiest foe for the golfers. Two days before the championship, Jones shot a two-under-par 70.

After the round, Jones said, "That was the first time since the Southeastern Open in Augusta that everything felt just right."

Walter Hagen felt he was playing well, but still needed a little more practice.

And he was exceedingly pleased with a new set of clubs. For the first time in a major championship, The Haig was playing with steel-shafted clubs. The consensus of the players was that the winning score would be 292, four over par.

On Thursday, July 10, the U.S. Open began. The temperature in the shade registered over ninety-five degrees, and the humidity was almost as high. Jones started off at 9:45. He played the front nine in a neat 34 shots; he played the back nine, in the hottest heat of the day, in just less than an hour and a half and 37 strokes. His score, a neat 71, stood as the lowest of the day until late that afternoon when Macdonald Smith and Tommy Armour both posted 70s.

So intense was the heat that Armour rubbed his face and forehead with a pack of ice before each shot. Ed Dudley and Chick Evans experienced spells of dizziness. Jim Barnes walked beneath a large green umbrella. Hagen, who never played with a hat, simply because he got paid handsomely for endorsing a particular hair tonic, stated that he wouldn't stir the next day without a big straw hat.

For those who might wonder where dignity goes when it melts, there was Cyril Tolley. The big seal of an Englishman, who had given Jones such a fierce battle in the British Amateur in near-gale winds, lost nine pounds that first day. A woman watching him walk slowly up a hill, his clothes soaked with perspiration, said, "Mr. Tolley looks like an iceman who has carried one hundred pounds of ice up five flights of stairs and found that the lady of the house was not at home." Tolley shot an 80.

Jones had dressed in light gray knickers, a white cap, a white shirt, and a red foulard tie. He carried a half dozen red-colored tees in his pocket. After his round, his knickers were so saturated with perspiration they were almost black, and the red tees had stained one leg of his knickers. His red tie had run all over his shirt.

The next day brought a cooling eastern breeze, and the humidity dropped; now the temperature was only in the low nineties. Jones played the front nine almost exactly as he had the first day, except for a bogey 5 on the long first hole, a 478-yard par 4, and a birdie 2 on the par-3 fifth.

On the ninth, a 485-yard par 5 with a big blue lake in front of the green, Jones hit the most controversial shot of the tournament. After a long drive down the right side of the fairway, Jones faced a spoon shot to reach the green. In practice and in the first round, he had reached the green easily and made birdies.

As usual, there were more than 8,000 spectators; Jones literally was hitting down a human alleyway. Just as Jones reached the top of his backswing, his eye caught a sharp movement in the gallery—two little girls were running ahead—and instinctively he flinched. He half-topped his shot. The ball took off in a low trajectory and didn't climb. It was heading straight for the lake. Now the best Jones could hope for was a bogey. But when the ball hit the water, it skipped twice and landed on the bank. From there Jones pitched to within four feet of the pin and holed his putt for a birdie.

For more than twenty-five years, until Jones denied it, the spoon shot was known as the "lily pad shot," because thousands of spectators claimed Jones's ball had actually struck a lily pad and then skidded onto the bank. There was no lily pad involved. With its low trajectory and the force with which it hit the water, the ball came in precisely like a flat stone being skipped across the surface. For sure, it was a stroke of luck, but in this championship, luck would even out. The unluckiest blow came at the worst possible juncture.

Jones played the back nine in 39, three over par. He bogeyed the seventeenth, the longest par 3 in U.S. Open history. It was a mean golf hole of 262 yards that called for a precise drive or brassie shot to a small green guarded on either side by bunkers. The right side of the fairway up to and beyond the green sloped toward a lake. In the whole tournament, only two birdies were made on the hole, one by Walter Hagen. The hole had a weird effect on Jones, one almost as strangely instinctive as that on a horse wanting to return to a burning barn. During the championship, Jones played the seventeenth in four over par.

At the end of the second round, Horton Smith, with a total of 142, led Jones by only two shots, hardly a very safe margin. Within five shots of the leader were four former U.S. Open champions: Jones, Tommy Armour, Johnny Farrell, and Walter Hagen. Collectively, they had won twenty-four major championships.

On Saturday morning, with thirty-six holes scheduled, the USGA posted a sign: "Play-off thirty-six holes 10 A.M. and 2 P.M. Sunday." It was a likely forecast. The last three U.S. Opens had been decided by play-offs. Jones had been involved in two.

For two days Jones had played well within himself. Not being the leader, he wasn't, as he would later write, "oppressed by that feeling of having something to protect." His tactic was to break quickly from the pack. Except for the mean seventeenth, there wasn't a hole that had him baffled.

Jones's third round was almost a perfect fusion of his mental and physical powers. Except for a slight faltering on the last two holes, the round was brilliant. Jones burned with a gemlike flame. He missed only three greens in regulation figures and only three fairways. He had nine one-putt greens; the longest putt he holed was a 10-footer on the first hole, and in all he took only twenty-seven putts. He scored six birdies, ten pars, and two bogeys. So accurate was his play with the mashie niblick (7-iron) that the aggregate distance the ball stopped from the pin was more measurable in inches than feet. His three shots with the club put the ball an average of thirty inches from the pin.

Jones also had the psychological edge on the field, now cut from 143 starters (there were 1,177 entries) to 66, by having an early starting time: 9:15. As Jones made birdie after birdie, the cheers from his huge gallery echoed across the course. It had an almost devastating effect on the other players. They started to press. On the sixth, Walter Hagen three-putted from four feet. And then there was poor Willie MacFarlane, not quite out of it, nine strokes off the lead at the start of the third round, who three-putted four greens in a row and eleven in all to post a third round total of 82.

After Jones holed his 10-footer at the long first hole for a par, he clicked off two more pars. Then on the par-5 fourth, Jones faced a delicate third shot, a pitch over a bunker to a green sloping steeply away from him to the pin, itself placed less than fifteen feet from the bunker. With the touch of a hairdresser, Jones played the pitch perfectly, landing the ball just over the bunker on the edge of the green and letting it slowly run down the slope. It ended four feet past the pin. A birdie. Jones easily parred the fifth. Then came the crescendo. On the sixth, Jones faced a second shot to an elevated green guarded by steep-walled bunkers. Out came the mashie niblick. The ball flew straight toward the pin and stopped twenty-three inches away. Again a birdie. On the next hole, from the rough, another mashie-niblick shot; this time the ball stopped five feet from the pin. Another birdie. He finished with two pars for a 33.

He parred the tenth, made two birdies at the back-to-back par 5s, the eleventh and twelfth, then three more pars. At the par-4 sixteenth, Jones's second shot was another mashie niblick. Again the ball went straight at the pin and dropped as softly as a grapefruit six inches from the pin. Another birdie. Two pars would give Jones a 66, a record U.S. Open round; but on the seventeenth, his brassie tee shot caught the right-side bunker, and after a poor explosion shot, he failed to get down a 14-foot putt for his par. He bogeyed the eighteenth after badly slicing his drive. He posted a 68, still the lowest round of the tournament.

The field not only backed off from Jones, but from par. There were only two other sub-par rounds that morning. Horton Smith and Walter Hagen slipped to 76s. Tommy Armour posted a 75. Jones led by five shots. Now it was no longer anyone's championship; it was Jones's. At least, so it appeared once again. But then, Jones so often had seemed to have won so many Opens.

Bobby Jones—The Gentleman from Georgia

from *Golf: The Marvelous Mania* by Alistair Cooke

Jones, Robert Tyre Jr. Lawyer, engineer, scholar, amateur golfer.

b. March 17, 1902. Son of Robert Tyre Jones, lawyer. For first five years was enfeebled by a puzzling disease, but at age six, won Atlanta East Lake Club's children's championship. At fourteen, was Georgia amateur champion and went through to quarter-final of US Amateur championship. In following two years, won Southern amateur. Throughout 1918, the sixteen-year-old toured in exhibition matches on behalf of the Red Cross and War Relief.

Ed. Public schools of Atlanta till age of fifteen, when he entered Georgia Institute of Technology. Graduated three years later with degree in mechanical engineering. At age eighteen, in 1920, began to enter open golf championships, and continued to play in them for next eight years, during the summer vacations from his studies. 1923, honours degree in English literature, Harvard; won his first US Open championship. After a brief fling at real estate, in 1926 he entered Emory University Law School and after three semesters passed Georgia bar examination. He consequently withdrew and set up law practice, which he maintained for most of his life. He was essentially a weekend golfer, in the fall and the spring. In 1924 he married Mary Rice Malone, of Atlanta. They had three children.

Between 1923 and 1930, Jones entered twenty major championships, won thirteen and came second in four. During that time, the leading two professionals of the day, Walter Hagen and Gene Sarazen*, never won a British or United States Open that Jones entered. In eight years of Walker Cup competition, he won all his singles matches. In the summer of 1930, he won in succession the US Open, the British Open, the British Amateur and the US Amateur, subsequently called 'the Grand Slam', a feat never performed before or since. Jones thereupon retired from competitive golf at the age of twenty-eight. In 1930, a group of friends purchased an abandoned southern nursery, which had served as the fruit farm for the Confederate armies. On these 360 acres, Jones, with the help of Scottish architect Dr. Alister Mackenzie, designed the Augusta National golf course. With financier Clifford Roberts, he founded the Augusta National Golf Club and a Jones's invitational tournament, later called (against Jones's wish) the Masters.

In the Second World War, although deferred as a forty-year-old father of three and suffering a medical disability, he was commissioned in Army Air Force intelligence and served in Europe under Eisenhower's command. In 1948, a painful back compelled him to give up golf. After two operations, he was diagnosed with a rare degenerative disease, which progressively paralysed him. In 1958, he was given the freedom of the city (burgh) of St Andrews, Scotland. He died in Atlanta, in December 1971.

On the centennial of the birth of Mr Justice Holmes, I was asked to write a commemorative piece for a liberal weekly. By that time, his reputation as a liberal hero was as secure as Jane Austen's new reputation as a pioneer

---

* Gene Sarazen (1902–1999): Won seven Majors, played in six US Ryder Cup teams. From 1984 till 1999 played the honorary opening tee shot at the Masters in company with Byron Nelson and Sam Snead.

feminist, an elevation that, if she were within earshot, would—as she might say—'vastly astound' her. Holmes had been so exhaustively written about, so firmly established as the Great Dissenter, that there seemed very little to say about him. I accordingly said very little and summed it all up in the title of the piece: 'What Have We Left for Mr Justice Holmes?' It took many years, and the leisure to look him over freed from his obituary pigeonhole, to make the alarming discovery that the cases in which he voted with the conservative majority as against it were in the ratio of eight or ten to one; and that two notable scholars succeeded each other in spending years preparing his biography only to abandon it to a third man who saw what they had seen in Holmes, but one who also had the courage to say it out loud: that Holmes's political philosophy was (his concern for free speech apart) as fine an intellectual approximation to Fascism as you would care to find among the savants of the Western world.

I have come to a similar hurdle with Robert Tyre Jones Jr, though one nothing like so formidable or alarming. I don't suppose any other athletic hero, certainly no one in golf, has been written about so often and with so much reverence. The same admirable anecdotes are repeated whenever his name is mentioned: his debunking of the teaching clichés ('never up, never in'); his famous putdown by Harry Vardon ('did you ever see a worse shot than that?'); his identifying the enemy as 'Old Man Par'; his calling a two-stroke penalty on himself to lose a championship ('you might as well praise a man for not robbing a bank'). And on and on. I have heard these stories a hundred times and concluded long ago that fresh anecdotes about Jones are as few and far between as new funny golf stories. This must be, then, a small memoir of a short friendship in the last years of his life and what I gleaned about him and his character.

In the summer of 1965, when I had been for nearly twenty years the chief American correspondent of the (then *Manchester*) *Guardian*, our golf correspondent, Pat Ward-Thomas, for some reason or other was unable to cover the US Open championship, which was being held, I believe for the first time, at Creve Coeur in St Louis. I filled in for him and my last day's dispatch eventually appeared in the *Guardian*'s annual anthology of the paper's writing. Somehow, a copy of it got to Jones. He wrote me a letter saying, as I recall, he was unaware that 'golf was another string to your bow'. Why he should have known anything about my 'bow' was news to me. But he mentioned that he had been a regular viewer of *Omnibus*, a ninety-minute network television potpourri of drama, science, politics, history, ballet, and God knows what, which I hosted in the 1950s. Jones's letter was, of course, highly flattering to me, especially since this was the first piece I had ever written about golf. I had taken up the game only one year before, at an advanced age (in my mid-fifties—hopeless, I know); but, being a journalist, I started to write about it, just as when you run into a man who is an expert on the manufacture of heels for ladies' shoes—as was a man I met in Rainelle, West Virginia—you write about him.

There was another short exchange or two, in one of which Jones characteristically started a letter: 'Dear Alistair (don't you think we ought to put an end to this minuet of Mr Jones and Mr Cooke?)' and went on to ask me to be sure to call on him whenever I was down in Augusta or Atlanta. Which I did, most often in the company of Ward-Thomas.

My first impression was the shock of seeing the extent of his disability, the fine strong hands, twisted like the branches of a cypress, gamely clutching a tumbler or one of his perpetual cigarettes in a holder. His face was more ravaged than I had expected, from the long-endured pain I imagine, but the embarrassment a stranger might feel about this was tempered by the quizzical eyes and the warmth his presence gave off. (He kept on going to Augusta for the Masters until two years before the end. Mercifully, for everyone but his family, we would not see him when he could no longer bear to be seen.)

After that first meeting I never again felt uncomfortable about his ailment, and only once did he mention it, which was when he spoke a sentence that has passed into the apocrypha. Pat well knew that Jones never talked about his disease, but on that day he really wanted to penetrate the mask of courage and know just how good or bad things really were. Pat's expression was so candid that—I sensed—Jones felt he would, for once, say a word or two. He said that he'd been told that his disease occurred in two forms—'descending and ascending', that luckily his paralysis had been from the waist and his extremities down, so that, he added, 'I have my heart and lungs and my so-called brain'. He spoke about it easily with a rueful smile, and no more was said. The familiar punch line, 'You know, we play the ball where it lies,' was not said in my presence and, I must say, it sounds to me false to Jones's character, as of a passing thought by a screenwriter that Hollywood would never resist. Let us thank God that Hollywood has never made a movie about Jones; it would almost surely be as inept and more molassic than the dreadful *Follow the Sun*, the alleged 'epic' about Ben Hogan.

About the disease. At a tournament Jones was playing in, in England, Henry Longhurst, the late, great rogue of English golf writing, was standing beside a doctor who, marvelling at Jones's huge pivot, the long arc of his swing and the consequent muscular strain that sustained it, predicted that one day it would cause him grievous back trouble. Longhurst wrote and retailed this comment to Jones, who responded with a good-tempered note saying, with typical tact, that Henry was good to be concerned but the trouble was due to a rare disease. This sad turn in Jones's life has also received several versions. So far as I can discover, from tapping the memory of his oldest surviving friend, the inimitable Charlie Yates, and checking with the expertise of several medicos, the true account is simple and drastic.

In the summer of 1948, Jones remarked to Yates, in the middle of what was to be his last round ever, that he would not soon be playing again because his back had become unbearable and he was going to have an operation. It was, in fact, the first of two operations and it revealed damage to the spinal tissue that could not then be tagged with a definite diagnosis. A year or two later, Jones went up to Boston and, after being examined at the Lahey Clinic, had the second operation, during which a positive diagnosis was made: syringomyelia, a chronic progressive degenerative disease of the spinal cord, which, as we all know, Jones bore for twenty-two years with chilling stoicism. The scant consolation for the rest of us is that anyone falling victim to the same disease today could expect no better outcome. The aetiology is still unknown and there is no cure.

When I first went into the sitting room of Jones's cottage at Augusta, I noticed at once a large picture over the mantelpiece, a framed series of cartoon strips by the best, and throughout the 1920s and 1930s, the most famously popular English sports cartoonist, Tom Webster. No American I knew (and no Englishman under seventy) had ever heard his name, but the drawings—of Jones and of Hagen, I believe—served as a taproot into Jones's memories of Britain and British golf in the 1920s. He enlightened me about the character and skill of various old heroes I brought up: Braid and Duncan and Tolley and Roger Wethered* and, of course, Hagen. (Though I played no golf I followed it—from the papers, the newsreels, and the Webster cartoons—as zealously as I followed county cricket.) This talk brought up, one time, the never-ending controversy about the essential characteristic of the good golf swing. Jones distrusted 'keep your eye on the ball' almost as much as Tommy Armour did. His preference was for Abe Mitchell's 'the player should move freely beneath himself'.

Jones never recalled to me, as all famous athletes are apt to do, the acclaim of his great days, though once when I had just come back from St Andrews, he remarked again what a 'wonderful experience' it had been on his later visits 'to go about a town where people wave at you from doorways and windows'. Otherwise, he never said anything that made me doubt his friends' assurance that he was uncomfortable with the spotlight and was grateful to

* All British golfers in the early twentieth century. James Braid won five Open Championships; George Duncan won the Open in 1920, the first to be played following the First World War; Cyril Tolley was British Amateur champion in 1920 and 1929 and represented Great Britain in the Walker Cup six times. Roger Wethered was runner-up in the 1921 Open, British Amateur champion in 1923 and played in the Walker Cup five times.

have room service in the hotels of towns where he would be recognised on the streets. He did not flaunt his trophies at home, and he kept his medals locked up in a chest.

Our talks were mostly about books, people, politics, only rarely about golf, whenever Ward-Thomas was eager for another Jones quote for his bulging file of golfing wisdom. In the winter after my first meeting, a book came out entitled *Bobby Jones on Golf* and I reviewed it under the heading 'The Missing Aristotle Papers on Golf,' remarking along the way that Jones's gift for distilling a complex emotion into the barest language would not have shamed John Donne; that his meticulous insistence on the right word to impress the right visual image was worthy of fussy old Flaubert; and that his unique personal gift was 'to take apart many of the club clichés with a touch of grim Lippmannesque humour'. Shortly after the piece appeared, Jones dropped me a letter beginning: 'Offhand, I can't think of another contemporary author who has been compared in one piece to Aristotle, Flaubert, John Donne and Walter Lippmann!'

Much was made—rightly—when the book came out about the extraordinary fact that Jones had written it himself. This is only to remark, in a more interesting way, how phenomenally rare it is for a scholar to become a world-class athlete. The same dependence on a ghost is true of actors and actresses, as also of ninety per cent of the world's—at least the Western world's—best politicians. The exceptions are rare indeed. Churchill, after a Washington wartime meeting with Roosevelt, flew home in a bomber, alternating between the controls and the composition of a speech on a pad. He was no sooner in London than he appeared at the BBC and broadcast across the Atlantic a majestic strategical survey of the world at war. To his horror, Roosevelt heard it in the White House while he was working on his own promised broadcast with the aid of three ghost-writers. One of them, Robert Sherwood, consoled the president with the sorrowful thought: 'I'm afraid, Mr President, he rolls his own.'

When I think back to those Augusta talks, I recall most vividly the quality of irony that was always there in his eyes and often in his comments on people and things. I asked him once about 'the master eye' without knowing that he had written about it. I'm sure he said what he had said before: he didn't believe in it or in the ritual of plumb bobbing.* The main thing was to 'locate the ball's position . . . I'm told a man can do this better with two eyes than with one'. The last time I saw him, I told him about a rather morose Scottish caddie I'd recently had who took a dim view of most things American, but especially the golf courses, which—he'd been told—had lots of trees. We were sitting out on the porch of his Augusta cottage and Jones looked down at the towering Georgia pines, the great cathedral nave, of the plunging tenth fairway. 'I don't see,' he said deadpan, 'any need for a tree on a golf course.'

Towards the end of one Masters tournament, Henry Longhurst took suddenly very ill. He lay grumpily in his hospital bed and, lifting his ripe W. C. Fields's nose over the bed sheet, predicted that it was 'closing time'. Happily, it turned out not to be, but Pat and I stayed over through the Monday to watch out for him. In the early afternoon, when the place was empty, we called on Jones and he suggested we collect some clubs from the pro shop and play the splendid par three course. We were about to set off when Cliff Roberts, cofounder of the club, came in. He was shocked at the generosity of Jones's suggestion: 'Bob, you surely know the rule—no one can play without a member going along.' 'Don't you think,' Jones asked wistfully, 'you and I could exercise a little Papal indulgence?' Roberts did not think so. And although he'd recently had a major operation, he went off, got into his golfing togs and limped around with us through six holes, by which time he was ready for intensive care and staggered away accepting the horrid fact of the broken rule.

---

* Plumb bobbing: a method of reading putts where the player generally squats and dangles the putter (head down) from the fingers (like a surveyor's plumb line) in front of him to check the line to the hole.

Because of the firm convention of writing nothing about Jones that is less than idolatrous, I have done a little digging among friends and old golfing acquaintances who knew him and among old and new writers who, in other fields, have a sharp nose for the disreputable. But I do believe that a whole team of investigative reporters, working in shifts like coal miners, would find that in all of Jones's life anyone had been able to observe, he nothing common did or mean.

However, a recent author, in a book depicting the Augusta National Golf Club as a CEO's Shangri-la, does not spare the patron saint of golf from his lamentations. He attacks Jones on two counts. First, for his being 'weak and irresolute' in bowing to Cliff Roberts's expulsion of a player for violating the etiquette of the game. (On the contrary, Jones was disturbed by the man's behavior for six years. Only when, after three requests, the man properly apologised, did Jones welcome him back.) This criticism reflects a serious misconception about Jones's function. In the running of the Masters, Cliff Roberts's power was absolute. What Jones brought to the tournament was the prestige of his immense popularity, not to mention a saving contribution of seed money when the club was on the verge of foundering. Otherwise, it was understood from the start that Roberts was the prime mover and shaker, the organiser of the staff and the commissary, the recruiter and commander of the course patrols, the boss of the course officials and of crowd control, the inventor of new conventions of scoring, and even (over Jones's protesting pleas) the final judge of the architecture of a hole.

So the view of Jones as the impotent puppet king of a cabal of CEOs is both melodramatic and quite wrong. In the beginning, Jones and Roberts wrote to hundreds of friends, acquaintances and strangers 'to buy a share of the club' but recruited only a minuscule membership; a hundred dollars a head was hard to come by in the pit of the Depression. Incidentally, the slur also blandly ignores the deepening agony of Jones's illness throughout the last twenty years of his attendance at 'his' tournament. (His private view of the tycoon's preserve that Augusta was to become was never, I believe, vouchsafed to his friends, but it was after a hearty get-together of board chairmen, celebrated in a photo opportunity more theirs than his, that he confided ruefully: 'They say I love people. I don't. I love a few people in small doses.')

The second charge is more familiar and these days has become inevitable when a young author reacts to warm praise of an old southerner. It is the charge of 'racism'. This is so pretentiously silly that I have to swallow hard to choose to meet it. It is the old fallacy, which every generation is subject to, of judging a man outside his time and place. Franklin Roosevelt now, I imagine, is thought in retrospect to have had a very callous streak since he never protested the separation of the races. Many shocked readers of this piece would have felt the same indifference if they had been born a half century earlier. I know. I was there. During my first two years in America, I was curious about, but not outraged by, the social status of the Negroes. In my most enlightened moments I should have thought of them as an aberration in an otherwise admirable system. The Negro was not yet a crusade, even among bloodshot liberals.

I look back on the southerners I knew and admired. I was lucky to have travelled far and wide in the South in the 1930s and 1940s, and I had many friends in many southern places. Jones belonged to those fine ones who were incapable of condescending to a black or being ever less than conscious of their lowly status. When things went wrong for their servants—sickness, debt, delinquency—the family took anxious care of them, of its own. By contrast, we in the North hired daily help in good conscience and hoped they stayed well. Their private afflictions were their own. The northern Negro might be permitted more public chutzpah than his southern brother, but the North took it out in tuberculosis.

For myself, I can now say simply that in my life I can count four human beings who radiated simple goodness: my father; a Franciscan priest; a university professor; and Robert Tyre Jones Jr. Maybe 'radiated' is too strong a word, for one striking thing about good human beings is their gift for not being striking. Jones had an instinct for noticing, and attending to, the shy one in any bubbling company. His capacity for shifting the spotlight away from himself was remarkable even in the one performance where you would expect him to be authoritative: in the act of teaching golf. In those precious film shorts he made for the Warner brothers, in which a lesson in the use of the brassie* or mashie† is tagged on to a ludicrous plot about a golf widow or other domestic strain, he never says, 'you must do this . . .' or 'it is essential to do that'. He is careful always to say: 'I've found that if I move the ball an inch or so . . .' and 'perhaps if you tried . . . it works well with some people'.

The last indelible memory of him, for those who had the luck to be in St Andrews in the late autumn of 1958, was his acceptance of the freedom of the city. The Provost was careful to say that he was being saluted not only as 'the first golfer of this age . . . but as a man of courage and character'. In response, Jones put aside the notes he had painfully written out and spoke freely, first of the Old Course, which had enraged the nineteen-year-old and come to enchant the man; then he talked with the slightest tremor of the curious lasting friendship he had acquired for a city and a people 'who have a sensitivity and an ability to extend cordiality in ingenious ways'.

He hobbled off to his electric golf cart and began to propel it down the centre aisle, as the audience stirred, picked up the cue of a tentative voice, and rose to sing 'Will Ye No' Come Back Again?' The start of the hobble and the fact of the cart were enough to remind them that he never would. It was a moment of suddenly shared emotion that upset the most cynical. Herbert Warren Wind remarked: 'It was ten minutes before many who attended were able to speak with a tranquil voice.' During those minutes, he seemed to one onlooker to qualify for Frederick Buechner's definition of goodness as 'valour and unnatural virtue'.

---

* Brassie: a 2-wood, so named because the clubhead was originally faced with brass.
† Mashie (niblick): a lofted iron used for medium distances, similar to a present-day 7-iron.

What we are left with in the end is a forever young, good-looking southerner, an impeccably courteous and decent man with a private ironical view of life who, to the great good fortune of people who saw him, happened to play the great game with more magic and more grace than anyone before or since.

Reading and Some
Major Wins

from *How I Played the Game* by Byron Nelson

My Inverness contract was again an improvement over what I was making at Reading, but also a lot more responsibility, larger membership, and a well-known championship course. As you can imagine, I was flying pretty high. I also signed an endorsement contract with MacGregor in June 1939. Tommy Armour was the pro at Boca Raton, and his clubs were the main ones MacGregor was making then. We pros were all at Boca at the time for a meeting, and afterwards I went to Tommy's pro shop and picked out a set of his irons, called "Silver Scots." Two weeks later, I won the Open with those irons and kept them quite a while—at least till I had MacGregor make some with my own name on them.

The Open that year was held at Philadelphia Country Club, which at that time had two courses: Bala Cynwyd in town, and the Spring Mill Course out in the country, where the tournament was to be held. I felt I was playing rather well, hitting my irons great, and in the practice rounds, I scored close to par. It was normally a par-71 course, but the USGA wanted to make it more difficult, and changed two of the short par fives into par fours, which made it a par 69—about the only time such a "short" course has been an Open site. One of the redesigned holes was the eighth, and the other was the twelfth. This was in the days before clubs would spend money to change a course just for a specific tournament.

You might be interested to know that despite a par of 69, those par fours were far from easy. They were 480, 454, 453, 449, 447, 425, and 421 yards, so you know we were using those long irons a lot.

I was very nervous in the first round and played poorly for the first seven holes. The eighth was a long par 4, slightly uphill. I hit a good drive and a 2-iron on the green and almost birdied it. On the 9th I hit a long iron to within eight feet of the pin and made it, which encouraged me. I really did hit my irons well, though I never holed a chip or pitch the entire time. In the four regulation and two playoff rounds, I hit the pin six times with my irons, from 1-iron to 8-iron.

We played thirty-six holes the last day, and I was paired with Olin Dutra, who'd won in '34 at Merion. We were both well in contention. My friend from Texarkana, J. K. Wadley, was following us, and also knew Olin. After our first eighteen, he offered to buy us lunch. Dutra ordered roast beef with gravy, mashed potatoes and all the trimmings. I said, "I'll have the same," and Mr. Wadley said, "No, you won't." He ordered for me—a chicken sandwich on toast with no mayonnaise, some vegetables, iced tea, and half a piece of apple pie.

That afternoon, it was hot and muggy. Dutra played badly, and I shot a 1-under-par 68, which got me in a tie with Denny Shute and Craig Wood. That taught me a good lesson, not to eat too heavy a meal before going out to play, and I've abided by it ever since.

I was very fortunate to get into that playoff. Snead, who was worried about Shute playing behind him, made a poor club selection on eighteen. He thought he needed a birdie to win when he only needed a par, but he ended up with an 8, so he missed both winning and getting into the playoff.

In the first playoff, Shute struggled to a 76, while Craig and I tied at 68. On the last hole, Craig was leading me by a stroke and tried to reach the green at 18 in two, but hooked his second shot badly, and hit a man in the gallery right in the head. The man had been standing in the rough to the left, and the ball dropped and stayed there in the rough, about thirty yards short of the green. The fellow was knocked out, and they carried him across the green right in front of us while Craig waited to play his third shot. Of course, his ball would have been in even worse trouble if it hadn't gotten stopped, but that didn't make Craig feel any better. He hit a pitch shot then that left him with a six-footer for birdie, while my ball was eight feet away. I would putt first.

As I stood over my ball, suddenly the thought popped into my head of all the times when we were playing as caddies at Glen Garden and we'd say, "This putt is for the U.S. Open." Now I was really playing that dream out, and it steadied me enough that I sank my putt. But Craig left his just one inch short, so we were tied.

That meant another 18-hole playoff in those days, and the committee asked us before we played that afternoon whether we would be willing to go to sudden death if we tied again. We both said, "No, we'll go a full eighteen." They weren't real happy to hear that, because the folks working on the tournament had to get back to their jobs, and of course the members wanted their course back. But we both felt the same way, that we didn't want to win based on just one or two holes. So they agreed.

On the second playoff, I hit a bad second shot at the first hole and ended up in the deep right bunker, but I got up and down all right. On the second, a long par three, we had to use drivers, and had to carry the green. I pushed mine into some deep rough, while Wood's tee shot landed on the green. I got out with my sand wedge and saved par, and Wood two-putted. The next hole I birdied while Craig parred, and on the fourth, I hit a good drive, then holed a 1-iron for an eagle, while Craig made another four.

When I was lining up to play my second shot, I wasn't thinking at all about holing out. But I'd been striking my irons so well, had just birdied the third hole, and I felt I could hit this one close and make birdie again. Sure enough, the ball went straight up to the green and straight into the hole like a rat. There were a lot of folks in the gallery, and they whooped and hollered quite a bit, though they were still quieter than the fans are now. You know, when you're on the golf course and hear the spectators cheering, you learn quickly that the applause for an eagle is different from a birdie, and of course it's even louder for a hole in one. No matter where you are, you can tell by the applause just how good the shot was. What you don't want to hear the gallery do when you're playing is give a big groan—because that means you just missed a short putt.

Anyway, as I walked off the green, I remember thinking very vividly, "Boy, I'm three strokes ahead now!" But I knew it was no time to turn negative or quit being aggressive. I knew I had to continue playing well. As it happened, I then bogeyed a couple of holes but so did Craig, and that three-stroke lead proved to be my winning margin, 70 to 73.

Harold McSpaden—who was really the best friend I had on the tour—walked along with me through both of the playoff rounds, helping me get through the gallery and just being there. Naturally, he didn't say anything, but his presence and support sure were a big help to me.

Mr. Giles, my boss and friend from Reading, was there with quite a few of the members, so you might say I almost had my own gallery. George Jacobus was there too, and was nearly beside himself with excitement. He said to me afterwards, "You remember, Byron, we talked about this, and I said, 'You're going to be the National Champion one of these days.'" I was kind of in a trance for a few days before I fully realized I was indeed the U.S. Open champion and had accomplished another dream.

After I got back home, the members of all three clubs—Berkleigh, Galen Hall, and Reading—gave Louise and me a wonderful party. They presented Louise with a large silver bowl that had her name engraved on it. Then they gave me a handsome, solid gold watch by Hamilton, engraved on the back "Byron Nelson, Winner U.S. Open 1939–40, Members of Reading Country Club." I still have both of them. They also gave me a Model 70 Winchester 30.06, a mighty fine rifle. That was arranged by Alex Kagen, a member at Berkleigh, who owned a sporting goods store and had once asked me if I hunted. When I told him all I had was a shotgun, he came up with the idea for the Winchester. I used it every time I went hunting, and kept it until just recently, when I sold it to my good friend, Steve Barley.

So there I was, the U.S. Open champion, with a contract I'd signed two weeks before to go to Inverness, just like when I signed the contract to go to Reading one week before I won the Masters. Some people would say I needed an agent to help me capitalize on my wins, but hardly anybody had one in those days. Hagen was the only one I knew of who did—a fellow named Bob Harlow, the golf writer who started *Golf World* magazine.

Shortly after the Open, Ben and Valerie Hogan came to visit and stayed a week. We practiced a lot and played some. I had to work, of course, but Ben played a couple of times with Mr. Giles, and he really enjoyed getting a chance to play with Ben, who was playing much better by then.

As it happened, my next tournament was the Inverness Invitational Four-Ball, which involved seven two-man teams. It was an interesting format, where you scored only plus or minus over seven rounds and four days of play. I was paired with McSpaden, and we tied for first at plus 6, then lost on the first playoff hole. This was my first real chance to see the course and the club where I'd be working the next year, and I enjoyed myself.

One week later, I won the Massachusetts State Open. McSpaden wanted me to come play in it because he knew the course real well, and because we were such good friends. I went, and in the last round, Harold and I were battling it out pretty tight. Along about the middle of the last nine, there was a long par 3 with a bunker on the right. I pushed my tee shot into the bunker and holed it from there. That kept me going good and I won by four shots. I won $400 plus $250 appearance money. There weren't many events that paid appearance money then, and I'm glad the PGA stopped it, but it sure did come in handy back when most of us were just barely making ends meet.

The PGA that year was at Pomonok, Long Island. The World's Fair was in New York, and my mother came to see me play and see the fair, too. It was the only tournament she ever saw me play in. I beat Chuck Garringer, Red Francis, John Revolta, and Emerick Kocsis—brother to Chuck, a wonderful amateur who still shoots better than his age—to get to the quarterfinals. Then I went up against Dutch Harrison, and either I was playing awfully well or he was way off his game, but after the 26th hole, I was 9 up, and as we came to the 27th hole, Dutch said to me, "Byron, why don't you just birdie this one, too, and we won't have to go past the clubhouse." I thought it was a good idea. As it happened, I did birdie, and beat him 10 and 9.

In the finals, though, I had my hands more than full with Picard. I was one up coming to the last hole, and Picard laid me a dead stymie. It was a short par 4, and I had pitched to three feet. But Picard's shot stopped twelve inches from the hole directly in my line, and since we were playing stymies, you didn't mark your ball or anything—the other fellow had to figure out a way to get over or around you and in the cup. Unfortunately, I didn't make my shot go in, and we tied.

Picard won on the first extra hole, but there's a little story connected with how it happened. This was the first tournament ever that was broadcast on radio. It was just short-wave, and it was done by Ted Heusing and Harry Nash. Ted Heusing was an excellent broadcaster who my good friend Chris Schenkel admired a great deal, and Harry Nash was a fine golf writer for the *Newark Evening News*.

On that first extra hole, Picard hit his drive into the right rough, and Ted and Harry were riding in a sizable four-wheeled vehicle, right close by. They didn't see where Picard's ball had landed, and drove right over it. The officials ruled that he should get a free drop, which was only right, and he put his next shot twenty feet from the hole and made birdie to win.

I took the next week off, missing the tournament in Scranton, to make sure things were in order back at the club and to practice some for the Western Open, another major I had my sights set on. It was at Medinah #3, and I drove exceptionally well—seldom ever got in the rough at all. I won by one shot, and it meant even more to me because the trophy had been donated by my friend J. K. Wadley.

Though the North and South and the Western Open aren't considered majors now—the North and South doesn't even exist anymore—you knew then which ones were more important because the golf club companies would award bonuses for them. I got $500 from Spalding that year for the Western, which was always considered somewhat more important than the North and South because it drew from all around the country. The other was always played at Pinehurst, and a lot of the players from the western part of the country didn't go. Another reason the Western was ranked higher was that the tournament contributed money to the Chick Evans Scholarship Fund, which added prestige and publicity. Evans, an excellent golfer, was always there, too, and his name meant a lot of good things to golf. He'd won the Open himself, and had been a caddie like most of us, so I felt really good about winning the Western.

The next regular tour event I played well in was the Hershey Open several weeks later. The tournament was sponsored by Mr. Hershey himself, who was the president of the club and a very nice man. Par was 73. I was 5 under and leading going into the fourth round, and paired with Ed Dudley and Jimmy Hines. We came to the 15th hole, where you'd drive down the fairway and over a hill. Well, I drove right down the middle of it, but when we got to the place where my ball should have been, it was nowhere to be found. There wasn't any confusion about it, because my golf balls had my name imprinted on them, and everyone there had seen mine go absolutely straight down the fairway and disappear over the hill.

I had no choice but to go back and hit another ball. But with that two-stroke penalty I ended up in fourth place. Afterwards, I was talking to the press in the locker room and told them what had happened. Fred Corcoran was managing the tour then, and always trying to get publicity, so he got all the papers he could to pick up the story.

About ten days later, I received an anonymous letter stating that the writer's guest and friend at the tournament, a young woman who knew nothing about golf, had picked up my ball and put it in her purse. After the tournament, as they returned to New York on the train, the woman opened her purse and showed him the ball she'd found on the course, and the gentleman realized then what had happened. Since these were the days before gallery ropes, people walked all over the course in front of you and in back of you and right alongside you. The young lady had apparently been walking across the fairway at the bottom of the hill after I drove, saw the ball lying there, and simply picked it up.

The letter was postmarked from the New York Central Post Office, and the man included money orders totaling $300—the difference between third prize in the tournament and fourth, where I finished. The money orders were signed "John Paul Jones"—clearly fictitious. I never did find out who did it, but whoever it was, it was a nice thing to do.

I guess I got a lot of media attention for that time but it was very little compared to what goes on now. I was glad for the attention, but since I hadn't talked to the press much after beating Lawson Little in San Francisco in '35 and winning the Masters in '37, it took some getting used to. I was even being interviewed on radio now, though we always had to go downtown to the station to do it.

I've always been fortunate with the publicity I received, and have had very little inaccurate reporting. Might be because I was always a little on the shy side, and didn't really talk very much or very fast, so the reporters couldn't get much wrong. I'd have to say, overall, that I enjoyed the attention. After I won the Open especially, people in the gallery would say, "Boy, you're sure hitting your irons good," or some such thing, and that would encourage me. Then I'd try even harder, because I didn't want to let them down.

With three majors to my credit, 1939 was definitely my best year so far. My official winnings were $9444, making me fifth on the money list. My stroke average was 71.02, good enough to win the Vardon Trophy, which was an added bonus.

The year I'd have in 1945 was a little more unusual, but with the quality of the tournaments that I won—three majors—and the way I played, 1939 was right up there with '45. And naturally, I had no idea what would happen in '45 was even possible. No, at that point, I was simply looking ahead to the winter tour and wanting to do my best for the folks at Inverness the next spring.

So Louise and I packed up and went back to Texarkana, where I practiced and played some with my friends or with the pro there, Don Murphy. Looking back on the whole year, I was more than satisfied with my accomplishments. . . .

Canterbury was a good course, and as usual for the national championship, it was tough. The rough was long, the fairways narrow, and I knew inside that this was going to be my last shot at really trying to win it again. I was playing well, hitting my irons as well or better than ever before, including the Open in '39. In the first round, on the front nine I never missed a fairway or had a putt more than ten feet for birdie, but I two-putted every one and had nine straight pars.

In the second round, Cliff Roberts and the great writer Grantland Rice were in my gallery. On the 15th hole, you drove into a valley and had a blind shot to the green. I got up there in good position for birdie, hit my putt perfect, but the ball swung in and out of the hole. I was walking toward it thinking I'd made it, and couldn't believe it didn't go in. I was told later that Rice said to Cliff right then, "He'll never win." When Cliff said, "Why? He's playing beautifully." Grantland said, "Yes, but the ball's not rolling right for him. He's not getting any breaks at all." As it turned out, he was right, but not because the ball wasn't rolling right.

In the third round, on the par-5 13th hole, I hit a good tee shot and a good second, but I laid up on it a little because if you hit it too far you'd be on a downslope. As soon as I hit it, naturally, the caddie went quickly toward it. Remember now, they didn't have the fairways roped off then for most of the tournaments—the only ones I recall for sure were the '45 PGA and the Masters. The spectators would walk right along with you till you got to your ball, and the marshals would then put a rope up to hold the fans back just enough to give you room to swing, really. Sometimes, if the crowd moved too fast, the marshals couldn't get there ahead of them, and that's exactly what happened this time. My caddie got there and ducked under the rope the marshals were holding, but the rope was too close to my ball; my caddie didn't see it, and he accidentally kicked it about a foot. Since I was leading the tournament at the time, Ike Grainger, one of the top USGA officials, was there as my referee, and we talked about the situation and what it meant. We were both pretty sure it meant a penalty stroke, but Ike said he preferred to talk to the committee before he made a ruling, though he said I had the right to have the decision right then. I said it was okay to wait, which was my mistake, and in my mind that was what cost me the tournament, not the delay itself. Because then I was trying to play with all that on my mind. I was pretty sure I would receive a penalty stroke, but not having it settled right then, I played two over par from there in, and then had the penalty stroke added on besides.

I didn't make up any ground the last round, though I had a good chance or two. On the 17th, a long par 3, I hit my 3-wood just beautifully, but it went over the green and ended up on the fringe—actually, in a lady's hat she had put on the ground next to her. Back then, they allowed people fairly close to the green itself, much closer than they do now. They ruled that I could pick up the ball so the woman could remove her hat, then replace it with no penalty, but the lost time and distraction of all this made me lose my concentration again. I chipped from there and it rimmed the hole, spun out three and a half feet, and I missed the putt. I was a little upset by that, and my tee shot on 18 went down the left side of the fairway, where it landed and bounced further left and into the rough, which was really tall and thick. It was only about a foot into the rough, but it was so thick that I had to use an 8-iron to get out. Then I got to the green and missed a twelve-footer for par, so I ended with two bogeys to tie with Lloyd Mangrum and Vic Ghezzi.

One other unusual thing happened there—we three were in and already tied, but on the 72nd hole, Ben Hogan and Herman Barron were on the green with medium-long putts for birdie to win. Both of them three-putted, but if they'd even two-putted, there would have been a five-way tie.

Now we were in the playoff, and on the 4th hole, the first par 3 on the course, Vic and Lloyd both had thirty-footers. They both made theirs while I missed my own ten-footer. I made up that stroke, but we all played very steady golf and ended up tied again at 72. In the second playoff, on the par-5 9th hole, Mangrum hit his drive out of bounds on the left. He got disgusted with himself, hit again, then put a fairway wood on the green and made an 80-foot putt. He ended up with a 71 to Vic's and my 72's. I'd have to say it was the best I played to lose a tournament my whole life. My concentration was probably not as good as it should have been, because I'd made up my mind ahead of time that if I won I would announce my retirement then and there, so that may have been too much on my mind.

One thing I'd like to say here is that Lloyd Mangrum was the most under-rated player of my time. He won twenty-one tournaments, including the '46 Open. He was a fine player, but he had a kind of unusual, funny sarcasm that he used, and if you didn't know him and understand it, it made him sound kind of tough. Some years ago, Susan Marr was doing some radio during the tournament at Westchester, and she asked me to go on the air with her. She said, "I've been asking people all day who are the seven pros who've won twenty-one or more tournaments, and nobody's been able to name them all. Can you?" I said, "I'll try." I'd been doing a little studying for my own broadcast work and got through all of them, including Lloyd, and she said I was the only one who'd remembered Mangrum. I won the prize, which was a "Thank you."

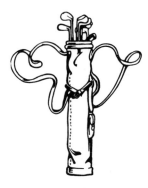

THE MODERN
ERA

Merion

from *Ben Hogan: An American Life* by James Dodson

Ben and Valerie checked into the stately Barclay Hotel, overlooking Philadelphia's sun-dappled Rittenhouse Square, a week before play commenced. The Barclay was Philly's "society" hotel—small, elegantly worn, sophisticatedly shabby, and probably twice the room rate of the other downtown hotels where the other name players and their wives dropped baggage. The hotel was a half-hour's drive out the Main Line by car to the golf course and home to Frank Sullivan, the crusty but brilliant bachelor lawyer who worked for Lippincott, publishers of Hogan's *Power Golf.* As Merion's genteelly Republican membership went, Sullivan was an unusual bird—a gruff, straight-talking city dweller who represented, among other notables, the state's brawling Democratic Party. He was, in short, Ben's kind of guy, a tough insider with no-nonsense, iconoclastic views. He also stirred one hell of a martini.

Hogan admired and gravely respected Merion, which at around 6,600 yards wasn't long by typical National Open standards but basically threw everything in the book at a player. Designed by an insurance man and club golfer named Hugh Wilson (who had a hand in shaping Pine Valley, a course Merion resembles), who spent seven months in England and Scotland studying great golf course design elements before agreeing to lay out then–Merion Cricket Club's "new" course in 1911, the par-70 Ardmore gem meandered over modest, thin, clay-covered hills and the rocky remains of an old granite quarry, an engaging mix of cleverly short par-4s that bent left and right, thoroughly testing par-3 holes of varying lengths, several tough par-5 holes including one stretching over 600 yards, and three concluding holes many regarded as the finest finishing trio in all of championship golf. To give the course the look and feel of its distinguished British antecedents, Wilson and the course's original superintendent, William Flynn, used bedsheets to strategically place bunkers in the most penal spots and loaded up the framing terrain with bursts of rough Scotch broom and spiky native grasses. As with all Open sites, Merion's tidy, marbleized putting surfaces and brutal rough made precision shotmaking critical. Intelligently plotting one's way around the golf course—what Hogan had taken to calling "course management"—was absolutely essential.

The story goes that during one of Ben's early practice rounds in the week before the 1950 Open festivities got under way, meticulously hitting three shots to different spots on every hole, playing mostly alone, he drove his ball to a plateau slightly over the right fairway bunker on the short and ingenious 8th hole, to a flat shelf just over the brow of the hill but well back of the spot where most players aimed to deposit their tee shots, sternly admonishing his young caddie to "carefully replace the divot, son, because I plan to be here every round."

Though no one has ever been able to confirm the story, the anecdote is a beloved part of Merion lore and certainly illustrates Hogan's methodical manner of strategically memorizing every feature of the golf course beforehand, selecting his preferred lies and directional angles to the flag and thoroughly digesting every possible variation so that no shot required of him during the tournament would come as a surprise.

Before the opening round of the National Open's golden anniversary edition got under way, in order to satisfy the sponsoring USGA's fourteen-club rule, Ben pulled the seven-iron from his bag proclaiming, "There are no seven-irons at Merion." In place of it, he inserted a one-iron, a bread knife for keeping the ball low and penetrating in the wind and a club few players had either the skill or nerve to carry.

Because he had gone from national champ to near-death and battled his way back to golf's most elite arena in just over sixteen months, perhaps more than any player before him—including Jones and Hagen in their prime—Hogan was now considered and treated like a demigod who gave the unassailable impression that he knew exactly what was humanly required to win. When reporters quizzed Ben on what score would take the Open, with or without a seven-iron in the bag, he declined to give a firm number but predicted the winning score would be "unusually high."

"From day one you got the feeling that everyone there was watching to see how Ben would hold up," remembers Skee Reigel, the '48 USGA national amateur champion who subsequently turned pro. "Sam was probably the favorite, and some thought Demaret and Mangrum would be right in it. But Ben was the one we were all really watching. He was like some figure from another planet."

When an obscure pro from Birmingham, Alabama, named Lee Mackey knocked off ten one-putt greens en route to a stunning 64 in the opening round of the tournament—a new eighteen-hole Open record—Ben was briefly paragraph-two news, especially after he limped home with a 72. Under normal circumstances, Hogan's two-over score would probably have placed him somewhere near the top of the leaderboard, but he was clearly having difficulties figuring out Merion's rock-hard greens and demanding slopes. At one point during the first round, facing a downhill putt, for example, he opted not to sole his putter so he wouldn't be penalized if the ball moved. It was a wise strategy, since his ball did exactly that, suddenly trickling down the hill and four feet closer to the cup. Hogan straightened and glanced sharply over at the watching USGA rules official, who informed him that no penalty would be leveled because he hadn't grounded his putter. Afterward, facing reporters in the warm and cramped players' locker room over the club pro shop, Ben told them that Merion's greens were as hard and fast as he'd ever seen at a National Open. Whoever won would have to find a way to handle them, he said flatly.

The next day, after being unable to sleep because of his excitement, leader Lee Mackey blew to an 81 and began a rapid disappearing act (he finished in a tie for twenty-sixth place), while Ben shot 69 and climbed into fifth place at 141 behind Dutch Harrison, Johnny Bulla, former PGA champ Jim Ferrier, and a darkly handsome accountant beginning his U.S. Open career, sweet-swinging Julius Boros. On the way out of Merion's main entrance, a wan Hogan suddenly instructed lawyer Sullivan to pull over. Overcome with nausea, he cranked open the car door and vomited in the grass. "When we heard about that," Skee Reigel remembers with a chuckle, "I told some of the caddies they ought to go mark the spot."

Back at the Barclay, Hogan unwrapped his throbbing legs and soaked them in a tub of Epsom salts for an hour. His 69 had not come without a price. The soaking reduced some of the swelling of his calves and ankles, but it didn't lessen the general fatigue he felt rippling dangerously through his body, which was why he and Valerie chose to eat early with Sullivan in the hotel's private dining room and turn in just after darkness fell on the lights of Rittenhouse Square. During their supper, Hogan admitted to Sullivan that he dreaded the next day's infamous double-round finisher. Privately, to Valerie, he expressed doubts about whether he would even be able to finish.

Hogan's preparatory routine—warm bath, stringent leg rubs, the elastic bandaging routine from crotch to ankle, downing a single aspirin with either fresh-squeezed orange juice or ginger ale—required at least two hours, followed by the thirty-minute drive to Ardmore Avenue. Accordingly, Ben rose at five-thirty and made it to the course by eight. Merion's one flaw was its lack of a serious practice area, so players warmed up at a flat spot above the left-hand fairway bunker on 18, where they were permitted to hit balls toward the 14th fairway. Hogan, some recalled, shortened his normal forty-minute warm-up routine in favor of more time on the practice green, trying to get a feel for Merion's murderous greens. Even as the first players teed off, the work crews of Merion superintendent Joe Valentine were busy dumping several wheelbarrows of fine beach sand onto the 12th green and working it into the turf with bamboo poles, watering and rolling the surface to make the lethally hard green even more hostile. On this same green later that day, Sam Snead rolled a short putt from three feet above the cup off the green and a dozen yards back into the fairway.

Saturday morning was lovely and warm in eastern Pennsylvania, with gentle warm breezes coming out of the southwest and puffy white clouds floating like dreamy battleships overhead. Thirteen thousand spectators wandered like ants at a picnic over Merion's tidy, magnificently groomed 108 acres, hoping to see history made on the National Open's 50th birthday.

The contenders all played cautiously that morning, including Hogan, who carded another 72 for a fifty-four-hole total of 213, three over par, placing him in a tie for second place with Johnny Palmer and his playing partner that Saturday, Cary Middlecoff, and two strokes behind the tournament's new leader, Lloyd Mangrum.

After a bowl of soup with Valerie on the club's covered terrace, Hogan started his afternoon round with a 4 on the 1st hole, a par. "I was terribly worried about him going back out," Valerie admitted to a Philadelphia society reporter who chatted briefly with her on the porch as she settled in to sip iced tea and wait nearly six full hours for her husband to finish whatever he was intent on finishing. "I don't think his legs are really up for this."

Her concern was well founded. As one by one the leaders gave ground to par, Hogan trudged slowly to an outward nine of 37, one over, and was visibly having difficulty as he paused for relief at several points and clasped his legs as he negotiated some of Merion's steeper hills. The front nine of his final round was far from spectacular, but under the circumstances it was considerably better than Mangrum's, Harrison's, or Middlecoff's. Fighting their own war of attrition, fidgeting Cary slipped to 39 while the others recorded disappointing 41s. By the turn, though he was now four over par for sixty-three holes, Hogan had backed into the lead of the golden anniversary National Open.

Almost entirely unnoticed in the excitement building in the huge throngs trailing Ben and Cary was the fine finish that scrap-metal dealer and part-time Cadillac dealer and PGA touring pro George Fazio made on the historic old course where, in the summer of 1930, Bobby Jones had capped off his own Grand Slam quest by whipping Eugene Homans 8 and 7 to win the U.S. Amateur Championship and subsequently announced his official retirement from the game. For his part, Fazio finished with 287, seven over par, and immediately went to get an iced cocktail in the players' locker room.

Jones's famous Merion match had reached its dramatic conclusion at the marvelous 11th hole, a 378-yard gem that conclusively established that a hole doesn't require length to be great. From the tee, the fairway rolls out rather innocuously for 200 yards before dropping to a lower shelf some 20 feet below and slightly to the left. The green from this point is no more than a stout pitching iron for most skilled players but reposes beguilingly above a narrow winding creek, flanked by a steep bunker on the left and trickling waters on the right and behind. "It is a teasing hole," writes USGA author Sommers, "that invites birdies but collects a stiff price from those who take the chance and fail."

It was precisely here in the Open of 1934, Sommers notes, that a cruising Gene Sarazen attempted to play cautiously with a two-iron off the tee, hooked his ball into the creek, took seven on the hole, and lost the National Open to Olin Dutra by a stroke.

Now, with a second National Open well within his grasp, Ben Hogan nearly failed to make it through the hole as well. His legs were so stiff and achy that Middlecoff had to lift his ball from the hole for him, as he'd already done at least twice in the previous holes. Hogan's face was a mask of stifled pain. He narrowly missed a birdie from twelve feet and hobbled through the little patch of hard woods to the 12th tee, now leading Fazio in the clubhouse by three, as the other contenders began to fall back.

"For by now," Philadelphia golf historian Jim Finegan wrote after watching the moment unfold before him, "every step had become agony. Hogan was managing to put one foot in front of the other, to advance down the fairway on a straight line—oh, he was striking the ball squarely and his swing still had the accustomed zip, the takeaway rather faster than most players could handle effectively, the exaggerated extension of the straight right arm far down the line on the follow-through swing something most players can only dream about—but here, obviously, was a man whose legs were near to buckling under him."

As Ben lashed his drive on 12, he felt both legs seize up in severe muscle spasms; he staggered and nearly toppled to the ground, only managing to spare himself that indignity by grabbing hold of someone's arm. "Let me hold on to you," he supposedly gasped, adding, "My God, I don't think I can finish."

"I thought he was going to collapse," Middlecoff said later.

Only those spectators who bothered to look back at the tee saw the little man stumble and nearly end his day and his Open comeback quest then and there. But muscle spasms were not the only reason he nearly fell: new turf had recently been installed by the club grounds crew, and the ferocity of his swing had caused the shaded turf beneath his spikes to slip. One of those who witnessed this incident was Bill Campbell, a fine amateur and the reigning West Virginia Amateur champion who'd fired rounds of 80–73 to miss the cut in his second U.S. Open effort. Campbell was standing only a few yards away and saw Hogan grab Middlecoff's arm, though other witnesses claimed it was a Hogan friend named Harry Radix (a wealthy Chicago golf enthusiast who paid for the diamond cuff links annually given out with the Vardon Trophy) whom Ben reached out to and seized. So much of what happened that day got wrapped in the gauzy fabric of legend. *Whoever* provided the supporting arm, as Campbell says, "Ben looked nearly finished. He couldn't even bend over to pick up his ball."

"The reason not many saw him stumble," injects Merion historian John Capers, "was because so many were already making a mad dash for the twelfth green." Campbell himself reached the green's edge just as Hogan was preparing to putt his ball twelve feet or so down the slope to the hole. His approach shot had been one of the few mistakes he'd made all day, leaving him dangerously above the hole on the stone-hard green. His ball rolled five feet past the cup, and he three-putted to reduce his own lead by a third.

Crossing sleepy Ardmore Avenue and ascending the steps to the slightly elevated 13th tee at the dazzlingly short par-3, Hogan's legs seized up again. He paused and rubbed his thighs. His caddie teed up his ball, and Hogan made a crisp swing that was remarkable, under the circumstances. His ball wound up ten feet from the cup. But after holing out for par and vacating the green, his legs seized up again, doubling him over.

"According to the story everyone tells around here," historian Capers picks up the tale, "Hogan turned to his caddie and said, 'That's it. I'm finished. You can take my clubs back to the clubhouse.'"

The caddie, whose name no one recalls, the Merion legend goes, supposedly turned to his client and said: "No, Mr. Hogan. You can't quit. I don't work for quitters. I'll see you on the 14th tee, sir."

Like so much else that people swore they witnessed that warm Saturday afternoon, the touching story may or may not be true. One account even has the incident taking place during Hogan's morning round. Regardless, after making his par at 14, Hogan limped on and played the daunting 15th nearly perfectly from tee to green, leaving himself a mere eight-footer for birdie. But then, unaccountably, he three-putted away the second stroke of his lead, missing a putt from less than eighteen inches.

The margin was now one, with perhaps the toughest three concluding holes in championship golf left to play. On the signature "quarry" hole at 16, his approach missed the green, but he chipped to within four feet and made the putt to save par. He bunkered his tee shot, however, on the long par-3 17th. He blasted to within six feet of the cup and took an unusual amount of time sizing up the putt to salvage another par, walking back and forth three times before he finally settled over his ball. He stroked the putt and saw it stop one full revolution shy of falling in the hole. Another bogey. His lead was officially gone.

At that instant, though he didn't yet know it, Ben's longtime Texas nemesis Lloyd Mangrum was already safely inside the Merion clubhouse with 287, tied with George Fazio and Hogan for the Open lead.

Now he faced the toughest tee shot on the golf course, a blind drive that required players to carry 220 yards up over the snarling rock lip of the old quarry to a heaving bosom of turf that would still leave the average Tour player a demanding long iron or fairway wood to the slightly elevated putting surface of the home hole. Hogan hit a beautiful drive that soared over the edge of the cliff to a flat spot on the brow of the hill. The gallery exploded in cheers and applause.

By the time he'd slowly made his way up the path to the upper tier of the fairway, his followers were preparing to close ranks behind him. Stopping by his ball, gray-faced and winded, pinching a smoldering cigarette, Hogan pondered what kind of shot he needed to hit to get safely home in two, and turned to see pro Jimmy Hines and Tour manager Fred Corcoran standing nearby in the gallery.

"What's low?" Hogan grunted at Hines, who told him 286.

"No," Corcoran corrected him, "287 is low. Fazio."

"Mangrum too," someone chipped in. Hogan gave a faint shake of his head. A par 4 would get him into the house in a tie with them at 287; a birdie would win it outright. But under the circumstances, the hole was probably among the toughest to birdie on the golf course.

As Hogan stared at Merion's final hole and considered his options, tournament marshals permitted spectators to fill in directly behind him. For the first and only time ever, the USGA had replaced the club's distinctive teardrop-shaped baskets with conventional flags, and the flag at 18 was fluttering in a light afternoon breeze up on the right rear portion of the green, guarded by a large bunker in front.

The math was pretty simple.

Par to tie, birdie to win.

Arguably nobody in golf ever hit the four-wood better than Hogan. But a four-wood shot that cleared the bunker and got back to the hole also risked the danger of running off the back side of the putting surface into the punishing rough. That would make a par, and a spot in a play-off, very hard to come by.

Though the idea of a Sunday play-off made him positively queasy to contemplate, Ben Hogan hadn't come as far as he had in golf—and in life—by taking ridiculous chances. Golf was a game of mistakes, and he was the man who normally came out on top by not doing something stupid when it counted most.

Hogan thumbed away his smoke and reached into his bag and pulled out his butter knife, the one-iron that had replaced his seven. In doing so, he chose wisdom over valor. If he aimed left of the bunker and hit it perfectly, the ball might reach the lower center of the green, leaving him a lengthy but reasonable shot at birdie, with little or no chance of running over into the deadly rough.

Kneeling just behind the Hawk, twenty-year-old Jim Finegan, a former caddie and a junior on the La Salle College golf team, had wiggled to the front of the six-deep crowd spanning the fairway and now feasted his eyes on every move the great man made, squinting through the filtered afternoon light to see what club Hogan had chosen. Finegan calculated that the Hawk had walked no less than nine miles since breakfast that morning.

Upstairs in the locker room above the pro shop, Skee Reigel and several other players came to the window overlooking the final green. Reigel remembers the scene being "unbelievably quiet—like 10,000 people sitting in a church." A few feet from Finegan, *Life* magazine photographer, Hy Peskin, a talented and aggressive New Yorker, suddenly plopped his camera on a fellow spectator's shoulder and insisted, "Don't move, pal."

Finegan watched Hogan take his stance, heard him inhale and exhale, then glance once at the distant flag for several seconds. His swing was a violent slash that "seemed like a blur" to the impressionable college boy. At that instant, Peskin's shutter lens opened and closed, freezing Hogan in his immaculate follow-through, a shot that became the greatest shot of Peskin's career and probably the most famous golf picture ever taken.

The elegant black-and-white photograph provides rich visual detail of what many consider to be the most marvelous clutch shot ever played in the throes of Open competition. The perfect balance of the slim, imperially tanned figure beneath the upraised hands and tilting white linen cap, the shadowed creases of Hogan's immaculately pressed tan gabardine trousers that suggest the faintest traces of the elastic supports within, the right foot en pointe, almost like that of a pirouetting ballet dancer—the signature thirteenth spike visible beneath the ball of his foot—and the way perhaps half of the solemnly watching multitudes (some wearing linen caps just like their hero) are turned away from the man striking the shot and already following the tiny white dot as it lifts toward the center portion of the green, while the greenside crowds stare intently back at Hogan, thousands of eyes attempting to pick out the tiny ball speeding at them from the sinking Pennsylvania sun. Four and a half seconds after the picture was snapped, Hogan's golf ball landed on the front portion of the putting surface and danced slightly left as it scooted a few yards up the slope to the left-hand corner of the green. His ball stopped rolling forty feet from the cup.

A surf of sustained applause and cheers rose along the fairway as Hogan slowly made his way toward the 72nd hole of the fiftieth United States Open Championship. As he did so, excited fans behind him broke and ran for a spot, any spot, close to the putting surface, oblivious to players still at work on the course, including Frank Stranahan, the former Augusta bad boy, who had his tee ball rudely knocked off its peg by overly enthusiastic Hogan fans as he prepared to hit his tee shot over on the 14th tee.

"Hogan," says Bob Sommers, "was a pathetic figure as he limped up the rise before the green. He had been on the course for six hours in this one round, and the last nine holes had been agony. He had thrown away a three-stroke lead over the last six holes, and right now he was as close to not caring as this tough, hard, determined man could ever be."

As deep quiet once again settled over historic Merion, Hogan took the measure of his forty-footer and rapped the ball firmly, believing it would fall off slightly to the right as it crossed the putting surface. Instead, the ball broke left and stopped four feet past the hole, sending anxious murmurs through the giant gallery. Moments later, whether out of disappointment with his collapse or a simple desire to get the ordeal over with one way or another, Hogan took half the time he normally required to size up a putt, assumed his crabbed stance, and rolled the ball into the left side of the cup to a burst of jubilant cheers.

There would be a play-off for the National Open between Mangrum, Fazio, and Hogan at 1:00 p.m. on Sunday, the sixth three-way tie in tournament history.

Hogan totaled and signed his scorecard, shook hands with and thanked Middlecoff, paid his caddie by the pro shop and asked the boy to leave his clubs there on the rack, then wearily mounted seventeen steps to Merion's players' locker room to collect his street shoes. He accepted congratulations from several players, Skee Reigel remembers, "but he looked completely beaten, as bad as I'd ever seen a man look after a tournament. I wouldn't have bet you a buck he was capable of playing any more golf that week."

At one point, Mangrum drifted by him and said, "See you tomorrow, Ben."

Hogan looked up, stone-faced.

"Yep," he replied, "see you tomorrow."

"I had given up on his being able to play in the play-off," Valerie told journalist Dave Anderson nearly five decades later. "But I couldn't tell him that."

While Hogan was putting on his street shoes and combing his hair, someone who clearly had a sense of history but no scruples pinched his one-iron from his golf bag. For years, the story went—proving how Hogan tales have a way of growing and changing shape with each telling—the thief supposedly also swiped his golf shoes from the same bag, even though he would clearly have worn them upstairs to the players' locker room.

To make matters even more confusing, there were some who later contended that the missing club was actually a two-iron Hogan fired so exquisitely to the final hole. Hogan himself said as much in *Five Lessons*, the famous instruction book he later wrote with Herbert Warren Wind, although Hogan eventually insisted that the club had been a one-iron and the copy in the book was a typographical error. George Fazio, for one, who stood nearby in the gallery and watched Hogan execute the shot, always maintained it was a two-iron he used, and so did veteran New York sportswriter Al Laney, who was also standing near the scene. Many years later, a member of Shady Oaks Country Club also swore Hogan personally told him it had been a two-iron. Future USGA president Bill Campbell, on the other hand, who was in the gallery directly behind golf's most mythical shot, says there's no doubt that it was a one-iron.

In hopes of clearing up the confusion, Merion members eventually wrote to the man himself, asking for clarification on the club he used that unforgettable afternoon, as well as for better particulars on how the club and shoes went wandering off into the mists of legend. Hogan wrote promptly back to the Merion membership: "It was a one-iron I played to the 72nd green. After hitting my shot, my one-iron was stolen. I haven't seen it since. Also, that night my shoes were stolen out of my locker and I haven't seen them either."

"This area," says Merion historian John Capers, fifty-two summers after the fact, "has created a real challenge to Merion's superintendents."

Kneeling by a modest granite marker set in the lush turf of Merion's 18th fairway (where, through a complex set of measurements it was eventually determined that Hogan hit the shot that got him into the play-off), Capers points to half a dozen recently repaired divots and explains that memorializing Hogan's feat with a modest stone plaque turned out to have a downside.

"Almost everyone who comes by here feels compelled to drop a ball and try and replicate the shot—measure themselves against Hogan that afternoon," he explains. The simple stone marker reads:

June 11, 1950

U.S. Open

Fourth Round

Ben Hogan

One Iron

"I suppose you can't blame them," Capers allows with the fractional proprietary smile of a true flame-keeper, noting that even he has a cherished connection to that unforgettable Sunday on the cusp of the decade's first summer. His mother, Mary, a Merion ladies' club champion, was selected to serve as one of three scorers who accompanied Hogan, Mangrum, and Fazio on their historic play-off round.

But as Valerie Hogan pointed out, it was a play-off many doubted Hogan would be able to show up for.

After finishing his work that warm Saturday afternoon, Hogan returned to the Barclay Hotel and soaked his aching frame in bathwater for an hour, downed several martinis to cut the pain, ate an early dinner, and went to bed. "To make matters worse," Valerie said, "I woke up in the middle of the night to the noise of jackhammers slamming into the street below, but he slept so soundly he never heard them."

As luck would have it, Pennsylvania blue laws—in effect since the days of William Penn, they prohibited businesses and sporting events from operating until the last scheduled church service was concluded on Sunday morning—provided Hogan with extra hours to sleep in and rest his weary legs, enjoy a good breakfast, browse the *Inquirer*, and perform his ritual morning soak.

When he woke that morning, according to Valerie, "he was fresh as a daisy." Glancing out their hotel window at Rittenhouse Square, where a sunny day only slightly cooler than Open Saturday was developing, he showed few lingering effects of his brutal Saturday march and even casually remarked, "Isn't it a lovely day, Val?"

A pack of reporters and sportswriters waiting in the lobby of the Barclay was just as surprised as anyone when Hogan suddenly appeared among them a little before ten that morning, looking both refreshed and rejuvenated. Once again, they'd apparently underestimated the willpower of golf's most dominant figure since Bobby Jones, and many of the scribes offered him their hands and best wishes as he left the Barclay. A few even applauded his recovery.

Both Hogan and Mangrum finished the first nine holes in 36, while Fazio, who struck the ball better than either of his competitors but had less to show for it, completed his opening nine with a frustrating 37. With five holes left to play, Hogan, showing the first traces of fatigue (having to pause and rest with his hands on his knees) but no visible performance letdown, began to pull away from his competitors. As his adrenaline surged, Fazio began to overshoot greens and make bogeys, while Mangrum made a pair of poor approach shots that resulted in costly bogeys at 12 and 14.

"I've never seen a threesome with only one person in it," Mary Capers later commented to her young son John. "Hogan was in a separate world."

By the 16th tee, though, Mangrum was still hanging tough. A birdie at 15 put him only one stroke behind Hogan with the three tough finishing holes to go. Hogan hadn't cracked but looked just about ready to, Mangrum decided, figuring that if the little man made a mistake, he could pick up that stroke and maybe snatch the Open straight out from under Hogan at 18. Nothing would have given Lloyd Mangrum more pleasure than that.

Following a sloppy approach shot and a weak chip that left him nine feet to negotiate for his par on the 16th green, Mangrum marked his ball and waited for Hogan and Fazio to putt out. As he stood over his ball, Lloyd noticed a bug crawling on it and, without thinking, used the toe of his putter to mark the ball's position while he picked up his ball and blew off the critter. He replaced the ball and holed the putt, then proceeded on to the 17th tee, believing he was still only one stroke behind Hogan with two holes to play. Still within reach.

As he teed up his ball, though, USGA president and match referee Ike Grainger pushed through the crowd and called out, "Just a moment, Mr. Mangrum. Mr. Hogan has the honors."

Mangrum paused, perplexed, glaring at Grainger. Like many regular Tour journeymen, Lloyd generally considered the gentlemen who ran the United States Golf Association a bunch of overbred aristocrats who probably argued passionately over how many Greek olives made the perfect martini. Lloyd was a straight whiskey drinker who didn't care much for tournament officials and match referees.

Grainger, a suave New York banker by occupation and the sponsoring organization's in-house champion of what he called "the rule of equity"—the belief that a sense of fair play should always govern any decision—patiently explained to a visibly seething Mangrum that by illegally marking his ball a *second* time, he had incurred a two-stroke penalty.

(Curiously, like the other moments that were misreported or embellished in the aftermath of the most thrilling Open finish since Ouimet beat Vardon and Ray, news reports widely portrayed the "bug" incident as the source of the two-stroke infraction. As Ike Grainger was careful to explain to Mangrum, though, the USGA did not believe in "double jeopardy," so only the *first* infraction of the rules would be observed and penalized. In effect, under existing conditions, though he did improperly "clean his ball," as widely reported, it was marking his ball a second time that got Mangrum in trouble.)

For a long moment, Lloyd gave the USGA's gentle, fair-minded Solomon of the rules a cold and penetrating stare. Then he stepped back and shook his head. "I guess we'll all eat tomorrow," he muttered with a bitter little smile beneath his riverboat moustache, glancing off at the gallery.

Hogan, now three ahead, teed up his ball and wasted little time. He stroked his ball onto the 17th green and, minutes later, eased the pain of Grainger's ruling by sinking a mammoth uphill fifty-footer to ice the golden anniversary cake.

Not far away, Valerie Hogan, who was having her umpteenth glass of iced tea on the Merion porch, began softly crying. After hearing the gallery's roar on 17, someone had told her, "Ben won," and now another emissary explained to her that it was official. He had indeed won his second National Open. The "miraculous" comeback was complete.

An elderly couple seated at an adjoining table leaned over and politely inquired if they could do anything for her. She seemed so distressed.

"I'm all right," she replied, dabbing her eyes, before getting up to go join Ben for the awards ceremony. "I'm just happy for my husband. I'm crying with joy."

Sensing history about to be made, many of the tournament's biggest names came back to Merion that Sunday afternoon to watch how the drama played out. Skee Reigel remembers sitting in the locker room moments after the play-off's completion, having a celebratory cocktail with Demaret and Middlecoff ("We all wanted Ben to do it," he says) and several others, when they suddenly heard Hogan's name being paged on the club's public address system. Ben was being summoned for the formal presentation of the trophy and the first-place check of $4,000.

"Hell," Jimmy barked, rattling his ice cubes, "he's already up at Oakland Hills practicing for *next* year's Open!" The overwarm locker room erupted in laughter.

Minutes later, a large contingent of players joined one of the largest galleries ever to attend the awarding of the National Open gold medal and trophy. Hogan was more gracious than ever, his voice breaking slightly as he talked about what his Merion comeback meant. "I know a lot of people wondered if this could ever happen again," he said to Ike Grainger at one point. "I'm just so relieved to have it done."

Under the circumstances, even Lloyd Mangrum was reasonably gracious, making only a few choice comments about needing to learn the rules for marking his ball before he played in another National Open.

The following week out in Hollywood, as it happened, shooting began in earnest on the soundstages and back lots at Twentieth Century Fox on the Hogan film project, newly titled *Follow the Sun*.

Diffident, mumbling, politely inoffensive Glenn Ford and veteran film actress Anne Baxter had been picked by Lanfield and producer Sam Engle to play Ben and Valerie Hogan. Edward Hazlitt Brennan was putting the finishing touches on a script he had developed from his own swooning profile of Hogan in *Reader's Digest*, with helpful field notes from the scriptwriters at Riviera and Valerie Hogan's own substantial scrapbooks. Among the more unconventional terms of the movie deal, Hogan refused to sign a contract until the movie was completed entirely to his satisfaction.

After a train trip down to Palm Beach to play in the round robin with chum George Coleman, Hogan went north to suburban Detroit for the Motor City Open and then headed off to the golden West to make sure his life was properly conveyed to film.

According to the film's archivists, he became such a nuisance and perfectionist on Lanfield's set—once spoiling an entire day of filming by insisting that the clubs Ford was rather ineffectually swinging weren't the same models he used that particular year—that Sidney Lanfield began making rueful jokes about murdering the film's hero with his own pitching wedge.

By autumn, when Ben wasn't busy pestering Lanfield about some acutely minor detail of the bedroom set where the ailing Hogan character was struggling to get back on his feet and chase the Tour, he was coaching the distinctly unathletic Ford on Hogan swing principles out at Riviera, where most of the outdoor golf shots were filmed, or beating balls into a cage specially built on a back lot at Twentieth Century Fox.

Hogan thought Glenn Ford was a hell of a nice guy but a walking embarrassment when it came to filming his golf swing. So he personally worked with Ford for several days before permitting the swing sequences to be filmed.

At one point during a break in filming, Hogan and Ford, mentor and pupil, sat having a drink together in a studio bar when an excited publicity man rushed in to show them one of the studio's advertising fliers for the new film, which producers hoped to release early in 1951. Among other absurdities, the ad described Ben and Valerie as "two rollicking kids from Texas," at which point, Ford later recalled, Hogan became so angry he threatened to "wash his hands" of the entire movie debacle. "If somebody called us 'rollicking kids,'" Ford quoted the Hawk as fuming, "we'd have been laughed off half the courses in the country."

The ad copy was quickly changed. Moreover, unable to coach Ford to an acceptable level of competence, Hogan did all of the long shots himself on the film, as well as many of the close-ups. A special rubber mask was created that made the lower portion of Hogan's face resemble Ford's—a rather peculiar case of life imitating art imitating life. Or better yet, Ben Hogan simply playing himself.

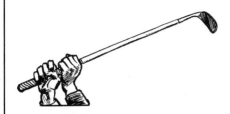

To Kill a Monster

by Dan Jenkins, *Golf Digest*, June 1985

It was the kind of course where you could lose your feet in the rough. Yeah, your feet, Foot-Joys and all. When you walked across the fairway of a par 4, you only took about 19 steps—and you were back in the rough again, looking for your feet, which might be standing on somebody's ball. And on those frequent occasions when the competitor would find himself on the "wrong side" of a green, there was usually something between him and the cup, either the Sahara Desert, played by an intruding bunker, or the Himalayas, played by the undulations of the putting surfaces.

This was Oakland Hills back in 1951, a layout doctored so severely that only Ben Hogan could have won the U.S. Open championship, which, of course, he did. Hogan won it over the final 18 holes with a 3-under-par 67, the greatest single round he, or anyone else, ever shot. And it was after that round that Ben supposedly made a remark for the ages: "I finally brought the monster to its knees." Nice editing on the part of the sportswriters. Some of us don't remember Hogan using the word "monster" on that sweltering Saturday of June 16, 1951, on the outskirts of Detroit. It sounded more like he said, "I finally brought the !#$%&@)! to its knees."

Actually, he may have said, "I got mad at this course, and I went out to bring the #$&%! monster to its knees."

Or maybe it was a writer in the Oakland Hills locker room who said, "By golly, Ben, you brought this stupid !$#&% course to its silly #$%&! knees, didn't you?" and Ben smiled in agreement.

What I *do* remember is how tough the course was and why.

Before the '51 Open, both the U.S. Golf Association and the Oakland Hills members had been afraid of what the pros might do to the old Donald Ross layout. Fourteen years earlier at the 1937 Open, Ralph Guldahl had set the 72-hole record of 281 at Oakland Hills, and for 11 years, or until the mark was bettered by Hogan at Riviera in '48, Oakland Hills had lived with the shame of being the club that surrendered the record. If the pros could shoot 281 in '37, what might they shoot in '51 unless changes were made? Enter now three men chosen by destiny to "protect" Oakland Hills in order for the club to stage a "proper" championship: Joseph C. Dey Jr., then the executive secretary of the USGA; Robert Trent Jones, the architect hired to "modernize" Donald Ross; and perhaps most important, John Oswald, chairman of the greens committee at Oakland Hills. An engineer at the Ford Motor Company, Oswald pushed harder than anyone for a rugged, if not impossible, golf course. "The Open is the greatest title there is," Oswald said to Dey and Jones. "The course should be so hard, nobody can win it."

Henceforth, Trent Jones removed 80 Ross bunkers that were no longer in play and added 60 new ones that *were* in play for the modern pro. He placed pot bunkers in the very center of some fairways, forcing the golfer to drive to the left or right of the bunker, to a narrow slit in the fairway, where it would usually take a bounce and wind up in the snarling "Open rough." On most long holes, Trent's fairways were only 19 paces wide at the landing area. Further, Jones reshaped all of the greens, creating a definite "wrong side." Par was trimmed from 72 to 70, a final psychological taunt for the competitor.

From the moment they arrived in town, the pros howled and complained, unlike they have at any Open since.

Cary Middlecoff said, "The only way to walk down these fairways is single file!"

Hogan said, "If I had to play this course for a living every week, I'd get into another business."

To fully appreciate Hogan's epic 67, you have to know where he came from. Sam Snead's 71 led the first day. Ben shot a 76, which left him five strokes and 31 players behind. "I made six mistakes," he said, "and paid for all of them." Hogan shot a 73 on Friday ("Three mistakes") as Bobby Locke, the South African, seized the lead at 144 for 36 holes. Ben was still five back.

"A couple of sixty-nines might take it tomorrow," a friend said to him that evening. "I'm afraid it's out of reach," he replied.

In those days, they played 36 the last day—"Open Saturday," as it was known. Hogan almost whipped the course in the morning round. He was 3 under going to the 14th, but he finished with a double bogey and two bogeys for a 71. He was hot, to say the least, both at himself and the course, but he was creeping up on the leaders. Locke and Jimmy Demaret were tied at 218 at noon. Hogan was at 220, now only two strokes behind.

Ben went out in 35, even par, in the afternoon, playing flawlessly, hitting "the slits." At the long 10th, he hit a driver and a "career" 2-iron to within five feet of the cup. Birdie. At the 13th, he birdied again with a 6-iron shot and a 14-footer. He took three from the edge for a bogey at the 14th. At the 15th, where he made a double bogey in the morning, Hogan drove with a 4-wood and then hit a 6-iron to within five feet of the hole and made it for a birdie. And he birdied the 18th with a driver and another 6-iron and a 15-foot putt for his 67 and winning total of 287. Clayton Heafner's 69 and 289 brought him second place. Hogan and Heafner were the only players to break 70 in the tournament, the only players to break 290. Locke finished third at 291. Poor Demaret collapsed with a 78, tied for 14th.

Ben Hogan shot many scores lower than 67, so why was this the greatest 18 ever played? Well, the average score of the field that afternoon at Oakland Hills was 75, give or take a fraction. In that sense, you can say that Hogan's 67 was actually 8 under par on the "monster"—and it *was* the last round of the Open, right? Case closed.

'53

The United States Open, June 11–13, Oakmont, Pennsylvania

from *Hogan* by Curt Sampson

Ben Hogan had won three of the five previous Opens, but the USGA required everybody (except defending champion Julius Boros) to participate in a thirty-six-hole qualifying tournament on the two days before the main event. Making Hogan qualify for the U.S. Open was like running a credit check on John D. Rockefeller, an insult and a waste of time. And although Hogan made the field without much trouble with a 77 at Pittsburgh Field Club and a 73 at Oakmont, the extra rounds cost him some of his limited supply of energy and a pulled muscle in his back.

Monumental and forbidding, Oakmont was the Mount Everest of golf courses. A river ran through it, the Allegheny; as did a turnpike, the Pennsylvania. Some of Oakmont's huge trees met at the top to form canopies, breaking the light into kaleidoscopes of sunshine and shadow. The shifting patterns were pleasant to contemplate even when your ball was hunkered down in the too-tall grass near a too-big tree or buried in a bunker with *furrows* in it for godsakes, like a freshly plowed field. The first, tenth, and twelfth greens tilted *away* from the fairway, a difficulty almost as maddening as the unplayable sand pits. Architect Henry Clay Fownes designed Oakmont in 1903 to be the toughest course in the world and he succeeded. Shots that strayed from the straight and narrow indicated an evil heart, Fownes seemed to say from across the years. Suffering was called for.

Salvation lay not on the greens, which undulated like a belly dancer. Although they were less steep than those at Augusta National, Oakmont's carpets were even quicker. Golf writers searched for similes involving hockey rinks and pond ice. Snead joked that the dime he used to mark his ball slid off one green. Grantland Rice wrote of seeing quite a number of the world's best players take five putts on some greens during the 1935 Open at Oakmont. He even witnessed a *six-putt*—from *ten* feet.

Hogan began memorizing and analyzing the old course nine days before the tournament started. "I have no practice system," he told a *Pittsburgh Press* writer, then described his practice system. "I go over the course a couple of times to decide what type of golf I'll have to play. Then I work on that." For most of three days he practiced high four-woods, for the second shot to the tenth.

Hogan debuted a black cigarette holder in the first round, during which he burned the usual two packs of butts. In warm, sunny weather that had most of the spectators thinking about sunburns and tans, Hogan wore the only sweater on the grounds, a gray cashmere cardigan.

Skip Alexander played in the threesome behind Hogan's. He strode into the locker room after the round and announced, "I know how to shoot 67 on this course."

"Okay, Skip," Fred Hawkins said, "how?"

"You hit every goddamn fairway and every green about ten feet from the hole. Like Hogan did."

Hogan had five birdies—three of them tap-ins—no bogeys, and his chip onto the only green he missed hit the flagstick and stopped two inches from the canister. His 67 led by three over Frank Souchak, a local amateur, and George Fazio, who had been in the U.S. Open playoff with Mangrum and Hogan at Merion.

Hogan said he had no problem with the back after the fourth hole. "I'm filled with ointment and I kept my back warm with this sweater. . . . Don't forget I'm forty years old. I'll have a new ache tomorrow—and I'll still have this one."

Drama returned to the Open the next day. Sam Snead shot 69 to pull into second place, and bitching by the pros reached an unpleasant crescendo. Snead produced the kind of brilliant putting round Hogan never had anymore. He used only eleven putts on the final nine holes and capped it off with a sixty-five-foot, seven-iron chip-in on the last green. Hogan, exhausted from being on the golf course too long, hit uncharacteristically poor iron shots on sixteen and eighteen for two bogeys. His 67-72 and Snead's 72-69 set up a showdown of the two best players in golf for the national championship in Saturday's double round. Just behind them lurked the third-best player, Lloyd Mangrum, and former Oakmont assistant pro Jay Hebert. Who could ask for more?

The USGA could. Actually, it asked for less—less dawdling by the participants, some of whom had spent almost five hours to get around Oakmont in the first round. USGA president Totten Heffelfinger, executive secretary Joe Dey, and others took positions on the course and played traffic cop, and the inevitable PGA-USGA blowup resumed. First it had been those irritating qualifying rounds, then the course itself (Mangrum called the hard, furrowed sand in the bunkers "a disgrace" and the greens "a runaway freight train"), now this.

"We played in three hours and seventeen minutes," said white-haired, red-faced Denny Shute, a normally pacific man who collected stamps. "I want to see them rush Hogan the way they did us."

Clayton Heafner also claimed selective enforcement. "I want to see what they do with Ben Hogan this afternoon. We played in three and a half hours. . . . It took Hogan four and a half hours yesterday. I told one official I was going out and clock Hogan this afternoon and see how fast he plays."

If Heffelfinger and Dey felt intimidated by Hogan, as Shute and Heafner implied, that would hardly have been unusual; Hogan scared everybody. Perhaps he should have been asked to get the lead out. He had been playing very carefully, looking at the clouds, the trees, and the smoke from his cigarette for clues about the wind strength and direction. On the greens he had slowed down to a crawl. His threesome required four hours and fifty minutes to get around Oakmont on Friday. But the snail's pace had just as much to do with delays caused by the ten thousand people watching him as with his own speed, or lack of it. How many had watched Heafner?

The feeling among his peers that the USGA favored Hogan continued on Saturday. Hogan began play at 9:00; Mangrum, 9:30; and Snead, 10:00. "It's unfair," said Cary Middlecoff, "and I don't think it's accidental." The good dentist quit in a snit halfway through the third round, because, he said, he was mad about starting times. "The late starters have to play on a course that's chopped to pieces by ten thousand people," Middlecoff said.

"They shouldn't give the leader the early schedule all the time," agreed Snead. "They ought to give everybody a fair chance."

Despite a three-putt from eight feet at the eighth, Snead took the lead with three front-nine birdies, and thousands of Hogan watchers fell back to watch the new leader. Snead held the lead until he reached the par-four seventeenth, an uphill and heavily bunkered hole just 292 yards long. You could drive it if you could hit and hold a convenience store roof from three blocks away. Snead could. But he went for his eagle-two too hard and three-putted. Ben had chipped to a couple of inches for a three on the same hole an hour before. Hogan led by a shot with one round left.

He ate a lunch of salad and fruit, a diet that had helped him lose twenty pounds since February. Between bites, he told a writer the outcome might hinge on holes fifteen, sixteen, seventeen, and eighteen, "the toughest part of the course."

Hogan still led Snead by one when he reached the 458-yard fifteenth. He drove into one of the cornrow fairway bunkers and had to wedge out. Then he hit his third with a two-iron into a bunker by the green. Another wedge, and still he faced a twenty-foot putt for bogey. But he holed the putt. Then he grabbed the Open by the throat, finishing three-three-three—par-birdie-birdie. Just when he might have been expected to lose his edge to fatigue, he hit a cut two-wood into a right-to-left crosswind on the 234-yard sixteenth, drove the green on seventeen—"I never hit a ball harder in my life," he said—and staked a five-iron to two yards on eighteen.

Snead had unraveled by then and would finish second in the U.S. Open for the fourth time. Hogan's final putt would win it by six shots. He stood over it, and again it was like he had seen Medusa. After an eternity, he hit the putt and made it.

Writer Charles Price asked Hogan what took him so long. "I couldn't see it going in," he said.

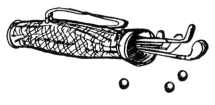

Cherry Hills

from *A Golfer's Life* by Arnold Palmer with James Dodson

A week after winning the 1960 Masters and playing my first round of golf with President Eisenhower, *Sports Illustrated* declared that an "authentic and unforgettable hero" had emerged in the pines at Augusta National, and *Life* weighed in with the verdict that I had replaced Hogan and Snead as the brightest star of the golf world.

What a wonderful moment it was for me, in some ways the fulfillment of my wildest childhood dreams. To have the press writing such breathtaking things about my exploits, to have people suddenly treating me as if I really was the best player of my generation—all I can say is, thank God I had Winnie and Pap and the folks back home to keep me humble. Even my Pap, though, was uncharacteristically moved to admit I'd done "pretty well" down in Augusta.

He knew better than anyone, though, that in my eyes the job was only partially done. My sights were set on the next big prize in golf, the United States Open Championship. The preeminent golf championship in the world was being contested that year at Cherry Hills in Denver, a course I knew a little bit about thanks to President Eisenhower, who happened to be a member there. President Eisenhower loved the course and predicted that I would do pretty well there. After nearly winning the Houston Classic, I didn't even worry too much about the mini-"slump" my game fell into during the month-long run-up to the Open. With reporters and photographers constantly underfoot both at Latrobe and on the road, I suppose the distractions of success took their toll on my ability to remain properly focused—a pattern that would increasingly become a problem for me in the coming years.

I played in my first Open championship at Oakmont in 1953, while still an amateur, firing 162 to miss the cut. I missed again in 1954 but finally finished the complete seventy-two holes at Olympic in 1955, the year Jack Fleck pulled off his miracle finish to beat Ben Hogan out of a record fifth Open trophy. I tied that year for twenty-first, so at least I was heading in the right direction. The next year, at Oak Hill, I was actually a threat for a while to Cary Middlecoff, before tapering off to seventh. After failing to make the cut at Inverness, I was never a factor at Southern Hills. The next year at Winged Foot, I finally made a decent run at the championship, but a weak finish, a 74, left me in fifth place.

But almost from the beginning, 1960 had a different feel about it. My confidence level had never been so high, my desire to go out and *play* the golf course so intense. Cherry Hills stretched 7,004 yards, but because of the added distance a ball would carry on a course that is located 5,280 feet above sea level, some believed Hogan's twelve-year-old tournament record of 276 might be in jeopardy. If the plus side of the equation was that a ball flew anywhere from ten to fifteen yards farther in that thinner atmosphere, the downside was that the decreased oxygen supply could sap your strength in no time flat. As a result, Hogan himself developed headaches and carried his own canister of oxygen with a breathing apparatus, and the sponsoring USGA arranged for similar supplies of oxygen to be made available to players at special facilities set up around the course. Something like forty players took advantage of these unusual arrangements.

Despite my surging confidence, I was in trouble from the opening swing, but breathing wasn't my problem. During two practice rounds, I'd driven the first green, a downhill par 4 measuring just 318 yards on the card, and I made up my mind to go for the putting surface in every round. Unfortunately, I pushed my first tee shot and the ball bounced into a small stream, Little Dry Creek, as it was fittingly called. The USGA had arranged to have water pumped energetically through the ditch, however, and by the time I arrived on the scene, frowning at my poor fortune, the stream had swept my ball farther down the hill toward the green. I remember commenting in jest to Joe Dey, the USGA's meticulous executive director and the rules official on the scene, that I would just "wait and follow my ball down the creek until it stops and take a drop there."

Joe clearly didn't think that was proper—or particularly amusing. After a bit of confusion determining where my ball had crossed the margin of the hazard, a spot was determined and I took a drop with a one-stroke penalty. My next shot glanced off a tree, and my fourth attempt flew over the green. I chipped five feet short of the hole for my fifth, then sank the putt for a nice fat opening double-bogey six.

You could have fried an egg on my forehead at that moment. I was so furious with myself for blowing a hole I clearly should have birdied. As we walked to the next tee, I remember hitching up my trousers and having a sharp exchange with my caddie. Bob Blair, who often carried for me, had somehow engineered the assignment to my bag (in those days, the USGA assigned caddies, who were mostly from the host club or local area, at random to players beforehand)—and I still don't think I want to know what kind of maneuver Bob pulled off to get on my bag. I don't remember what Bob had said that got my dander up, but whatever it was it even caught the attention of my playing partners, Jack Fleck and Cary Middlecoff. I was obviously steamed, and I stayed that way. Several factors contributed to that.

Perhaps due to the thinner air, play was much slower than the normal slow pace of an Open, and it didn't help matters that Fleck and Middlecoff, Open champions both, were two of the most deliberate players on tour. They could sometimes seemingly anguish over the ball for a small eternity before pulling the trigger on a shot. That habit was anathema to my style of play—once I'd made up my mind what I needed or wanted to do, which was usually pretty quickly, the last thing I wanted to do was stand around and *think* about it some more. It was better, in my view, to make the shot believing it would work and deal with the consequences if it didn't.

In any case, the three of us wound our way tediously around the golf course over the next five hours. I had several moments when my putting stroke failed and my frustration deepened. I was fortunate to finish the opening round with a one-over 72, a respectable score that placed me four strokes behind leader Mike Souchak. Afterward, my friendly nemesis Bob Drum growled at me to summarize the round, and I reflected that I felt "wobbly and scrambling" all day long and never found my pace. Cary Middlecoff used those same words to describe my round when he wrote about our trio's frustrating escapades for his hometown newspaper. What I didn't come right out and say was that by my calculations the poky play of my partners had cost me four strokes on the round, because anytime I wasn't moving forward on a golf course my nervousness and anxiety level increased twofold and my scoring usually paid the price. That day, the agonizing pace of play seemed even too much for Cary. He could manage only a painful 77 for his afternoon's labors.

Of course, the real trophy for loss of composure under pressure that day went to Tommy Bolt, who in a rage of frustration flung his driver into the pond in front of the 18th tee after knocking two balls into the water, clearing the head of an astonished Claude Harmon by either inches or yards, depending on which account of the famous incident you choose to accept.

In the press tent, I was asked if I thought I was still in contention, and I wearily replied that I only hoped I would still be within four shots come Saturday afternoon. As tradition had held since 1895, the Open finished with two rounds on Open Saturday, a practice that would continue until 1965. Noting my poor start on the day, someone else wondered if, given the opportunity, I would use my driver again on the first hole, and I politely assured him I certainly would because you never could tell what could happen when you hit the green off the tee—you just might make a hole in one.

I know some observers thought that, under the circumstances, that was a foolish strategy. The course was playing a lot tougher than most had expected, and scarcely anybody was now thinking that Hogan's record was in danger of tumbling. But I meant every word of it, and I couldn't wait to get back to the first tee and take my revenge on the hole.

Winnie wasn't with me in Denver. She and the girls were visiting her parents at the family's cottage at Shawnee-on-the-Delaware, taking a breather from the rigors of tour life. I suppose it's a little ironic that, after being on hand for virtually every important tournament I'd played in since the day we met, she would miss one some would later describe as the greatest ever—where three eras of the game collided in the persons of Ben Hogan, Arnold Palmer, and a young amateur named Jack Nicklaus, and I would pull off the most dramatic charge of my career.

But, of course, we had no way of knowing ahead of time how things would play out and had already decided to leave the girls (then four and two) with Winnie's parents while we went on to the Canada Cup and the British Open at St. Andrews. The decision, from a family standpoint, made good sense.

My second circuit of the Cherry Hills course was hardly more encouraging than the first; I shot 71 and fell even further back of the hard-charging Mike Souchak, who tore around Cherry Hills in 67, setting a thirty-six-hole record of 137 in the process. I made several bold escapes from the rough and five birdies, but I failed to convert several pars at critical moments (including the par-3 12th, which I felt jinxed me all week) and was fortunate, I suppose, that my day's total wasn't any worse. I honestly felt I'd deserved better than the course gave me, but other observers, like the ever-downbeat Drum, said I was very lucky to finish at even par. The only good thing about losing ground to the leader was that I wouldn't be paired with slowpokes Fleck and Middlecoff again. I must admit, the two of them nearly drove me crazy at times.

Saturday, the day of the double finishing rounds, dawned sunny and warm, a perfect Rocky Mountain morning, and Mike showed the first signs of cracking, finishing his morning round with a two-over 73. His score was still good enough, though, for a two-stroke lead over Julius Boros, Jerry Barber, and Dow Finsterwald. Ben Hogan, who was still the man to beat in my mind, hit all eighteen greens in that third round, as I recall, but his unpredictable putter was betraying him.

That morning, I woke up telling myself that if I was going to lose the Open, I'd do it kicking and screaming, so it didn't surprise anybody when I pulled out my driver on the first hole and went for the green. My ball landed in the short grass just in front but then rolled into the deep collar grass around the green. I made a poor chip and needed three more shots to get down in bogey.

Not the way to start Open Saturday.

I finally got birdies at three and five, bogeyed six, birdied seven, and parred the difficult and long eighth. I had yet to par the tough uphill ninth, made another poor chip from the rough by the green, ripped off my golf glove in disgust, and holed out for a careless double-bogey six. Despite three birdies going out, I'd managed only a mediocre 36. The struggle continued on ten, where I barely got out of the bunker and had to make a dangerous twenty-foot downhiller to save par. I pulled back to even par with a birdie on 11 and—finally—managed to par the watery 12th, the par 3 that had been trouble all week long. My fifth birdie of the round came at 13, but I knew I would need at least two, possibly three, more birdies to have a reasonable chance of catching Souchak and the eight or nine others ahead of me.

Of the remaining five holes, only the 17th offered a realistic birdie opportunity. I parred 14 and 15 and went for broke on 16—making bogey instead. To compound my woes, I settled for par on the "easy" 17th and followed that up by making a bogey on the finishing hole.

A disappointing one-over 72. At that moment, with eighteen holes to play, I was exactly where I had been at the start of the third round. I was still eight back of Souchak, and on top of that, four players in the two pairings that finished just ahead of me—Boros, Hogan, Player, and the kid Nicklaus—had all gained ground on the nervous leader. A few minutes later, thanks to a spectator taking an unauthorized photograph—only the credentialed members of the press are allowed to use cameras on the premises—Souchak hooked his drive out-of-bounds on 18 and finished the hole with a double bogey for 73 and a three-round total of 208. That nudged all of us a bit closer to the lead, but thirteen players stood between me at 215 and Mike at 208.

Needless to say, I was angry with myself for my weak finish in the third round. I stalked into the clubhouse to get a hamburger and a Coke to try to cool down and compose myself for the final eighteen. I was brooding on the fact that I'd made twelve birdies in fifty-four holes yet was two over par.

I can't say I knew this at that very moment, but history was hardly on my side: In the fifty-six Opens that had been contested over seventy-two holes since 1895, no player trailing by more than five strokes after fifty-four holes had ever come back to win the championship. Still, Mike was clearly vulnerable—in the locker room he admitted to several reporters that he felt he'd just blown his chances with the double bogey at 18, a terrible thing to do to his confidence, in my view, what with Hogan, Nicklaus, Finsterwald, and Boros hot on his heels. After playing as brilliantly as Mike had, this was the moment to keep all negative thoughts out of his head.

I suppose I was looking for some consolation for my own self-inflicted troubles, or at least some reassurance that all wasn't entirely lost yet, so I took my burger to where Drum sat talking to Dan Jenkins and Ken Venturi and a couple of other players in the locker room.

I remember someone, possibly Ken, wondering if Souchak would fold. Somebody shrugged and reflected that anything could happen in golf—especially in a U.S. Open. That was true enough, we all agreed.

"What if I shot sixty-five?" I spoke up, chewing my burger. "Two-eighty always wins the Open. What would that do?"

I meant exactly what I said. But they all looked at me as if I'd grown a second head, and Drum gave his usual cynical snort of derision.

Drum and I had already locked horns on the course, when he barked at me to quit fooling around by trying to eagle the first hole; I knew he'd also thought it was a big mistake going for any of the par 5s in two, as I routinely did. Maybe he'd been right, but as I pointed out to him in the locker room, I still had a shot at 280, and 280 traditionally won the Open.

Drum looked at me with more amusement than sympathy.

"Two-eighty won't do you one damn bit of good," he pronounced bluntly.

I'd only taken a couple bites of my burger, but I stopped chewing, ready to explode with anger at his remark. I'd come looking for support and encouragement from a man I considered a friend—a man who was planning to accompany me and my wife to Britain in a matter of days, no less—and essentially he'd dumped a bucket of cold water over my head.

"Oh, yeah?" I said. "Watch and see."

I put down my sandwich, turned and left, yanked my driver out of the bag as I marched to the practice tee, teed up a ball, and slammed it to the back of the range. Still seething mad, I hit maybe one or two more such monster drives before I heard my name being paged, the official summons to the first tee.

I walked straight onto the tee, pegged up my ball, and drove it onto the front of the first green.

There was an explosive cheer from the gallery on the tee and around the green, producing one of the strongest thrills of my career. Marching off the tee, I felt a powerful surge of adrenaline, maybe the greatest I had ever experienced. By the time I reached the green, I knew something big was happening to me. The eagle opportunity was long and not the easiest to read from that position on the green, but I coaxed it close enough to make people gasp and then made a lengthy comebacker for a birdie—a vastly better start than the previous three visits to the green. Around me, the gallery was running to find places on the second tee and fairway. There, I missed my approach shot to the green, but I chipped in for a birdie from the fringe, producing another pulse-quickening roar. A good wedge approach at three left me only a one-footer to convert for my third consecutive birdie, and I followed that up at the fourth with an eighteen-footer that dropped for my fourth birdie in a row.

I was back in the Open now, two under for the tournament and only three back of Souchak. I'm told that some of the large galleries waiting for the tournament leaders to tee off heard the commotion of what has been described as the wildest cheering ever heard at an Open and broke away to go see what was happening.

On the par-5 fifth, 538 yards long, I blocked my tee shot a bit and drove into the right rough, hit a 3-wood into the greenside bunker, blasted out to twenty feet, and took two putts to get down—my first par of the round. I remember feeling let down a bit—mentally kicking myself for not making five in a row.

I went back to work at the sixth, nailing a curling twenty-five-footer for birdie, then followed that up with a strong chip up and tap-in birdie at the seventh. The gallery went wild, I'm told, but all I could think about was the difficult eighth, a long uphill par-3 of 233 yards. The pin had been moved from the morning round to a spot that was down front and left, and I chose to gamble and go at it; I went with a 2-iron and pulled the shot slightly, landing my ball just on the front of the green, and watched the slope send it back into the bunker. I blasted out and two-putted for bogey.

As I stood in that eighth-hole bunker, Jack Nicklaus was walking off the ninth green, also in the process of tearing up the course. He'd gone out in 32 and was five under for sixty-three holes. I was four under, but so were Souchak, Hogan, Boros, Fleck, Finsterwald, Jerry Barber, and Don Cherry.

For the next hour or so, the entire leader board was in utter chaos. Behind me, Ted Kroll and Jack Fleck were also blistering the course. Up ahead, leading the tournament by a stroke after twelve holes, Nicklaus was sizing up a dangerous downhill putt for par on 13 when his inexperience caught up with him. Aware of Hogan's gruff response to what he considered stupid questions, Jack, barely twenty years old at the time, was uncertain whether under the rules he was entitled to repair a pitch mark directly in his putting line. He was—but was too timid to ask either Ben or an official. He tapped the putt, and the indentation threw the ball off line and caused it to just miss the hole. The error shook Jack's confidence, and, still rattled, he three-putted the 14th as well.

It was around 4:45 in the afternoon when I finally got a share of the lead, tied with Hogan and Fleck at four under par after a birdie at 11. I cooled off a bit at that point and made five consecutive pars, arriving at 17 at four under after seventy holes of golf.

At one point before the turn, I looked over and saw wordsmiths Drum and Jenkins following along in the Army. Smiling at them, I couldn't resist a well-aimed barb: "Well, well. What are you guys doing here?" I don't recall if or what they may have answered, but the staggering tension was visible on their faces as well.

The 17th was a 550-yard par 5 with an island green sitting in the middle of a still lake. The hole's design forced even long players like me to go with an intelligent drive, careful lay-up, and safe pitch to the putting surface. The pin in the afternoon final round was positioned dangerously close to the front of the green—and the slope that led to a watery doom in front. A typical fourth-round Open pin placement, set up to make someone either a hero or a goat. Ben Hogan's putter had been shaky all week. Perhaps that explains why he, the premier precision shotmaker of all time, decided he needed to get his third shot as close as possible to the hole for a reasonable chance at birdie or even a two-putt. In a daring attempt that had some people scratching their heads for years, he went directly for the flag, his ball barely clearing the band of water in front of the green. It was almost a phenomenal shot, but he and the gallery watched in horror as it spun backward and trickled down the slope into the water.

You have to credit Ben. He did what a champion does at such a crucial moment: play the shot he thinks will work best and the devil take the consequences. Facing disaster, he didn't hesitate to remove his shoes and socks and wade into the water to slash the ball out and onto the green—exactly what I would have done under the same circumstances. He somehow got the ball onto the putting surface but missed his par putt, and I think that finally took the steam out of him. At 18, his drive found the water a foot or so short of land and sank his hope of a fifth Open championship.

Behind him in the fairway, I saw much of what was unfolding and tried to keep Pap's stern injunction to "take care of my own business" in my mind, meaning I needed to keep my focus where it ought to be—on the next shot and nothing else. Even after I'd been informed that I alone was leading the tournament, and even after I successfully negotiated the moat and putted out for par at 17, I quietly sweated bullets.

One more par.

That's exactly what I was thinking. *Concentrate on the next shot,* I told myself. *Don't get ahead of yourself. Try to stay calm and keep your head still.*

I wanted to win a United States Open so badly. I'd dreamed of winning the Open as a small boy, and now all I had to do was make *one* par to achieve that dream. I don't recall whether I knew it or not, but two holes behind me, Jack Fleck was the only guy with a realistic chance of catching me. As he'd proven by stunning Ben Hogan at the Olympic Club, the man was capable of producing miracle finishes.

I hit a 1-iron across the pond and safely into the fairway at 18, feeling a massive surge of relief. I'd avoided the hazard that had undone Bolt and

Hogan and God knows how many other world-class players that week. A few moments later, I felt my emotions seesaw when I pulled my 4-iron approach shot and wound up to the left of the green. The ball was eighty long feet from the cup and in the rough. United States Open rough, no less. I walked up and stared at the lie for several moments. I took a couple of deep breaths, trying to gain as much composure as possible.

If I got up and down, I'd have my 280. If not, Fleck or someone else would probably at least tie or might pass me.

You can wait your entire life for a moment like this. I took out my wedge, set up over the ball, and made a crisp little chip that sent the ball rolling slowly toward the pin. It stopped a couple of feet from the hole. On my way to the ball, I paused to repair a pitch mark and then straightened up and studied the line. When I finally stood over the ball, my hands were moist from the heat and the tension, and those couple of feet looked more like two miles. But I kept my head dead still, took the putter back slowly, and rolled the ball into the heart of the cup.

I suppose I didn't believe, for an instant, what I'd just done. After half a beat of silence, the air around the green exploded, fractured by wild cheers and whistles. I glanced around, took a step or two to the hole, and lifted my ball from the cup, then turned and flung my white visor toward the gallery at the back of the green.

I later learned that, in the excitement, an NBC announcer had prematurely announced to his audience that Arnold Palmer was the new National Open champion. But that certainly wasn't the case, with Souchak, Cherry, and Jack the Giant Killer still out on the course.

With my heart beating wildly, I signed my card and went into the press tent to get a Coke. I took a seat at the interview table and the place erupted into a noisy den of questions and activity. A few minutes later, word reached us that Don Cherry had gone for the green at 17 in two and topped his ball into the water, while Fleck, two back then thanks to a missed one-footer at 16, could do no better than par. He would need an eagle at 18 to force a playoff. Instead, after what felt like an hour, he tapped in for bogey and the U.S. Open championship was mine.

Somehow I got a call through to Winnie from the noisy pressroom to her parents' house in Coopersburg. They'd been on the road, as it turned out, when they heard on the radio that Arnold Palmer was about to pull off one of the biggest comebacks in Open history. By then, of course, the verdict was in amid the long shadows of that Denver afternoon. My final-round 65, in fact, had overtaken fourteen players and at that time was the best finish ever by an Open champion, beating Gene Sarazen's 1932 finish by one stroke.

When I finally got Winnie on the phone amid the hubbub of excited voices, my heart was still thumping wildly. I decided to skip most of the details, though.

"Hiya, lover," I said to her. "Guess what? We won!"

Some would say the arrival of Jack Nicklaus in my "backyard" at Oakmont in Pittsburgh, two years later, was almost the match of Cherry Hills for sheer quality of drama. Though I didn't care for the outcome, I can't disagree. The Open that year had all of the classic elements: a hometown favorite son at the peak of his form, a brilliant tour rookie everyone feared, highly partisan crowds, and the intensity of a National Open on the line.

I'd had a great year, my best start ever, leading up to Oakmont—including back-to-back wins at Palm Springs and Phoenix (where I enjoyed a 12-shot margin of victory, the largest of my career), followed by my third win at the Masters in April, then those three consecutive wins at the Texas Open, the Tournament of Champions, and the Colonial.

The pre-tournament consensus had me as the man to beat, and the home-field advantage of Oakmont, a course I knew intimately, seemed like a storybook setting for a second Open championship. Frankly, after playing poorly and finishing twelfth at Oakland Hills in Detroit the previous year, I was determined to do well in front of the homefolks in Pittsburgh. But as I was careful to warn the writers and anybody else who would listen to me prior to that week, "Everybody says I'm the favorite, but you'd better watch the fat boy."

I wasn't trying to insult Jack. In fact, as I think back on that comment, I realize I was mimicking much of what was being written about Jack's weight and appearance, and his apparent threat to my dominance of the Tour. Since joining the Tour at Los Angeles the first week of the year and winning $33.33, Jack had steadily climbed the leader board, and it was clear to anybody who'd witnessed his power and finesse and almost unearthly ability to focus on his game that Jack Nicklaus's moment had arrived. Whatever image problems he had early on regarding his weight or appearance or personality were, in my mind, completely irrelevant. I knew he was perfectly capable of taking the Open at Oakmont, because golf courses play no favorites and young Mr. Nicklaus simply had the look of a champion about him. I could see it, and so could anybody else who cared to look beyond the image baloney. As I privately expressed to Winnie and a few others from Latrobe, I really did view him as the one man I feared could snatch away the second Open title, one I dearly wanted to win in front of my hometown fans—a prophetic hunch, as it turned out.

I suppose if I had an ace in the hole where Jack was concerned, it was simply that Oakmont was a dangerously narrow golf course, with punishing rough that could turn errant tee shots into major disasters. Jack had something of a "flying elbow" in those days, a tendency to get wild off the tee with those huge, high-power fades of his. U.S. Open rough, of course, is the great equalizer of the championship. Anybody who misses fairways probably has no chance to contend in a National Open.

I was pretty sure the heavy partisan fan factor wouldn't bother Jack; in fact, it might even be a motivating factor in his favor. With that year's Masters title already in my pocket, and the goal of a modern Grand Slam intensely set in my mind, the pressure was really on me to prove to the world that I deserved a second Open title. On top of that, the tournament was being held on ground that held great meaning for me. It's ironic that it was this same rugged Open rough, specifically the rough around the greens, that gave me fits and ultimately proved to be my downfall. Oakmont's glassy putting surfaces also played a part in my undoing. At best, I was a mediocre putter on very fast greens, and I probably should have practiced on a similar putting surface prior to the Open. But I didn't, and that oversight took its toll.

Almost from the opening bell, my fears began to materialize. Jack and I were paired together for the first round, and an estimated gallery of 12,000 spectators lined the first fairway, anxious to watch us do our things. Jack started with three consecutive threes, all birdies, but I gave my fans precious little to cheer about. After just three holes, I trailed Jack by five strokes and it looked as if the day would be a long one. Fortunately, I righted the ship and ripped off my own string of birdies while Jack faltered just a touch. I shot an opening-round 71, and by the end of the day I stood one better than Jack for the championship. Both of us trailed reigning Open champion Gene Littler, who shot 69 in a round that included an eagle on the par-5 ninth. But Gene had trouble figuring Oakmont's mighty lethal greens, too, and the next afternoon Bob Rosburg and I surged to the front of the pack, I with a 68 and Rossie with a 69.

After sixteen holes of the morning round on Saturday, Rossie took the lead, but I regained it a hole later by driving the green at the short 17th and making the putt for an eagle two. Unfortunately, I gave a stroke back with a birdie attempt that was too bold on 18, missing the comebacker for par and suffering yet another three-putt bogey. The 73 dropped me into a tie at 212 with Bobby Nichols.

I went to fetch a ham sandwich and Coke, feeling let down. Though I still had a piece of the fifty-four-hole lead, all those careless three-putts were killing my psyche. Jack, on the other hand, two strokes back, hadn't had even one of them. He'd putted brilliantly over some of the most treacherous greens in championship golf. The sandwich and Coke refreshed me. I even downed a pint of chocolate milk for an energy boost and walked back to the first tee, where my final round was set to begin.

"Go get 'em, Arnie!"

The whooping and cheerleading had intensified.

I remember being aware of how large the crowds had grown. By early afternoon, some 22,000 fans were on the grounds at Oakmont, and by the end of the tournament something like a total of 25,000 more spectators than had ever attended an Open before would come to Oakmont.

Some of them could have used crash seminars in proper sportsmanship—or basic civility. I didn't witness much firsthand, aside from the crowd's unusual boisterousness, but I later heard of several instances when zealous Palmer partisans called out unflatteringly to Jack and even cheered when he—and other contenders, for that matter—missed a shot. This was deeply distressing both to Jack's father and to mine, both of whom were in the gallery that week, and when I heard about some of the incidents they made me angry. There is no room for such shenanigans in the game of golf. But it also played right into Jack's hands, as far as I was concerned.

At the ninth hole of the final round, I faced an opportunity to put the Open out of reach. I was two under for the round at that point, three under for the championship. If I could reach the par-5 ninth in two and make birdie—better yet, eagle—that might cinch the deal. I don't suppose it surprised anyone that I went for the green, pounding a 3-wood right on the screws. The ball drifted a little too much, though, and settled in the heavy rough just off the green, about pin high. All I still needed to do was make a solid little flip chip and a putt for birdie; that just might be enough.

I don't recall being particularly concerned about the chip shot. I mean, U.S. Open rough is like no other, but, frankly, I was used to playing out of the longer grasses where careful players seldom ventured. Even so, this week the rough was giving me nightmares. I took my stance and aimed at the pin and drew back my wedge. The unimaginable happened. I stubbed the shot. The ball popped up and settled in the rough mere inches from where it had been. The gallery around the green groaned and then grew so eerily quiet I swear you could hear the blood pumping angrily through my veins. I glared at the ball and tried again, producing another poor effort that left the ball eight feet from the cup. Instead of an excellent shot at birdie I now had to scramble like crazy for par. I missed the putt, grazing the right edge of the hole. I'd turned a surefire birdie into bogey, which under the circumstances felt like a double bogey. Even worse, it gave Nicklaus just the opening he needed.

He birdied nine and 11, and when I bogied the par-3 13th, we were tied for the championship. Jack made a great recovery from the bunker on 17 and nearly holed a birdie at 18 to finish with 69 and a seventy-two-hole total of 283.

I knew what I needed to do and was in position to do just that. From tee to green, I'd played almost as well as I ever have, missing only four greens that day, twice reaching critical par 5s in two. All I needed was a birdie at 18 and I would have my second U.S. Open title in storybook fashion. But the hole is hardly a cream puff. It measures 465 yards and is studded with menacing bunkers. I hit maybe my best drive of the day to the heart of the fairway, then slashed a superb 4-iron shot to ten feet of the cup. I was certain I would make the putt, but once again I didn't.

After the regulation seventy-two holes of play, the United States Open Championship was tied, with a playoff scheduled for Sunday.

Winnie, Pap, and I drove home afterward to Latrobe, an hour away, and I remember feeling a little drained by my experience, replaying in my head blown opportunities and my failure to make a birdie when I needed it. On the other hand, despite all those depressing three-putts, I was relieved to still be in the hunt. By the finish, I would collect thirteen three-putts to Jack's one—and therein lies the tale, as far as I'm concerned.

The point is, as we all understand, that you never know what will happen in golf. The conventional view is that Oakmont was an Open I should have won because I was the better player at the time. Well, "should have" and "did" may be neighbors, but they don't always get along. Still, I was going to do my level best at Oakmont to make sure they did. Winnie, Pap, and I had a quiet dinner, and I slept well and got up early, ready to charge to the golf course in Pittsburgh and take care of business.

But I fell behind right from the start, and after Jack rolled a birdie into the cup at the sixth hole, I was already four strokes down. The crowds were eerily silent at that point, as though they were spectators at a state funeral. When I rallied, though, they rallied and cheered me on. I briefly got a charge going with birdies at nine, 11, and 12. That drew me to within a stroke of Jack. As my playing history showed, that was my preferred position, having to mount a charge and close hard upon the front-runner.

But, suddenly, that equation was different—or should I say the front-runner was different. In the past, whenever I mounted a charge I could almost *feel* that the player I was chasing was going to collapse and give ground. It sounds a bit odd, but it was almost as if I could will the leader to move over and permit me to pass. As I've said on numerous occasions, I was a far better closer than a front-runner. So it can be argued that after a trio of birdies got me back in the hunt, I was exactly where I needed to be.

But Jack Nicklaus was a different animal altogether, completely unlike anybody I'd ever chased. For one thing, he didn't seem the slightest bit bothered by the electricity of my charge and the lusty cries of my supporters. If anything, they seemed to drive him further into that hard cocoon of concentration he showed the world. But it would take the world years to fully appreciate how difficult a chore that was and how well he executed it. I had never seen anyone who could stay focused the way he did—and I've never seen anyone with the same ability since. In my view, that's why Jack Nicklaus became the most accomplished player in the history of the game.

You just couldn't crack that concentration. He had his own game plan and he stuck to it, come hell or high water—or even noisy hometown fans.

Once again, though, it was my own traitorous flatstick that did me in. I three-putted the 13th green, fell two strokes, and never recovered. Despite a drive into the rough at 18, Jack won his first U.S. Open, and a little bit later

I reflected to a reporter, "I'll tell you something. Now that the big guy is out of the cage, everybody better run for cover."

Then I went and found Winnie, who gave me the same big kiss she always gave me, win or lose, and we drove home to Latrobe.

The popular historical view is that I was a dominant force in the next four Open championships and a major factor in Opens for at least the next decade. I would agree with that assessment, and note that by my own calculations, poor chipping and putting on Open greens cost me at least three Open titles, maybe even a shot at the fourth.

Not long ago, Doc Giffin asked me an intriguing question. "Arnold," he said (because he always calls me "Arnold"), "if you could have one mulligan anywhere in your career, where would you use it?"

I thought about it a moment and cheekily replied, "I'd divide it several ways."

Certainly the eight-footer to win at Oakmont would be the first part.

The second part I'd spend at Brookline, the very next summer, in 1963.

I arrived at the Country Club, on the fiftieth anniversary of Francis Ouimet's miraculous 1913 win over Harry Vardon and Ted Ray, in a virtual dead heat with Jack Nicklaus for the Tour money title, and, thanks to a rare month off, my game was rested but pretty well tuned. In thirteen tournaments I'd already registered four wins and five other top-ten finishes, one of my strongest starts ever, but Jack was also winning tournaments at an impressive clip, causing some in the press to openly wonder if I was beginning to slip a notch or two. The truth is, I was distracted by a seemingly endless array of new business deals brought my way by Mark McCormack, my business manager, by a new airplane, and by other factors that come with the kind of success I was suddenly enjoying. But my game, as my record that year indicated, was essentially fine. I simply needed that four-week rest from the public eye, and I got it, and I came back raring to go.

The week before Brookline, after defeating Paul Harney in a playoff to take the Thunderbird Classic, I traveled to Massachusetts and immediately liked what I saw of the Country Club's old-style meandering course, which placed a premium on accurate driving and intelligent shots to small greens. I hoped the more northern grasses would also mean the putting surfaces were a touch slower, and therefore more to my liking, though that didn't turn out to be the case.

The weather was a major factor in producing unusually high scores, cold blustery winds that constantly shifted direction, tossing balls hither and yon. Meanwhile, the USGA was up to its old tricks with the greens and rough, difficult to read, harder to play. I didn't play particularly well, in the first three rounds going 73-69-77. Most unexpectedly, Jack failed to make the cut, and I remember feeling slightly out of synch, never quite able to find my stride and get my rhythm going. I was lucky enough to hang on with a final-round 74 and find myself in a three-way tie with Jacky Cupit and Julius Boros at the end of regulation play. Our 293s were the highest scores to lead after seventy-two holes since 1935, when Sam Parks won at Oakmont with 299. Perhaps five other men had an opportunity to win it outright, including Tony Lema, Paul Harney, and even young Bruce Crampton. But none of them could convert when they needed to, and the Open did an odd reprise of its celebrated 1913 three-man playoff.

For me, the critical moment in the playoff came in the 11th-hole fairway. Boros, typically chipping and putting like Old Man River, was four strokes ahead, and if there was a moment for me to make my charge, it ought to have been then. After a bogey at the tenth, I tried to put some extra mustard on my drive, but it strayed, and I found my ball sitting in a rotten stump off the left side of the fairway.

I had three choices: accept the penalty, which amounted to two strokes, drop out of the stump or hit another drive, or else play the ball as it lay. There was doubt in my mind what I needed to do. But I had no margin to squander strokes, so I took out a 4-iron, figuring to simply advance the ball back onto the fairway and make a good recovery from there.

I hacked three times at the ball before I freed it from that damned stump. Once again my bold style of play had mortally wounded me. I made seven on the hole and finished six strokes back of Julius with a dismal 76. If I had it to do over—or if I had one of Doc's magic mulligans—I might have gone back to the tee and hit my drive over, because you never know what might happen. I might also spend my "do-over" on the short putt I missed at 17 in the final round, a devastating miss that might have given me the championship outright.

But golf is not a game of what might have been. It's a game of who did what when it counted.

What happened, of course, was that Julius Boros glided home with that magnificent flowing swing of his to become, at age forty-three, the second-oldest man since Ted Ray to capture an Open championship. It seemed oddly fitting, given all the history surrounding that hallowed ground.

But for the second year in a row, I'd lost the Open in a playoff, and frankly it hurt like hell.

The next year, at Congressional Country Club in Washington, I was the only man to break par 70 in the opening round of the U.S. Open, on a lush, green, newly irrigated course that had been stretched to 7,053 yards, making it the longest Open test ever. Washington was in the midst of a terrible heat wave and a drought that wilted the hopes of almost everybody, including me. My scoring grew worse with every round, and I finished in fifth place. Coming back from years of disappointment, Ken Venturi walked slowly home, dazed by the hundred-degree heat, and heroically claimed his well-deserved U.S. Open title.

When I shot 76-76 and missed the Open cut at Bellerive in St. Louis in June of 1965, the talk that my game was foundering reached a near-fever pitch in the press. I heard it nearly everywhere I went and I saw it in people's faces: I wasn't striking the ball with the same old zest and derring-do; I wasn't fearless over putts anymore; I didn't attack golf courses the way I always had. . . . *What on earth is wrong with Arnie?*

The Big Slump had struck. That's what was wrong with Arnie. My desire to win golf tournaments was as strong as it had ever been, but I suddenly couldn't seem to get the ball in the hole when it counted.

This is as good a point as any to talk about something I've been thinking about, in this respect, for many years. Namely, why did I begin in late 1964 to lose that magical ability to charge and capture major golf tournaments? As my record indicates, I played extremely well in most of the major championships for the next decade, but it's undeniably true that, as the press detected, something *was* different about my game.

Most golfers win tournaments, and certainly U.S. Opens, by avoiding mistakes. But I typically won my most important tournaments by overcoming mine. Charlie Sifford once noted that I was the most aggressive player in the history of the game. It's entirely possible that's true.

If the downside of that signature trait is that I was capable of risking—and losing—everything on a low-percentage shot that could take me from hero to goat in one swing, the reverse was also equally true. Faced with a situation like the one that I found at Cherry Hills, it never entered my mind that I *couldn't* pull off a so-called miracle finish. The doubt never entered my mind.

When Sam Snead commented that every time I drove the ball, it looked as if I was trying to hole my tee shot, he wasn't far off the mark. The way I looked at any shot was that if you played it as boldly as you could, you were guaranteed to have the results you desired at least some of the time. In my mind, that far outweighed the benefit of playing conservatively. It was precisely this quality, I'm convinced, whatever that elusive mental "it" may be, that enabled me to win the tournaments I won—certainly the majors.

Magnified by the unprecedented media coverage my life and my career received, the historic charge that made Cherry Hills such a memorable Open for my fans and transformed my life also made my inevitable collapses (like losing the Masters to Gary Player the very next spring, as well as the National Opens I all but had in my grasp) all the more vivid and painful for people to watch. In time, those major disappointments and losses even took a toll on me. Permit me to explain.

Before I had the hopes of an entire *Army* resting on my shoulders with every shot, the consequences of failing to pull off a successful charge were pretty much mine alone to bear. Prior to 1964, it hurt like hell to blow a big tournament the way I did at Brookline or three-putt my way out of the championship the way I did at Oakmont in '62. But the disappointment never lasted long and certainly didn't affect the way I attacked a golf course. By nature, I simply wasn't prone to dwell for long on failure or moan about my fate. That was the Deke Palmer in me, I guess.

But after Cherry Hills, the British Open titles, and three more Masters championships came my way, I can see now, from the vantage point of many years, there was a subtle but perceptible shift in my playing consciousness. Yes, the distractions of fame and demands of a burgeoning business life were many, and I'm certain they had some impact on my ability to focus during a golf tournament, though how much I still can't say. But the truth is, as Mark McCormack once pointed out, it was nice to have those distractions on which to blame my slump, like the one that struck me hard in 1965.

But here is the critical point. Somewhere about the time I won my last major championship in 1964—and I'm still not certain when this phenomenon began to occur—even I became slowly aware that I wasn't playing tournaments with the same indifference to consequences that had carried me to the summit seven times (eight if you count my National Amateur title, which I do).

Not to place too fine a point on it, somewhere along the way, the elusive "it" that defined my style of play and enabled me to go for broke after any prize I hungered for began to change, slip away, or simply evade my summons. For example, I would step up to a long putt, pause a moment, and think about the potential danger of running a bold effort too far past the hole—something that once would never have been part of my thought process. Furthermore, I would stand on a tee studying a difficult fairway and—without even realizing what was going on at first—feel deep inside that, above all else, at this critical juncture of the tournament, I didn't want to disappoint my fans by making a poor shot or a gamble that failed. In simplest language, I began to sometimes get careful when I shouldn't have. Without even realizing it, I was playing defensively—playing, at times, not to lose rather than to win. Frankly, once I started down that road, it was all but impossible to come back.

Maybe the thing I hated and feared most was the feeling that people might feel sorry for me. I still had the desire to show them what I could do, and I knew I still had the shots to do it. But as I admitted to several close confidants beginning in about 1965, every time I'd get close to a major prize, my hands would begin to shake, and for a moment or two, when it counted most, the demons of doubt would whisper in my ear and I honestly wondered if I could win again.

As a result, 1965 was a genuine torment from beginning to end. At age thirty-six, for the first time, I had major body pains to go with the mental anguish, particularly in my shoulder, where I was plagued by bursitis most of the year. I no longer smoked on the golf course, but I ate more to try to fill the nervous void. As a result, I put on extra weight that made me feel sluggish, out of sorts, slower, more cautious—not old, exactly, but no longer young, either. I know enough star NFL quarterbacks to know that this was how they felt when they realized it was almost time to hang up the spikes.

By year's end, I'd managed to win only one tournament in nineteen months, the Tournament of Champions, and for the first time after five consecutive years of ranking first or second on the Tour earnings list, I'd fallen to tenth place—almost $90,000 behind Jack Nicklaus.

I've often said, as others have before me, that the true test of a champion comes not when he's winning, but when the chips are down and he can't seem to find his way.

After my steep fall-off in 1965, Winnie and I did some serious soul-searching about where I was headed in my playing career. I know she felt one factor contributing to my decline was the growing length of the PGA season, which now stretched from Los Angeles the first week of the year to November and even early December. The Tour I had joined in 1955 was pretty much a six-month affair, but now, thanks to lucrative exhibition matches and a host of growing "unofficial" events and foreign tournaments anxious to capitalize on golf's booming popularity, it was possible to play golf without a significant break almost from Christmas to Christmas.

During my peak performance years, I'd always relished the chance to get away from the Tour and go home and do nothing but putter around the house and my workshop, play with the girls and go hunting with Pap, have dinner with friends, and be a nuisance underfoot to Winnie as she prepared the house for the holidays. One thing that was clearly missing now, as she pointed out, was that month of rest I once customarily took after Thanksgiving.

I was reluctant to admit she was right—but, as usual, she was right. We agreed after that disappointing "slump" year of 1965 finally came to an end that I needed to get back to the basics of family life, slowing down to enjoy it more.

I canceled a lot of engagements and took the rest of the year off to be with Winnie and the girls. It was almost like the old days, and the rest clearly did me good.

In the first tournament of the new year, 1966, Los Angeles Open, I birdied seven holes in a row en route to a third-round 62, matching my career low and producing a three-shot victory over Miller Barber and Paul Harney.

I kept telling reporters and just about anybody else who would listen that my only focus for the year was winning golf tournaments, and in successive weeks, falling briefly off the cigarette wagon and puffing the odd coffin nail here or there on the sly, I placed second in the Crosby, third at the Lucky International, and lost in a playoff to Doug Sanders at the Bob Hope Desert Classic.

My Army was clearly pleased that "Arnie was back," and I wasn't at all disappointed myself.

After sixty-two holes at the Masters, I was tied for the lead, but I faltered and faded to fourth. Still, heading into the 66th U.S. Open at San Francisco's Olympic Club, our destination when Winnie and I had made our first big trip west more than a decade before as newlyweds, I was pleased that I'd made one of my best starts ever.

This time we stayed with our friends Ed and Rita Douglas, in their lovely home not far from the University of San Francisco. The Douglases had become close friends of ours over the years, and it was Ed, a regional manager for Pennzoil, who helped create a strong commercial affiliation that I enjoy to this day.

I'd made a few changes to my swing, learning to hit the ball with a slight fade that would fit Olympic's predominantly left-to-right features. It seemed to work pretty well, though I completed my first round in 71 despite some typically shaky putting on those billiard-table-fast greens. The first-round magic belonged to Al Mengert, a part-time tour professional from Washington State, who shot 67.

The next day I caught fire, and if I hadn't missed putts of less than four feet on each of the closing two holes, I would have matched the Open record of 64. As it was, my round of 66 and 137 total left me in a tie for first with Bill Casper.

Bill—as I preferred to call him instead of Billy—was a bit rejuvenated himself, having shed a lot of weight on a strange diet that reportedly involved buffalo and bear meats. The story goes—and I've never asked Bill about this, so who knows if it's true—that one morning before his round he ate swordfish and tomatoes, which would be enough to give me serious stomach distress. But the point is, Casper was leaner and meaner and had a more serious look in his eye than most of us had ever seen before. He was also one of the best short-game players who ever walked on an Open course, especially in the putting department.

For reasons both commercial and logistical in nature, the USGA's executive committee had decided to abandon "Open Saturday's" double rounds. Starting with Olympic, the tournament would conclude on a fourth day, a move most players applauded.

My third round wasn't particularly sensational, a steady 70, but it allowed me to open up a three-shot bulge over the slimmed-down Bill Casper, who completed his round with 73.

I felt the old adrenaline pumping, and I was once again attacking the golf course as I had in my younger days. Going into that final round, my feeling was that Olympic's front nine was more difficult than the back nine. If I could post a low score there on Sunday, I could play home with the confidence that it would take an extraordinary feat of shotmaking—or at least a spectacular collapse on my part—for somebody to catch me.

Everything just seemed to click. The shots were solid, the putts dropped. I'd posted a 32 by the turn and opened a commanding seven-stroke lead over Casper. To be perfectly honest, though, I wasn't thinking too much about Bill and what he might have to do in order to catch me. He was a steady player and sensational putter, but frankly not the sort who was known for last-minute heroics. The guy I had my eye on, and feared most, quite honestly, was a couple of strokes back of him: Jack Nicklaus.

How do you explain what happened over the next ninety minutes or so? I've spent nearly three decades attempting to do just that—explain to myself and to a lot of other sympathetic people the rhyme and reason of what transpired.

The simplest explanation is that, believing I had the Open already won, I quit playing Bill and Jack and started playing Ben Hogan's old 1948 Open record of 276. I'd done the same thing at Augusta when I almost gave away the Masters while chasing his mark there. I knew that if I could just finish the back nine in 36, a stroke above par, the new record of 275 would belong to Arnold Daniel Palmer.

In retrospect, it was the biggest mental error of my career.

In daring to think about breaking Hogan's record, I violated the very rule Pap had spent all those years drilling into my head—never quit, never look up, and, most of all, never lose focus until you've completely taken care of business. As we started together down the tenth fairway, Bill looked at me and made what sounded an awful lot like a concession speech. No doubt feeling Jack in hot pursuit, he reflected:

"I'm going to have to go just to get second."

"Don't worry, Bill," I replied, uttering the words I was doomed to have to eat. "You'll finish second."

The nightmare began at that same hole, a bogey for Palmer at ten. Bill parred. Advantage Casper.

After that, like some ghostly newsreel playing in my head, I recall it going like this: I birdie at the 12th, but so does Bill. I remind myself that I'm still six ahead of him with six holes to play—no place to panic. At the par-3 13th, I miss the green with my tee shot and settle for bogey four. Maddening, but not fatal. We move to 14, where we both make pars; I'm still five up, but thanks to that bogey I now must par my way home to beat Hogan's old mark.

Fifteen is another par 3. The pin is tucked in the right-hand corner behind a bunker. Instead of playing safe, I decide this is the moment to put the tournament on ice. I attempt the perfect shot and go straight at the flag, watch my ball catch the edge of the green and tumble into the bunker. Another bogey. Then Casper, who has played safely to the middle of the green, thirty-five feet from the pin—I remember being annoyed by his strategy, wondering what he had to lose by *not* going for the pin—smoothly rolls home another birdie putt.

Thoughts of Ben Hogan and his record instantly vanish from my mind, replaced by the first rising vapors of genuine alarm. For the first time, it dawns on me that Bill Casper is the real threat here, not Ben Hogan. My lead has dwindled to three. We walk on to the 16th, the big par 5, 604 yards with a sweeping right-to-left curve that fits my natural ball flight. Most golfers would settle for two safe hits and a careful pitch to the putting surface, but all I can think at this point is how irritated I am that Casper has been "playing safe" and is catching up on me. I tell myself there is no way I can allow that to happen. There is *no way* I'm going to allow him to beat me by playing safe. I decide I will win or lose exactly the way I've won or lost every golf tournament I've ever played.

The long draw is my bread-and-butter shot, but either nerves or perhaps the fact that I've been hitting fades all week finally takes a toll. An untimely duck hook sends the ball off a tree into the deep left rough. I compound the situation by trying to slash a 3-iron out of the heavy rough. The ball squirts across the fairway, advancing less than a hundred yards. It stops once more in the heavy grass, leaving me no chance to reach the putting surface on my third. Now I still have over three hundred yards of fairway to negotiate and only three shots left for par. I chop the ball back to the fairway with my wedge and drill a 3-wood into the greenside bunker. You don't want to know what's going on in my mind here. It feels as if a volcano is about to erupt in my head. I blast out of the bunker and am fortunate to make no worse than six. Bill, playing impeccably safe golf again, scores his second consecutive birdie.

I have now lost four strokes on two holes, and my lead is one.

On 17, the hardest hole at Olympic, 435 yards uphill to a small green on the shoulder of the hill, I hook my drive into the long grass again, miss the green on my approach, but finally make a decent chip that leaves me ten feet for par. My putt just grazes the right edge of the hole. Bill, meanwhile, makes his par 4 and we are suddenly tied for the lead at the 66th U.S. Open.

At 18, Bill plays quickly, splitting the fairway with his drive. I tell myself there is still no reason to panic but certainly a need to get the ball into the short grass. I choose a 1-iron for accuracy but am so wound up I even pull that shot. I stare after the ball with a slumping heart as it scampers into the heavy left rough and disappears from my sight. What I wouldn't have given for an L&M cigarette about then.

Walking down the fairway, shaken to the core, I doubt if I have ever felt as alone or as devastated on a golf course. I know what a train wreck the world is witnessing, but I tell myself that I am *still* in the thick of it. I can glance at faces in the gallery and see their shock and grief, too. People call out reassuringly, and I don't even know if I acknowledge them. Perhaps I scan the crowd for Winnie, because her emotional thermometer is always set on seventy-two degrees and it never fails to calm me to see her. (Mark McCormack, on the other hand, was often such a visible nervous wreck, it made me feel nervous just to look at him—he often left the course at such moments to make business calls, for both our sakes.)

I try to relax and remember my father's lessons about keeping my head and body still, making a slow backswing and solid contact. All I need is one good shot. This one looks almost impossible, but I must somehow get it on the putting surface. I know Bill will get his shot on the green, and if I want any hope of making a playoff, I simply must have a par.

I decide on a wedge and set up over the ball, then hit it hard, slashing it out of the long grass. An instant later, still leaning over, I glance up to see where it is going. I watch the ball fly extremely high and appear to settle somewhere in back of the dangerously tiny green. The gallery there lets out a roar, and I know I've still got at least a chance to save par and halve the hole.

On the green, I face a difficult thirty-footer downhill to the cup across the lightning-fast putting surface. After a moment or two sizing up the situation, I stroke the putt and slightly misjudge the line a bit, leaving myself as tough a side-hill six-footer as I've ever faced to salvage par. Under the rule then in effect, I am forced to putt out first, which I do, then I step back to wait and see if Bill can beat my four. He misses his birdie attempt and we both finish with 278.

As Bill and I shake hands, all I really feel is a sense of deep relief and perhaps a bit of disbelief at what has just happened. My anger at myself will come later. In time, I realized I knew what Hogan must have felt like when Fleck caught him in exactly the same spot in 1955, forcing a playoff at the final hole of the Open—a tournament the greatest player in the game at that moment felt confident he'd won. My own confidence now shaken, I sign my card and walk slowly to the press tent, where a hundred unanswerable questions await. My friends in the press corps all look a little embarrassed to have to ask them. I can't wait to get to Ed and Rita's place for a drink.

There will be yet another U.S. Open playoff for me.

The playoff was an eerie reprise of the fourth round. Once again I played solid shots and went out in 33 against Bill's 35, and once again he started picking up strokes the way he had the previous day. He dropped a dramatic fifty-footer for a birdie two at 13, going ahead for the first time. In all the high drama of my collapse, it's sometimes forgotten that Bill Casper played almost flawless golf down the stretch. That point can't be driven home enough. I didn't just lose the 1966 U.S. Open—Bill Casper's brilliant play won it.

He finished with a 69 and I managed a 73, once again letting an Open championship slip through my fingers. Afterward in the pressroom, the shock of the previous day's free fall had begun to wear off, and I detected a swell of great sympathy about what those on hand had witnessed, the most historic collapse in Open history. As a postscript, or epitaph, to the event, some would write that the disaster only humanized Arnold Palmer even more—simply proved he was more like the people who admired him than any professional golfer in history.

I don't know whether that's true or not. All I know is that, curiously, afterward I was bitterly disappointed but I didn't feel the least bit sorry for myself. Why should I? It wasn't a disaster. A plane crash or an earthquake is a disaster. This was a golf tournament—admittedly a huge one and one I'd desperately wanted to win. But, as I consoled myself, I'd won it before and would probably have a chance to win it again. I was only the second man in history to break 280 and not win a U.S. Open. (Jimmy Demaret was the first, in 1948, losing by three to Hogan.) I'd played well enough to win the Open. But Bill Casper had played slightly better. That's all I can really say about it.

Fact is, I really felt worse for my fans and for those people with long faces waiting for me at Ed and Rita's house. I walked in following the playoff and discovered Winnie, both Douglases, and Mark and Nancy McGormack sitting silently around the kitchen table, as if they were at a wake. I didn't want anybody feeling sorry for me. That feeling extended to my own friends and family.

"What's wrong with you people?" I bellowed at them, forcing a half-hearted smile. "You look like you've been to a funeral."

I guess they thought they had.

Well, that's golf. My kind of golf, anyway.

Losing three Opens in playoffs was tough, but life is tough, and even though I felt emotionally drained and a little cheated by Old Man Par at Olympic Club, I wasn't through with the United States Open, nor it me.

The next summer, 1967, I chased Jack Nicklaus and his painted white Bullseye putter around Baltusrol's Lower Course and was tied for the lead with him for 54 holes. I shot a 69 to his 65 in the final round, becoming the second player in history to twice break 280 and fall short of victory, this time by four strokes.

At Champions Golf Club in 1969, I three-putted the 15th hole after making a great recovery from the woods. A birdie there would have put pressure on the leader (and eventual winner) Orville Moody; maybe that would have created an outcome more to my liking. Instead, I wound up three strokes back, in sixth place.

Playing the 14th hole at Pebble Beach in 1972, I had a putt of about eight feet for birdie that would have placed me in the Open lead with just four holes to play. Nicklaus was sizing up a similar-length putt on 12 for par. If I had made my putt and he had missed, the Open would probably have been mine. Instead, he converted and I failed—and the Open was his.

If only I could have had one of Doc Giffin's magic mulligans . . .

Then there was my return to Oakmont the very next summer. By then, of course, a host of new names were regularly pegged to the leader board: Lee Trevino, Raymond Floyd, Johnny Miller, even a bright young prodigy from Kansas City who looked as wholesome as a face off a cornflakes box. His name was Tom Watson.

At the par-4 11th hole during the final round, I was four under, facing a short, four-foot birdie opportunity that would have put me five under and in command of the tournament. I made what I thought was a good stroke, and watched in disbelief as the ball grazed the hole, staying out. Two more shocks to the system followed. First, thinking I was still in the lead at four under, I glanced over at a distant scoreboard and could make out that someone else had just posted a red five. I asked my playing partner, John Schlee, who that could have been. "Miller," he answered, meaning twenty-six-year-old Johnny Miller, who'd just finished with a sensational 63.

A few moments later, I struck what I was sure was a terrific drive at 12, only to discover a few minutes later that the ball lying in the fairway, which I thought was mine, really belonged to Schlee. Much to my surprise, my ball had caromed left instead of right and was in deep grass on the 603-yard hole. Now, instead of being tied for the lead and in good position in the fairway at a hole where I often made birdie, I was a stroke behind and facing a desperate situation. All I could do was thump a medium iron shot back to the fairway. With a four-wood, though, I attempted to reach the green but pulled the shot into the deep rough above a greenside bunker, pitched well past the hole, and made bogey six. I felt devastated and it quickly showed—two more bogeys at 13 and 14. I finally birdied 18 but it was meaningless. Once more I'd been unable to rally from my own mistakes, and someone else's good golf had cost me the Open.

Following a pair of top-ten finishes in '74 and '75 at Winged Foot and Medinah, respectively, my Open career began to fade. I played hard and never gave up; I gave my fans a few thrills here and there, but somehow I could never summon back any magic.

Then, in 1984, I came up two strokes shy at sectional qualifying on the outskirts of Cleveland. That ended my streak of thirty-one consecutive U.S. Open appearances, a record I shared with Gene Sarazen. I'm still very proud of that.

In the summer of 1994, by special invitation from the USGA, I made one final journey to Oakmont, where I had played my first National Open, as an amateur (failing to make the cut), in 1953, for my last appearance at the U.S. Open. What an emotional roller-coaster ride that week was, with parties and dinners and private conversations with old friends who'd followed my Open escapades for several decades. I must have signed a thousand autographs. The letters and telegrams poured into the Latrobe office, and it was all I could do to keep myself together emotionally, if not on the golf course.

I shot 77-81 and as most people expected, I guess, missed the cut. In the pressroom afterward, as I mopped my brow with a small towel, I was asked to reflect on my long and illustrious Open career. The proper words were difficult to find. I wanted to express so much about the wonderful way I had been treated by fans and the USGA and what playing in the National Open had always meant to me. I began by talking about the tournament's great traditions and my own beginnings at Oakmont in 1953, moved on from there to say a few words about how grateful I was to have won at Cherry Hills and to have had a crack at winning probably seven or eight other times, then finally . . . I lost it.

I apologized and bowed my head, too choked up to go on.

As I got up to leave, the members of the press accorded me a great honor, something I had never seen or heard of them doing before. One by one, they stood and applauded—and kept applauding. It's traditional for writers to give the Open winner a standing ovation when he enters the pressroom after his victorious final round.

This time they gave me a standing ovation after my final Open round.

It was like having one of Doc's magic mulligans, after all.

Redemption

from *Getting Up and Down: My 60 Years in Golf*
by Ken Venturi with Michael Arkush

I arrived in Washington, D.C., on Monday. Being gone for four long years made me appreciate every moment of U.S. Open week. Like many blessed to be a professional golfer, I didn't completely realize my good fortune until it was taken away. I wasn't going to make the same mistake again.

My top priority the first few days was getting to know the golf course better. Congressional, in my initial assessment, seemed to be the perfect setup for my game. At 7,053 yards, the longest course in U.S. Open history, it would require excellent long iron play, which was my forte. Nonetheless, I needed to absorb as much as possible about Congressional's subtleties, about where I should try to hit it, and, just as important, where it was safe to miss it. How much knowledge I picked up would depend heavily on my caddie, which is where I received my first big break of the week.

In 1964 a tour player wasn't allowed to bring his regular caddie to the U.S. Open. Instead I picked a name out of a hat from a list provided by the host club. The name I picked was William Ward, who just happened to be the course's highest-rated caddie. I was delighted, although William, I could only imagine, didn't feel quite the same way. William had a lot of kids to feed. Drawing Arnold Palmer or Jack Nicklaus, who would offer the likelihood of a more lucrative payday, is closer to what I'm sure he had in mind.

"William, I know you're not too happy about having me, but I think I can win this tournament," I said.

William could tell I was serious.

"I'll do the best for you, Mr. Ken," he said.

"We'll give it a good, hard try."

On Tuesday morning I played a nine-hole practice round with Paul Harney, who was surprised to see me.

"Aren't you going to the White House?" he asked.

I didn't have a clue of what he was talking about. The White House, he told me, was hosting a lawn party for the favorites, the leading contenders, and the past champions. I didn't have a clue because I wasn't invited. No problem. I used the rejection as a motivating factor. Thank you, President Johnson.

"It's more important for me to get in a practice round," I told Harney.

Another 9 holes with Paul Harney on Wednesday—it was too hot to play 18—provided me with additional insight. I was as ready as I would ever be.

Finally, play began. Paired with Billy Maxwell and George Bayer, the U.S. Open pressure got to me, simple as that. I considered myself one of the game's finest bunker players, but on the front nine I failed *twice* to get the ball out on my first try. Fortunately, with my second try, I got up and down each time to save bogey. Doubles would have been disastrous. I was 3 over at the turn, with the tougher nine yet to go. But demonstrating the kind of grit that was missing from my game for so long, I scrambled for a 2-over 72. I was four shots behind Palmer, but at least I could see him.

My second round was a marked improvement. All aspects of my game were working. Except for the first hole, I drove it without using a tee. I kicked up the turf, hitting sliders off the ground that, essentially, helped me eliminate the left side of the course. My approaches found the right spots on the greens, and I made my share of crucial putts. Throughout my slump, all I wanted to do was get the ball close enough for a par. Now I was thinking birdie.

So was my good friend Tommy Jacobs, who shot a remarkable, record-tying 64, highlighted by a 60-foot putt on 18. Palmer, after a 69, was within one. After an even-par 70, I was six back. In the old days, I would have been very disappointed to face such a large deficit at the halfway mark. But these were new days, difficult days, days of lower expectations. I had told my caddie I could win, but winning wasn't really on my mind. I came to Congressional to make a strong showing, to qualify for a return to Augusta and perhaps the 1965 Open. So far, so good.

Over the next 24 hours everything changed. Forever.

It started with a letter I found in my locker. The letter, six pages long, came from Father Murray. I read it in the car on my way to the hotel. I read it over and over and over:

> If you would win the U.S. Open, you would prove to millions of people that they can be victorious over doubt and struggle and temptation to despair. . . . Your success would be a world of encouragement to everyone. . . . You have always had the ability, and since the beginning of the year this ability has been getting sharper and steadier. . . . You want it for your own satisfaction, after suffering humiliation and frustration in the past . . . to show the world that you are made of championship caliber. . . . You are truly the new Ken Venturi . . . now wise and mature and battle-toughened.

Father Murray went on to make specific suggestions:

> Keep your mood from getting emotionally disturbed from elation or disappointment.

> Make the clear determination and make the act of your will to follow that definite plan of action.

> Give yourself over entirely to the fulfillment of your one shot at hand.

Trust in your swing and in your ability.

Get the birdies during the early holes. When you see you are in contention it will give you more spirit and inspiration to fight consistently and bravely and hopefully.

Father Murray demonstrated a surprisingly acute knowledge of the game, advising me to practice with only one ball on the putting green, not two or three, which was my routine. "The reason for this," he wrote, "is to simulate playing conditions where you only have one putt at the hole. Also it forces a man to concentrate solely on the one practice putt."

His advice made so much sense. Suddenly, I felt a kind of peace I had never felt before. I decided to go to church that evening. Praying in a hotel room wouldn't do.

I found a Catholic church close to the hotel, but it was locked. Fortunately the priest was gracious enough to open the doors. I stayed for nearly an hour, going back and forth between reading Father Murray's letter and reciting my own personal prayers. I didn't ask God for a victory. God doesn't care who wins the U.S. Open. "Please let me believe in myself," I said. "I know that my faults are many, but please let me play well and comport myself like a man, no matter what happens."

I walked outside and thanked the priest. "Good luck, tomorrow," he said.

Back at my hotel, I found more inspiration. I watched *Champion*, a film starring Kirk Douglas as a boxer who refused to surrender. He kept getting himself up off the mat, which was exactly what I was trying to do.

When I woke up Saturday morning, the peace I felt was even more profound. I was about to tee it up on the final day of the game's most prestigious championship, and I was as relaxed as if I were getting ready for a practice round at Harding Park. Tony Lema, one of my best friends on tour, noticed the change in me right away. "You look great today, Ken," he said on the putting green. "You know something, I have a feeling it's going to be your day."

"I sure hope so, Tony," I said.

I kept putting, practicing with only one ball, as Father Murray suggested.

If he ever got tired of the priesthood, it occurred to me, he might have a future in the golf business.

The final day of the U.S. Open is always the game's most exacting test, 36 holes of trying to negotiate narrow fairways, deep rough, fast greens, and fragile emotions. On every hole, par, as the cliché goes, is a good score. This year's contest would be even tougher than usual. No fault, to be fair, of the USGA. The blame belonged to Mother Nature. It was hot, really hot, and it would get even hotter. Today was going to be a challenge just to survive.

My playing partner was Ray Floyd, a promising 21-year-old kid. I remembered when I was a promising 21-year-old kid—a lifetime ago.

On the opening hole, I received a sign that maybe Tony Lema was right. Maybe today was going to be my day. I sent my approach on the par-4 to about 12 feet and hit what I thought was a wonderful putt. But the ball stopped on the lip, refusing to take one more small dive into the hole. I stared at it for as long as I could under the rules, hoping to will the ball into the cup. I gave up, finally, and walked over to tap it in. At that moment, the ball disappeared. A gift, I decided, freeing me to toss aside my conservative game plan. "You have one shot to play with," I told myself. "Fire at every flag until you lose that shot."

Making that putt also made an impression on a certain spectator in the gallery, Vince Lombardi. Lombardi, the legendary coach of the Green Bay Packers, told a friend that he was convinced I would be the champion.

"How can you tell?" the friend asked.

"Just take a look at him," Lombardi said. "His eyes are dead. They're the coldest I've ever seen. He beats them going away." (Over the years, a few of his players told me that Lombardi often brought my name up during his halftime speeches to motivate them. "You look into that guy across from you on the line," he would say, "and his eyes better know that your eyes own him. The greatest eyes I ever saw in my life were Ken Venturi's when he stared at that ball. I feel he made the ball move." Last time I saw Lombardi, about four years later, he was still talking about it. "I'll never forget that look on your face," he said.)

The change in strategy kept paying off. My card for the front nine was one to be framed: 3-3-4, 3-3-4, 3-3-4, a total of 5-under 30. I was getting my birdies early, just like Father Murray advised. Given the circumstances, it has to be, without a doubt, the finest nine holes of golf I've ever played. More importantly, with Palmer struggling and Jacobs cooling off a bit, I was right back in the tournament. I picked up another birdie on 12 to go 6 under for the day. Six more pars and I would match Tommy Jacobs with my own 64.

But I would not finish with a 64, or, for that matter, a 65. I would, in fact, be fortunate to finish at all.

The heat—the temperature had risen to near 100 degrees—was getting to me. I wasn't used to this kind of weather. I was a product of the Bay Area, familiar with fog and rain and mist—you know, Crosby weather.

After making pars at 15 and 16, I hit my approach at 17 to within about 15 feet. I missed the putt, leaving me about a foot and a half for par. But as I lined it up, my whole body began to shake. I thought I was going to faint. I pulled the putter back but had no idea where it was going. I missed, needless to say, notching my first bogey of the day. At 18, after being short of the green, I chipped to about three feet. Again I was shaking and could hardly see the hole, resulting in another bogey; 64 had quickly turned into 66.

My score was the least of my problems. There were still another 18 holes to play, and it wasn't going to get any cooler.

I dropped the putter and staggered to a station wagon for the drive up the hill to the clubhouse. From then on, except for a few brief moments, I can't remember a single thing that happened until I reached the 16th hole about four hours later. All I can do is go by what others have told me. Following is their account:

I joined Jay Hebert in the front seat. "Think you can make it back to the clubhouse?" Hebert asked me. "Your eyes are rolling in your head." I did make it to the clubhouse, where I was promptly greeted by Dr. John Everett, a Congressional member and chairman of the Open's medical committee. Dr. Everett was asked to check me out. What he found was not good. I was suffering from heat prostration. Despite the unbearable conditions, I didn't drink any water during my round or take any salt tablets. The only salt I knew about was the kind they put on eggs. Pretty naive, huh? I guess so. I suppose the only explanation is that I was so focused on the task at hand.

Dr. Everett stretched me out on the floor next to my locker and gave me some salt tablets and iced tea. I was too sick to eat lunch. He then gave me something else to digest.

"If it were up to me right now, Ken, I would take you to the hospital," he said. "You can't go out there. It could be fatal."

"It's better than the way I've been living," I responded, and got off the floor.

I wasn't referring only to my golf game. I was referring to my whole life. The situation with Conni was more torturous than ever. While in San Francisco, I spent many nights during the week on a buddy's boat. A divorce was inevitable. Now, with everything that was on the line at Congressional, I had come too far to back down.

I could tell Dr. Everett was still worried. I told him that I would sign anything to absolve him of responsibility. It was not necessary, he said.

And back out there I went, into the heat, into the biggest round of my career, with nothing—and everything—to lose. My 66 had put me only two strokes behind Jacobs, who shot a 70. Palmer, with a 75, fell six back.

When I arrived at the first tee, some fans were relieved, as a rumor had spread that I wasn't going to be able to continue. Only 50 minutes had gone by since my bogey at 18. I could've used a much longer break, but it wasn't up to me. Besides, everybody else had to cope with the same time frame.

Dr. Everett went out there with me, carrying the cold towels he would put around my neck, and he had an abundant supply of salt tablets.

I split the fairway with my drive on the opening hole and went on to par the first five holes. In retrospect, being so out of sorts was a blessing. My mind was too vacant to wander to the wrong places, to the old demons. I played strictly on instinct. All I tried to do was what it always takes to win the United States Open: fairways and greens, fairways and greens. I know it's a cliché, but I was concentrating on one shot at a time, again like Father Murray suggested. I trusted my swing, unaffected by any pressure. Even a bogey at the 6th didn't throw me off my game plan. Heading to the 9th hole, I was tied with Jacobs, who doubled the second and bogeyed another hole. The game was on.

At the 9th, the 599-yard Ravine Hole, I smacked a solid drive and a good 1 iron, almost too good—the ball stopped only a few yards from the edge of the ravine. On my approach, I aimed right for the flag at the back of the green. The gamble paid off, the ball coming to a halt about nine feet from the pin. The tricky downhill putt broke right to left, caught the low side, and rolled in. I was the sole leader of the U.S. Open. Looking back at the old, grainy, black-and-white footage—boy do I wish there were VCRs in 1964—my reaction after that putt went in reveals a lot. I lifted my arm ever so slightly to celebrate and then abruptly stopped. I wish I could recall exactly what I was thinking, but I'm pretty sure I was merely following another piece of Father Murray's excellent advice: "Keep your mood from getting emotionally disturbed from elation or disappointment." There was a long way to go.

I came up with a huge save at 10, converting a short putt for par, and followed with pars at 11 and 12. I was a machine. Whenever I asked William for the yardage, he issued his standard reply. "You don't need the yardage, Mr. Ken," he said. "You're at the same exact yardage you were at in the morning." In fact, for my approaches to the green, I used the same club I did in the morning 14 times. By today's standards, I wasn't hitting it particularly long, perhaps about 250 yards, but it was good enough. More important, I was finding the fairways, and every time I faced a critical putt, I relied on Philly Garnett. "Come on Philly baby," I said, "we really need this one." Philly almost always came through.

At the 13th hole, a very exacting, 448-yard par-4, I hit one of my best drives of the day, a beautiful 6 iron to within 18 feet. I was told I took a long time to look over the putt, but I suppose it was worth the wait. When the ball fell in, I closed my eyes. There was only one person who could beat me now: me.

Which, I knew, could very well still happen, especially with the way my body was reacting to the heat. The American Red Cross reported numerous cases of heat prostration that day. One could barely breathe. On my way to losing eight pounds, I was moving slower and slower.

Too slow, I worried, which is why I approached Joe Dey, who, along with future Masters chairman Hord Hardin, was following our group.

"Joe, I'm having a hard time walking," I said. "I know that if I get too slow, I might be penalized, but let me know if I need to speed up."

"You're doing just fine," Dey said.

Soon I was on the 18th tee. For the whole round, I had purposely avoided the leader boards. There was already enough to worry about.

But after hitting my drive, it was time. I approached Bill Hoellie, a good friend whom I had known since my junior golf days in San Francisco.

"How do I stand?" I asked him.

"Just stay on your feet," Hoellie said. "We've got it."

Coming down the fairway, I finally looked at the board. My name was the only one in red, under par, which meant my lead was at least two strokes. It was, I soon found out, actually even larger. I was home free. The only way I could blow the Open was if I were to do something really stupid, such as hit my approach into the pond left of the green. Therefore, I intentionally put a slight block on the second shot with my 5 iron, steering it to the right of the green. The ball took a bad bounce off the slope and ended up in the bunker. The important thing was that I was dry.

I started my triumphant walk toward the green, doing something I had never done before the final putt dropped. I took off my white cap. "Hold your head high, Ken," Dey said, "like the champion that you are." The applause was unlike anything I ever heard. I wanted it to last forever.

Moments later, I saw something I had never seen before—two marshals rolling around in the bunker. One was working the 18th hole. The other came over from a different hole to catch all the drama. One guy kicked the other in the face. My only thought was a selfish one: don't roll on my ball! They didn't.

The bunker shot was not especially difficult. The lie was clean and there was very little lip. No problem. But, with the way I chose to execute the shot, it could have been a tremendous problem. Instead of chipping it, I did what was ingrained in me and hit the standard explosion shot, catching the sand behind the ball. Over the years, every time I watch a replay, I break into a cold sweat, aware of how easily I could have skulled it over the green into the very same water I had avoided with my approach. I could have finished with a six or seven, which would have been one of the biggest choking acts of all time.

But there would be no choking today. This was 1964, not 1956.

The ball stopped about 10 feet from the cup. I read the putt to break left to right. I pushed it about two inches too far right, but somehow it went left and fell in, only fitting that the day would end as magically as it began. I dropped my putter, and suddenly it all hit me: "My God, I've won the Open," I said. I stayed pretty composed until I looked into the eyes of Ray Floyd, who picked the ball out of the hole for me. Floyd was sobbing, and that's when I lost it.

There was one thing left to do, and it was important: sign the card. I needed to be extremely careful. One mistake and everything I worked for would mean nothing. While someone in the tent called off my scores, I started to get a little nervous, reflecting back to my good friend, Jackie Pung, the apparent winner who was disqualified in the 1957 U.S. Women's Open for signing an incorrect card. I became even more nervous when I couldn't remember if my scores were accurate. I was so out of it that when I handed Floyd his card, there wasn't one number on it. To this day, I can't tell you about a single shot he hit.

I then felt a comforting hand on my shoulder.

"Sign the card, Ken, it's correct," the voice said. I looked up, and it was Joe Dey.

After that everything happened so fast. I received congratulations from Jacobs, the man whom I had shared Christmas dinner with in Austria 10 years earlier. "Tommy, I really mean this, but if it couldn't have been me, I wish it could have been you," I said. "No," he responded. "It should have been you." I took a call from my parents, who had watched on television from California. My mom was crying so hard she could barely say a word. She was crying in victory, her son's victory. My dad, of course, the stoic one, did have something to say.

"Now you've got to prove it was no fluke," he said. Typical Dad.

"I'll show you," I told him.

Next, a U.S. Royal representative handed me a check for $10,000, the bonus the company handed out to any of their players who captured a major. I was extremely grateful. Contrary to the Jantzen company, U.S. Royal stuck by me when I went through hard times. They didn't think I was "over the hill," and, by golly, now they were being rewarded for their loyalty.

I was escorted to meet with the press, the group I hadn't been too crazy about since the unfortunate incident in 1956. We talked about Father Murray—I suggested splitting the trophy with him—the 1956 Masters, my long slump, and how I survived on this incredible day. I don't recall most of what I told them, except for a line that received a lot of play. "The last three years," I said, "when they've talked about Arnie's Army and Nicklaus' Navy, all I've had were Venturi's Vultures."

One new admirer I picked up that week was my caddie, William Ward. There is absolutely no way I would have won the Open without him. He always knew, like any good caddie, when to talk and when to be quiet. His knowledge of Congressional was invaluable. Early in the week, he took a tape measure over the course so that he could give me exact yardage. When the tournament was over, I gave him a check for $1,000. He, in turn, gave me a compliment I would cherish just as much.

"Mr. Ken, I don't mind telling you, but when you picked my name out of the hat, I wasn't too pleased," he said. "I wanted to get one of the favorites, but I want to tell you something. You're the damnedest golfer I ever saw in my life." (For several years, I spent a little time with William whenever CBS covered the Kemper tournament at Congressional. He shagged balls for me when I hit chip shots and putts for about a half hour, and I always gave him $100. The last time I saw him, he wasn't feeling too well, but he wanted to see me. I told him I wasn't in the mood to hit any balls. I hit a few putts, gave him a hug and placed in his hand two $100 bills. "Mr. Ken," he said, looking down at his hands, "it is always good to see you, and you're still the greatest.")

Finally, Conni and I left Congressional. I think we closed the place. When we arrived at our hotel, there were so many calls to return from Byron Nelson, Toots Shor, and others. I was up for hours. I was still excited from the call that came earlier in the day from Bing Crosby. "I'm so proud of you," he said. When Bing got off the line, he handed the phone to Bill Worthing, who would later be my best man when I married Beau: "I never saw him shed a tear in his life," Worthing said, "but he was sitting here crying." Another well-known entertainer was also touched by my performance—Ed Sullivan. I was booked for the following night, four months after the Beatles had made their historic appearance.

After I slept for a few hours, the phone rang again. The woman on the line was extending a very important invitation: "The president of the United States would like to have you to lunch to personally congratulate you on winning the Open," she said.

I was very excited. The White House doesn't call every day. But, believe it or not, I told her I couldn't meet President Johnson for lunch on Sunday. "No disrespect to the president," I said, "but please tell him I'm unable to make it." I had to rush to New York for the Sullivan show and lunch the following day with Toots Shor.

Before flying to New York, there was one more stop I needed to make. I went back to the same church I had attended on Friday night. So much was different now. With Mass already under way, I took a seat in the back.

I didn't come to pray. I came to simply thank God for giving me a new life. "You're unbelievable," I whispered. "I don't know why you chose me, but I will never forget you for it. I promise that I will find a way to give back."

On Sunday afternoon Conni and I arrived at the studio for *The Ed Sullivan Show*, the same auditorium that David Letterman uses today. I was scared to death, to say the least. I was the one, remember, who always gave short answers, and here I was about to talk on national TV—and live, no less! I was way out of my comfort zone. Fortunately I felt much better after we rehearsed for over an hour. Sullivan, who was going to read his questions from a teleprompter, couldn't have been more accommodating. He and I had once been partners in a pro-am. This time, I was the one who needed the strokes. Finally the show started.

"Mr. Ken Venturi," Sullivan said, in that distinctive voice. "How are you doing?"

"I'm doing just fine, Ed," I said. "Thank you very much."

Live or not, this wasn't so hard. Just then, the teleprompter broke. Sullivan was at a total loss.

"So, Ken, uh, how many salt tablets did you have yesterday?" he asked. "Eighteen," I said.

That was the whole interview. There was nothing to do but go to a commercial break.

"I'm so sorry, Ken," Sullivan said.

So was I. I was on the air for less than a minute, my first experience in the pitfalls of live television. It would not be my last.

No matter. The next day I was off to the big celebration with Toots Shor. Three weeks earlier I had shown up for dinner a desperate man who almost had to beg for a sponsor's exemption. I was returning as the United States Open champion. When I arrived, the applause was overwhelming. I felt as if I were back on the 18th fairway at Congressional. Toots told me later that it was the only standing ovation he had ever seen in all of his years at the restaurant. "I knew you'd be back," he said. I was greeted by comedian Joe E. Lewis.

"Vennie," Lewis said. He always called me Vennie. "I saw you win the Open. Staggering around, dropping your putter, passing out. It's the greatest act I ever saw in my life." I've borrowed that line ever since.

I received wonderful reactions the whole time I was in New York. As I walked up 52nd Street in Manhattan, motorists blew their horns at me. Cab drivers stopped right in the middle of the street and ran over to hug me or give me a kiss. Yes, New York City cab drivers! I went to another popular hangout, the "21" Club, and everyone applauded. The most amazing tribute came when I saw the Broadway hit *Hello Dolly*. The star, Carol Channing, whom I had never met before, performed a slightly different rendition: "Kenny," she sang, "it's so nice to have you back where you belong." I also attended a musical that starred Steve Lawrence and Eydie Gorme. Before their last curtain call, Lawrence addressed the audience. "We never do this," he said, "but please turn the house lights up. I want you all to meet the United States Open champion, Ken Venturi."

Carol Channing was right. It was so nice to be back where I belonged. For the longest time, I doubted I would ever belong on the tour again. Even with all the supporters—Bud Ward, Bill Varni, Father Murray—who cheered me on, and with the countless hours at California Golf Club, I was never far removed from my deepest, darkest fears: did I squander my talent forever? Would I ever make up for the way I lost the 1956 Masters?

But with the performance at Congressional—my 2-under 278 was the second-lowest score by a winner in U.S. Open history, behind Hogan's 276 in 1948—those fears were gone, presumably for good. I was ready to build on my four-shot victory and become, once again, one of the best players in the game. The future, uncertain for so long, was filled with exciting new possibilities.

At my hotel, hours after the Open victory, I did something I hadn't done in nine months. During that whole time, I had kept my promise to Dave Marcelli, the bartender from San Francisco. I wouldn't take another drink until I won again.

I had a glass of white wine.

Seven Ahead, Nine to Go, and Then?

Arnold Palmer blew the '66 U.S. Open not once but twice, giving unflappable Billy Casper an unbelievable victory

by Rick Reilly, *Sports Illustrated*, June 15, 1987

Somebody once asked Arnold Palmer why his army was so feverishly devoted to him.

"Well," Arnie said, "maybe it's because I'm in the rough so much I get to know them all personally."

And therein lies a good part of the reason Arnold Palmer became America's favorite—not best, not winningest, just favorite—golfer. For in Arnie you had an athletic god who could come down from the heavens and screw up royally, and the nation loved him for it. When Palmer stood over a three-iron in weeds as long as his inseam, needing to carry that pond way up yonder, you had the feeling that even he had no idea what would become of the ball. It might land three inches from the pin or three blocks from the clubhouse. What made it impossible not to watch Arnie is the same thing that makes it impossible to put down a good book—suspense.

Either way, coming or going, Palmer always tried uproariously hard. He swung as if slashing his way out of a Brazilian rain forest. His face contorted with every tortured heave. Golf is an unplayable game. Why fool around pretending it's not? And everything about Arnie—from his untuckable shirttail to his uncombable hair—screamed it out. Arnold Palmer did for finesse what Oliver North did for procedure.

And so it was that Arnie could bank on fans' forgiving and forgetting. If he could come from seven shots behind on the last day to win a U.S. Open, as he did heroically at Cherry Hills in 1960, then he had the inalienable right to blow one of equally colossal proportions. Twenty-one years ago this month, he did.

Leading by seven shots with nine holes to play in the Open at the Olympic Club in San Francisco, he committed perhaps the grandest golf gaffe in history, ultimately falling to Casper and the Ghost—the putting of Billy Casper and the legend of Ben Hogan—in a loss that never healed in his psyche. Palmer never won another major after that, and some people say he hasn't been quite the same since.

The Olympic Club, a storied institution boasting an athletic and social club in San Francisco as well as the country club about 10 miles away, has had its sporting moments. Gentleman Jim Corbett was a member in 1892 when he beat John L. Sullivan for the heavyweight title. Olympians in a variety of sports have called it home.

But on June 19, 1966, on the fourth day of that year's U.S. Open, Olympic was golf itself.

Here was golf's past in the becapped Hogan, returned to the scene of his most famous flop, his 1955 Open loss to the widely ignored Jack Fleck, who is said to have had only $3 in his pocket when he beat Hogan that week. Hogan lost the playoff when his tee shot at 18 went awry. He said his foot slipped, but some said it was his heart. Fleck was barely seen on golf's map again. Yet here they were together again in 1966—Hogan by invitation, Fleck as a qualifier—both of them living apparitions at old, shadowy, haunted Olympic.

Here was golf's future, too: Hale Irwin, Bob Murphy and Deane Beman all played the '66 Open as amateurs. Then there were two unlikely newcomers, a quiet El Paso pro playing in his first major and a 19-year-old amateur who had signed up to caddie but instead qualified—Lee Trevino and Johnny Miller.

Miller, a junior member of Olympic, played two practice rounds with Jack Nicklaus himself.

"What do you think of our kid?" a member asked Nicklaus late Wednesday.

"Not bad," said Nicklaus. "But we'll see how he reacts with the heat on him."

So nervous was Miller that on the first day he overslept and his mother had to wake him. Trevino's week was unremarkable, but Miller finished eighth, the low amateur.

The story line, however, was golf's present. And golf's present then, golf's everything, was Palmer.

Trevino stood at the entrance to Olympic one day and stared as Palmer drove up in a Cadillac.

"I remember he couldn't get out of his car because so many people were trying to get his autograph," says Trevino. "They pushed past me. And I thought, I never dreamed this is what it could be like."

But if Palmer was far and away the people's choice, Nicklaus, 26, was fast becoming history's. Ten years Palmer's junior, Nicklaus had already won five majors to Arnie's seven, owing partly to Palmer's alarming knack for fumbling away majors at the goal line. *Sports Illustrated*'s Alfred Wright once called Palmer "that cataclysm with legs," and, indeed, Palmer's bumbling down the stretch was getting to be a habit. Three majors had slipped through his big knuckles in the early '60s. At the 1961 Masters, Palmer led by a shot with his ball in the middle of the 18th fairway on Sunday (he had even accepted a congratulatory handshake from a fan as he walked to his ball), then made a double bogey to give away the green coat to an astonished Gary Player.

He went glare-to-glare with Fat Jack at Oakmont in the 1962 Open and lost in a playoff. The next year at the Country Club in Brookline, Mass., he lost another Open in a playoff, this time against Julius Boros and Jacky Cupit; Boros won.

No wonder that even with a three-shot lead after three rounds at Olympic, even playing, as he put it, "some of the best golf in my life," Palmer felt jittery. When someone asked how he felt about the remote chances of a playoff, Palmer said, "I'd just as soon not be in one."

But as Palmer walked to the 10th tee on Sunday, a playoff was as unthinkable as snow. He had birdied four of the first nine holes, and led the world and Casper by seven shots. He had now been playing with Casper for 27 holes, and nothing in Casper's style rattled Palmer. He and Casper had been tied after Friday, but Palmer put three strokes between the two of them on Saturday and turned the front nine in a sporty three-under-par 32 to Casper's 36.

No, in Palmer's mind, Casper wasn't the competition. The competition was the man who at that moment was putting out at the 18th hole for what would be 12th place, Ben Hogan.

It was Hogan's U.S. Open record of 276, set in 1948 at Riviera, that Palmer longed to break, and he needed to play the back nine in only one-over-par 36 to do it. "I knew what the record was, and I knew I had the British Open record [276 at Troon in 1962]," Palmer says now. "I thought it would be nice to have both."

Such a lock was Palmer that Casper wandered over to him as they walked to the 10th tee and asked for help. "Arnie," Casper said, "looks like I'm going to have to work some to finish second."

Casper was only two up on Nicklaus, who was playing in the group ahead of him, and on Tony Lema. Golfers can be elevated by a hot partner, and Casper was subtly asking Palmer to keep cranking out birdies, hoping that the suction would take him right along. Of course, this works only up to a point. In the final round of the 1964 Masters, Palmer was walking up the 18th fairway with a five-shot lead when he turned to his struggling compatriot, Dave Marr, and said, "Anything I can do for you?"

"Yeah," said Marr, with a smile. "Shoot a 12."

This time, Palmer said to Casper, "Don't worry, Bill. If you need some help, I'll help you."

Twenty-one years later, Palmer recalls his offer with a wince. "Boy, I helped him right on, didn't I?"

Fate, thus tempted, turned. Maybe Fate doesn't much like golfers giving acceptance speeches after 63 holes of a 72-hold tournament. And what better pair of men to make up seem down and in seem out? For Palmer and Casper could hardly have been more different.

Palmer was tan, Casper pale. Palmer was handsome, Casper plain. Palmer smoked, often on the green, and wasn't averse to hitting the 19th hole and occasionally staying through the 27th. Casper was straighter than a one-iron. He buttoned his golf shirt at the neck and, as a recently converted Mormon, eschewed drink, tobacco and caffeine. Palmer was a Pennsylvania shot-and-a-beer guy, big-boned with huge hands and shoulders and narrow hips that were forever and famously failing to keep up his breeches. Casper was devoutly religious. "At that time, Billy thought he could convert the world," remembers Miller, also a Mormon. (After the '66 Open, Casper announced he was giving 10% of his first-place check as a tithe to his church. Sighed Palmer, "Yeah, well, I'm giving 10 percent to my business manager.")

Palmer was a regular guy. Casper was considered a little strange. Because of allergies, Casper was on an exotic diet—a mooseburger here, an elk or buffalo cutlet there—thus earning the nickname "Buffalo Bill." He had spent most of his adult life, by his own admission, cranky and fat. The mooseburgers had helped him cure his headaches and lose 50 pounds in the 18 months before Olympic.

Palmer was publicly emotional. His mood swings on the golf course looked like today's Dow-Jones average. Casper was as expressionless as a Soviet news anchor. Palmer was the hacker's hero, swinging at the ball as if to unscrew his cleats from his shoes, bent on proving that the shortest distance between A and B was a straight line, trees and condominiums be damned. Casper played holes exactly the way the diagram said to play them. He liked short grass and clear views. He could go years without getting sand in his shoes. Palmer was as allergic to the safe side of the green as Casper was addicted to it. To ask Palmer to try to arrive at a par-5 in anything more than two was abhorrent to his dimpled soul.

Casper was the anti-Arnie. One of the best putters in history, he was caution itself. "Billy was one of the greatest percentage players I've ever seen," says Miller. And why not? For Casper to take the putter out of his own hands would have been madness; he made his living laying up on par 5s, then draining sidehill 30-footers for 4s. With such skill, Casper left the death-defying two-irons to the daring young men on their flying trapezes. Sometimes it seemed to Casper that he spent half his life waiting on greens while brave men tried to extract themselves from trouble they well deserved.

But at 3 p.m. that Sunday, there was no need to think anybody would be doing any comparing. Palmer was going to grant the most interviews to the press and his caddie the second most. As Casper would say, "I was praying . . . praying for second place."

And so it was that as the two men began on the back nine in the 1966 U.S. Open, Casper's mind was on second, Palmer's was on Hogan and nobody's was on winning the tournament. As *The New York Times* columnist Arthur Daley put it, "The chief requirement for rabbit pie is this: First catch the rabbit. Arnie let him escape."

At the par-4 10th, Palmer made an indifferent chip to the green—he was considered one of the lesser wedge players—and missed an indifferent 10-footer for an indifferent bogey. The lead was six with eight to play.

After both men parred 11, Palmer's lead was seven again for half a minute when he birdied 12, with Casper still to putt. Looking back, Palmer said, "The worst break of all could have been that birdie. It convinced me I could break the record." Casper made his birdie, too. Six up with six to play. Yawn, snore.

At the 191-yard, par-3 13th, Palmer was still chasing Hogan. "I tried to go at the hole and pulled it a bit." The four-iron shot hit on the green and bounced into deep rough. The pitch went by the hole and he two-putted. Casper, the tortoise, made par. Five with five to play. Yawn but no snore.

Both players made par at 14, leaving Palmer only to par out the rest of the way to better Hogan's record. Why, then, on the par-3 15th, did Palmer again try to dent the flagstick? Why, then, did he not learn from Casper's elegant shot, a simple hook away from the bunker that guarded the green, tucking calmly 20 feet from the pin? Why was Palmer obsessed with trying to stick it inside the leather?

"I guess because I grew up thinking that's what you are supposed to do," Palmer says today. "I mean, I really enjoyed shooting at the pin . . . I never thought about knocking it to the middle of the green. Never."

Recalling the shot in his book *Go for Broke* in 1973, Palmer wrote, "I was trying to play the perfect shot—going for the record, not just the title." The perfect shot tarried on the edge of the green and then trickled, to the gasps of the crowd, into the bunker. Bogey. Casper made the 20-foot downhiller. Three with three to play.

"That was the key," Casper says now. "I think that hole changed everything. He then realized he could lose the Open. Up until that point, he was swinging free and easy. After that, he tightened up. I remember thinking, 'I'm three behind. Now I've got a chance.'"

At 16, a monstrous 604-yard par-5 dogleg left, Casper, hitting first, drove away from trouble down the right side. Safe, not sorry. It galled Palmer. "Here's a guy trying to catch me and he's playing it safe," he wrote.

Palmer's turn to hit. "I knew I could play it safe and shut Billy off completely," he wrote. "I could take out a one-iron and bump and nudge the ball down the fairway, keeping it under control . . . and get my par. Then I thought of how I'd look to myself: 'There goes Arnold Palmer, playing it safe with a one-iron when he's got a three-stroke lead with three holes to play.' It seemed silly . . . I couldn't do it."

'Twas vintage hitch-up-your-pants thinking—bold if not brilliant—and Palmer swung as if to arrive at the green in one. "I swung too hard," he says now. The ball described a pattern that looked like Turn 3 at Indy. It hooked viciously, wreaked pain on some branches 150 yards away and plunked straight down. "Now," recalls Palmer, "I knew I was in deep you-know-what."

The lie was such that nobody in his right mind would try to blast it out in hope of making a birdie. Anybody else would have taken a seven-iron and plopped it back into the fairway, leaving a long iron to the green and not much problem making five. Palmer, naturally, took a three-iron.

Casper: "I would've played out. I have a rule. When I get in the rough, if I can't hit it with my four-wood, I drop to a five-iron. There was no way to get a three-iron out of it. I think he was still going for the record."

That 3-iron shot was never warmed by sunlight. It cut a swath of vegetation for maybe 100 yards and collapsed, this time in even nastier rough. "I misjudged that [second shot] lie," Palmer says with remorse. "It was deeper than I thought. It was down in there." Palmer was forced to take a nine-iron and lay it back into the fairway. Now the ball rested 280 yards from the green and had already been slashed at three times.

Palmer drew out a three-wood and hit it with a stupendous blow—perfectly—carrying 270 yards . . . sailing, sailing, sailing . . . smack into a greenside bunker. What is it the ancient Greeks said? "Those whom the gods wish to destroy, they first make mad." Now Palmer found himself with a fried-egg lie and lying four.

While Palmer was thrashing about, Casper was a kind of golfing Muzak, a background hum you didn't notice until you stopped to think about it. He had used a driver, two-iron and five-iron to get within 13 feet. It was quite possible he could pick up three strokes on this one hole.

Palmer exploded beautifully 40 yards out of the sand to within four feet. Casper calmly sank his birdie putt ("I knew I was going to hole it"), and now Palmer needed his four-footer to keep from being tied. He made it. "One of the greatest sixes the game has ever seen," says Casper. One with two to play.

Pandemonium rattled the cypress trees. The unthinkable was being thought. "The army was in desertion," Casper says. "Now you've got Casper Converts. Arnie is really going through it. What I think happened was that at 15 he lost the opportunity to break Hogan's record and he panicked."

Palmer tried to talk himself down. "People started running then," Palmer remembers. "The word was out: 'Arnie is caving in.' But I'm thinking: 'I've still got a one-shot lead with two holes to play.'"

At the 443-yard 17th, Palmer missed the fairway, short and left in deep rough. "A terrible swing," Casper says. Then again, Casper's wasn't exactly a video instructional. He hit so badly it was good. The ball went so far right it landed on gallery-trodden weeds, a perfectly fine lie. Funny game.

The two players crisscrossed with their second shots, both short of the green. Casper faced a delicate pitch, which he knocked to four feet. Palmer's chip had to come from deep rough, go over a bunker and then bite. He hit it to eight feet. "One of the finest recovery shots I've ever witnessed, under the circumstances," said USGA executive director Joe Dey, who was following the group as one of the tournament referees.

Palmer's putt was straight uphill. "I was nervous, but I had myself under control. I hit that putt dead in the hole."

And dead short, one inch. "One lousy inch," says Mike Reasor, Palmer's caddie and later a Tour player. "I think it was the first putt in 71 holes he'd left on the short side of the hole."

Casper made his putt. Tied with one to play.

As the two men walked to 18, their thoughts were literally worlds apart. Casper was thinking about Vietnam. He had spent 16 days there in February and March visiting hospitals and battle posts and putting on exhibitions for American soldiers. At Da Nang one day, he hit some shots into a field and, when he was finished, told the soldiers they could keep any balls they retrieved. Nobody moved. "Nobody wants the balls?" Casper asked.

"Thanks anyway, Mr. Casper," one soldier said. "But that field is full of mines."

He hit balls off an aircraft carrier. He was even shot at once while in a helicopter. And as he walked to the 18th tee, he was thinking about Vietnam. "Just for a second, I was thinking about those guys on the carrier," Casper says. "Those guys were like lions basking in the sun. They'd wait there, calmly, but when the situation came, they were ready to fight. I think I was sort of the same way. Here was my chance."

As for Palmer, he had given up five shots in the last three holes. One could imagine how many he would give up now as he walked to that infamous 18th. "I thought about Hogan," he says. About Hogan and the record? "No, Hogan and Fleck."

On 18, Casper drew a driver for the first time all week and slapped it down the center of the fairway. Also for the first time all week, Palmer didn't grab a driver. Instead, he took a one-iron. "I'm just thinking, 'Get this son of a bitch in the fairway.'" Such is the pressure of an Open. Casper was now bold and Palmer timid.

Palmer's swing was too fast, and the ball flew left, into deep, monstrous rough. Olympic was getting eerie again: Palmer had hit it where Hogan had hit it 11 years before.

From *Go for Broke*: "My ball was caught deeply in the tangled rough, and it would take a high-lofted club—the 9-iron—to dig it out of there. And the way the ball was sitting, it figured that I wouldn't hit it much more than halfway to the green with that club. But I put everything I had—every muscle that could be brought to bear—into that nine-iron shot."

Reasor: "I've never seen such an ugly lie. I took a look at it and I said, 'This guy would do well to hit it in the front bunker.' The veins were bulging out of his neck. He took a swath of grass you couldn't believe. The ball barely flew over the lip of that bunker, but it came out with no spin and rolled clear to the back of the green. It was the greatest shot I've ever seen."

Casper: "Arnie must've taken out about three feet of grass. He took a swing that you couldn't believe. It was a tremendous shot . . . a fantastic shot."

Even so, Casper had knocked a wedge only 17 feet away, hole high, and Palmer was 25 away—with a downhill putt on a heartlessly slick green. "I really thought the tournament was over," Reasor says. "I think everybody did."

That year, in an effort to speed play, the USGA was experimenting with a rule that called for golfers to continue putting until they holed out. Palmer's first putt stopped three feet short of the hole, and now the crowd realized he had to putt again, three feet, straight downhill, with the U.S. Open on the line.

Two of the spectators, Marr and Nicklaus, had signed their cards minutes before and taken a seat on the hill to watch. As Palmer readied his putt, Nicklaus turned to Marr and said, "If he misses this, there goes the rule."

Palmer: "I remember looking at that putt and thinking, 'Everything is on the line here. My pride. My business. My livelihood.' And there I was making it even harder."

Palmer never was much good at doing it the way people figured he would. He rammed his ball in the hole. "Maybe the greatest putt Arnie ever made," said Marr.

Now the boxer had a 17-footer to put the puncher away for good. "I thought to myself, 'You've picked up seven shots on one of the greatest players the game has ever known,'" Casper recalls. "'Maybe you better just lag this up and putt it in.'" And he did. Playoff on Monday.

Neither player said a word as they walked like zombies into the scoring tent to sign their cards. "Two of the most garbled signatures you ever saw," says Reasor.

When Casper was finished, he looked up to say something to Palmer, but his lips were so parched he couldn't get the words out. Arnie marched, glaze-eyed, for the clubhouse. Palmer later said, "All I could think was, 'I've just lost a 7-shot lead in the U.S. Open, and now I've got to tell the press exactly how I did it.'"

It wasn't easy. He had shot 39 on the back to Casper's 32. He had missed three of six fairways and five of nine greens, and, most of all, he had forgotten the lesson his golf-pro father had taught him. "Never forget your main objective," Deacon Palmer would say. "You get someone down, you keep on pressing."

"Anybody can make up excuses," Palmer says today. "Everybody's different. Some days you can handle the heat and some days you can't. I don't think I've ever met anybody or heard of anybody who could handle it every single day, day in and day out."

Palmer spent a quiet—very quiet—few hours that night at the home of his host, Ed Douglas. "We never brought up the tournament," Douglas recalls. They retired early. Casper was taken immediately from the press conference to a Mormon "fireside chat" in which he spoke and answered questions until 11:30 p.m. with nary a mooseburger for a man to eat until midnight. He wasn't in bed until one and swamped Palmer by four shots that morning in the playoff. Go figure.

Actually, the playoff was an afterthought and is mostly forgotten. "The momentum was with Billy," says Miller, and even though Palmer had a two-shot lead going into—ta da!—the 10th, it was simply a matter of waiting for Popeye to open up a can of spinach and get on with it. And so, with his magic wand, Casper calmly dropped a 40-footer with a 6-foot break on 11 (startling Palmer so much that he missed his par putt), then a real white-knuckler—50 feet—on 13. Now Casper was ahead for good. He even three-putted three times—his first three-putts of the week—and he still lapped Palmer. On 18, Casper made birdie, his 33rd one-putt of the tournament. For the back nine on the last two days, Casper shot 66, Palmer 79.

And from that final putt on, the 1966 Open has been known as the biggest one Palmer ever blew, with Casper looked upon as chief beneficiary. "They can say what they want," Casper says. "I've got the check."

And yet Casper may go down in history as one of the most accomplished golfers we never knew. "Casper has never been given credit for the kind of golf he played in the mid-'60s," says Trevino. Indeed, from 1964 through 1968, Casper won more tournaments than Palmer. And from 1960 to '68 one or the other of them won the Vardon Trophy for low stroke average, Casper five times to Palmer's four. Casper is one of 15 men to win at least two U.S. Opens, which is one more than Byron Nelson, Tom Watson and you-know-who.

As for Palmer, it has gone like this: After the awards ceremony, he made it to the clubhouse and sat dejectedly next to Reasor in front of his locker. Tears were collecting in their eyes. After a long pause, Palmer put his arm around Reasor and said, "Sorry, Mike."

Reasor figured he shouldn't be sorry at all. "Time will pass," the caddie told the legend. "You'll get over it." And so Palmer has. In fact, as he says, "Things turned out pretty well." His estimated worth is somewhere near $55 million, give or take a bank. His Q (positive-recognition quotient) rating is one of the highest in advertising, sports figures or no. He has designed upwards of 100 golf courses, owns three more, the latest of which, Isleworth in Orlando, Fla., is so lavish that the floors in Palmer's office there are made of leather.

After Olympic, Casper went on to win the 1970 Masters, but Palmer never won another major. Arnie was close, yet never closed. At the 1967 Open at Baltusrol, he went head-to-head with Nicklaus and got cleaned. At the 1968 PGA, he had an eight-footer on 18 to tie Julius Boros and missed. At the 1972 Open at Pebble Beach, he had a putt on 14 that could have given him the lead, and he missed it.

Yet none of those failures, including the '66 Open, has spoiled the man's popularity. If anything, what happened at Olympic cemented it. It may have been the turning point of his career, for in this incredible defeat he became real to fans, more human than ever. "I think they saw someone who was at least out there trying his hardest," Palmer says.

America was happy to forgive. "Had anyone else done what Arnie did at Olympic, they would have been labeled a huge choker, a guy who had committed one of the biggest boo-boos in the history of the majors," says Miller. "But with Arnie, it's 'Oh, Arnie was going for the record.' He's got the world by the tail."

And so, given that Arnie's losing is more interesting that almost anybody else's winning, we gather around Palmer, pop open a malted beverage and cry until we laugh. "The losses aren't so bad," he says today. "I mean, without them, I think there'd be a void in my life."

To wit, one last story. Once, on a Friday at the L.A. Open, Palmer needed only a par on the last hole to shoot 69. He hit his second shot out of bounds, then the next one, and the next one and the next one. He made a 12 and missed the cut.

Hearing of this, the press summoned him for an interview.

"How in God's name did you make a 12 on the last hole?" somebody asked.

"Well," said Palmer. "I missed a 20-footer for an 11."

"What's Wrong with Jack Nicklaus?"—Round 1

from *Jack Nicklaus: My Story* by Jack Nicklaus
with Ken Bowden

I must have been asked a thousand times over the years for my rating of golf's four major championships. Here's how I feel about them.

It is sometimes argued that the Masters should not be included among the majors because it is not the championship of anything, and I know that its founder, Bob Jones, was sympathetic to that viewpoint. The truth is that Bob had no intention when he started the tournament of it being anything but an enjoyable springtime outing for his friends. His modesty was such that he insisted the inaugural event be called the "Augusta National Invitation Tournament," and in the years I knew him he disliked any reference to his creation as a "championship." As he invariably pointed out when such matters came up, it was the media that named his tournament "The Masters" and elected it a major.

For all of those reasons, even though the Masters is the major I enjoy playing the most, I have always placed it fourth, behind the U.S. Open, the British Open, and the PGA Championship, when pressured to rate the big four.

I rate the U.S. Open first for numerous reasons that I will get to in a moment. Heading them is the fact that, as an American, it is the championship of my country. I also believe it is the toughest of the four to win.

To me, the British Open earns its number-two rating as the world's oldest golf championship, as the championship of the country where the game began, and as the most international of the majors. The unique challenge of the big links courses it is traditionally played on makes it for me the second most enjoyable of the four, only slightly behind the Masters.

The PGA is third in my ranking because of its age, and because, when American players dominated golf, it often enjoyed the strongest fields of all tournaments worldwide.

Largely, I suppose, because they had played the game the longest, the British and their Open championship dominated the scene until about twenty years after the game had taken solid root on this side of the Atlantic. In 1913, however, American players received a boost that in a relatively short time led to a superiority that lasted for more than half a century. This was, of course, the victory in our Open of a nineteen-year-old, virtually unheard-of Boston amateur and ex-caddie by the name of Francis Ouimet over the legendary English golfers Harry Vardon and Ted Ray, in a playoff at The Country Club of Brookline on the outskirts of Boston.

Before Ouimet's victory, only one native-born golfer had won the U.S. Open, Johnny McDermott in 1911 and 1912, to twelve victories by players emigrating from Scotland and four from England. After Ouimet's sensational achievement, foreigners would win our championship only four times in the next sixty-seven years. Also, over that period, Americans, with previously zero victories in the British Open, would capture twenty-four out of fifty-six, along with all but five of the sixty PGA Championships and the forty-two Masters played. Although the best foreign players in recent years have become the equals and sometimes the betters of the top Americans, it was obviously this long U.S. dominance of golf that, most of all, gave our national championship its preeminence. There are, however, some additional reasons for its stature.

Number one is the quality of the courses over which it is generally played. The better the course, the more enjoyable the playing and the greater the fulfillment in winning. Throughout most of its history, and certainly in my time, U.S. Open courses have generally been the finest in the nation. Excepting the fixed-location Masters, this is true of no other old-established tournament.

Number two is the condition of those courses. The traditionally narrow fairways, heavy rough and firm ground conditions of U.S. Open courses annually present players with their most severe mental and physical examinations. Win the U.S. Open and you know you have survived golf at its most demanding.

Number three is the field. Any golfer with fire in his belly dreams of winning the championship of the world's largest golfing nation, which means the best players of every era almost always participate. This again is not true of any other event, including even, I'm sad to say, because of its limited invitational field, the Masters.

Fourth is a factor you rarely hear much about but which I think is an important contributor. More than any other top event, the U.S. Open is still pure, straight golf, with a minimum of commercial hoopla. In an age where money increasingly dominates all sport, and despite the corporate tents of recent years, the U.S. Open's single objective remains identifying the best player. For me, that gives it an aura and a flavor unattained by any other championship. Over the years there have been some justifiable criticisms of the Open's organizational standards, but, if less than operational perfection is the price to be paid for minimal commercialism, then fine and dandy with me. If money ever becomes more of a factor in the U.S. Open than generating enough to stage it decently, that will be the day it begins to slide off its peak among the world's great golfing occasions.

You can probably tell from these sentiments that the U.S. Open has always been extra special for me, and it was never more so than in the spring and early summer of 1967. As in the past, I felt a thrill of anticipation every time I thought about the championship. Unfortunately, though, that feeling tended to get wrestled aside by another emotion that was both unfamiliar and unpleasant: anxiety. Not only was I coming into the Open off the worst six months of my career, but also with my weakest record in a major since turning pro. In 1963 at Brookline I had missed the cut. Twelve months later, at Congressional, I had tied for twenty-third, seventeen shots behind Ken Venturi. In 1965, at Bellerive, after an exceptionally thorough study of the course with friend Gary Player, he had won and I had tied for thirty-first, again seventeen strokes off the pace. Then, at Olympic, in my last try, I had fumbled at least a slim chance of victory with a sloppy final round to finish third behind Casper and Palmer.

I had heard it said by old hands about the U.S. Open that any half-decent golfer on a hot streak might luck out in it once, but that it took a real champion to win it a second time. As I flew north from Florida the week ahead of the championship for my first look at Baltusrol, I let my mind dwell on that thought as an extra stimulus.

Baltusrol Golf Club is located in Springfield, in the rolling hills of central New Jersey, about twenty miles southwest of Manhattan. Founded in 1895, it played a prominent role in the formative years of American golf, and today is rivaled by only one other old-timer, Oakmont, as our leading host of national championships.

In 1967 we would play the Lower Course, designed by one of America's finest golf architects, A. W. Tillinghast, and opened in 1922. In most respects I liked it immediately. To begin with, the course had the same settled, mature feeling as the one where I grew up, Scioto, opened in 1916 and thus one of the older clubs in the Midwest. Additionally, the layout had a natural, uncontrived, un-prettied-up quality, particularly on the less wooded stretches from the seventh through the sixteenth holes, that reminded me a little of the great British links courses. I decided this more than made up for the handful of semiblind drives and eight or nine approaches where you couldn't see the bottom of the flagstick.

What I liked most about Baltusrol, though, was its condition. For a reason I never discovered, the United States Golf Association had not narrowed the fairways to a point where they eliminated or severely limited the use of the game's most exciting club, the driver. Here we generally had between thirty-five and forty yards of short grass to aim at from the tees. And what fine grass it was. Composed of bent and *Poa annua* cut very low, the fairways were the best I had encountered for playing iron shots, the ball sitting cleanly on top of them, enabling you to get all the way down to its bottom with no risk of trapping grass between blade and ball. There would be few if any "fliers" here, which was excellent news. Equally good, due to a long spell of dry weather, was the reasonable height and consistency of the rough. Miss those gorgeous fairways and you generally had a chance of advancing the ball with something more than a sand wedge and a prayer. All in all, I felt this was the best balanced U.S. Open course I had yet encountered: consistently demanding from the tee, invariably challenging on approach shots, never a cinch if you missed a green, but, taken in the round, a fair and enjoyable test of golf.

Liking a course always increases one's desire to play well, and Baltusrol added to mine. But, in one respect, it also worried me. The less penalizing the conditions, the better the chances of a larger number of players, and the more contenders, the greater the impact of putting on the outcome. After two days of practice, I was certain that putting would be a critical factor in the 1967 U.S. Open. Considering my recent efforts in that department, this was not good news.

Well, it sure is great to have friends! I had played both of those days with Deane Beman, and—surprise, surprise—here comes little Deano to my rescue yet again.

For most of the previous year I had used a Ping putter, and had persevered with it on the well-known principle that poor putting invariably derives from the "puttee," not from his implement. Nevertheless, I had brought half a dozen other putters to Baltusrol. Following our Friday round, still trying to figure out which one to use (and how), on the spur of the moment I picked up a spare center-shafted Bull's Eye of Deane's, and decided immediately that it might be the answer to my prayers. Seeing the covetous look in my eye, Deane, one of golf's all-time great putters, quickly reclaimed his trusty weapon, but the next morning dug a selection of similar clubs from the trunk of his car and invited me to take my pick. Naturally, none of them felt as good as Deane's second-string putter, and I was about to return to my Ping when Fred Mueller, a pal of Deane's from Washington who was on the green with us, told me that Deane had worked on his Bull's Eye, and that I was welcome to try it if I cared to. I accepted the offer, and knew on the first stroke that it was identical with Deane's with the exception of having an all-white head (Fred had painted the brass to prevent sun glare). Recognizing how much I liked it—and probably how much I *needed* it—Fred offered to let me keep it. I thanked him, promised him some MacGregor putters in return, and took the club home to Florida and practiced with it over the weekend. By Sunday night, I couldn't wait for the Open to begin.

By Tuesday evening, back at Baltusrol and back on the putting green after my practice round, I was at square one again. I had struck the ball beautifully getting to the greens, then performed on them like a beginner with a hangover. "White Fang," as the putter came to be known, still felt good—but there was still something seriously wrong with the fellow using it.

Like everyone who has enjoyed any success at this game, I have had the good fortune on more occasions than I can recall to just happen across a tip at a moment of extreme need that fixed a seemingly insoluble problem. In this instance, the bearer of good tidings was Gordon Jones, an old friend from Ohio and a periodic tour player with a fine knowledge of technique. After watching me for a while not even hit the hole from no more than ten feet, Gordie suddenly said, "Jack, why don't you try taking a shorter stroke and hitting the ball harder?" For months I had been trying to do exactly the opposite, taking the club back long and flowingly in an effort to obtain the necessary distance by a free-swinging pendulum-type motion rather than by force of strike. But what the heck . . . as an amateur, I'd mostly swung relatively short and popped the ball . . .

The moment I tried Gordon's suggestion, orchestras began to play and angels to sing. I have never believed in miracles, but this was close. I worked on the shorter backswing for an hour or so, and couldn't get the silly grin off my face all through the rest of the evening. The next day, in my final practice round, despite closing with two par fives, I holed almost everything I hit for a round of 62. Practice round scores are, of course, meaningless beyond whatever they may—or may not—do for your confidence, but low ones always seem to make headlines, so Thursday morning I got a big share of the sports section's large type. However, Friday's papers had a very different slant.

During my peak years, it became almost commonplace for an "unknown" to lead the U.S. Open after the first round. The 1967 championship was no exception, but this time there was an extra dimension to further excite the fans and the media. Marty Fleckman, who had opened with a smooth 67, was not only a new name to almost everyone at Baltusrol, but an amateur barely out of college. With the last victory by an amateur in the U.S. Open being Johnny Goodman's in 1933, for the three days that Marty remained in the thick of this one he received enormous attention. Unfortunately, all the fuss, along with his inexperience, finally exacted a price: an unhappy final round and a slide to a tie for eighteenth place. But it was a valiant effort by the young Texan, and one that increased the excitement of the championship for all involved.

I excited nobody that first day, and particularly not J. W. Nicklaus. The full shots were not coming off the clubface quite as easily and sharply as the day before, but basically I had arrived on the greens in decent numbers. Also, I was pleased not to have hit one hook or even a draw. My problem, yet again, was on the greens: a complete reversal of the previous day. Then, I had drained everything. Now, I could make nothing. The result was a one-over-par 71. What annoyed me as much as the thirty-five putts was the missed opportunity in such fine scoring conditions. It had become and would remain stiflingly hot and humid. ("Hot?" commented Ben Hogan. "Hell can't be any hotter, and I'll check that out one of these days.") Nevertheless, nine men had broken 70, including Arnold Palmer, Bill Casper, Gary Player, and Deane Beman. Working on my putting after the round, it was tough not to get despondent. I heard that Arnie had canned a monster for a birdie after two poor shots, then, pumped up, immediately made a couple more snakes. I would have given a lot for one of those morale-builders.

It arrived on the fourth green early the next morning.

After opening with a bogey and two pars, I had not been in the best of spirits sizing up the tee shot. Number four is generally regarded as Baltusrol's prettiest hole, but it is also one of the trickiest: 190 yards with a stone-walled pond immediately fronting the shallow green and four bunkers in back. Distance is thus the critical factor, and I had gotten that part right in choosing the 3-iron. But overanxious and hurried (the two are synonymous), instead of fading the ball, I'd drawn it into light rough to the left of the green, then fallen asleep on the chip. Now I had an eleven-foot putt for par. Studying it, the predominant thought in my head was that if I missed and went three over for the championship, I could almost certainly wave it good-bye. There were simply too many fine players firing low for me to be able to bridge a big gap.

It is probably kind of dumb to suggest that a single stroke can win a championship, but this one still sticks in my mind that way. When that putt dropped, everything changed. Despondency turned into elation, doubt into confidence, sluggishness into momentum. I birdied the next hole from four feet, the eighth from twelve feet, the twelfth from fifteen, the sixteenth from twenty-five, and the 545-yard eighteenth with two putts from forty feet after a great drive and 1-iron, for my then-lowest round in a U.S. Open of 67. At the end of the day there was only one golfer ahead of me: Arnold Palmer.

In one respect, this was excellent news, because nothing then more inspired me than doing battle with Arnie. That evening, however, I also had some less positive thoughts on a couple of counts, neither of them relating to his one-stroke advantage.

The United States Golf Association's pairing system for the last two rounds of the Open was then and is still strictly arithmetical: first plays with second, third with fourth, and so on. This meant that Arn and I would be paired together for Saturday's third round. My first concern was the extra burden this imposed on us of focusing on besting the course and the field rather than just each other. Not since the Open of 1962 had we been paired in a major championship with both of us contending, but it had happened on numerous occasions in regular tour events. No matter how strong our resolve—and we had discussed the problem candidly—with so intense a rivalry it had proven impossible for us not to end up going at each other head-to-head, which invariably had cost us both. I knew I would have to fight hard to prevent it happening again the next day.

My second concern was speed of play. When I got behind in those days it made me try to hurry, which led to mistakes, which compounded the problem by making me take even more time over shots. Being overtly timed by officials in the previous year's Open at Olympic had made me fretful, and, as mentioned, I had been penalized for slow play only a few weeks earlier in Houston. Thus I had made a vow on the eve of this championship to keep myself moving along, to, if necessary, force myself to stay up with the group ahead. However, while Arnie himself certainly would not interfere with that—he was always a fast player—we now had to contend with the large and boisterous New York/New Jersey battalion of his famed Army. Inevitably, the bigger and more excited the crowds accompanying them, the harder it is for players to giddyup. All I could do was hope the officials would take this factor into account if we began falling behind.

I had one more thing to dislike that evening: television. This was about the time that the networks began to exert the pressure on golf's administrators that today has given them almost total control over the timing of weekend tournament rounds. The broadcaster had decreed seven o'clock finishes for the 1967 Open, which meant that Arnie and I would not tee off until three in the afternoon. It was a challenging prospect and it proved a challenging reality. I remember Barb and I yawned through *Casper the Friendly Ghost*, then *The Winsome Witch*, then a Bob Hope movie, then most of Randolph Scott in *Riding Shotgun* before it was even time to leave for the course. B-o-r-i-n-g, not to mention the impact on the nervous system.

As things turned out, thanks largely to fine crowd control, the slow-play problem never materialized. Both of us striding as fast as we could between shots, we got around on Saturday in three hours forty minutes (spurred toward the end by a threatening storm, we would improve on that by fifteen minutes the next day when we also played together). But, whether subconsciously or not, that old head-banging bugaboo got to both of us yet again in round three. On the eighth tee, Arnold finally suggested we stop playing each other and start playing for the championship, and I agreed wholeheartedly. By then, though, it was too late for either of us to change the mind-set. Compounding the problem, perhaps for him almost as much as for me, was the size and vola-tility of the "Army." It was the biggest and noisiest I had ever played before, and also by miles the most blatantly partisan. I knew I had some fans out there, too, because they had been rooting for me the first couple of rounds, but on Saturday they were mostly invisible and inaudible. Conceivably that's because I could give them so little to get excited about. Birdies on seventeen and eighteen kept my final tally out of total disaster range at 72, which bettered Arnie by a stroke. But both of us had produced basically miserable displays of golf.

The only consolation was that Casper, who had carved himself a four-stroke lead leaving the fourteenth green, had backpedaled into a tie with us by the time he left the eighteenth. But all this was inside-page stuff. The big news once again was the Byron Nelson protégé, Marty Fleckman. Most people had been expecting him to follow his opening 67 with an 80-something, and, when that didn't happen in the second round, were sure it would in the third. Instead, Marty, with a fine 69, had ended up in the lead.

Regardless of how I have played, throughout my career I have almost always spent some time on the driving range following tournament rounds. One reason is simply to "wind down" my nervous system—to let off steam, if you will. Another is to seek a solution while the memory and senses are sharp if something is off kilter, or to reaffirm and reinforce the good moves or feelings if I'm swinging well. In fact, I've generally been able to achieve more with my swing following tournament rounds than at any other time.

By the time we got through the interviews and other postround chores that Saturday evening at Baltusrol, there was not much daylight left, but I was determined to get in a solid session. Sloppily as I'd played, I still believed I had some fine golf in me, and I wanted to prove that to myself before going to bed. As on the course, the first few swings did not feel right—okay, but a little forced. After a few more shots reviewing my basics, I discovered why. To fade the ball, you need to align the body a little left of target. As so often over the years, I had been creeping to the right in my setup. With a slight change in shoulder alignment, everything suddenly fell in place. I went through the entire bag just to be sure, then moved over to the putting green. On the course I had sensed I was quitting with my left hand through impact. I worked on that until I lost the hesitant feeling, then wended my way back to the motel to wait out another challenging starting time—3:08 p.m.

One of the great moments of anticipation in golf occurs when you walk onto the practice tee before the final round of a major championship when fully in contention. That's because within a minute or two you will have a pretty accurate idea of your chances from the feel of your golf swing. The Sunday of the 1967 U.S. Open is still one of my happiest warm-up memories. The first few wedges were perfect. So were the other short irons, then the medium irons, then the long irons, then the driver. On to the putting green and, there again, a great feel. Down they went, easy as shelling peas. "Well, Nicklaus," I said to myself, "maybe you can finally play golf again. Let's go find out."

No doubt helped by the good practice session, my qualms of the previous day about playing with Arnold had evaporated. As always in those days, when he was in contention I saw him as the man to beat. That being the case, I was now happy to be playing alongside him. His presence would heighten my concentration, force me to keep my mind 100 percent on the task at hand. The Army was in full force and song again, but I resolved to have it serve as a spur rather than a distraction.

By the time we arrived at the fourth tee, my anticipation of a two-horse race appeared to be materializing. Fleckman and Casper, playing immediately behind us as the final pairing, had both begun poorly. Following a steady opening par, I had bogeyed number two, but then sneaked a twelve-footer in the side door at the third hole for birdie. That had tied me with Arnie again, and given me the kind of lift I'd gotten the previous day with the saving putt on number four. Now I enjoyed a couple more boosts, with a perfect 3-iron to four feet for a second straight bird, then a fifteen-footer at the fifth hole for a third. That put me two ahead of Arnie and alone in the lead.

I will always believe that the next three holes decided this Open.

At the first of them, number six, Arnie made his sixth solid par in a row while I bogeyed, missing from seven feet. It was a tricky putt and I fretted less over missing it than about reopening the door for my toughest adversary. Arnold's drive at the rugged 470-yard seventh hole confirmed the boost he had received: Dead straight and absolutely nailed. I hit a solid one, too, and when we got to the balls was delighted to find mine a couple of steps ahead.

Even off a good drive, the second shot to this hole is one of Baltusrol's most challenging (the members play it as a par five but it's a four on the Open card). The green is oval-shaped and drops away at the back, and the bunkers fronting it hide the bottom of the flagstick. Arnie hit what he would later describe as one of the best shots of his life, a superb 1-iron that came to rest no more than twelve feet behind the cup. I followed with a high, faded 2-iron that ended up about twice as far away.

The Army had gone nuts over Arnold's great shot, and became even wilder as he strode onto the green. My thoughts as I followed him were very much on the psychological impact of what would happen next. If I missed and he made, we would be tied again, and he would be all set for another of those legendary "charges." I decided this was not a moment for playing safe. "Whatever else, get it there," I told myself, and stroked the ball firmly. As soon as it took off I thought, "That's in," and as the ball got to within five feet I started to walk after it, certain I'd made it. The look Arn gave me as I picked the ball out of the cup is one I will never forget, and he told me later that this putt "absolutely crushed" him. When he missed his own birdie effort by a whisker, suddenly I was again leading by two strokes.

The perfect tee shot at number eight on Baltusrol's Lower Course is a driver started down the left side of the fairway with a slight fade. Now, really pumped, I could not have played a better one in a hundred tries. And then came another opening. Obviously reacting to the unexpected turnaround on the previous hole, Arnie hit what he later described as his only bad tee shot of the championship, overcutting the ball into the right rough, where it stopped behind the trunk of a tree. He had no option but to pitch out sideways, and from there was unlucky to trickle off the fringe of the green into a bunker. Thus he now had played three strokes to my one, and would have his work cut out to make better than a bogey five.

The shot facing me was a pitch of eighty-five yards, definitely not my strongest suit. However, while trying to refind a golf game during those miserable weeks after the Masters, I had discovered that my chief problem on short pitch shots was an insufficiently firm left arm both swinging back and swinging through. By doing some strengthening exercises and keeping the arm almost rigid, I'd found I could keep the clubhead on a consistent path. Applying that technique now with the sand wedge, I stopped my ball almost where it landed four feet from the hole. When the putt dropped, I'd picked up another two strokes on Arnold and was leading the Open by four.

It had happened before and it has happened since, and it will probably happen again. Despite my good golf and large lead, all of a sudden on the back nine I could not shift my mind off the possibility of a disaster. The trigger, unquestionably, was number ten. The hole is a long par four with a tight driving zone, particularly for a fader of the ball, and the previous two days I had blocked myself out from the tee and bogeyed it. Now it cost me three putts, and, walking down the eleventh fairway, even though I'd hit a fine drive, I experienced a bad burst of jitters. Two solid pars helped to reduce them somewhat. Finally, after a pitching wedge to three feet at thirteen and a 7-iron to five feet at the next hole for a pair of easy birdies and a five-stroke lead, self-doubt became idiotic and was dispelled.

Baltusrol's Lower Course par for Opens is 70, and the birdie at fourteen had taken me to four under for both the round and the championship. Leaving the green, it occurred to me that Ben Hogan's seventy-two-hole record for the Open, set at Riviera in 1948, was 276, and that I could break it with three pars and one more birdie. I told myself to resist any impulse to try to force the birdie. Arnold had told me that the real reason for his stumbling golf over the final nine holes at Olympic the previous year was focusing too much on breaking the record, rather than on winning the title (he finally tied with Casper and lost in their playoff). With that in mind, I decided four pars in for 276 and the title would do just fine, and resolved to work on them speedily enough to beat an imminent and nasty-looking thunderstorm.

The first three of those pars came safely enough. On the 542-yard par-five closing hole, even though a good drive would have set me up to reach the green in two (I'd done so with a drive and 4-iron the previous day), for safety's sake I decided on the 1-iron for the tee shot. I felt a little foolish about it, but Arnie had birdied seventeen to cut my lead to four, and there was big trouble down the left side. Most of all, I knew I had a better chance of making six, which would still give me the championship even if Arnie eagled, off a missed 1-iron than a missed driver.

Miss the 1-iron I did, at least a little bit. Started straight rather than left, and faded too much, the ball finished just in the right rough close to a television cable drum. I was permitted a free drop clear of that obstruction, and knew as soon as I'd taken it I could forget the heroic option. The only intelligent shot from a lie as bare and tight as the one I had given myself was a punch out short of the water hazard 120 yards ahead. I took the 8-iron, choked down, made a nice compact three-quarter backswing, looked up halfway through the downswing, hit the ground about three inches behind the ball, and dribbled it all of fifty yards. Trying to relieve my embarrassment, I walked over and said to Arnie: "That was stupid, wasn't it?" Diplomatic as ever, all he offered was, "You said it, I didn't."

I guess if you have enough of it, pride will sometimes come to your rescue. I figured I now had 238 yards to the pin, uphill, all carry, and against the wind. Mathematically, that indicated the 3-wood. Emotionally, because of the greater confidence I've always had in it, I chose the 1-iron. The swing felt perfect, and, absolutely nailed, the ball carried the bunker, landed a few feet short of the green, and ran up onto it to finish twenty-two feet from the hole. It was certainly the longest 1-iron I've ever hit in competition, and quite likely the best.

Walking up the hill, knowing I had won the Open, there was now no reason not to let myself think about the record. This putt would do it, and I decided to be bold on it. When it dropped, giving me a 65 and 275 total, I let go with a mighty kick—the biggest spontaneous burst of emotion I had shown in a moment of victory. It was my lowest and best-played round in the Open, but the big thing was I had won the championship for that critical second time.

At last I could stop asking myself, "What's wrong with Jack Nicklaus?"

"Who Is That Guy?"

from *They Call Me Super Mex: The Autobiography of Lee Trevino*
by Lee Trevino and Sam Blair

But by the time I headed for Rochester and the U.S. Open at Oak Hill in June, I had some momentum. I had finished second in my last two tournaments at Houston and Atlanta and I felt I was at the top of my game. As I passed through Utica, New York, I saw some kids playing baseball in a park so I stopped, got myself a Coke and a hamburger and watched the whole game. I had been in Stamford, Connecticut, practicing for a few days and I was in no hurry. I stopped several times, just to enjoy a ball game or the scenery. It's a ten-hour drive but it took me two days.

I had come very close to winning my first tour title in my home state. I led the Houston Open at Champions, with two holes to go, but I was really nervous. I was playing with Roberto de Vicenzo, the fine player from Argentina who had lost a shot at the Masters championship a few weeks earlier when a scorecard error kept him from a playoff with Bob Goalby. I caused my downfall on the 16th hole, a par-3 with the pin over the bunker on the left, when I hit a 4-iron eight feet from the hole but missed the putt that would have given me a two-shot lead on Roberto. The two closing holes at Champions are difficult. I bogeyed the 17th, a long hole with a lake on the left, and Roberto parred to tie me. Then on 18, I shanked a 3-iron from the middle of the fairway and my ball almost went on the driving range. From there I putted the ball to three feet from the hole, but I missed the next one and Roberto won by a shot.

I shook hands with him and he looked at me with those big, soft eyes. In his broken English he said, "I thank you very much. You are young and you win many tournaments. I am old and maybe never have another chance to win one." I didn't feel all that bad, finishing second.

When I came in second again at Atlanta, it bothered me more. I shot a 74 the first round and I was solid hot when I walked off the 18th green. Clyde was standing there and she asked me a question, but I paid no attention to her. I hit a rope on the gate and it flew up and hit her in the eyes. It was a terrible, stupid thing for me to do. I felt so bad that I told her, "I'm going to win this tournament for you." I came close. I shot the next three rounds in the 60s, but Bob Lunn still beat me by two shots.

After spending some time practicing with my pals Joe Iazzi and John Homorsky in Connecticut, I felt relaxed and confident when I reached Rochester. I'd never been there, but I'd heard about Oak Hill, one of the top courses in America. It just turned out to be one of those weeks when everything went right.

To begin with, I stayed in the home of a family I hadn't met. I hadn't tried that before because I have my own way of relaxing away from the course. If I'm in a motel room I like to lie in bed and watch television or hit balls on the carpet until one or two o'clock in the morning. But when Paul Kircher wrote and told me his kids had picked me as the player they wanted to stay in their home during U.S. Open week, I accepted. With all those people around, I figured I'd always have somebody to talk to.

Paul had been a pitcher in the New York Yankees' farm system and was a good amateur golfer. He had done well in the insurance business in

Rochester and he and Barbara had five children then. They have seven now. They're a sweetheart of a family—Catholic and very religious.

They really knew nothing about me when they decided to invite me. Paul said later they picked me because I was new on the tour and they thought I might need some help with my expenses. They didn't even know if I could speak English.

When Paul took me to their home it was a hot afternoon and Barbara was wearing a black bathing suit like she was going swimming. Paul said, "Don't mind Barb. She dresses like this all the time." She was a very attractive lady and I couldn't help looking at her, walking around the house in a bathing suit.

Then I saw what she was doing in the kitchen. She was unpacking a whole box of canned Mexican food she ordered from El Paso. I told her I really didn't like Mexican food that much unless it was homemade and that I just liked some grapefruit and a little toast and bacon in the morning. I'm sure she still has that box of Mexican food to this day.

Maybe it was because the Kirchers made me feel comfortable at home that I felt so good at Oak Hill. I played practice rounds with Doug Sanders, who was one of the best players of the time. I was driving the ball extremely well and my putting was really good, I was using an old Tommy Armour putter with a gooseneck that my friend Dennis Lavender, the pro at Cedar Crest municipal course in Dallas, had fixed up for me a few weeks before when I was playing the Byron Nelson Classic. I'll never forget his words: "I'm going to fix you a putter you can win the Open with."

I was paired with Deane Beman and Gay Brewer the first two rounds and shot 69–68 to go three under par. Oak Hill was a very difficult course but I was splitting every fairway with my tee shots. My chipping and putting were strong. I had my game under control. Still, I didn't know if I had a chance to win.

Brewer was the real star in our threesome because he had won the Masters in 1967 and was another of the top players of that era. He had that perfect loop in his swing, which is a lot better than trying to take the club straight back and then bring it straight ahead to the ball. That's like trying to walk a straight line when you're drunk.

Beman had tremendous courage and an exceptional short game, but he was small and didn't have the strength to hit the ball well out of the rough. He had to lay up and sacrifice shots. If he'd had the strength of players like Nicklaus, Palmer, Player, Tom Watson or me, he never would have become the commissioner of golf. He'd be one of the superstars of the game.

But I was the one who was hot, and after two rounds I was second in the field, one shot behind Bert Yancey. We played together in the third round on Saturday and I shot 69 but Bert had 68, so he led by two when we teed off on Sunday. I was really pumped up. I knew that I was the underdog and that nobody expected me to win. We had a gallery following us, but there was a much bigger gallery behind us. The USGA had Palmer, who was almost in last place in the tournament, in the final twosome that day.

It's customary for players with high scores to tee off early in the round, but they changed it at Oak Hill because Palmer was so popular. That probably would bother me today because that big gallery walks up on you when you're putting. But I didn't pay any attention to it then.

I was wearing a red shirt, red socks and black pants that day, and for a long time after that it was traditional for me to wear those colors on Sunday. I called them my payday colors and I made them so popular that a lot of my gallery wore black and red on Sunday. Later I won the Chrysler tournament in Sydney, Australia, and received a new car, which I gave my mother-in-law. She asked for a black and red one and named it Payday.

But that day I was still just an unknown golfer who was dressed kinda strange. Palmer was playing right behind me and Nicklaus just ahead. A few times one of them gave me a puzzled look. It was like Butch Cassidy and the Sundance Kid watching that railroad detective who tracked them across the country and asking themselves, "Who is that guy?"

I believe that in his heart Yancey thought he had it won because I was the only person giving him any heat. Nicklaus was five shots behind me. But Yancey didn't know my outlook on life, and how I always had been an underdog. I knew I could shoot 80 and nobody would be surprised, but if I played well, it put pressure on Yancey, who was expected to win. I liked my position but I was still mighty nervous when we teed off.

I hit a low screamer and the ball barely got over the rough and onto the fairway. I took a bogey and I'm sure Yancey never dreamed I would play the next 17 holes two under par.

He didn't play well that day, but you couldn't tell it by watching him move around the course. He had gone to school at West Point and he always looked the same out there, a military man who walked down the fairway like he was marching. He was self-disciplined, a tall blond guy with a beautiful swing that made him the Gene Littler of that era—a machine. He also reminded me a lot of Don January . . . never in a hurry. He had one flow. Not so with myself. I get excited and I get a little fast.

Yancey's downfall came on 11, 12 and 13. I birdied the first two and he 3-putted 13, a par-5 that I also birdied with a 6-foot putt. That blew it open. I went to 14 with a 5-shot lead and all I wanted to do was finish. I parred that hole and then on 15, a relatively short hole, I hit the flag with an 8-iron. I'll never forget that because I asked my caddie, a kid named Kevin Quinn, "What do you think I ought to hit here?" "Five-iron," he said. And I said, "Man, you've got to be joking. My caddie's choking worse than I am."

As it was, an 8-iron was too much club. The ball bounced 15 feet from the hole but I 2-putted for a par. On 16 I made a nervous 7-footer for par, and then on 17 I hit the ball with my old Tommy Armour gooseneck and sank a 20-footer for a par after chipping up short. On 18, I missed the fairway to the left and when I wanted to get it out of the rough and back into the fairway with a sand wedge, my caddie wouldn't let me.

"You don't want to be remembered as the U.S. Open champion who laid up on the last hole," he said.

I took a 6-iron but I couldn't get the ball out of the rough, and I lost a stroke. I was solid hot so I took a sand wedge and took the hardest swing I could. The pin was set right by the bunker and I was aiming at the right of the center of the green just to get it on the green. The ball came out of that tall grass, went straight at the flag and stopped two feet from the hole. Then I realized if I made the putt I'd be the first man in history to shoot four rounds in the 60s in the U.S. Open. I made it. I had another 69 and won by four shots over Nicklaus, who had shot 66 to beat Yancey out of second place.

My 275 for 72 holes also tied the record set by Nicklaus at Baltusrol the year before, one that stood until Jack went back there and won the 1980 U.S. Open with 272. Nobody could say I backed into it.

Yancey had to feel miserable but he was nice to me. He put his arm around me, shook my hand and congratulated me. The most pleasing thing about winning that day was when Palmer finished the 18th and came over to me. He gave me a little hug and said, "Congratulations. You won the big one."

Then he finished his card out. As he walked off he hitched up his pants and the people fell out of the stands.

There were thousands around the green and five policemen escorted me through the crowd to the clubhouse. I hadn't had so much attention from the cops since I backfired my 1949 Ford on North Central Expressway when I was fifteen.

I had about twenty minutes to try and calm down in the USGA office before we went out for presentations. At the ceremony I sat next to Nicklaus and I can't remember what we talked about. I had seen him before but I had never talked to him.

The U.S. Open victory meant a big silver trophy, $30,000 prize money and the opportunity to win it again someday and prove my week at Oak Hill wasn't just a fluke. It also meant the mass-interview treatment in the press tent. I was still nervous and I was a completely different person, not smiling and answering questions straight on. Later I loosened up and we had some fun.

Someone asked how I would spend the prize money.

"I may buy the Alamo," I said, "and give it back to Mexico."

Hey, people remembered that back in Texas. When I went to San Antonio for the PGA championship a few weeks later everyone kept mentioning the Alamo, so I took a tour of it. When I came outside, I said, "Well, I'm not gonna buy this place. It doesn't have indoor plumbing."

I got away with that one better than I did my wisecrack a few years later when I went back to Rochester to be inducted into the Oak Hill Hall of Fame. They plant an oak tree in your honor and put your name on a plaque in front of it. So there was my tree out there with Walter Hagen's and Ben Hogan's.

"Thanks very much," I said, "but it probably will be my luck that this is the only tree the dogs use."

I never dreamed that tournament would do so much for my career. It gave me a tremendous amount of confidence. One, because it was the first one I ever won, and two, because of the caliber of the golf course, tournament and players. And since it was the U.S. Open, it gave me the impression that other tournaments wouldn't be as hard to win. Still, I never dreamed I would win twenty-five more tour championships in the next thirteen years.

When we were finished with all the celebrating in Rochester, I called Bill Eschenbrenner in El Paso and told him I wanted to come home soon and play golf with all my friends. I thanked Bill and Herb Wimberley for helping me get my Class A card, and he told me he'd get everybody together whenever I could get there.

A few weeks before, when I had been at Horizon Hills, I noticed Martin Lettunich was having trouble with his swing. I tried to help him. "Lee," he said, "I don't know any Mexican who can play golf."

I walked off, took a thirty-gallon barrel of balls to the other end of the range and started hitting them at him. Martin thought it was funny.

Well, when I went back there as U.S. Open champion, Martin asked me on that same practice tee, "Lee, what am I doing wrong?"

"Martin," I said, "I don't know any Mexican who can play golf."

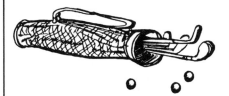

Super Mex, Super Mess

from *They Call Me Super Mex: The Autobiography of Lee Trevino*
by Lee Trevino and Sam Blair

When I arrived at Merion in June of 1971 I was thinking about what Nicklaus told me in March: "You just don't know how good a player you are. You can win anywhere." I also remembered what Walter Hagen once said: "Any player can win a U.S. Open, but it takes a helluva player to win two."

I had thought about that a thousand times since I won at Oak Hill three years before. Merion is a great old course on the Main Line in the Philadelphia suburbs, and as soon as I played a practice round there I felt this might be the time for me to move up in class.

I thought I had an excellent chance of winning because my game was starting to peak. At some point in the year your game will always peak, and mine had started to do it the past few weeks. Until then I had been in a semislump that started back in 1970.

That may seem a crazy thing to say about a year when I led the money list and won the Vardon Trophy, but a lot of my success came early in 1970. I won both my tournament championships during the first three months of the tour and then fell back. That's why I didn't qualify for the Tournament of Champions in April of 1971. There the field is made up of winners dating back to the previous Tournament of Champions. That week I said, "What the hell, I may as well go to Tallahassee and play."

Those people down in Florida put on a fine golf tournament for the guys who don't qualify for the Tournament of Champions. My game was sharp at Tallahassee and so was my attitude.

The night before the pro-am a young magazine writer came by my motel room to interview me for an instruction article. "I don't think you'll ever see me in a tournament for losers again," I told him. "It's time I started winning. I can feel it coming."

I won at Tallahassee and started rolling. I played well in Houston, Dallas and Fort Worth and then I won again at Memphis. When I reached Merion I had my putting stroke back, and my confidence. Merion suited me best of all the courses I had played at that time. It was relatively short—just over 6,500 yards—but with extremely high rough and small, well-contoured greens it demanded accuracy. And, like at Oak Hill, I got a break when it rained during the week. That softened the greens so that I could stop my low ball, which I always hit. With my flat swing I've never been able to hit the ball high.

A great example of how those soft greens helped was the 9-iron shot I hit on the 12th hole in the fourth round. The ball landed 20 feet past the flag, but I put backspin on it so it sucked back and stopped about four inches from the hole. With the kind of play around the greens, it came down to accuracy off the tee in order to win the tournament. If I kept my ball in the fairway, I had a fine chance.

I played extremely well that Sunday. I started the round in third place, two shots back, and I played in a twosome just ahead of Nicklaus and Jim Simons, the young amateur and college star. Simons was leading when we teed off but began to falter. It came down to Jack and me to decide the championship.

I played a little better than Jack, but he kept making some par-saving putts behind me to stay close. I had a one-shot lead through 17, and I felt if I could par 18 I would win because that was a helluva tough one for anyone to birdie. Merion's 18th probably was the most difficult finishing hole in U.S. Open history—a 458-yard par-4. You had to carry a small brook with your tee shot and the fairway started about 180 yards out. There was a double-tiered green with the lower tier in back, a very deep bunker on the right and a couple of bunkers on the left. And out-of-bounds was only about 15 feet left of the green. If you hit your ball over there, it might wind up on the veranda of the clubhouse.

I had just made a difficult downhill putt to par 17 and I hurried to the 18th tee, anxious to get on with it. I teed up my ball, stepped behind it and threw some grass up to see which way the wind was blowing, never taking my eyes off the driving area. That gave me a mental picture of how I wanted the ball to go. Then, with my eyes still fixed ahead, I put my hand out for my driver. This was a habit with me. I expected my caddie to put the grip right in my hand, where I could grab it, put it down and hit my ball.

Well, nothing hit my hand. I put my hand out again and nothing hit it. So I took my eyes off the fairway and looked around for my caddie. He wasn't there.

Just then, he squeezed through the crowd with my bag. He was a young law student who hadn't done much caddying and the pressure was getting to him. He had stopped for a drink of water.

"My God, where have you been?" I said.

Once I finally hit the ball I cut it just a little too much. It was a low fade down the left side of the fairway and my ball stopped half in the semi-rough, half in the fairway. As I studied my shot I heard a huge roar from the gallery back at 17. Nicklaus had made a helluva putt for a par, and to a lot of people it looked like he was going to steal the tournament.

If the ball had been sitting up clean, I probably would have hit a 2-iron or 1-iron and tried to roll it to the green because there was an opening between the bunkers in the front. But I decided to hit a 3-wood, cut it low and try to run the ball through the opening to the flag, which was in the back of the green. It was too much club and the ball hit near the gallery in back and bounced. There were so many people they couldn't move and my ball went into the crowd. I had a pretty good lie because all the grass was stepped down and my ball was sitting up. I chipped it up short and was left with a 6-foot putt. It was the type I dislike the most, one breaking from left to right, but if I made it I had a par and Nicklaus would be under tremendous pressure to birdie the hole and tie me.

I walked around it, stalked it and got ready to hit the ball. There must have been 20,000 people around the green but they were so quiet you could hear a pin drop. There was a sign that said, "No Cameras, Please" nailed on a tree behind the green. A young man had climbed up and was sitting on it about six feet off the ground. Just as I got ready to hit the putt the damn nail came loose and he fell. It distracted me and I pulled away from the putt.

"Is he all right?" I asked. Somebody said, "Yes. No problem." But my concentration was broken. I didn't hit a good putt and missed it to the right.

I holed out for a bogey, giving me par-70 for the round and 280 for the tournament. Now Nicklaus could beat me with a birdie. He already had hit his drive long down the middle of the fairway, and it looked like he could hit a 5- or 6-iron into the green. The pin placement wasn't that difficult. It was in the dead middle, and if he pitched his ball in front, it was going to run down to the hole because of the slope.

I signed my card and ran into the locker room. Nicklaus had left his iron shot 14 feet short of the pin, and if he sank the putt, he had won another U.S. Open championship. I couldn't stand to stay out there and watch him.

It was a very warm day and the locker room wasn't air-conditioned, so all the windows were open. I heard the crowd go silent and I stood there with my eyes closed. Then I heard thousands of voices go up: "Ah-h-h-h . . ." And then down: "Oh-h-h-h!" I opened my eyes and grinned. "Now we've got a playoff," I said. I began thinking about another 18 holes on Monday. This is the only U.S. tournament that has not changed to sudden-death.

I saw the putt on film and to this day I don't know how it stayed out. He hit a great putt down that slope but it hung on the left side of the cup and slid two inches past.

In the press conference afterward, we were kidding back and forth and someone asked me, "What do you think your chances are in the playoff?"

"My chances are just as good as Jack's," I said. "The pressure is on him. He's the best ever, the odds-on favorite. If I lose, people expect it. If he loses, it makes me look like a hero."

What the hell, I thought, I might as well try a little reverse psychology.

When we waited at the first tee the next day, I felt it was my time to win. He had scrambled a lot in the fourth round to tie me. But I was nervous. We had five minutes until tee time and my glove was soaked from sweat.

I was joking with the crowd while I reached in my bag for a fresh glove. I found a rubber snake in there that I bought my daughter at the Fort Worth Zoo a few weeks earlier. I had pulled it out on the 18th green at Colonial and scared Miller Barber's caddie, Herman Mitchell, so bad that he damn near ran into Crampton's Lake.

I slipped on the fresh glove and then held up the snake. Everybody laughed, including Nicklaus. "Throw that over here and let me see it," he told me. I tossed the snake to him, he looked it over, shook his head and threw it back to me. The next day a lot of stories said I scared him with that snake.

The way I played the first hole you'd have thought *I* was scared. I pushed my 9-iron into the bunker and then missed my putt, causing me to settle for a bogey. Jack drove the middle of the fairway, left his second shot 15 to 20 feet from the hole and two-putted for a par.

But on the next two holes he hooked his ball into the left bunkers and hit some poor shots, trying to get out. I parred both holes and took a one-shot lead. But, more important, I realized he was nervous, too.

But when I bogeyed 6 he pulled even. Then on 8 I left my second shot six inches from the hole and birdied to take the lead again. I was in control the rest of the way. I made a 35-foot putt on 12, a 25-footer on 15 and then I rolled a 65-footer just inches short on 16 to save a par. I believe Jack could see he had run out of holes. He bogeyed 17 and I took a 3-shot lead. This time I had no trouble on 18. I hit an iron into the front bunker but I blasted the ball out and it landed just four feet from the cup. It was the easiest putt in the world.

I finished with a 68, still three shots ahead of Jack, and I had my second U.S. Open championship. Hello, Walter Hagen!

Jack was very gracious when he congratulated me. "You played absolutely fantastic," he said. And the crowd loved it, even though it was mostly the wealthy, country-club set. The American dream is to see the underdog win, but you find that happening less in a sport like golf. And I believe my victory pleased the average fan across the country. I represent the public golf courses, the working man, the blue-collar worker.

That playoff taught me something else. The good Lord doesn't give you everything. He kept one thing from Jack Nicklaus: his sand wedge. He's a poor wedge player, out of the fairway and out of the bunker. If he had been a good wedge player, I sure wouldn't have beaten him that day at Merion. He left his ball in two bunkers and chili-dipped two wedges.

But the Lord kept a hook from me. I might even have won the Masters if I had that.

I had to fly to Cleveland that night, so my only celebration was drinking a few Scotches on the plane. But the next day during a practice round I enjoyed one of the special moments of my life.

Bob Goalby and I never had been close. When I first came on the tour he didn't appreciate my loud, outgoing ways. When I won the U.S. Open in 1968 he wasn't impressed. "In five years," he told someone, "we'll be playing benefits for that guy." But now he was running across two fairways to see me.

"I want to shake your hand," he said, "and I want to tell you one thing. That was the greatest exhibition of golf I've ever seen. I'm proud of you."

The Best Round Ever?

from *U.S. Open: Golf's Ultimate Challenge* by Robert Sommers

Nicklaus had now won thirteen of the major tournaments, the same number but not the same events as Bobby Jones had won. It is difficult for men with the driving ambition and enormous egos necessary to reach apogee in any field to have heroes, but if Nicklaus had one, it was Jones. Jack had grown up in Columbus, Ohio. His father, Charles Nicklaus, was the owner of several pharmacies and held a membership in the Scioto Country Club, where Jones had won the 1926 Open. When Jack was a young boy, his father had told him stories of Jones. Indeed, Jones was a hero to the entire club, and so it was only natural for young Jack to set him up as an idol.

When he retired after winning the original Grand Slam, Jones had won thirteen national championships—five U.S. Amateurs, one British Amateur, three British Opens, and four U.S. Opens. By the beginning of 1973, Nicklaus had won two U.S. Amateurs, four Masters Tournaments, two British Opens, two PGA Championships, and three U.S. Opens. He had not won the British Amateur.

At what point an idol becomes a rival is difficult to say. Indeed, it is not altogether certain that Nicklaus ever looked on Jones as anything other than a hero, but nevertheless Jack was driven to surpass Bobby's record, and by June of 1973 hardly anyone doubted he would.

The key goal was that fourth Open. Twenty years had passed since Hogan had won his fourth in 1953, and eleven years had gone by since Jack had won his first in 1962. Hogan had won his last and Nicklaus his first at Oakmont, and now the Open was back to that homely old course in the rolling hills of western Pennsylvania.

Oakmont was seventy years old by then, but it was expected to be just as tough as ever. It was twenty-seven yards longer than it had been in 1962, its fairways were still narrow, it was well bunkered—perhaps even excessively bunkered (thirty-three new ones had been added, bringing the total to 187)—and its greens were still the fastest in American golf, cut at three thirty-seconds of an inch for everyday play and even shorter for the Open. To emphasize driving accuracy, the USGA set fairway widths to an average of thirty-five yards—some short holes were narrower, some long holes were wider—but Oakmont members must have a masochistic streak in them, because the USGA ordained that two fairways had to be widened; they were too narrow for the Open field.

Oakmont made one other change, revising the 17th, which had always been its weakest hole. Hogan had driven the green in the last round in 1953 and birdied, and Palmer had driven it in the third round in 1962 and eagled. A new tee was built back in a wooded hollow behind and to the left of the old tee, the fairway was shifted to the right, and instead of 292 yards, it played now at 322 yards, with a big, sweeping right-to-left curve that brought into play the bunkers that framed the elevated green. The approach now had to carry those bunkers and hit and hold a shallow green. The 17th was much more satisfactory than it had been; no one could drive it now. But someone did.

Anticipation was at an unusually high pitch as the championship approached, the feeling more feverish than it had been in years. The reasons were varied. In addition to the game's having become a more popular spectator sport to begin with, Nicklaus was going for his fourth Open, his fourteenth major championship, and Palmer was still able to generate excitement, especially so close to home. This had been the scene of the confrontation of 1962, when Nicklaus had beaten Palmer, and Pennsylvania golf fans wanted revenge.

The weather for the first round was ideal for golf. The air was warm and light, and a little breeze blew from the west, helping the tee shots on the 17th. When he had finished sixteen holes, Nicklaus was two over par and unhappy, and seeing a chance to make up the strokes he had lost, he went for the 17th green. Drawing back his driver in his usual high arc, Jack swung with a combination of sheer power and perfect timing. The ball soared off in a high parabola, came down twenty yards short of the green, took one big bounce over the bunkers, and rolled ten feet from the cup. He holed the putt for an eagle 2 and finished the day at 71, four strokes behind Gary Player, who shocked the gallery by shaving four strokes from a sturdy par of 71 and shooting 67.

For Player to be at the front of the field was somewhat surprising, because he had been hospitalized for twelve days in February for surgery on his bladder, and had played in only three tournaments in five months. His 67 was a remarkable score, for Oakmont had been its usual difficult self, yielding birdies grudgingly. Player was enjoying a three-stroke lead over Lee Trevino, Jim Colbert, and Raymond Floyd, the only other men under par. Only six others matched par, and some of the scores were startling. Billy Casper shot 79, Bruce Devlin 76, Dow Finsterwald, Doug Ford and Bob Murphy, 77, Tony Jacklin 75, and Orville Moody 78. It looked as if this would be another trying week.

Then something happened overnight, and Oakmont was a different course on Friday. The greens had become soft, and the players were firing at the flagsticks without fear. The golf course was defenseless; it had never seen a day like this. Early in the day Gene Borek, a club professional from Long

Island who was in the field as an alternate, shot 65 and broke the course record. Altogether nineteen men broke par. Brian Allin shot 67, Colbert 68, and nine others had 69, including Vinny Giles, the National Amateur champion, who had a great finish. Against a par of 4-3-4-4 he shot 2-3-3-3, holing a full 6-iron on the 15th, barely missing a birdie on the 16th, and holing short birdie putts on the 17th and 18th.

The sprinkling system was blamed. Unlike those at Pebble Beach and Merion, Oakmont's greens are large, and to be at their best, they must be firm and fast. Simply hitting them shouldn't be enough; you should be forced to hit the right spot. Reaching those spots is difficult if the greens are firm, but Pittsburgh had had a rainy spring, and on the Tuesday night before the championship began, Oakmont was hit by a thunderstorm. The weather had been clear and dry since then, and the course was becoming fast, just as it should be. When he shot his 67, Player said that by Sunday everybody would know just how good a round that was. Both P. J. Boatwright, the man most responsible for running the Open, and Harry Easterly, then the chairman of the championship committee, were satisfied the greens had the proper pace, and after a conversation with Lou Scalzo, the club's greenkeeper, they agreed to sprinkle for only five minutes overnight. Exactly what happened was never clear, but most likely someone made a mistake and allowed the sprinklers to run longer than they should have. Oakmont was never right again.

In the easier conditions, Player went around in 70, and while he clung to his lead, he was only a stroke ahead of Colbert, with 137 to 138. It was evident by now that Player's game was not as steady as his scores implied. With only twenty-nine putts for the round, he should have done better than 70, but five times he had to one-putt to save pars. Because he had been away from the game for so long, he did not have his usual competitive edge.

Nicklaus was hardly playing any better, but he was sharper competitively, and he could score. He birdied three of the last six holes, shot 69, and climbed to within three strokes of Player with 140. Palmer stood two strokes farther back after a second 71, but he was erratic. Every time he birdied, he threw the stroke away with a bogey. In thirty-six holes, he had had eight birdies, eight bogeys, and twenty pars.

Already saturated, Oakmont was hit by another storm early Saturday morning. Rain began falling heavily at about 5:30, stopped briefly three hours later, but began in earnest once again at about 9:30. It stopped in time for the first starting time at 10:20, but then fell heavily off and on throughout the day, occasionally interrupting play. While the greens had been soft on Friday, they were like mush on Saturday. Where the ball hit, it stopped. The course was playing easier than it ever had, but Player's game collapsed, and he shot 77. Six men broke 70, and when the round ended, four shared the lead at 210, another had 211, and three others had 212. Eight men were bunched within two strokes.

Jerry Heard was one of those at 210, after shooting 66, the low round of the day. A strapping six-footer who had dropped out of college to join the pro Tour in 1969, Heard said hitting irons to the greens was like throwing darts. He was tied with John Schlee, a lean, sandy-haired veteran with a flat, unattractive swing, fifty-three-year-old Julius Boros, and Palmer.

With so many bunched so close, and with Palmer among the leaders, a dramatic climax was shaping up for Sunday's final round, but some spectators who flooded through the gates came only to see Arnold. They had only a vague acquaintance with golf. To wit:

One man ran up to another and asked, "Where's the next par?"

Another wondered, "Do they change the pins for every group coming through?"

Still another looked at Arnold with green envy. Watching how the female spectators reacted as Palmer strode by, he turned to his companion and said, "Can you imagine being Arnold Palmer and single?"

Sunday was an uncomfortable day. Clouds hung low and the humidity pressed down, and because the overcast blocked the sun, the greens remained soft and receptive, raising the probability of low scoring. Nevertheless, no one was prepared for what happened.

Johnny Miller, a lanky, blond Californian who hit wonderfully straight and crisp irons and who had won two tournaments since dropping out of Brigham Young University to join the Tour in 1969, left the 1st tee an hour before the leaders. When he had left his motel that morning, he had told his wife to pack and be ready for a quick exit from Pittsburgh; after shooting an untidy 76 on Saturday, Miller had 216 for fifty-four holes and stood six strokes behind the leaders. To reach the top, he would have to pass twelve men; clearly, he was going nowhere.

Miller began the last round by playing a straight drive down the middle and then drilling one of his pretty, precise irons—a 5-iron here—five feet from the cup and holing the putt for a birdie.

"That's not too bad," he told himself. On to the 2nd.

After another straight drive, Miller almost holed his 9-iron; the ball sat down six inches from the cup for another birdie. On the 3rd he looked out at the Church Pew bunkers and smacked another long, straight drive and a 5-iron twenty-five feet past the hole. The putt fell; three under.

The fairway of the 4th, a 549-yard par 5, swings in a long crescent through a narrow opening past the Church Pews on the left and a grouping of five other bunkers on the right, through coarse and heavy rough to another slick and undulating green set at an angle to the approach. After another fine drive, Miller tried to reach the green with his second, but his 3-wood drifted into a greenside bunker on the right. He almost holed his recovery and had his fourth straight birdie. He had begun the day three over par and now he was one under for fifty-eight holes. For the first time it occurred to him that he could win.

No one was paying attention to Miller yet though, because at about this time the leaders were going off the 1st tee. Schlee was paired with Palmer, playing ahead of Boros and Heard, who were the last two men off. After Saturday's round, Schlee had tried to explain why he was playing so well. A disciple of astrology, he said, "My horoscope is just outstanding. Mars is in conjunction with my natal moon." Something must have tilted overnight, because he pushed his drive out of bounds and made 6 on the 1st hole. He would be back, though.

With so many players grouped so tightly, and almost all of them playing so well, it was impossible to tell what was happening through the first nine holes. Nicklaus set off a roar when he birdied the 2nd, but then so did Colbert, Trevino, Bob Charles, and Tom Weiskopf. From then on through the end of the first nine, the situation changed quickly and repeatedly. Caught up in the frenzy, spectators dashed back and forth as one man after another went ahead, then fell back. Three men held the lead at one time or another—Heard after he birdied the 2nd, Palmer after a birdie on the 4th, then Boros after birdies on the 4th and 6th. As soon as they grabbed the lead, they lost it. After nine holes, Boros, Palmer, and Weiskopf shared the lead at four under par, and Trevino, Schlee, and Heard were three under.

Miller, meantime, had cooled off. After reeling off routine pars on the 5th, 6th, and 7th, he three-putted the 8th from thirty feet. Three under for the day now, he was four strokes behind the leaders, but he could pick up one with a birdie on the 9th, a short, uphill par 5. A drive, then a 2-iron, and he was on the green, but forty feet from the cup. A good lag putt put him close, and he holed the short second putt for the birdie. Out in 32 and four under par for the round, one under for sixty-three holes. Now he was closer, but a quick glance at the scoreboard showed him how tight the race had become. No one was folding; he needed more birdies.

A drive and 5-iron to twenty feet on the 10th. No birdie there. Then a break on the 11th. His wedge from the crest of the hill stopped fourteen feet away, and the putt fell. Five under for the day, two under for the distance. Closing in. Now for the 12th, 603 yards winding through wiry rough and deep bunkers. A drive into the rough, his first off-line drive of the day. No chance to do anything with this shot; just play it out to safety. A 7-iron to the fairway, then a marvelous 4-iron to fifteen feet. The putt dropped. Six under for the day, three under for the distance. Almost there.

Most of the gallery was still across the Pennsylvania Turnpike following

Palmer, Boros, Nicklaus, and the others, but as word of Miller's hot streak spread, they raced for the footbridge that spans the Turnpike, clogging the approaches and cramming their way through. Risking serious injury, some fans climbed onto the foot-wide railing and crawled across on hands and knees while cars and trucks whizzed past below at mile-a-minute speeds. Others slipped off the course and fought their way through heavy traffic inching along a road that borders the club, then cut back onto the Oakmont grounds.

Miller kept up the pace. A 4-iron to five feet on the 13th and another putt dropped. Seven under for the day, four under for the distance. He'd caught up, and now only Palmer was tied with him. Another birdie chance on the 14th from twelve feet, but the ball stopped an inch from falling. Now for the 15th, one of the strongest holes in American golf, a 453-yard par 4 with a narrow fairway only thirty-four yards wide, bordered on the left by a smaller version of the Church Pews and on the right by a mammoth bunker that begins twenty yards ahead of the green and runs almost to the back edge. Putting something extra into the shot, Miller drove his ball 280 yards. Now a 4-iron. The ball hit the green, hopped once, and skidded ten feet away. Miller rolled the ball into the center of the hole. Eight under par for the round and finally into the lead at five under par for sixty-nine holes. Only three holes left.

Palmer, meanwhile, was coming up the 11th not aware of Miller's surge. He was four under par then, and after a good tee shot he played a lovely pitch just four feet to the right of the hole. It seemed just like old times. If he kept playing as he was, he would surely win and have that second Open he had tried so hard for all those years. He was forty-three years old then, and he would probably have no more opportunities; he had to take advantage of this one. When he made this putt, he would be five under par, and that should be good enough.

Arnold was about to suffer three shocks that upset him so badly he never recovered.

First, he missed the putt and remained four under par. It hurt, but he believed he was still leading by a stroke over Schlee, Weiskopf, and Boros. Still confident, he strode over to the 12th tee and played what he thought was a perfect drive, shading the left side where the ground slants to the right and will kick the ball to center-fairway. He was so confident he had played the shot perfectly, he hitched his pants, and with an assured, tight-lipped smile, he turned away and didn't watch the ball land.

Then, as he and Shlee left the tee, Arnold glanced at a scoreboard. Squinting through the branches of a tree, Palmer made out a red 5 down on the bottom of the board indicating that someone was five under par and a stroke ahead of him. He couldn't quite make out the name.

Palmer was stunned. His confident grin faded and, bewildered, he asked Schlee, "Who's five under?"

"Miller," Schlee answered. "Didn't you know?" Shock number two.

Then, as he and Schlee approached the landing area, they saw only one ball in the fairway. Assuming it was his, Arnold strode up to it, but when he looked down, he saw it was Schlee's. Instead of bouncing right, Palmer's ball had jumped left into heavy rough. Shock number three. He bogeyed the 12th, then followed with two more bogeys on the 13th and 14th. There would be no second Open.

Now it was only a matter of Miller's holding on. A 3-wood to forty feet on the 16th and two putts for a par 3; a 1-iron and a wedge to ten feet on the 17th and another par; then a huge drive on the 18th, a 7-iron to twenty feet, and two more putts for his final par. Out in 32, back in 31. A 63, the lowest round ever shot in the Open.

Miller finished with 279, four strokes better than Hogan had shot in 1953 and than Nicklaus and Palmer had shot in 1962, and twenty strokes under Sam Parks's 299 of 1935.

But it wasn't over yet; two men could still catch him.

Schlee had rallied after his 6 on the 1st hole, and now he could tie Miller with a birdie on the 18th. His second shot rolled over the green into clumpy rough about fifty feet from the hole. He would have to chip. The crowd hushed and Miller stood and watched as Schlee set himself. He played a courageous shot, gauging the distance just right, but he pulled the ball a trifle left of the hole and made 4.

Miller relaxed. Only Weiskopf was left, and he would have to hole his second shot on the 18th to tie. He didn't, and Miller was the champion. Schlee finished second, one stroke behind at 280, and Weiskopf was third at 281. Palmer, Trevino, and Nicklaus all shot 282, and Boros and Heard finished with 283, tied with Lanny Wadkins.

Miller had played a phenomenal round. He had hit every green and had missed only one fairway on the driving holes. His irons were inspiring. He had hit five shots inside six feet (two of them inside one foot), two more to ten feet, and three others to fifteen feet or less. He had birdied nine holes and had bogeyed only the 8th, where he had three-putted. His 63 had broken the record set first by Lee Mackey at Merion in 1950, then matched by Tommy Jacobs at Congressional in 1964, and by Rives McBee at Olympic in 1966.

As soon as Miller posted his score, a natural question arose: Was it the greatest round ever played in the Open? Did it rank with the 65 Arnold Palmer shot at Cherry Hills in 1960, the round that carried him to the championship from seven strokes behind, or with Ben Hogan's closing 67 at Oakland Hills in 1951?

No, it didn't. While it was an extraordinary score, it was done over a course softened by rain. Miller's shots required nowhere near the control of Palmer's and Hogan's, because they played their rounds over fast and firm courses. For them to hold those hard greens, Palmer and Hogan had to play to certain spots on the greens and apply fierce backspin to stop the ball. Miller didn't have to do that: Oakmont's greens were so soft and mushy, any kind of shot would hold.

Nevertheless, Miller had played the course as he found it, and he had played it better than anyone else. As for controlling his emotions, while it is true he had no thoughts of winning when he had begun in the morning, he had realized he had a chance after he birdied the first four holes, and he had birdied five more after that. Furthermore, a 63 on no matter what kind of course is something special, and even though Oakmont was playing easier in 1973 than it had ever played, it was still among the more challenging tests in American golf.

Miller's 63 wasn't the best ever, but it was close.

Sunday, June 16

Tom Watson and Hale Irwin: Two for the Title?

from *Massacre at Winged Foot: The U.S. Open Minute-by-Minute*
by Richard Schaap

If someone had wagered before the start of the 1974 United States Open that the two leaders going into the final round would be two men born in the same state, he would have had a pretty good offbeat bet. He could have won with Jack Nicklaus and Tom Weiskopf, both from Ohio; or with Johnny Miller and Jerry Heard, both from California; or with Lee Trevino and Frank Beard, both from Texas.

But he never would have suspected that he would win with two men from Missouri—Tom Watson, born in Kansas City, and Hale Irwin, born in Joplin.

Watson and Irwin will be the final twosome to tee off on the final day of the Winged Foot Open, and despite similar geographical backgrounds, they have arrived at this point through two totally different routes. As one of the top fifteen performers on the 1973 PGA tour, Irwin was among the twenty-nine exempt players who automatically qualified for the Open. Watson had to fight his way into the tournament. He competed in the sectional qualifying round two weeks ago at Charlotte, North Carolina, and shot 72-73 for 145. If he had taken one more stroke, Watson would have been forced into a playoff for an Open berth. (Back in 1936, a little-known pro named Tony Manero struggled through a qualifying playoff to reach the U.S. Open, then won the whole tournament by two strokes.)

Although Irwin has won only twice on the tour and is virtually unknown except among dedicated golf fans, he is, at the age of twenty-nine, one of the most successful golfers in the world. In 1971, he won $99,473 and placed thirteenth on the money list; in 1972, he won $111,539 and again placed thirteenth; in 1973, his finest year, he finished in the top ten twelve times (including his second victory in the Heritage Classic), won $130,388 and place seventh on the money list; already in 1974, he has posted two seconds and two fourths (including a fourth in the Masters) and has won $96,936, putting him eighth on the list. Not bad for an unknown.

Irwin's lack of image can be traced partly to his appearance and manner. He wears glasses, dresses smartly but conservatively and could pass for a college marketing major, which he was. He seems mild and businesslike, which puts him among the majority in his sport. His skill as a college football player might distinguish him from his fellow pros, but he was a defensive back, and collegiate defensive backs rarely win headlines; besides, he now weighs fifteen pounds less than he did in college and, at six feet and 165 pounds, he does not look like an ex–football player. His skill as a college golfer might distinguish him—he did win the national collegiate championship in 1967—but NCAA champions are no rarity on the pro tour; a new one shows up almost every year. The trouble is there is nothing dramatic about Irwin, nothing flamboyant. He is, in many ways, the typical touring golf pro—too typical.

Tom Watson, on the other hand, is not a typical golf pro. True, he is twenty-four years old, just like Lanny Wadkins. And he was born during the first ten days of September, just like Arnold Palmer. And he comes from Missouri, just like Larry Ziegler. And he went to college in California, just like Jerry Heard. And he majored in psychology, just like John Mahaffey. And he married a Jewish girl, just like, well, Bruce Fleisher.

Yet Tom Watson is unique. For one thing, he is the tour's only twenty-four-year-old Missouri-born, Stanford-educated, psychology-trained Virgo with a Jewish wife. For another, he may be the only professional golfer who rooted openly for George McGovern to win in 1972 against Dwight D. Eisenhower's former caddy.

Watson is a liberal—with everything except his golf strokes—and that automatically sets him apart from his fellow pros, most of whom shared Frank Beard's feeling, a few years before Watergate, that the ideal national political ticket would have to include Spiro Agnew, Martha Mitchell, William Buckley and perhaps, as a sop to the radicals, Richard Nixon.

Tom Watson comes by his political interests naturally. His grandfather, Isaac Newton Watson, helped to break up the corrupt Prendergast machine in Kansas City.

He comes by his golfing instincts naturally, too. His father, a prosperous insurance broker, got as far as the fifth round of the U.S. Amateur in 1950, two weeks before Tom was born.

Tom began playing the game when he was six and, in his teens, won the Missouri amateur championship four times. He competed often in the U.S. Amateur, but never finished higher than fifth. In 1969, the year he placed fifth, he came in six strokes ahead of Bill Hyndman, the man whom his father had defeated in the same tournament, at match play, nineteen years earlier.

In 1974, Watson's game is maturing. He is one of the most consistent golfers on the tour. He has played in eighteen tournaments, and he has survived the cut eighteen times. He has not once taken more than 288 strokes for seventy-two holes, and he has finished among the top ten in seven tournaments, the top twenty in twelve, including his last seven in a row. He has shot only one round higher than 75 all year, and nothing higher than a 74 in almost three months.

If Watson's consistency is a strong asset on the last day of the 74th U.S. Open, his record under pressure is not. He has been in position to win several times, and so far, he has not. He started the last round of the Los Angeles Open one stroke behind winner Dave Stockton and finished fourth, the last round of the Doral Open three strokes behind winner Bud Allin and finished ninth, the last round of the Byron Nelson classic two strokes behind winner Bud Allin (again) and finished second, and the last round of the Memphis Open two strokes behind winner Gary Player and finished fourth.

In 1973, his second year on the pro tour, Watson came even closer to victory: he led the Hawaiian Open after each of the first three rounds, but then faded to third; he shot an incredible 62 in the fifth round of the two-week $500,000 World Open and led the field after the fifth, sixth and seventh rounds, then staggered home in a tie for fourth.

Of course, in the World Open, only a $100,000 first prize was at stake. Today, Tom Watson is bidding for something bigger: the most prestigious title in golf.

9:15 A.M.

Linda Watson is in the coffee shop of the White Plains Hotel, eating breakfast with two pro golfers, Leonard Thompson and Tommy Aaron (who missed the cut and is not playing today). Her husband is still up in Room 206, sleeping. He slept through the night surprisingly well; Linda knows, because she didn't. She is more nervous than her husband. "You're choking, Linda," says Tommy Aaron with a smile.

9:30 A.M.

It is raining at Winged Foot, a steady drizzle which could, if it worsens, force Tom Watson and Hale Irwin and Arnold Palmer to spend another twenty-four hours thinking about their positions in the U.S. Open or, if it lessens, could make putting on the Winged Foot greens almost a pleasurable experience.

The rain is holding down the crowd, and attendance today will reach only 12,831, the lowest of the four days of actual competition. The attendance for the week is about 75,000, not spectacular for any major golf tournament, but not surprising in the metropolitan New York area, where other distractions, some more interesting than golf, are available.

10:11 A.M.

The first twosome of the fourth day of the 74th U.S. Open goes off the first tee: Andy Bean, the Florida college student who briefly held first place two days ago, and Bill Hyndman, the Philadelphia stockbroker who has competed in national championships against two generations of golfers. They are two of the three amateurs still in the Open, and they are tied for last place, each twenty-three strokes over par. The other amateur, Jay Haas, Bob Goalby's nephew, is twenty over. Each of the trio is guaranteed a golf medal, but, still, each wants to be low amateur—for the prestige and for the automatic berth in the U.S. Amateur in August.

10:32 A.M.

Jay Haas is on the first tee, paired with pro Jim Simons, who was the low amateur by eleven strokes going into the final round at Merion three years ago. Haas is an undergraduate at Wake Forest, Simons an alumnus; the school has seven representatives among the sixty-six men teeing off today, including Arnold Palmer and Lanny Wadkins.

10:39 A.M.

John Buczek and Barney Thompson stand in the drizzle on the first tee, wet and forgotten. Two days ago, both were in strong contention for the U.S.

Open championship. Now they are both nineteen strokes over par, sixteen strokes behind the leader.

11:40 A.M.

In the press tent, Sandy Tatum of the USGA is wearing a windbreaker instead of the USGA blazer he has been seen in all week. He is wet from walking in the rain, but his pipe is still lit. He picks up a walkie-talkie and says, "This is Sandy Tatum, to all USGA officials. Will you please make sure to tell me when there is an accumulation of water on any green that is affecting the conditions of play?"

Someone asks him what the prospects are for getting the round in, and Tatum looks gloomy. "We're receiving reports from the local airport," he says, "that the weather is going to continue like this for two days. So our decision about whether to continue play is affected by the fact that it is only going to get worse.

"There are two factors involved here. One is that we want to complete our championship in the scheduled time. The other is that we want it to be a true test of the skills we think are necessary for a champion."

Tatum puffs on his pipe. "We're thankful," he goes on, "that we've had three days of weather that allowed the course to be played as we would like it to be. And this includes the effects that the wind had yesterday. We are not running a tour event. I don't mean to be demeaning. Surely, the success of the tour events shows something. But we have certain feelings about what a champion should be required to do.

"Those feelings begin on the tee. We feel the golfer should be able to drive the ball within an area forty to forty-five yards wide. If he does not, he should be penalized half a stroke. His next shot should be placed properly on the green."

Tatum looks out at the darkening skies. "People can be critical of us in two ways," he says. "They can be critical of the concept—or they can be critical of the execution of that concept."

It seems a reasonable explanation for the massacre at Winged Foot.

11:45 A.M.

For many of the contestants, there is no hope of winning, but a strong reason not to give up. "I'm only three shots out of fifteenth place," says David Glenz, who is at 225. "I sure could go for playing at Augusta and 'here' again next year." To qualify for the Masters, a golfer must make the top *sixteen* in the Open; to qualify for next year's Open, a golfer must make the top *fifteen*.

Not far from Glenz on the practice tee, Mike Reasor is entertaining similar thoughts. He is at 223, tied for sixteenth place, only a stroke out of fifteenth. "I'm thirty-two years old," says Reasor, "and it's about time I played in a Masters."

12:05 P.M.

Halfway through the battle for low amateur, Jay Haas clings to the lead, one stroke ahead of Andy Bean and six ahead of Bill Hyndman.

12:10 P.M.

He will not tee off for two hours, but Forrest Fezler is already in the locker room, staring out at the rain. He seems nervous, or pensive. He is not unfriendly, but he stays to himself, near his locker, reading a letter and responding to any questions with quick, one-word answers.

12:11 P.M.

Hale Irwin steps out the front door of the White Plains Hotel, looking for the courtesy car that will drive him to the golf course. He unbuckles the umbrella that is attached to his red and white golf bag. The rain is coming down hard.

"You'll need that today," someone says.

"You'd better believe it," says Irwin.

12:38 P.M.

As Jack Nicklaus prepares to drive off the first tee, a spectator calls out, "Jack, you need a 60 today."

"No, I don't," say Nicklaus, smiling. "I need a 58."

Both of them will be proven wrong. What Nicklaus really needs is a 61.

12:42 P.M.

Arnold Palmer enters the upper locker room and begins to thumb through his mail. He picks up a telegram, holds it at arm's length and still can't read it. A sportswriter offers his glasses. "Want to borrow these?" he says.

Palmer smiles. He seems relaxed, comforted by the knowledge that, at forty-four, he can still threaten to win a U.S. Open.

"You want to play today?" someone asks.

"Yes," says Palmer.

"You feel strong?"

"Yes."

"You feel like you can win?"

"I don't see why not," says Palmer.

12:55 P.M.

Creamy Carolyn is the clubhouse, holding court for a group of friends and reporters. Now he thinks his man can win. "After twenty-five years of golf," says Creamy, "he knows how to play in the rain. You just have to pull out a longer club. A four-iron is not a four-iron today. A three-iron is a four today."

Creamy is equally confident that next year touring caddies will be allowed to work in the Open. "I was talking to a USGA official," he says, "and we both agreed it's a big, big business. I asked him, 'When you go to a tournament, do you hire a waitress to be your secretary?'"

1:05 P.M.

Johnny Miller and Jerry Heard are paired, as they expected, and just for the sake of consistency, Johnny Miller bogeys the first hole for the fourth straight day.

1:10 P.M.

Hale Irwin looks out the locker room window at the gray skies. The drizzle has just about stopped. "The greens won't be slow," Irwin says, "but they'll be less quick. You never know exactly what it's going to be like. It's a whole new ball game."

"Do you mind playing in the rain?" a reporter asks.

"In the past," says Irwin, "I haven't played too well in the rain. But that's because I let it bother me."

The implication is clear that Irwin will not let the rain bother him today.

1:14 P.M.

As he comes to the first green, Hubert Green spars with the crowd. "What happened this week, Hubert?" someone asks.

"I've made mine already," Green snaps back, not very graciously. "How much have you made this year, pal?"

Green has a bit of a cruel streak, aggravated probably by his score and by spending time in New York, one of his least favorite places. "Anyone who lives around here deserves a medal," Green tells the gallery.

1:15 P.M.

Hale Irwin is trying on golf gloves. He picks out six that he likes and puts them in his golf bag. He'll change gloves whenever one gets slick. "Do you think Watson's a little anxious?" someone asks.

"I assume he is," says Irwin, "but a few others are, too."

"Is it possible for him to win, considering he's never won before?"

"It doesn't take a winner to win in a pressure situation," says Irwin. "But—it is difficult for Tom to have played an exceptional round yesterday and, hopefully, have to shoot an exceptional round today."

1:16 P.M.

The lockers assigned to contestants are arranged alphabetically, and several rows away from Hale Irwin, Tom Watson is sitting in front of his locker. "I spent a very restful night," he tells his own cluster of reporters. "More restful than I expected, actually."

Watson smiles. "I'm not thinking about the money," he says. "I'm thinking about the championship. Trevino and Nicklaus had their first victories in the U.S. Open. I'd like to do that."

1:17 P.M.

"Hale," a newspaperman says, "what does your middle initial stand for?"

"Nothing," says Hale Irwin. "It's just a middle initial S. My father's middle name is Spencer, but I just have S."

Irwin grins. "It can stand for stupid," he says, "or sometimes for smart."

Someone asks Hale Irwin if his football experience has helped him on the pro tour. "I can't say it's had any direct bearing," says Irwin, "but just the idea of competition, a challenge to overcome, that has to be some help. This golf course is a series of challenges."

"Were you drafted by an NFL team?"

"No," says Irwin, "but the St. Louis Cardinals sent me a questionnaire. You know, How big are you? How fast are you? When I saw the one about how fast are you, I threw it away."

1:20 P.M.

"You worried about the rain?"

"I shot a 68 in the last round at Memphis in the rain," says Tom Watson.

1:21 P.M.

"What was your instant reaction to the rain when you woke up?"

"My instant reaction was expletive-deleted," says Hale Irwin, deleting the expletive himself. "Rain gear, gloves, umbrella—it's a pain."

1:22 P.M.

"Did you ever imagine you'd be playing against Arnold Palmer for the U.S. Open title?"

"I think everybody dreams that," says Tom Watson.

1:23 P.M.

"I'm nervous," says Hale Irwin, "but I'm not shaking with anticipation."

1:24 P.M.

"My only philosophy," says Tom Watson, "is, I like my position."

1:25 P.M.

Hale Irwin closes his locker. "Excuse me, gentlemen," he says. "I have work to do."

1:26 P.M.

Tom Watson closes his locker.

"Do you like all this attention?" someone asks.

Watson nods. "Yes," he says, "I do. I'd like to give this kind of interview every week."

1:32 P.M.

On the second hole, Hubert Green watches his second shot hit the green and stop dead, thanks to the rain. "That sure is nice for a change," says Green.

1:35 P.M.

Seated in his office just off the veranda of the clubhouse, Sandy Tatum of the USGA seems to have relaxed. The rain has subsided. "Well, we've made it now," Tatum says. "The sky's going to hold up for us."

1:43 P.M.

On the third hole, Hubert Green watches his tee shot hit in a bunker and bury. "We sure won't miss these bunkers," says his wife, Judy, who is following him. "It was a lot more fun last week, in Philadelphia."

1:44 P.M.

A little-known professional named Bruce Summerhays, who was the first man to tee off in the 1974 U.S. Open, completes his fourth round with an 83, for a total of 315, a score that will stand up as the highest for seventy-two holes at Winged Foot.

Summerhays finished one stroke below the 316 that A. W. Tillinghast, the man who designed Winged Foot, shot in the 1910 U.S. Open.

1:55 P.M.

Jay Haas emerges from the scorer's tent as the low amateur in the Open, seven strokes ahead of Bill Hyndman and Andy Bean. Hyndman and Bean both closed with 81's, Haas with a 77 for 307.

"Are you thinking about turning pro?" a reporter asks Haas.

"On the basis of what I've seen here," says the youngest man to survive the cut, "I don't think my game is strong enough yet."

2:02 P.M.

Before the tournament began, Andy Bean said that if he did well, he would consider turning pro. "Right now," he says, as he empties out his locker, "I'm seriously considering an advanced degree in marketing."

2:05 P.M.

Lanny Wadkins hits out of the Winged Foot rough on the fifth hole, and his playing partner, Hubert Green, shouts, "It couldn't have been too bad a lie. I could still see your knees."

2:P.M.

Five strokes off the lead, awaiting his turn to tee off, Frank Beard stands on the small putting green near the first tee, holding his putter, but not practicing. "It's okay not to putt," says Beard.

"The only reason I ever do putt is because I see the big-name pros doing it. I don't worry about my putting—it's the Chinese fire drill from tee to green that gets me."

2:09 P.M.

Arnold Palmer is the last man off the practice tee, and as he marches away, the tee looks like some primeval relic, muddy and deserted.

On his way to the putting green, Palmer is besieged by well-wishers, including a crowd of young boys who practically step on his toes. "Careful, boys," says Palmer. "I've got to walk on them all day."

A female reporter walks up and asks, "What are you going to do on the fifth tee, remembering yesterday?"

Palmer obviously remembers the damaging bogey, but he seems stunned by the bluntness of the question. He is more accustomed to "How do you feel, Arnie?" He stares at the woman, blankly.

"Are you going to play it differently?" she says.

"I thought you were my friend," says Palmer.

"That's a stupid question, lady," says one of the youngsters pursuing Palmer.

2:13 P.M.

Hale Irwin's caddy, Peter McGarey, is on the edge of the putting green, waiting for his golfer. McGarey is sixteen years old. He used to live in Larchmont, not far from Winged Foot, then moved with his family to Arizona. He came back East strictly to caddy in the Open, hoping that he would draw a contending golfer.

McGarey hands his blue jacket to a friend. "Hold this for me," he says, "but be careful. I've got some brownies in the pocket."

2:20 P.M.

As Arnold Palmer approaches the first tee, he is engulfed by fans and by thunderous applause. A few steps behind him, Hale Irwin is ignored, except by three USGA officials who ask for his autograph.

2:22 P.M.

Frank Beard finds his drive off the first tee smack up against a tree in the right rough. He has no choice but to chip out to the fairway. His third shot is short of the green, his fourth is on and then he three-putts for a triple-bogey that sends him reeling to eleven over and out of a tie for fourth place. He has not won a tournament in three years, he has never won a major championship and he does not look as if he is about to break either frustrating streak.

2:23 P.M.

The rain stops, on cue, as Arnold Palmer steps on the first tee. His fans welcome the omen with more cheers. Palmer's playing partner for the fourth round is Jim Colbert, who played the first three rounds with Jack Nicklaus. "I guess they want me to settle down the elder statesmen this week," says Colbert.

Colbert hits first, a long, straight drive, rewarded by polite applause.

Then Palmer hits longer and straighter, and the Army explodes, first in cheers, then in a mad rush for position to watch the next shot.

2:25 P.M.

As Lou Graham and Forrest Fezler walk down the second fairway, followed by a few obscurity-worshipers, one fan who doesn't recognize them says, "Look, these guys must be doing good. They've got marshals with them.

The early guys didn't even get marshals. Nobody watches them. They can cheat if they want to."

"Hell," says a companion, "they're so far back, even if they cheated, they couldn't win."

2:29 P.M.

Jim Colbert hits a lovely shot to the first green, and the gallery responds with cheers. But the cheers are not for Colbert. "C'mon, Arnie, baby," a few members of the Army yell. "Put it inside him."

Palmer, too, reaches the green, and the Army roars.

Both men two-putt for pars.

2:30 P.M.

On the eighteenth hole, Al Geiberger is three under for his round, needing a birdie for a 66 that would break the Open record at Winged Foot. Instead, Geiberger takes a bogey and comes in with a 68 for 297, a total that could put him in the top sixteen.

"You have two thoughts out there," says Geiberger. "First, put it in the middle of the fairway. Then put it anywhere on the green. You have no thoughts of putting it in the hole."

Geiberger's playing partner, Charlie Sifford, comes in with an 80, for 309, and his chances of ever playing in a Masters grow slimmer each day.

2:42 P.M.

Bert Yancey sinks a twenty-five-foot putt for a birdie on the second hole and moves to seven over par, alone in fourth place, four strokes off the lead.

2:45 P.M.

On the first hole, Tom Watson's thirty-foot putt for a birdie slides four or five feet past the cup. The putt coming back is not easy, but Watson makes it, and as the ball dives into the cup, Linda Watson says, "Argh!" Or something very close to that.

"I'm so nervous," she says. "If I can just get by these first four holes, I'll be all right."

The first four holes are tough on everybody.

2:47 P.M.

On the second hole, Jim Colbert and Arnold Palmer both have birdie putts, Colbert from eighteen feet, Palmer from ten. Colbert two-putts, and then Palmer strokes his birdie attempt two feet past the hole. He misses the two-footer and slips back to seven over. The Army is restless. "Send us home happy, Arnie," someone yells, but the prospects do not seem good.

2:50 P.M.

Lou Graham and Forrest Fezler come off the third green, each with two pars and a bogey so far. A man with a six-pack of Budweiser points and says, "That's Forrest Fezler. He finishes second all the time."

2:53 P.M.

As Tom Watson and Hale Irwin step onto the second green, each headed for his second par, a spectator points at Watson and says, "Who's that?"

"Watson," he's told.

"I know. But what's his first name?"

2:58 P.M.

For the third straight hole, Arnold Palmer has a putt for a birdie, but his twenty-footer fails and he taps in his par. Jim Colbert bogeys the short hole and goes to nine over.

3 P.M.

THE STANDINGS

GOLFER	SCORE	HOLES
Watson	+ 3	56
Irwin	+ 4	56
Yancey	+ 7	57
Palmer	+7	57
Colbert	+ 9	57

3:02 P.M.

With no one else within three shots of them, the focus tightens on the Tom Watson–Hale Irwin pairing. Irwin is wearing dark blue slacks and a blue checkered shirt. Watson is wearing light blue slacks and a white shirt. The motif for the day is obviously blue. Linda Watson is carrying a blue bag with a pin on it that says, Mrs. Tom Watson.

As Irwin hits his tee shot on the third hole to within thirteen feet of the cup, Mrs. Tom Watson applauds and says, "Great!"

Her husband also hits the green, and both men two-putt for pars.

3:07 P.M.

As the sun breaks through, Arnold Palmer, for the fourth straight hole, putts for a birdie, and for the fourth straight hole, fails to break through. He gets his par to stay at seven over, and Jim Colbert takes his second straight bogey to fall to ten over.

3:20 P.M.

After Hale Irwin misses a seven-foot putt for a par on the fourth hole, Tom Watson has a two-stroke lead. For thirty seconds. Then Watson misses a six-footer, and he, too, takes a bogey.

3:22 P.M.

Arnold Palmer makes it five for five. He misses another birdie putt. He has now hit five greens in regulation, he has had five putts at birdies, only one of them longer than twenty-three feet, and yet he is one over for his round, seven over for the tournament, three strokes off the lead.

3:26 P.M.

After missing a fourteen-footer for a birdie on five and a nine-footer for a birdie on six, Gary Player sinks a three-foot birdie putt on seven and moves to nine over, within five shots of the leader. Player's guess that he could win with a 68 still looks reasonable.

3:30 P.M.

Chi Chi Rodriguez, in with a 73 for an even 300, is getting ready to leave the locker room. "I've got to play this course one more time," he says. "I have to play tomorrow—with some customers of a building company I work for." Chi Chi shrugs. "It's like going back to hell for a second time," he says.

3:37 P.M.

On the par-five fifth hole, Tom Watson three-putts from sixty-three feet, Hale Irwin two-putts from thirty, and the two men are tied for the lead, each five over par. As Irwin's putt goes in, Linda Watson claps, bravely.

3:38 P.M.

On the sixth hole, Arnold Palmer's string of missed birdie putts ends. Instead, he misses the green, then misses his putt for a par and slips to eight over par.

3:46 P.M.

Tom Watson and Hale Irwin record routine pars on the sixth hole and remain tied, three strokes ahead of Arnold Palmer and Bert Yancey, who has just bogeyed the short seventh hole.

3:56 P.M.

Forrest Fezler rolls in a six-foot birdie putt on the eighth hole to move to even for the day, nine over for the tournament, still very much alive.

3:57 P.M.

After bogeying the eighth hole, Gary Player triple-bogeys the ninth, ending all question of a Grand Slam in 1974. He is now three over for his round, thirteen over for the tournament, eight strokes behind with too few holes to play.

3:58 P.M.

Tom Watson and Hale Irwin both par the seventh hole, Irwin with a gutsy six-foot putt, and keep sharing the lead.

4 P.M.

THE STANDINGS

GOLFER	SCORE	HOLES
Watson	+ 5	61
Irwin	+ 5	61
Yancey	+ 8	62
Palmer	+ 8	61
Fezler	+ 9	62
Colbert	+ 9	61
Beard	+ 10	62
Graham	+ 10	62

4:06 P.M.

After two good drives on the eighth hole, followed by poor second shots into the left bunker, Tom Watson and Hale Irwin both miss long putts for pars and both go six over.

4:11 P.M.

As Bert Yancey comes off the ninth green, after playing the front nine in even par and moving within two strokes of the lead, his ten-year-old son, Charles, comes running up to him. "Beautiful," says the youngster. "Now we really need a birdie."

4:13 P.M.

Arnold Palmer bogeys the ninth hole, his second bogey in a row, and slips to ten over, once again four strokes behind the leaders.

4:14 P.M.

On the par-three tenth hole, Bert Yancey puts his tee shot into the right rough, and his ten-year-old son curses, then walks dejectedly toward the green. Yancey chips on and two-putts for a bogey.

4:17 P.M.

Tom Watson and Hale Irwin are both on the ninth green with their second shots, both facing long putts for birdies. Linda Watson is nervously trying to peek through the crowd. "Tom made the turn three over Friday," she says, hopefully, leaving unspoken the wish that Tom might duplicate his 33 on the back nine Friday.

"What we can use now is a snake," says Linda. She has been married to Tom for only eleven months, but she knows the terminology for long, successful putts.

The snake strikes—but not for Tom Watson. From thirty-five feet away, over a ridge, Hale Irwin curls his putt into the cup and, as the ball falls, he breaks into a happy little dance, his first sign of emotion all day. Irwin's birdie is only the second on the ninth hole all day; Steve Melnyk got the first two hours ago.

Now Irwin is back to five over, and Watson starts to line up his twenty-five-foot bid to regain a tie. "There's a lot of pressure on this kid now," says a spectator, not realizing he's standing next to Watson's wife.

Watson strokes the putt, and misses, and slips to second place. "He birdied the tenth hole Friday and Saturday," says Linda Watson, hopefully.

4:18 P.M.

Hale Irwin's wife is beaming, fifteen hundred miles away, in Kirkwood, Missouri, near St. Louis, in their new home. Sally Jean Irwin is sitting next to packed crates and her sleeping two-and-a-half-year-old daughter, Becky, watching the Open on television. Sally Jean is eight months pregnant, which explains why she is not at Winged Foot.

Three weeks ago, Hale Irwin woke up one morning and told his wife he had just had a dream that he won the U.S. Open.

4:19 P.M.

Jack Nicklaus bogeys the eighteenth hole and comes in with a 69, his best round of the tournament by five strokes. He is the leader among the early finishers, at fourteen over, and he has a chance to win only if the weather suddenly shifts and everyone is forced to play the back nine in a tornado.

Nicklaus' finish comes only a few minutes after Arnold Palmer completed the front nine, and as one moves toward the clubhouse and the other toward the tenth tee, their galleries—the two largest on the course—intermingle, Arnie's Army and Jack's Pack, neither likely to enjoy any spoils today.

4:21 P.M.

Arnold Palmer—faced with his longest birdie putt—rolls in a thirty-nine-footer for the first deuce surrendered all day by the tenth hole. The Army lets loose the howl they have been saving since the first holes, and the sound rocks the tenth tee, where Hale Irwin and Tom Watson are waiting to hit.

4:25 P.M.

Hale Irwin misses the tenth green, and Tom Watson puts his tee shot a little more than twenty-five feet from the hole, in good position to gain back the stroke he lost on nine.

4:27 P.M.

Tom Place, the information officer for the PGA, walks into the press tent with a stack of xeroxed sheets. "We have some information on Hale Irwin," he says, and starts handing out the fact sheets.

4:31 P.M.

Finishing with a flourish, five pars in a row, Johnny Miller comes in at 77, only fourteen strokes higher than his closing round a year ago. He is twenty-two over par and, by his own admission, considerably over-golfed. "Let me say that it was a real thrill out there," says Miller, with heavy sarcasm. "Did you see all those birdies and eagles?" Then Miller turns serious. "I can see why a defending Open champion never repeats. There is just too much commotion around him all week. Too much pressure."

4:33 P.M.

Tom Watson three-putts for a bogey on the tenth hole, slips to seven over, but remains within a stroke of the lead when Hale Irwin also bogeys.

A spectator behind the tenth green points at Watson, nods his head knowingly and says, "He's choking."

Linda Watson is standing a few feet away. "I hate that word," she says. "I'd like to see them go out there and try it. If they only knew . . ."

Her words tail off.

4:34 P.M.

After reaching the front edge of the par-five twelfth hole in two and guiding his eagle putt three feet past the hole, Forrest Fezler rolls in his birdie and moves to eight under. He checks the nearest scoreboard, which has not yet recorded Irwin's bogey on ten, and thinks he is three strokes off the lead. "If

I play the next six holes even, or maybe one under," Fezler tells his caddy, "I could give Hale a lot of trouble."

4:35 P.M.

Still struggling, still fighting, Arnold Palmer comes up with a magnificent sand shot on eleven. He blasts the ball to the edge of the green and then, as the Army urges it on, the ball trickles downhill and stops only six inches short of the pin. Palmer taps in his par. He is back alive, three strokes behind Hale Irwin. His playing partner, Jim Colbert, with a tap-in birdie on eleven, is also at nine over.

4:39 P.M.

After a birdie on eleven and a par on twelve, Bert Yancey is even for the day, eight over for the tournament. He is still in contention and, amazingly, so is his playing partner, Frank Beard. After his triple bogey on the first hole, Beard has played the next eleven holes in forty-two strokes, one under par, and is now two over for the day, ten over for the tournament. "You're still in it, Frank," a spectator calls, after Beard's eighteen-footer falls for a birdie on twelve.

"Yeah," says Beard. "But I sure make it tough for myself. I'm getting in trouble on every hole." He has hit only six of twelve greens in regulation.

There are now seven men within four strokes of the lead.

4:40 P.M.

Forrest Fezler marches toward the thirteenth green, hearing strange sounds: people yelling his name. "Go get 'em, Forrest," someone shouts. "You can do it, kid," says another spectator, as enthusiastic as if he had been following Fezler all week.

Fezler smiles his appreciation. His tee shot left him more than fifty feet from the pin, but he two-putts to save par.

4:42 P.M.

On the eleventh hole, Hale Irwin rolls in a twenty-five-foot putt for a birdie, and Linda Watson claps politely. Her husband then strokes his birdie putt perfectly. The ball hits the hole and spins away, and Linda Watson groans. Tom taps in his par and stays at seven over, now two strokes behind Irwin for the championship of Missouri—and the U.S. Open.

4:46 P.M.

Bert Yancey blasts from one end of the trap on the right side of the thirteenth green to the other end of the trap. He takes a double-bogey five, so does Frank Beard, and now, with Yancey at ten over and Beard at twelve over, they are both out of contention.

4:50 P.M.

Jim Colbert bogeys the twelfth hole and, at ten over, he is out of contention. Arnold Palmer, with a par, stays barely alive at nine over.

4:51 P.M.

"Of course I'm disappointed," Jack Nicklaus tells the reporters lined up in front of him in the press tent. "I've been preparing for this ever since the Masters."

Nicklaus dismisses all charges against the course. "Nothing unfair about this kind of course," he says. "It's a severe test, but a fair test. There's an element of luck to it, but that's the kind of game golf is. It's my kind of course, a hard course, and all I did wrong was play bad."

"The IBM computer says you took 136 putts, and only one guy took more," a reporter says.

"I don't need IBM," says Nicklaus. "I could have told you how bad I putted. I changed my putter today for the first time in seven years. I just got the putter last week, but I felt what did I have to lose. It didn't make much difference. The new one's pretty much the same as the old one, just a little flatter, a little different feel. You know, there never are two putters or two drivers exactly the same."

"Just like violins," suggests a newsman.

"I don't know," says Nicklaus. "I never played a violin."

4:52 P.M.
Tom Watson hooks his tee shot on the twelfth hole into the woods, and a spectator says, "That's it for Watson."

Linda Watson winces.

4:54 P.M.
With a nifty chip and a four-foot putt, Forrest Fezler saves his par on fourteen and remains three strokes behind Hale Irwin.

4:57 P.M.
In the press tent, finished with his interview, Jack Nicklaus wanders over by a television set. The Open is on, but the sound is turned off. "Want me to turn it up?" someone asks Nicklaus.

"No thanks," says Nicklaus, turning away. "I've seen enough of that golf course for a long time."

4:58 P.M.
Hale Irwin two-putts for a par on the twelfth hole, and Tom Watson two-putts for a bogey. Watson slips to eight over, tied for second place with Forrest Fezler, three strokes behind the leader.

4:59 P.M.
"It was work," says Jerry Heard, sitting in front of his locker, after a 79 for 304. "I really did not enjoy it at all. This is the first time I ever felt this way at the end of a golf tournament."

5 P.M.

THE STANDINGS

GOLFER	SCORE	HOLES
Irwin	+ 5	66
Fezler	+ 8	68
Watson	+ 8	66
Palmer	+ 9	66
Yancey	+ 10	68

5:01 P.M.

Arnold Palmer bogeys the thirteenth hole, and the army surrenders. He is ten over, five behind with five to play, and he is out of contention.

5:02 P.M.

"An Open is never fun," says Hubert Green, sitting in front of his locker, after a 76 for 300. "It's a painful test, but you only have to go through it once a year."

"You disappointed?" someone asks.

"I didn't win, did I?" replies Green.

5:09 P.M.

Forrest Fezler has a testing four-footer to save his par on fifteen, and he passes the test. He has eleven pars and two birdies in his last thirteen holes, and his adrenaline is flowing. He is walking the fairways so fast his growing gallery can hardly keep up with him.

5:10 P.M.

"I think it's a magnificent course," says Larry Ziegler, sitting in front of his locker, after a 71 for 295. "But it's not a fair test of putting. When you're standing there scared that the putt's gonna run, and you don't have any idea how to stroke it, that's not right. But that's what they want here, and that's what they got."

5:11 P.M.

After his first truly spectacular shot of the day, a shot out of the bunker to within six feet of the cup on thirteen, Tom Watson misses the putt and goes to nine over. He has now bogeyed four of the last six holes.

Hale Irwin, who had reached the green with his tee shot and had been greeted by cries of "Go, you Buffalo," presumably from Colorado football fans, doesn't gain on his rivals. He three-putts from more than fifty feet and slips to six over, now only two strokes in front of Forrest Fezler.

5:13 P.M.

"What do I care?" says Johnny Miller, sitting in front of his locker. "I'm exempt for four more years."

5:14 P.M.

Linda Watson walks toward the fourteenth tee, her face showing her pain. She glances at the scoreboard and sees that Forrest Fezler—spelled "F3zl3r," because the scorekeeper has run out of *e*'s—is now alone in second place. "It's so unfair the way people get labeled," Linda says. "Forrest has gotten a 'choke' label, and it's so unfair. It's so hard to win out here. Especially the first time." She shakes her head. "I hope Tom doesn't get that label," she says.

5:15 P.M.

On the sixteenth tee, waiting to hit, Forrest Fezler paces back and forth, his head down, his arms folded, his concentration complete. Then he looks at the scoreboard, confirms his position and tells his caddy, "We can win," as if trying to convince himself.

Then he looks back, waiting for the birdie roar or the bogey groan from Hale Irwin's distant but burgeoning gallery.

5:18 P.M.

Hale Irwin and Tom Watson approach their second shots on the fourteenth hole. Irwin's ball is lying in the right rough, dangerous territory. Watson's ball is lying in the middle of the fairway, dangerous territory, too, the way he's been playing. "Come on, Tom!" Watson urges himself aloud.

Irwin hits first and breathes a sigh of relief as the ball comes down safely on the green. It is better than safe. It is five feet from the cup. "Great shot," says Linda Watson.

Then Watson hits and his shot stops fourteen feet from the pin.

5:21 P.M.

The thirty-two-year-old rabbit, Mike Reasor, who was caddying in the Open when he was Tom Watson's age, comes off the eighteenth green after shooting a 73 that puts him at 296, sixteen over par.

"I think you're gonna make it," says his wife, Caron.

It looks as if either fifteen over or sixteen over will put a golfer into the Masters and the 1975 U.S. Open.

"I don't know," says Reasor. "It's close."

"Susie Snead said you're going to make it," says Caron.

"What did she shoot?" says Mike.

Susie's husband, J.C., shot 75 and finished two strokes behind Reasor, at 298. Snead lost five strokes to par on the last four holes.

5:22 P.M.

Tom Watson's bid for a birdie that might put him back in contention rolls past the cup. "Get in the hole," he yells, too late to alter the ball's course.

Then Irwin steps up and sinks his birdie putt, and the difference between the two men widens to four strokes, with only four holes to play.

5:25 P.M.

Forrest Fezler one-putts on sixteen to save his par.

5:28 P.M.

After perfect drives, Hale Irwin and Tom Watson both miss the fifteenth green with their second shots.

5:32 P.M.

Forrest Fezler hits his second shot on seventeen into a bunker guarding the green. He shakes his head and tugs at his mustache.

5:33 P.M.

Hale Irwin and Tom Watson both bogey the fifteenth hole.

5:36 P.M.

From the left bunker, Forrest Fezler blasts to the seventeenth green, and his ball stops thirty feet from the pin. He stalks the green, studying the putt from every angle. Then he stops, sets himself over the ball and strokes it into the cup.

As the ball disappears, Fezler throws his fist and leaps in the air, his greatest display of emotion all day. He has every right to be excited. He is only two strokes behind, and he has only one hole left to play. Hale Irwin must still face the three murderous closing holes. Of the fifty-four golfers who have finished play for the day, fewer than half a dozen have gotten through sixteen, seventeen and eighteen without at least one bogey. The majority have had at least two.

5:40 P.M.

In Kirkwood, two-and-a-half-year-old Becky Irwin wakes up, her nap ruined by the constant ringing of the telephone. She can watch her father play the last three holes, if she's interested.

5:41 P.M.

On the sixteenth hole, Hale Irwin drives into the rough.

5:42 P.M.

On the eighteenth hole, Forrest Fezler drives into the rough.

5:43 P.M.

"I was beautifully keyed up this week," says Gary Player, sitting in front of his locker after a 73 for 293. "I was concentrating well. I never felt so cool in any tournament. I have no excuses. I tried self-hypnosis. I'm a great believer in self-hypnosis." Player nods, confirming his belief. "I don't think we've scratched the surface on that yet," he says.

"When you were paired with Palmer," says a British reporter, "did the noisy fans disturb you?"

Player smiles. "Well, Jerry," he replies, "you really shouldn't ask me that in front of these reporters."

Not one of the Americans blushes.

5:44 P.M.

On the sixteenth hole, Hale Irwin hits his second shot into a bunker on the right side of the green.

5:45 P.M.

From the seventeenth tee, Jim Colbert looks back, turns to Arnold Palmer and says, "Fezler might still catch him."

5:46 P.M.

On the eighteenth hole, Forrest Fezler hits his second shot into the heavy grass on the right side of the green.

5:47 P.M.

From the bunker, Hale Irwin blasts to within eight feet of the pin on the sixteenth. He walks onto the green, sights his putt very carefully—and misses.

He now has two straight bogeys and he is seven over, only a stroke in front of Forrest Fezler.

5:49 P.M.

From the heavy grass, Forrest Fezler chips fifteen feet past the hole.

5:50 P.M.

As Hale Irwin and Tom Watson prepare to hit off the seventeenth tee, a chipmunk runs up toward Watson. The ex-leader laughs and steps back. The present leader does not laugh.

The chipmunk runs back and forth across the tee, looking for an exit through the dense crowd. "Make way for the players, please," a gray-haired marshal says to the chipmunk. Everyone laughs except Irwin. "Get him out of here," he says, indicating the chipmunk. "Let him out."

Irwin shoos the animal away with a driver, and, finally, he escapes.

Watson and Irwin both drive into the rough.

5:52 P.M.

Forrest Fezler misses his fifteen-foot attempt to save par on the eighteenth hole. As he comes off the green, still with a chance to win the U.S. Open championship, he shakes his head. "Man, this course really takes it out of you mentally," Fezler says. "It just does things to your mind."

5:54 P.M.

In the rough alongside the seventeenth fairway, Hale Irwin turns to his caddy and takes a four-wood. "I can get through it better with this," Irwin tells sixteen-year-old Peter McGarey.

Then Irwin swings and doesn't get through the rough very well. He is still one hundred yards short of the green, but he has no complaint. At least he is out of deep trouble.

5:55 P.M.

After most of the reporters have left Gary Player alone, a straggler asks the South African one more time for an honest reaction to Arnie's Army. "I couldn't hear anything, I couldn't concentrate," Player concedes. "My ears were ringing." He is not a machine, not always.

5:57 P.M.

Hale Irwin hits a lovely chip shot, up to within twelve feet of the pin on the seventeenth green.

6:01 P.M.

Forrest Fezler comes out of the scorer's tent, after carefully adding and re-adding the round of 70 that has lifted him, at the moment, as high as second place. "What a strange day," he says. "When I started this day, I had a gallery of about three people. All I hoped to do was not slow down the groups behind me, and maybe finish in the top ten. Now, all of a sudden, I'm almost winning it. These are strange tournaments, these U.S. Opens."

6:02 P.M.

Hale Irwin lines up his twelve-foot putt on seventeen, and a reporter kneeling behind him says, "He'll never make it. It breaks a foot."

By now, Irwin knows that Forrest Fezler has bogeyed eighteen, that if he can make this putt, he will go to the final tee with a pleasant two-stroke lead.

He makes the putt and breathes another deep sigh of relief.

6:04 P.M.

Charged up equally by his putt on seventeen and the huge gallery lining the eighteenth hole from tee to green, Hale Irwin sends his drive straight down the middle of the fairway.

He marches to his ball, turns to caddy Peter McGarey and confidently takes his two-iron, the club that was ruining him on Thursday and Friday. Irwin hits the two-iron, and the ball stops running nineteen feet from the pin.

The U.S. Open is Irwin's. He can three-putt from nineteen feet, and he will still win. Forrest Fezler, waiting by the eighteenth green, sees Irwin's ball and knows that once again he is finishing second.

As Irwin strides toward the green, he raises both hands above his head, like a victorious boxer. The gallery booms out its applause, and Irwin waves his visor. Arnie's Army, Jack's Pack, Lee's Fleas—everyone joins in the cheers. Linda Watson claps as loudly as anyone, while her husband, already eight over par for the day, eleven over for the tournament, emerges from the woods, anxious to get his third shot onto the green, anxious to get out of the champion's way, anxious to get this round in the past.

Irwin plays the nineteen-footer the way a champion should. He strokes the ball to within an inch of the cup. He taps in, and Hale Irwin is the 1974 United States Open champion.

6:15 P.M.

Hale Irwin is not the only winner. His score is 287, seven over par for the West Course at Winged Foot. Forrest Fezler finished at 289, and no one else broke 290. Every man who finished within sixteen strokes of par—including Mike Reasor—qualified for the 1975 Masters and the 1975 U.S. Open.

Not in more than a decade, not since the 1963 Open at The Country Club in Brookline, Massachusetts, has a course so dominated the greatest players in the world.

6:17 P.M.

Jim Colbert stops at Arnold Palmer's locker to tell Palmer that he enjoyed playing with him. "Thank you," says Palmer. Then he adds a polite lie: "I enjoyed the game." Arnold Palmer never enjoys defeat.

6:26 P.M.

Tom Watson sits dejectedly in front of his locker, gathering up his things, getting ready to move on to the next tournament, the next chance for his first victory. After a bogey on eighteen, he finished with a 79, twelve over for the tournament. "I just played terribly," he says softly. "I just had no feel for the game today."

6:28 P.M.

Reporters crowd around Arnold Palmer's locker, looking for some final words of wisdom. "I really didn't think I played well enough to win. I felt I was making the best of what I had going for me. I've lost the Open a couple of times when I did play well enough to win."

Palmer explains that he didn't feel he was out of it until the last two holes. He reached that point ten over par, and he felt if he could make two birdies, and go to eight over, he would put a lot of pressure on Hale Irwin, playing behind him. Instead, Palmer made two bogeys and finished twelve over, tied for fifth place with Jim Colbert and his former exhibition opponent, Tom Watson.

"The young pros were rooting for you," someone says.

"That makes this whole business worthwhile," says Palmer. He smiles, "I'm looking forward to next year," he says.

6:45 P.M.

Forrest Fezler is hurrying to leave Winged Foot, not to flee from the West Course, but to catch a plane. "God, I tried," he says. "But, you know, it's a lot of money when you finish second alone."

Fezler has earned $18,000 for his week's work, his best week of the year. "I wouldn't mind coming in second every week," he says.

Then he writes out a check for $1,000 and gives it to his caddy, Jim Dever, a high school principal from New Jersey.

6:50 P.M.

Arnold Palmer turns to his press aide, Doc Giffin. "Give me a cigarette," Palmer says.

"Do you smoke?" says a writer.

"My first in six months," says Palmer. Then, as an afterthought, he says, "Nah, not really. I have one every now and then. But don't write it. My old man will be on my back."

And then Arnold Palmer lights up and relaxes.

6:52 P.M.

All the writers stand and applaud as Hale Irwin enters the press tent. He smiles, happily, and says, "I hope this answers any questions about whether I can win on any course besides Harbour Town.

"I think the putt on the ninth hole turned the whole thing around. And then on the seventeenth, I made the best putt of the tournament, a left-to-right downhill putt, just the kind you don't like to have."

"You think you're still going to be anonymous?"

Irwin laughs. "Well, I don't want to be anonymous," he says. "But I do think there is a time and place for everything. I'm not going to change now because I won the Open. This has done a lot for my ego, but it isn't going to change my personality. I won being the way I am and I'm not going to change that. I'm just going to have to reevaluate my goals. Now that I've got one major championship, I want two. If I get two, then I can worry about going after Jack's fourteen. I'm not anywhere close to being Jack Nicklaus, but why not have that as a goal?"

And then Irwin tells the writers about the dream he had, the dream he told his wife, the dream in which he won the United States Open championship. And hearing about the dream, one writer sits down at his typewriter and begins his story of the U.S. Open in the only possible way:

"Nobody ever dreamed Hale Irwin would win the 1974 U.S. Open . . . nobody except Hale Irwin."

The Tree That Didn't Qualify

by Dave Anderson, *The New York Times*, June 16, 1979

Toledo, Ohio, June 15—From the knoll behind the seventh green at the Inverness Club today, Lon Hinkle smiled when he saw the tree that had not been there in the opening round of the United States Open championship. When he strode onto the tee of the 528-yard eighth hole, a dogleg left, he stared at the 25-foot-high spruce tree that had been transplanted by the United States Golf Association in order to prevent golfers from taking a short cut through the adjoining 17th fairway, as he did yesterday in shooting birdie 4 there. But now Lon Hinkle pointed to the yellow gallery ropes.

"Take down the ropes over there for me," he called to the marshals. "I'm going that way again." Then he pointed to the 17th fairway the way Babe Ruth pointed to the Wrigley Field bleachers in the 1932 World Series. Teeing his ball to the far left and within the required two-club lengths behind the markers, the bulky touring pro from San Diego hit his driver.

His ball brushed the leaves of a tall oak on the left and kept going, but he only heard the sound of it grazing the leaves.

"Where is it?" he asked.

"It's perfect," he was told.

"Tomorrow," a man in the gallery said, "they're going to have to put ornaments on that tree."

"Tomorrow," another said, "there'll be a bigger tree."

With a smile, Lon Hinkle walked onto the 17th fairway, the hole that George Burns, John Schroeder and John Gentile were playing. Burns grinned when he realized that Lon Hinkle was shortening the eighth hole by perhaps 60 yards.

"Good for you," Burns said. "The hell with 'em."

SCORECARD PENCIL FOR A TEE

That was the way many people felt about the U.S.G.A. even before Lon Hinkle got another birdie 4 there today. In taking the short cut with or without the tree, Lon Hinkle was gambling. He had to hit his tee shot to the 17th fairway, then he had to loft an iron shot over high trees to the tightly bunkered eighth green. He won each gamble—with a 1-iron, a 2-iron and two putts from 70 feet in the first round; with a driver, a 7-iron into a bunker, a sand wedge to within eight feet and one putt in today's round.

But the short way is not necessarily the best way. Chi Chi Rodriguez, who teed his ball on a yellow scorecard pencil today for a higher trajectory, bogeyed it both times. And the other member of their threesome, Greg Norman of Australia, had an eagle 3 there today—the conventional way.

"I don't know what I'll do there tomorrow," Lon Hinkle said after his six-over-par 77 for 147 after 36 holes. "It'll depend on where the markers are and on who's on the 17th tee. Where the markers were today, that tree didn't look nearly big enough."

The issue was bigger than the tree. The issue was whether the U.S.G.A. was correct in importing a tree once the Open had begun. In advertising the Open as the world's most prestigious golf event, the U.S.G.A. always proclaims it to be the most democratic golf tournament. Aside from 42 prominent players granted exemptions because of various accomplishments, the remainder of the 153 contestants had to qualify for the Open—but the tree had not qualified. The tree had not been on the Inverness course when the tournament began.

JOYCE KILMER AND JIM HAND

Annually, the Open is a battle of wits between the golfers and the U.S.G.A. officials, who resemble soldiers of fortune from Brooks Brothers—armbands, red, white and blue striped ties and red and blue ribboned medals dangling from the left breast of their white button-down shirts. If a golfer is willing to gamble on outwitting the U.S.G.A., as Lon Hinkle did, the U.S.G.A. should be willing to accept the results of the roll of the dice.

If the U.S.G.A. had realized its mistake before the first round started and imported a tree, fine. But once the Open began, the U.S.G.A. was morally bound not to tamper with the design of the course, for better or for worse. In playing an Open course, the golfer must live with his mistakes. But the U.S.G.A. deemed otherwise.

"I think that I shall never see," Joyce Kilmer wrote, "a poem lovely as a tree . . .

". . . Poems are made by fools like me," he concluded, "but only God can make a tree."

Only the U.S.G.A. and God, it now develops. The tree itself was about 30 yards away from the blue tee markers, blocking most of the opening to the 17th fairway that existed yesterday. Someone jokingly called it a "Hinkleberry tree." Actually it was a Black Hill that had been trucked in from a local nursery and transplanted less than an hour before today's second round began. Beneath its lowest branches, wires from two steel stakes propped it upright.

From behind the tree, it appeared that the spruce, unlike anything else connected with the U.S.G.A., was leaning slightly to the left. But after Lon Hinkle's second birdie there, the U.S.G.A. was leaning to the status quo.

"There will be no further changes on No. 8," said Jim Hand, the chairman of the U.S.G.A.'s championship committee.

Sandy Tatum, the U.S.G.A. president, had explained earlier that "we had to do something to protect the integrity of the design of the hole; it would be improper for us to leave that avenue open." According to Tatum, it also would have been improper to move up the tee markers, thereby shortening the hole.

"There's no question," Jim Hand said earlier, "I should have seen that opening when I was here last year and when I was here a month or so ago."

Lon Hinkle saw the opening instead. And took advantage of it. When he saw the transplanted tree today, he took a gamble. And won again. But no matter who wins this Open, it will be remembered mostly for the tree that the U.S.G.A. created.

Pebble Beach and the Open: Watson

from *Following Through* by Herbert Warren Wind

Without a doubt the most thrilling U.S. Open in recent years was the one at Pebble Beach in 1982. Many people consider Pebble Beach the best course in the country, and there are those who rate it the best in the world. Halfway through the final round, all of the contenders had been dismissed except those two well-acquainted adversaries: Tom Watson, who had never won our Open, and Jack Nicklaus, who had won it four years, including 1972, the last time it was played at Pebble Beach. With four holes to go, Watson, playing just behind Nicklaus, led him by a stroke. He lost his lead when he bogeyed the sixteenth. On the par-3 seventeenth, Watson pulled a 2-iron into thick rough. It looked as if that error might cost him the championship but, as we know, it didn't. Bob Jones, who had some experience in these matters, came to believe that before the first shot has been struck in a tournament, fate has already decreed who will win it and who will not.

There are few experiences in sport that can compare with the thrill that the average golfer or the skillful golfer receives when he plays a famous course for the first time. Golf courses vary immensely as to how hard or how easy they are to comprehend for the first-time visitor. For example, the Old Course at St. Andrews, a sea of erratically rolling duneland, is replete with holes that give a golfer little or no clue in determining the correct line from tee to green. On many holes, a drive that whistles down the center of the fairway may end up in a pot bunker that is hidden from view at the tee. For another thing, there is no sure way of reading the undulations on many of the vast greens. When you study your line to the cup, what looks to be a definite break to the right turns out to be a slight swerve to the left. The Old Course must be memorized. There is no other way to learn the position of the hazards and the speed and roll of the various areas of each green. Inasmuch as this requires months of practice and application, the sensible procedure for a visitor is to take a caddie. Even then, the course manages to muffle a good deal of its personality. On the outgoing nine, your caddie will point out the salient features to aim at and the right club to use, and you must trust him. The same is true on the incoming nine, on which, after playing the loop, the golfer heads home, the old town looming in the distance like a watercolor of some medieval city. Down this stretch, the target that the caddie gives him on his drive and some of his other shots is more often than not a church steeple or an ancient building made of stone of a distinctive color. I once played a round with Willie Turnesa, a golfer of international stature, during which his drive on the thirteenth finished at the base of a rise so abrupt that all he could see was the sky. His caddie was resourceful. "Hit the middle of that big cloud," he said, pointing, as he handed Turnesa a 5-iron. Turnesa hit the ball exactly where he was told to, and when he climbed the bank and peered at the green, a hundred and seventy yards away, his ball was sitting eight feet from the pin.

On the other hand, when a golfer plays an exceptionally frank, straightforward course—three excellent examples would be Muirfield, near Edinburgh;

Portmarnock, outside Dublin; and Royal Melbourne, outside Melbourne—
the individual holes clearly disclose the perils he faces and the precise route
he should try to take from tee to green. Nevertheless, when one plays these
three courses, it is still advisable to take a caddie, for they are linksland
courses, and, what with the shifting winds off the ocean, distance is harder
to gauge than it usually is on inland courses. (Linksland is the stretch of
sandy soil deposited by the sea as it receded slowly over the centuries.
The soil drains well and produces splendid turf for golf.) Most of the
other genuinely great courses lie about midway between St. Andrews and
the likes of Muirfield, Portmarnock, and Royal Melbourne in the clarity
with which they present themselves. In any list of the top courses in this
country, the following would surely be included: Seminole, in North Palm
Beach; the Augusta National, in Augusta, Georgia; Merion, on the edge of
Philadelphia; Pine Valley, which is also close to Philadelphia; the Lakeside
course at Olympic, in San Francisco; and Pebble Beach and Cypress Point,
both of which are on the Monterey Peninsula, roughly a hundred miles
south of San Francisco. In their separate ways, the challenges that each of
these courses offers are stated explicitly, but it never hurts to have put in
some time becoming acquainted with the subtleties of the land. The key to
the endless fascination of golf is that it is the only game played on natural
terrain—or, at least, on land that, however unpromising it was originally,
has been fashioned to resemble attractive and interesting natural terrain.
The finer the course, the more enticing the shots it asks the golfer to play.
Moreover, on a great course on which many championships have been held
there is an invaluable bonus: history comes to life every step of the way, and
a golf pilgrim is continually reminded of the feats of the celebrated players
who trod the same holes long before him.

All of this is by way of leading up to the fact that if there is any one course
that is generally regarded as being the most dramatic in the world, and
quite possibly the best, it is Pebble Beach, where the United States Open

Championship was played last month, and carried off by Tom Watson after a tremendous duel with Jack Nicklaus that was decided by one of the most breathtaking shots in Open history. The official designation of the course is the Pebble Beach Golf Links, and this is odd, since it is not a true linksland course. It is made up of eight holes perched atop craggy headlands that overlook Carmel Bay and of ten fairly difficult, if less spectacular, holes, which are commonly referred to as the "inland" holes, although most of them lie within a driver shot of the bay. The moving force behind the creation of Pebble Beach was Samuel Morse, a shrewd, farsighted entrepreneur, who had been the captain of the Yale football team in 1906. In 1914, when he was in the employ of the Pacific Improvement Company, a subsidiary of the Southern Pacific Railroad, Morse got to know and appreciate the unspoiled grandeur of the Monterey Peninsula, with its pine-covered hills and its rockbound coastline. His assignment at the time was to liquidate the company's holdings on the peninsula and on the land adjoining it. He decided instead to form a firm of his own, the Del Monte Properties Company, and bought a tract of seven thousand acres of this land, including seven miles of coastline, for one million three hundred thousand dollars. Among the assets Morse acquired was the Del Monte Hotel, an immense Victorian structure above Monterey Bay, which at one time possessed—far more than any other West Coast spa—something of the cachet of Newport. Attached to the hotel was the pleasant if obsolescent Del Monte golf course. Morse had the astuteness to realize that the hotel had seen its best days, and that in order to attract the wellborn and well-to-do from San Francisco and elsewhere who might purchase property and build homes on the Monterey Peninsula a much more modern golf course was necessary—preferably one with such a superlative layout that its fame would quickly redound throughout the world.

To this end, Morse, instead of selling his prize property on the high cliffs above Carmel Bay for plush private estates, as most real-estate developers would have, reserved it for the golf course. In 1918, he made a startling decision. He did not approach either Charles Blair Macdonald or Donald Ross, the two outstanding golf-course architects in the country, or any other golf-course architect of reputation, to design his course. He entrusted this considerable responsibility to Jack Neville, a real-estate salesman who had worked for the Pacific Improvement Company and had continued with the Del Monte Properties Company. A tall, laconic man with a nice dry wit, Neville had won the California State Amateur Championship several times and was rated to be as good an amateur golfer as there was on the West Coast, but he had never built a golf course before. He set about his task with no fuss whatever. He walked the site daily, spending most of his hours mulling over how to use the extraordinary land above Carmel Bay to maximum advantage. After three weeks, he settled on the way that the holes he had in mind would be routed. He got it absolutely right. His inspired plan went like this: The first three holes would swing inland and then back toward the bay. Holes four, six, seven, eight, nine, and ten followed along the edge of the cliffs. The fifth, a par 3 framed by woods, did not. Holes eleven through sixteen were inland holes, but the seventeenth returned to the bay, and the entire left side of the eighteenth, a long par 5, was bordered by the rocks, sand, and water of the bay. The course was completed in 1919. The golfers who played it came away stunned by its scenic beauty and the cornucopia of astonishing golf shots it offered.

It is well worthwhile, I believe, to describe in some detail the eight holes along Carmel Bay which Neville visualized and executed so brilliantly. The first one that the golfer meets is the fourth, a par 4 that is 327 yards long. Despite its shortness, it is a worrisome hole. Along its right side, a cliff about twenty-five feet high drops down to a rocky beach. Since such features have a particularly powerful subconscious effect on people wearing spiked shoes, most golfers hook or pull their tee shot far to the left, into the rough or into a bunker. Even if his drive stays on the left side of the fairway, the golfer faces a touchy shot: he must feather a soft pitch just over a frontal bunker in order to stop it on the green, perhaps the smallest of the eighteen—and the greens at Pebble Beach are smaller than those at any other of the world's great courses.

The sixth, a par 5 that measures 516 yards, presents a similar problem. Off the tee, the golfer must avoid the right side of the fairway, for it is bordered by a cliff that ranges from thirty-five to sixty feet high. Most golfers, in their concern to avoid this hazard, again play their tee shot farther left than they had intended to, and many drives wind up in a long trap that hugs the left side of the fairway. This complicates matters. Approximately three hundred and fifty yards from the tee, the fairway climbs a sudden hill nearly fifty feet high, to a plateau, at the end of which the green is situated. On a windless day, a big hitter can reach the green in two, but for the average golfer, unless he finds the fairway off the tee, a 6 is a most acceptable score. The tee on the short seventh, a mere 110 yards, is set about five yards below the level of the sixth green but at the edge of a cliff almost seventy-five feet high. When the golfer is addressing the ball on the tee, he has no protection from the sometimes fierce winds as he attempts to hit and hold the tiny, heavily bunkered green, far below him. On stormy days, when the wind is buffeting the rocks just behind the green and sending spray high into the air, a 3-iron is not too much club for a professional. On quiet days, a pitching wedge will suffice.

After this, the course begins to get tough. In playing the eighth, where the tee is only a short distance from the seventh green, the golfer, who has now turned around to face inland, must produce a long, controlled drive to reach the high land at the top of the hill that he had approached from the opposite direction when he was playing the sixth. From the tee on this 433-yard par 4, he takes in the cliff rising sharply along the right side of the fairway. When he has climbed to the top of the incline—a good drive will finish there—what may very well be the most awesome sight in golf awaits him. Here the cliff plunges straight down a hundred and fifty feet or more into Carmel Bay. He sees this and also notices that up ahead the fairway jogs slightly to the left, but what transfixes his attention is the sight of the eighth green in the distance, across the waters of an inlet of the bay. The green is guarded by a cortège of five bunkers, but it actually doesn't need any of them, since it sits just beyond the continuing cliffline, approximately fifty feet high at this point. Depending on the weather, the tournament-calibre golfer, who will usually choose to lay up off the tee with a long iron or a 3-wood or 4-wood, is usually left with a carry of between a hundred and seventy and a hundred and ninety yards across the inlet on his second shot. The average golfer, of course, having hit a somewhat shorter or more errant drive, most times faces a longer carry on his second if he chooses to go for the green. To pull it off, he must summon nothing less than a career shot. He should give it a whirl nonetheless. After all, if he manages to get home in two he will have something to talk about for the rest of his life. On the other hand, if he is working on a tidy round and scoring well, prudence dictates that he take a long or middle iron for his second and play a conservative lay-up shot down the fairway as it begins to bend to the right and follow the curve of the inlet. He will then be in position to hit the green with a firm pitch on his third.

The eighth leaves a golfer emotionally exhausted, but he must pull himself together quickly in order to cope with the ninth and tenth, two extremely exacting par 4s—467 and 424 yards long, respectively—that continue southeast along the bay, which is on the right. On these two holes, the cliffs have dwindled to thirty feet, but this is enough to deter the golfer from flirting with the right side of the fairway. In addition, on both holes the fairway slopes from left to right, and, with the greens set close to the cliffs, hitting them in the regulation number of strokes in a swirling wind is no easy matter. I would guess that the eighth, ninth, and tenth constitute the most difficult succession of three par 4s in golf.

Pebble Beach has a formidable finish. The seventeenth and eighteenth return to the bay, and they can be destructive. The green on the seventeenth, a par 3 that is 209 yards long from the back tee, is situated on a rocky point that juts into the bay. The eighteenth is regarded by many experts as the premier finishing hole in golf. It curves like a scimitar along the bay, which flanks the fairway on the left. Out-of-bounds stakes patrol the right side practically from tee to green. As if the hole weren't stiff enough with these constraints, there are other hazards, such as clumps of trees and bunkers, that come into play with a strategic niceness. Then, there is the wind. Some days, it blows in so ferociously off the water that experienced golfers feel that the safest course is to aim their shots out to sea and let the wind bring them back onto the fairway.

The only trouble with emphasizing the grandeur of the seaside holes at Pebble Beach is that this may promote the impression that the inland holes are rather ordinary. They are not. The opening three holes are a short par 4 followed by a flat par 5 and another short par 4. Though original and provocative, they present good opportunities for birdies. As a matter of fact, the trick to scoring well on Pebble Beach is to get through the first six holes a shot or two under par, for, regardless of his skill, the golfer is almost certain to give a few shots back to par over the last twelve holes. Granted, life becomes a little milder after you walk off the tenth green, but each hole on the inland stretch from the eleventh through the sixteenth requires fastidious shotmaking. On the par-4 eleventh, for example, the drive must be placed on the left side of the fairway in order for the golfer to command the opening to the green on his approach. On the twelfth, a fairly long par 3, the surface of the green is hard and unreceptive, and the only way to stop a long iron or wood there is to hit the kind of shot that reaches the apex of its parabola above the green and floats down softly. On the thirteenth, a 393-yard par 4, the wide right side of the fairway beckons, but the tee shot should be played close to the large bunker on the left side, for otherwise you cannot come into the canted green from the correct angle. The fourteenth, fifteenth, and sixteenth also require knowledge and control. The greens, slippery and fast, as are all the greens at Pebble Beach, are full of quirky slopes and breaks, and you must place your tee shot—and on the par-5 four-teenth your second shot as well—with a good deal of care in order to be able to stop your approach on the proper part of the green in relation to the pin, and so avoid finding yourself in a position where there is almost no escape from taking three putts. All in all, the inland holes, with their emphasis on finesse, complement the seaside holes perfectly.

Before Neville worked his wonders on the marvellous land that Morse had set aside, there had never been a golf course quite like Pebble Beach. On the West Links at North Berwick, one of the older Scottish courses, there are a few cliffside holes. The green on the first is on an abrupt plateau twenty-five feet or so above the southern bank of the Firth of Forth. The second and third holes hug the shore, but the land drops quickly down from the high tee on the second and is only five feet or so above the water. Then, there is the fourteenth, the elegant hole called Perfection—a drive and about a 6-iron—on which the green is near the edge of a cliff some fifteen feet above the firth. At the beginning of the second nine, when the course heads back to the clubhouse, four other holes are situated close to the firth, but substantial hillocks and sand hills block off the sight of the water, and the golfer is hardly aware of its proximity. The course at Dunbar, near North Berwick, and the one at Stonehaven, twenty miles south of Aberdeen, also have some enjoyable cliffside holes. At Ballybunion, the renowned Irish course that winds through towering sand hills above the Shannon estuary, there are cliffs of a more heroic size, but they come into play on just three holes, and then only tangentially. After the First World War, when golf underwent a tremendous boom, Charles Blair Macdonald created Mid Ocean, the first course built in Bermuda. Formally opened in 1921, Mid Ocean is an imaginative layout, but for most golfers it proved to be a disappointment. They had assumed that such a lavishly publicized course on such a storied island would surely feature several arresting holes adjacent to the Atlantic, including a few in which the handsome coral cliffs were involved. Not at all. For example, the first three holes occupy a strip of land fairly close to the Atlantic, but the water is largely hidden by stands of trees, and when it is visible it plays a strictly decorative role. The only time a golfer really experiences the sensation of being next to the water at Mid Ocean comes when he walks onto the tee of the eighteenth, a grand finishing hole, where, just behind the back markers, the land drops vertically fifty or sixty feet to the ocean.

After the Second World War, the Ailsa course at Turnberry, in Ayrshire, Scotland, which is laid out over a glorious expanse of duneland along the Clyde estuary, and which during the war had been converted into an airfield for the R.A.F. Coastal Command, was revived and revised most successfully by Mackenzie Ross. Seven holes in a row—the fourth through the tenth—move along the coast, but for the most part a continuing ridge of duneland shuts off the view of the sea. The best-known hole, the ninth, has a tee that is set on a high, isolated crag, and it demands a fairly long carry over water to reach the fairway, but there were many other opportunities at Turnberry to build tees and greens at the water's edge, which were not utilized. I don't know the reason for this, but my guess is that in Scotland—and throughout the British Isles—improving on nature to this extent has not been seriously considered, because of the expense involved and because to do so would be impractical: on stormy days, holes that had been constructed too close to the sea might be inundated and damaged.

One course on which the popularity of Pebble Beach must have had an effect is Cypress Point, its neighbor on the Monterey Peninsula, which was completed in 1928. Cypress Point has an almost incomparable variety of holes: ordinary seaside holes, duneland holes, typical inland holes, pine-lined holes that climb and descend rolling hills, and, for good measure, three cliffside holes—the fifteenth, sixteenth, and seventeenth—which make magnificent use of the course's chunk of jagged coastline. Alister MacKenzie, who designed Cypress Point, was such a talented golf-course architect that he must have sensed on his first exploratory stroll of his acreage the possibilities of that wild corner where the Pacific beats against the cliffs, but if somehow he did not, the existence of Pebble Beach just a few miles down the road would certainly have thrust it into his mind. While there are a number of other courses around the world that have one or two or three memorable holes poised on cliffs by the sea, the only course that truly merits comparison with Pebble Beach is Campo de Golf Cajuiles, designed in the early nineteen-seventies by Pete Dye, on the southeastern shore of the Dominican Republic. As at Pebble Beach, a total of eight holes are strung along the sea, some of them with greens or tees built only a few feet above the water, others marching along coral cliffs, which Dye's Dominican crews patiently hammered into a workable substratum for the tees, greens, and fairways. On seven of these eight holes, it is necessary for the crack golfer to attempt risky carries across water on his tee shot or approach shot in order to match par. Campo de Golf Cajuiles lacks the dimensions and the majesty of Pebble Beach, but it is a remarkable achievement—a striking Caribbean version of the original.

And what about Jack Neville? After the smashing success of Pebble Beach, one would think that the world would have beaten a path to his door. For various reasons, this did not happen. He collaborated with George Thomas III on Bel Air, a superior course in Los Angeles, and, at Morse's request, he laid out plans for a number of other courses, none of which were ever built. Much later on, he designed a second nine holes at Pacific Grove, a nearby municipal course, and assisted in the design of the Shore Course of the Monterey Peninsula Country Club. All this time, he adhered to his old routine, selling lots for Del Monte Properties and living simply, almost forgotten. He was rediscovered in 1972, when the U.S. Open was held at Pebble Beach for the first time. Nearly eighty-one years old then, he remained modestly in the background during the championship, but there was no question that the tardy recognition he received as the man behind the masterpiece meant a great deal to him. He died at eighty-six, in 1978, not long after a banquet in his honor was held on the peninsula.

Down through the years, Sam Morse ran his beloved Pebble Beach as a home course for the residents of his private duchy and as a resort course for visitors—primarily those who were vacationing at the Del Monte Lodge, a hotel overlooking the eighteenth green and Carmel Bay, which was built to replace the old Del Monte Hotel. Technically, Pebble Beach was (and still is) a public course—the only public course, incidentally, on which the U.S. Open has been played—but, being well off the beaten path, in its early years it was seldom uncomfortably crowded. With few exceptions, a golf course's status depends to a large extent on whether or not it has been the scene of important tournaments. For instance, whenever the Royal and Ancient Golf Club of St. Andrews, which conducts the national championships in Great Britain, adds a new course to the rota of courses over which the British Open is played, this is tantamount to conferring knighthood on that course. A similar prestige accrues to courses in this country that are selected by the United States Golf Association for the U.S. Open. From the day that Pebble Beach was unveiled, knowledgeable golf hands thought that it would be a perfect venue for our Open, but it was not chosen until 1972 because the course lacked one fundamental requirement: it was not situated near a major center of population, and the general feeling was that an Open held there would not attract enough fans and bring in enough money in gate receipts to balance the considerable expense of staging the championship. The first significant tournament held at Pebble Beach was the 1919 California State Amateur Championship, which, incidentally, was won by Jack Neville. The site added incalculably to the event, and the California Golf Association was able to arrange for the championship to be played there annually, as it continues to be. In 1929, the course played host to its first national championship, the United States Amateur. This was quite a coup, for until then no national championship had been held west of Minneapolis. In those days, the Amateur was looked upon as Bobby Jones' personal championship. He had reached the final the five previous years and had won it four times. The 1929 Amateur is probably best remembered for the fact that Jones was eliminated in the first round, after a rousing match with the then unknown Johnny Goodman, who beat him one up over eighteen holes. The 1929 Amateur served to make golfers throughout the country much more conscious of Pebble Beach. Photographs of many of its spectacular holes appeared in newspapers from coast to coast and in magazines with a national circulation.

Pebble Beach's fame continued to grow. The United States Women's Amateur Championship was played there twice—in 1940 and 1948. The U.S. Amateur returned there in 1947 and again in 1961, when the young Jack Nicklaus dominated the proceedings from start to finish. There is no question, though, that the event that made Americans, non-golfers as well as golfers, aware of Pebble Beach was the annual P.G.A. Tour tournament that Bing Crosby devised and ran. Its official designation is the National Pro-Am, but it is usually referred to simply as the Crosby. Inaugurated as a thirty-six-hole competition before the war at Rancho Santa Fe, near San Diego, it was shifted to the Monterey Peninsula by Crosby in 1947. That year, it was extended into a fifty-four-hole tournament, with the golfers playing one round at Cypress Point, one at the Monterey Peninsula Country Club, and one at Pebble Beach. The critical year was 1958. The Crosby was further extended into a seventy-two-hole tournament, with the final round, appropriately, taking place at Pebble Beach. That winter, the Crosby became one of the first tournaments on the P.G.A. Tour to be televised nationally. From the start, it drew huge audiences. The presence of some movie stars in the lists and Crosby's personal popularity had a great deal to do with this—he did much of the commentary, fully indulging his penchant for polysyllables—but the main reason, I would have to believe, was the effect on the viewers of Pebble Beach's overwhelming beauty.

Apart from its high television ratings, the Crosby attracted large galleries. This undoubtedly led the U.S.G.A. to review its earlier position that holding the Open at Pebble Beach was too much of a financial risk, but for several other reasons as well the organization was ready to accept the invitation that Sam Morse tendered in 1966 and to agree, after some discussion, to hold the Open at Pebble Beach in 1972. In 1968, Morse and his son-in-law, Richard Osborne, who was associated in business with him, called in Frank D. (Sandy) Tatum, Jr., a San Francisco lawyer, to be responsible for the part of the course preparation which was the obligation of the Del Monte Properties Company. Tatum was an ideal choice for this assignment. When he was in his teens, he had spent his summer vacations working as a laborer on construction crews in Los Angeles, his home town, to accumulate enough money to play in the California State Amateur. "I'd blow it all in one wonderful week at Pebble Beach," he once told me. "It was one of the most intelligent things I've ever done." An able golfer, Tatum won the National Collegiate Championship in 1942, when he was at Stanford. At Oxford, which he attended as a Rhodes Scholar, he was a member of the university golf team. Few people of my acquaintance know as much about golf or are as exuberantly passionate about it. As a longtime admirer of Pebble Beach, he knew that no changes had been officially authorized since H. Chandler Egan was asked to strengthen the bunkering in the green area on some holes before the 1929 Amateur, but he also knew that bit by bit, from 1929 on, as has happened at many courses, the physiognomy of individual holes had been altered by greenkeepers and work crews, and, in the case of Pebble Beach, by understandably spotty maintenance during the Second World War. Tatum concluded that the soundest procedure was to get in touch with Jack Neville and to restore any features of the original layout that Neville thought were significant but that somehow or other had disappeared over the years. Neville suggested restoring the following: the bunker at the front left corner of the first green, which made the approach shot more exacting; the bunker in the drive zone to the left of the fourth fairway, which he felt would work best if it was elongated into an L shape and carried into the fairway, and, additionally, if a small pot bunker was placed in the angle of the L; and the bunkering on the left shoulder of the hill on the sixth, which influenced the playing of the second shot. Neville also recommended that the bunker on the edge of the right rough in the drive zone on the sixteenth be deepened, so that a golfer couldn't play a relatively routine recovery onto the green from it. He also felt that this bunker would pack more trepidation if it edged toward the fairway. Later on, P. J. Boatwright, Jr., the executive director of the U.S.G.A., came out to supervise the Association's part in preparing the course for the championship—a job he has done for years with enormous skill. Along with putting into effect such standard procedures for the Open as narrowing the fairways and letting the rough grow tall and dense, Boatwright proposed changes on the ninth and tenth that Tatum and Neville heartily concurred in. Both holes, exceptional par 4s, were playing extremely short at that time. The burned-out rough on the high, or left, side of their fairways was playing as hard as stone, with the result that on a solidly hit tee shot the ball would get so much bounce and roll if it landed there that the golfer would have nothing more than a wee pitch for his approach. On the ninth, new bunkering was established in the drive zone where the rough met the high side of the fairway. On the tenth, a new championship tee was built, on the left side of the ninth green, to add some length to the hole, and on the left edge of the fairway, some two hundred and thirty-five yards out, a long, irregularly shaped bunker that could not be carried was added. The effect of the new bunkers on these two holes was to force golfers to play for the fairway to the right of the hazards, and this put increased pressure on them.

The 1972 Open turned out to be everything that one had hoped it would be. The course played hard but well on the first three days, under blue skies and a warm sun and with a refreshing breeze coming off the water. It played perceptibly harder on the fourth, and last, day, when the golfers had to deal with a gusty wind that stirred up whitecaps in the bay. The 1972 Open had been expected to provide one of the most rigorous championship tests in years, and it did. For instance, Jack Nicklaus, who either was tied for the lead or held the lead from the first round on, posted a winning total of 290, which was two strokes over par. Only half of the hundred and fifty-two starters broke 80 on each of the first two rounds. On the windy fourth day, no one broke 70, and only two players broke or equalled par, 72. On that final round, there were several memorable moments. The first came when

Nicklaus was playing the tenth. He held a comfortable lead at this point, but his tee shot sailed out to the right, over the cliff, and down onto the beach. His third shot could well have done the same thing, but it stopped at the brink of the cliff. Nicklaus was extremely lucky to get out of the hole with only a double-bogey 6. Not long after this, he botched up the par-3 twelfth and was faced with sinking an eight-foot putt for a bogey 4. At that same moment, Arnold Palmer, who had played a good, stubborn Open, was on the fourteenth green lining up an eight-foot putt for a birdie. If Palmer made his putt and Nicklaus missed his, Palmer would move into the lead by a stroke. It went the other way: Palmer missed and Nicklaus holed. On the fifteenth, Nicklaus nailed down his victory with an authoritative birdie. He went on to birdie the par-3 seventeenth when his 1-iron shot hit the flagstick on its first bounce and stopped six inches away. This is the shot that most fans who saw that Open remember.

There was no question after the 1972 Open that the championship would be returning to Pebble Beach. Before it did so, this year, a number of changes in the ownership, condition, and atmosphere of the golf course took place. Following Sam Morse's death, in 1969, the Del Monte Properties Company was reorganized. Under the new management, the role of Pebble Beach was altered. It was regarded primarily as a source of income. The cost of a greens fee rose steeply, as did the cost of renting a golf cart. The golf course was also looked upon as a principal attraction for luring visitors to the Del Monte Lodge—which, inevitably, was renamed the Lodge at Pebble Beach—and for selling lots on the peninsula. In 1976, the Del Monte Properties Company became the Pebble Beach Corporation, and three years later it was sold to Twentieth Century–Fox. Along with Pebble Beach, the old Del Monte course and Spyglass Hill, a new Robert Trent Jones course, which was completed in the mid-nineteen-sixties, were included in the purchase. (Twentieth Century–Fox had an abundance of capital at its disposal at this time, chiefly because of the colossal profits racked up by *Star Wars*.) In 1978, no fewer than fifty-six thousand rounds of golf were played over Pebble

Beach. This total was attained by starting the groups of players off the first tee at nine-minute intervals. The average round took six hours, and under the constant tramp, tramp, tramp and whack, whack, whack the course took quite a beating. The installation in 1977 of a web of garish asphalt cart paths hardly improved its appearance. In 1979, a more enlightened attitude toward the course was observable. That year, the interval between starting times was increased to twelve minutes—a change that reduced the number of rounds to forty-two thousand. Pebble Beach gradually began to look like its old self again. This was due in a large measure to the work of John Zoller, an accomplished golf-course superintendent, who was appointed director of golf operations in 1978. (Before coming to Pebble Beach, Zoller, who had studied turf management at Ohio State, had been the course superintendent at the Eugene Country Club, in Oregon, for eighteen years, and then the course superintendent, and later the general manager, at the Monterey Peninsula Country Club. In 1980, Zoller became the executive director of the Northern California Golf Association, and, shortly after this, Tim Berg, who was also trained at the Eugene Country Club, was hired to be both the course superintendent and the professional at Pebble Beach.) One other change was in the offing. In June, 1981, Marvin Davis, a Denver oil man, bought Twentieth Century–Fox. Davis then formed a partnership with the Aetna Life & Casualty Company, and at the present time they operate holdings on the Monterey Peninsula and at Aspen, Colorado—ski runs, a ski school, a ski shop, and several restaurants. This year, the division that runs Pebble Beach hiked the greens fee at the course, which in 1979 had been raised from fifty to sixty dollars, to seventy dollars.

Pebble Beach underwent only minuscule changes in the months before the 1982 Open. After a visit to the course before preparations for the championship began, Tatum, who had meanwhile served as president of the U.S.G.A. in 1978–79, had a pair of recommendations to make. He believed that the shallow splash bunker that had been constructed before the 1972 Open in the angle of the L-shaped bunker on the fourth hole should be replaced by a classical pot bunker, sharp-sided and deep, since Neville had had that type of bunker in mind. And he believed that Neville had meant the bunker in the drive zone on the right side of the sixteenth hole to be more daunting from the tee and more punishing to play from. These changes were made. Apart from this, the 1982 Open course was really the same course that was played ten years before. This is evidenced by their over-all lengths: 6,812 yards in 1972, 6,825 yards this year.

The 1982 Open turned out to be one of the great Opens of all time. Before play got under way, there was a good deal of speculation about the chances of Craig Stadler, Severiano Ballesteros, Ray Floyd, who was on a hot streak, young Bobby Clampett, Tom Kite, David Graham, the defending champion, and a number of other players in the starting field of a hundred and fifty-three, but the two men at the center of most discussions were Jack Nicklaus and Tom Watson. No other golfer has played Pebble Beach as well as Nicklaus. In addition to winning the 1972 Open there, he scored his second victory in the U.S. Amateur there, in 1961, when he was twenty-one, overwhelming his opponent in the semifinals 9 and 8 and his opponent in the final 8 and 6. Aside from this, he has won the Crosby three times—in 1967, 1972, and 1973. Nicklaus's successes at Pebble Beach have been due in a large measure to his being that rare golfer, a power hitter with an instinctive sense of shotmaking. When he has been a bit off his game, he has been able to convert mediocre rounds into acceptable ones, because, first, he is an exceptional putter, as we have begun to appreciate more and more in recent years, and, second, he can concentrate under the strain of the big test like few other athletes. This uncommon amalgam of abilities explains why Nicklaus has won many more major championships than any other golfer—nineteen in all: two U.S. Amateurs (1959, 1961); four U.S. Opens (1962, 1967, 1972, 1980); three British Opens (1966, 1970, 1978); five Masters (1963, 1965, 1966, 1972, 1975); and five P.G.A. championships (1963, 1971, 1973, 1975, 1980). A proud man who is rightfully aware of his prodigious record, Nicklaus wanted very much to win the 1982 Open, for several reasons. Now forty-two and showing signs of slowing down, he was eager to bring his total of major victories to an even twenty. Then, too, if he carried the day at Pebble Beach he would become the first player to win our Open five times. (Willie Anderson, Bobby Jones, and Ben Hogan have also been four-time winners.)

As for Watson, he is the finest hitter of the golf ball to come along since Nicklaus's heyday. Over the past seven years, he has won five major titles—the British Open in 1975, 1977, and 1980, the Masters in 1977 and 1981. Watson is subject to spells of wildness, especially off the tee, but when he is in top form he can be dazzling. For a man of only medium size—he is five feet nine and weighs a hundred and sixty pounds—he drives the ball an astonishing distance, frequently more than two hundred and eighty yards. Around the green, he can improvise all kinds of stunning shots—a talent he has had since he was a boy. He is probably the outstanding bunker-shot artist since Gary Player. An attacking putter, he tends to be overbold, leaving himself plenty of those grisly four- and five-footers after running his approach putt past the cup, but he has streaks when he holes long ones from all over the place. Watson wanted to take the 1982 Open as badly as Nicklaus. Now thirty-two, he had failed in eight previous attempts to win it, although he was in a position to do so at Winged Foot, in Westchester, in 1974; at Medinah, outside Chicago, in 1975; and at Baltusrol, in New Jersey, in 1980. He knows only too well that since the mid-nineteen-twenties our Open has been the game's most important championship, and that a golfer cannot expect to be ranked among the great players in history, whatever his other accomplishments, unless he has won at least one Open. Many of us had begun to wonder whether the Open would always elude Watson, and I can well imagine that these same thoughts have gone through Watson's mind every day the last five years. Like Nicklaus, he has a special fondness for Pebble Beach. During the years he was attending Stanford University, which is only seventy miles or so away, he would hurry down to the Monterey Peninsula whenever he had a free weekend, and revel in the challenge of the course. Like so many young golfers who hoped for a career in the game, during his college days Watson used to fantasize about winning the Open while he was out on the course playing a round—"Tom Watson is now tied for the lead. To win this championship, he will need at least one birdie on the remaining holes. He has his work cut out for him. . . ." Watson was particularly prone to these fantasies when playing Pebble Beach.

As it turned out, in its final stages the 1982 championship was fought between Nicklaus and Watson, and was resolved by one of the Open's most exciting climaxes. It deserves to be described in some detail, but a few aspects of the first three days of play should be mentioned in order to set the scene properly for the stirring dénouement.

On Thursday, the day of the opening round, a fairly strong west wind swept over Pebble Beach. In the morning, the skies were gray and the air was chilly, and waking up to greet the new day brought one all the delight of rising in Glasgow in December. All during the morning and the afternoon, clouds from the fog banks in the bay rolled across the course. Apart from the fact that after the opening day the wind was appreciably gentler, the weather remained much the same throughout the tournament. The skies were generally overcast, and only now and then could one see the sun breaking through in Carmel Valley, fifteen miles away. It is testimony to the beauty of Pebble Beach that under such bleak conditions the course looked as handsome as ever. It was in first-class shape for the championship, the greens swift and smooth, the fairways tightly knit and resilient. The rough was not as high as it usually is in the Open, but it was thick, wiry, and sufficiently punishing. In one respect, Pebble Beach had a different mien: the bunkers were heavily fringed with shaggy, tall grass, which waved in the wind and gave the course a sort of Scottish look.

The tournament had hardly started on Thursday morning when Danny Edwards, a seasoned touring pro from Oklahoma, ripped off an eagle and three birdies to go five under par on the first six holes. As noted earlier, the first six holes at Pebble Beach are eminently birdieable, but one seldom tears through them the way Edwards did. However, after he had gone to six under par with a birdie on the eleventh, he double-bogeyed the fourteenth, bogeyed the sixteenth, double-bogeyed the seventeenth, and eventually had to settle for a 71, one under par. The lowest score that day was 70. There were two of them, one by Bill Rogers, the 1981 British Open champion, and the other by the veteran Bruce Devlin, a transplanted Australian who now lives in Houston. No one had looked for Devlin to make this much of a splash. Now forty-four, he is best known in the golf world these days as a commentator on the tournaments that NBC televises. Not many people remember that in the nineteen-sixties and the early nineteen-seventies he was one of the top dozen players in the world. When I think back to the period between 1955 and 1975, only two golfers come to mind who had the stuff to win a major championship but somehow didn't. Devlin was one, and Mike Souchak the other.

In the second round, on Friday, Devlin, instead of quickly fading from contention, birdied three of the last four holes for a 69, a total of 139, and a two-stroke lead at the halfway mark. Another pleasant surprise was the performance of Nathaniel Crosby, the twenty-year-old son of Bing Crosby. Smitten by golf at an early age, Nathaniel—everyone refers to him by his first name—is a slim, nice-looking, intelligent, and intuitive young man who attends the University of Miami. Last September, he astounded everyone by winning the U.S. Amateur Championship. His swing was so unimpressive that most observers felt there had to be at least a thousand better amateur golfers in the country. In many of his matches in the championship, including the final, he fell behind his opponent and seemed certain to be beaten, but he has courage and abiding determination, and in one crisis after another he produced the crucial shot or holed the vital putt and survived. Since the Amateur, he had done nothing to speak of. However, as the Amateur champion he automatically qualified for the Open, and he was paired on the first two rounds with two other automatic qualifiers, David Graham and Bill Rogers. This was a most attractive threesome, and I walked the second round with them. On the opening day, Nathaniel had shot a 77, which was not a bad score, but in order to make the thirty-six-hole cut, which seemed likely to come at either 150 or 151, he was faced with the necessity of playing a much lower round. I must confess that I did not anticipate golf of the quality he showed us. His technique had improved considerably since last summer. The arc of his swing was wider, his tempo slower and more rhythmic, his extension through the ball more assured. Indeed, there was little to choose between the shots he played and those of Rogers and Graham. Through the first thirteen holes, he was two under par. If he could stay close to that pace, he would almost surely qualify to play the last two rounds of the championship.

The fourteenth hole at Pebble Beach is a 565-yard par 5 that breaks acutely to the right in the drive zone and swings up to a very firm green, whose high left side, protected in front by a deep bunker, sits about ten feet above the fairway. In tournaments, the pin is almost always positioned on the left side, and so it was that day. Nathaniel's tee shot just failed to carry the bunker in the angle of the fairway, and he proceeded to play the hole about as badly as it can be played. He caught the lip of the bunker with his second shot. His third, from the bunker, was well out, but he hit his approach shot thin and it finished short of the green on the right side of the fairway. His fifth shot, a pitch with his wedge, rolled over the back of the green into deep rough. He tried to dig the ball out with his wedge but barely advanced it. He was on in seven with a deft wedge flip two and a half feet from the cup, but he missed the putt, and that gave him a 9. Now, according to my computation out on the course, in order to have a chance of making the cut he could not afford to drop another stroke to par. What a superb job he did! Quietly regathering his poise and his purpose, he played the last four holes flawlessly. On the par-4 fifteenth, he was on the green in two, twenty-two feet from the pin, and rolled in the putt for a birdie. He was on in two on the sixteenth, a dogleg par 4, and got down in two putts from about twenty-four feet. He had a crack at a birdie on the hazardous seventeenth, the 209-yard par 3, when he put his tee shot twelve feet past the pin, but his putt slipped by the cup. On the eighteenth, the par 5 that edges along Carmel Bay, he hit the narrow fairway with his drive, as he had done on both the fifteenth and the sixteenth. Safely on the green in three, he stroked his approach putt inches short of the cup, and tapped in for his 5. That was a 73 and a thirty-six-hole total of 150. Bob Sommers, the editor of *Golf Journal*, who is often a walking companion of mine at tournaments, thereupon lifted his shooting stick and speared the air in exultation. "A 73 with a 9! I won't forget this soon. You know, Nathaniel played so well after that disaster on the fourteenth that he could have birdied three of those last four holes." Nathaniel's 150 enabled him to make the cut, which came at 151. Only one other amateur, Corey Pavin, made it—at 151.

Nathaniel Crosby completed the tournament with creditable rounds of 76 and 77, and his four-round total of 303, a stroke lower than Pavin's, earned him the low-amateur honors. There is no knowing whether he will go on to become a truly outstanding tournament golfer, but I venture to predict that whatever he chooses to do he will do well.

The way to play a seventy-two-hole stroke-play championship is not to try to win it on the first three rounds. The main thing is to be patient those first three days, passing up the flamboyant or outright dangerous shot even when you may feel in your bones that you can bring it off. Your aim should be to be in a position at the end of the third round where you can win the championship on the fourth round. At Pebble Beach, both Watson and Nicklaus, working hard and carefully, played themselves into excellent position after fifty-four holes. Indeed, Watson, with rounds of 72, 72, and 68, for a total of 212, was tied for the lead with Rogers. He had been very lucky to escape with a 72 on the second round, for he had hit a number of loose iron shots. His putter had bailed him out: he sank two twenty-footers, a twelve-footer, and an eight-footer, and missed no putt he should have made. On the third round, his iron play was much sharper, but, then, the course was considerably more docile that day. Rain had fallen during the night and early in the morning, and, with the greens soft and holding, the players could fire right at the pin. The greens also did not putt fast, even though they had been triple-cut in the morning by the mowing crew. To further encourage low scoring, there wasn't so much as a puff of breeze coming off the bay. Incidentally, the galleries were so hushed and stayed so respectfully still that whenever a golfer was playing a shot on the holes along the bay it was impossible not to notice the movement and calls of the birds. The peninsula is well known for its many feathered species, but the only ones that I, a 36-handicap ornithologist at best, could identify were the California gull, the common swallow, and, I think, the lark sparrow.

One man who failed to take advantage of the easy scoring conditions on the third day was Devlin; after a birdieless 75, he stood at 214, two strokes behind the leaders, along with Graham, Scott Simpson, and George Burns. Nicklaus (74-70-71) was a stroke farther back. On his third round, Nicklaus had also failed to seize the day, and he knew it. He had played steadily and well from tee to green but had missed many holeable putts. "I'm not disturbed at the way I'm rolling the ball with the putter," he said at the close of the round. "These greens are very difficult to read." He added, with a rueful smile, "I've only been playing them for twenty-one years, and one of these years I'll learn to putt them." Twenty-one years ago, when he was twenty-one, Nicklaus was a different kind of golfer from what he is today. A heavyset, muscular athlete, he hit the ball "with the kick of a mule," as Bernard Darwin put it, and he sent it incredible distances. One year in the nineteen-sixties, he reached the green on the 525-yard fifteenth hole at the Augusta National with a drive and an 8-iron. In 1966, when he captured his first British Open, at Muirfield, the pivotal hole was the 528-yard par-5 seventeenth, the seventy-first hole of the tournament. Playing the small British ball and helped by a slight wind at his back, he set up the winning birdie by getting home with a 3-iron and a 5-iron. Nicklaus lost some of his power in 1969, when he took off twenty pounds, and over the last decade he has placed increasing emphasis on control at the expense of distance. Today, the ball doesn't explode off his club the way it used to, but he still hits it a long way. One other thing: he is still the most fearsome fourth-round player in the game.

On Sunday, under glum skies, Nicklaus, paired with Calvin Peete, started his fourth round at 12:38 P.M. His No. 1 son, Jackie, who is a student at the University of North Carolina, and is many inches taller than his father, was caddying for him. Nicklaus got off slowly, bogeying the opening hole, where his approach shot spun back off the green, and then missing his birdie on the second, a par 5 that is reachable in two. He appeared to be completely unfazed by this disappointing start. When he is out on the golf course during a tournament, you can practically feel the fierceness and continuousness of his concentration, and yet at the same time, despite being surrounded by pulsing thousands, he seems to be not only oblivious of the pressure of the contest but more relaxed than you and I are when we get home after work and watch the news in the living room with a drink in hand. On the third, Nicklaus holed a good-sized putt across the green for a birdie 3. That set him off. He birdied the fourth when he dropped a twenty-three-footer. For the first time in the Open, he was making some putts. He birdied the par-3 fifth after he stuck a 6-iron two feet from the pin. Continuing to roll, he birdied the par-5 sixth by reaching the hilltop green with a drive and a 1-iron, and two-putted from thirty-five feet. He birdied the seventh, the precarious 110-yard par 3, playing a crisp pitching wedge eleven feet from the pin and making the putt. His surge was stopped when he bogeyed the eighth, the hole across the inlet of Carmel Bay—here his iron to the green found the rough on the right—but, thanks to that rush of five consecutive birdies, he finished the first nine four under par for the tournament. He was in the thick of it now, tied with Watson and a stroke behind Rogers, who was the leader at that moment.

In the old days, news travelled slowly on a golf course, and the reports over the grapevine were not always reliable. Today, what with a large, well-operated leader board at nearly every hole, the players know almost instantly what their rivals are up to. Watson, paired with Rogers, certainly did. By nature a much more high-strung person than Nicklaus, he had felt a little nervous when he awakened on Sunday morning. After breakfast, he played for a spell with his two-year-old daughter, Meg, whom he adores. He then dug into two Sunday papers, taking his time as he read about the federal-budget controversy and the earthquake in El Salvador. He felt somewhat less tight when he put the papers down. He and Rogers were off at 1:05 P.M., three twosomes and twenty-seven minutes after Nicklaus. Throughout the round, Watson was two holes or a hole and a half behind Nicklaus, depending on the length of the holes they were playing. They were seldom in sight of each other.

Watson, who had started the final round four under par, turned the front nine still four under par. A bogey on the third had offset a birdie on the second. On the short seventh, he had wasted a big chance, muffing a two-and-a-half-foot putt for a birdie. This error obviously did not affect him as much as it might have, for on the eighth he made a difficult seven-footer to save his par. At this point in the round, Rogers was going through a very shaky passage, missing his pars on the ninth and tenth and, later, on the twelfth, and therewith dropping out of the race. By that time, Devlin, too, was out of it, a stout-hearted challenge by Graham was over, and the championship had become a two-man battle—Watson against Nicklaus.

In retrospect, the tenth hole looms large in Watson's eventual victory. On that 424-yard par 4 that marks the end of the glittering cliffside sequence, he managed to avoid a 5 and, possibly, a 6 or 7. This significantly changed the shape that his duel with Nicklaus took. Off the tee, he hit the narrow, slanting tenth fairway—it was only twenty-seven yards wide for the Open— but he hung his approach shot, a 7-iron, out to the right, and it found the bunker below and to the right of the green. That green is tucked close to the edge of the cliff, and if the ball had drifted a shade more it could conceivably have toppled over the cliff and down onto the beach. (Incidentally, in the distance beyond the tenth green one takes in the crescent beach of the town of Carmel, its bright white sand washed by the breaking slate-colored waves. It is something to contemplate. It looks the way one imagines the shore at Bali Ha'i might, except that one sees few people swimming, because the water is intensely cold.) From that sunken bunker on the tenth, Watson exploded to the edge of the green, twenty-five feet from the cup. Then he made the putt for his 4. This not only kept him four under par but boosted him into the lead, a stroke ahead of Nicklaus, who, minutes before, had three-putted the eleventh green from twenty feet.

Which player should one watch, Nicklaus or Watson? When in doubt, it is usually wise to go with the leader. I walked to the drive zone on the eleventh. This 382-yard par 4 runs uphill from the tee, but Watson, pumped up by holing that big putt on the tenth, whaled his tee shot two hundred and seventy yards up the fairway, at least forty yards beyond Rogers' drive. He was on with a pitching wedge, twenty-two feet from the pin. As he walked with his quick strides to the green, he acknowledged the gallery's applause with his ingenuous smile. Like Nicklaus, Watson is determined to play golf his way, and his way is to approach it as a game and to show in a natural manner his appreciation of the support that the spectators give him. The keystone of Watson's personality is his invariable honesty. This somehow comes through in his facial expression, and may explain why some people get the feeling that there is a certain vulnerability about him. It should also be noted that there is a lot of iron in his soul, for otherwise he would never have been able to accomplish the things he has. After studying the line of his birdie putt on the eleventh—close to the cup, the sidehill putt would dart from left to right—he stepped up and knocked it in. Five under par for the tournament now, a two-stroke lead on Nicklaus. Not for long. On the par-3 twelfth, 204 yards long, he left his iron shot out to the right and was bunkered. He played what was for him only an ordinary sand shot, leaving the ball fifteen feet short of the cup. He made a rather weak try for the putt. Back to four under par and a lead of only a single stroke on Nicklaus. Matters stood the same way after he parred the thirteenth. His tee shot on this hole must have been close to three hundred yards. Under tournament tension, Watson sometimes sprays the ball into trouble, because his hitting action gets too quick, but on this last round, swinging well within himself, he was clouting his drives a mile and dead straight.

The fourteenth, the long par 5 that swings to the right, proved to be another critical hole. After a good drive, Watson chose to lay up with an iron about eighty yards short of the pin, figuring that he would be able to put more backspin on a relatively full wedge than on an abbreviated wedge flip, and so would be able to stop the ball close to the pin, which, once again, was situated on the high left side of the green. I could not see what kind of lie he had, but, in any event, his shot had very little spin on it and rolled thirty-five feet past the pin to the back edge of the green. I think it was then—as Watson was walking to his ball—that most of us in his gallery noticed on the leader board adjacent to the green that a red 4 had gone up for Nicklaus on the fifteenth. This meant that he had birdied that hole and now stood four under par—tied for the lead. (We learned later that Nicklaus had holed a fifteen-foot putt for that birdie. The old Golden Bear is really a tough customer down the stretch in a championship.) Watson took a shade more time than usual reading the line of his thirty-five-foot birdie putt on this sleek, ripple-filled green. He hit the ball with a good-looking stroke. Halfway to the hole, the ball seemed to pick up speed. It was still moving fast when it dived into the middle of the cup. A terrific putt—especially in those circumstances. Five under par now, Watson had regained his one-shot lead over Nicklaus. Only four holes to play.

Up-and-down rounds are nothing new to Watson, but what was called for at this stage of the Open was sure, prudent golf: do nothing fancy, keep the ball in play, concentrate on hitting the green in the regulation number of strokes, get down in two well-thought-out putts. On the par-4 fifteenth,

Watson was letter-perfect: on in two, down in two from twenty feet. On the sixteenth, however, the 403-yard par 4, which slides downhill as it doglegs to the right and drops to a green shut in on both sides by trees and further protected by immense bunkers, Watson made an almost fatal mistake. Off the tee, he missed hitting the fairway for the first time during the round. He started the ball off to the right, and it stayed to the right, finally plummeting down into the recently remodelled bunker in the crook of the dogleg. This is one of the two bunkers that Sandy Tatum, remembering Jack Neville's suggestions before the 1972 Open, had asked to have fortified for the 1982 Open, so that it would more accurately fulfill Neville's wish that it be both more intimidating off the tee and more difficult to recover from. Now its front wall rose straight up three feet high, the upper two feet sodded like a Scottish bunker. Talk about irony! Watson has no more fervent admirer or devoted friend than Tatum. A contemporary of Watson's father at Stanford, Tatum has been close to Tom ever since he came West to attend Stanford. Looking gravely at this bunker after it had caught Watson's tee shot, Tatum turned to some friends in the gallery and said, "That's what this bunker was meant to do." On the third round, Watson's tee shot had ended up in the same bunker, but the ball had finished at the back edge, and he was able to fly his recovery shot onto the green. On this round, though, his ball lay only a foot and a half from the base of the perpendicular front wall. Attempting to go for the green was out of the question. After some thought, Watson concluded that the best he could do was to explode out sidewise onto the fairway, which he did. The ball trickled several yards down the hillside and came to rest on a fairly severe downslope. It is not easy to put backspin on a ball from a downhill lie, and, with the pin positioned only fifteen feet from the low front edge of the green, which slopes down from back to front, backspin was necessary in order to stop the ball near the pin. Watson's third, a wedge pitch of some eighty yards, landed near the pin, but the ball had no spin on it whatever, and it rolled another fifty-five feet on up the green. At about this time, I began to wonder whether Watson should have exploded backward out of the bunker onto a flat stretch of fairway from which he could have played an approach with backspin. However, this was strictly second-guessing. His lie in the bunker had been such that he probably didn't have room enough to swing the club back and play that kind of shot. Anyway, from the high back edge of the sixteenth green he would be fortunate if he could escape with a 5. He came through with a beautiful approach putt. He lagged the ball downhill over the skiddy surface with its subtle slide to the right, and it died barely fifteen inches from the cup. He tapped in for his 5. With two holes to go, he was again tied with Nicklaus at four under par. It could have been worse. If he had three-putted the fifteenth, he would have been trailing by a stroke. He walked to the seventeenth tee at about the same time that Nicklaus, to resounding applause, was walking off the eighteenth green and heading for the scorer's tent to check his card. Except for taking those three putts on the eleventh, Nicklaus had played an errorless second nine. From tee to green, he had thought his shots out painstakingly and had executed each shot the way he had meant to. If his putting had been up to his normal standard, he could easily have been a couple of strokes lower. He had made his birdie putt on the fifteenth, but then he had missed a shortish birdie putt on the fourteenth, and on each of the last three greens he had had a crack at a birdie from seventeen feet or less. In any event, he had given one more unforgettable demonstration of how a golfer should play the final round of a championship.

Watson won the Open on the seventeenth hole, just when it seemed that he might lose it there. On the final round, the back tee of this celebrated par 3 was used, so the hole played its full length—209 yards—into a moderate wind. (On the eighteenth, the wind was blowing across the fairway, off the bay. If it had been behind Nicklaus on that hole, and if he had got off a long drive, he might have tried to reach the green in two.) The seventeenth is a tester. The green is unusually wide and unusually narrow from back to front. It sits just above a very large front bunker. Beyond the green is a string of small bunkers, along with other trouble: the rocks and water on the left.

You really cannot play for the right side of the green, because you then have to deal with the dangerous ridge that divides the green into two sections. In tournaments, the pin is almost always set on the left side. It was on this day—ten feet from the left fringe, about halfway between the front edge and the back edge of the green. Watson first thought he would use a 3-iron but then changed his mind and played a 2-iron. He hooked it a shade—or, to use the current expression, he "came over" the ball, instead of hitting under and through it. The ball finished hole-high, twenty feet to the left of the pin and eight feet from the fringe of the green, in a growth of thick, resistant rough. He would also have to cope with a downhill lie. If you were standing out near the ropes on the right side of the hole, you could not see the ball. However, Watson later explained that though it was down low, it was lying on top of the grass. "I had a good lie," he said. "I could get the leading edge of my club under the ball." Opening the blade of his sand wedge and cutting under and slightly across the ball, he hit an exquisite shot. The ball came up softly, about two feet high, and landed just on the edge of the green. Curving a foot and a half from left to right with the contour of the green, it rolled straight for the pin, hit it dead center, and fell in. The moment the ball disappeared from sight, Watson threw his arms up and broke into a wild Indian dance. The spectators packed along the seventeenth, reacting almost as immediately to this sensational birdie, which put Watson in the lead by a precious stroke, began jumping for joy and shouting and howling.

Under the circumstances, Watson calmed himself down quickly. By the time he stuck his peg into the ground on the eighteenth tee, he looked composed and confident, ready to wrap things up. A par 5 on the 548-yard eighteenth would do it. He played the hole just the way he meant to: a 3-wood tee shot down the right side of the fairway; a 7-iron laid up in the center of the fairway a hundred and thirty yards from the green; a 9-iron that sat down pacifically twenty feet behind the pin. Watson studied the green with care. His putt was a touch downhill, and he wanted to be sure he had the speed right, so that he would leave himself the shortest of tap-ins. He had no intention of trying to hole the twenty-footer, but the ball slithered into the cup. He had won the Open. He had finally won the Open. The fact that his margin of victory was two strokes was irrelevant. He had won the championship by holing his sand-wedge shot on the seventeenth when it would have been an achievement to get down in two from the rough. (I think his ball would have rolled about seven feet past the cup if it hadn't hit the pin.) That little cut pitch out of the heavy grass may well be the greatest winning shot that has been played in the Open since 1923, when Bobby Jones, tied with Bobby Cruickshank as they came to the eighteenth in their playoff for the title at Inwood, on Long Island, summoned a perfect-plus 2-iron, from a poorish lie, that rose in a high parabola over the water hazard before the green, came down on the green, and stopped six feet from the hole. The scores of the leaders in the 1982 Open: Watson, 72-72-68-70—282; Nicklaus, 74-70-71-69—284. Two strokes farther back, at 286, were Rogers, Clampett, and Dan Pohl.

Nicklaus, after walking off the eighteenth green, watched Watson's tee shot on the seventeenth on the TV monitor in the scorer's tent. When he saw the ball hook into the thatchy rough, he felt that the percentages were heavily against Watson's getting down in two from there and saving his par. He turned his attention to checking his scorecard, thinking that now he would probably win the Open and that the worst that could happen was a playoff, if Watson somehow birdied the eighteenth. When Nicklaus next looked at the monitor, what he saw was Watson dancing across the green. His first reaction was that Watson's recovery had probably lipped out of the cup.

Twelve minutes or so later, when Watson walked off the eighteenth green, Nicklaus was waiting there to congratulate him. "You little son of a gun, you're something else," he said as they shook hands. "That was nice going. I'm really proud of you, and I'm pleased for you." The two men have enormous respect for each other. They also like each other. In the last Ryder Cup match, they were always together. Nevertheless, it took an extraordinary sportsman to do what Nicklaus did at the conclusion of a championship that, not many minutes before, he had thought he would win. There is no other loser in sports as gracious and warm as Jack Nicklaus has shown himself to be. This quality is due in part to training he received from an exceptional father and in part to Nicklaus's own character and sense of sport. He and Watson had previously fought three memorable battles down the stretch in major championships. In the 1977 and 1981 Masters, Nicklaus, trailing at the start of the final round, had mounted valiant rallies only to see Watson fight back successfully. In the 1977 British Open, Watson and Nicklaus happened to be paired on the third round. They both shot 65s. As the two leaders, they were paired again on the fourth round. Nicklaus had a 66, Watson another 65, with Watson prevailing on the final green. I can still see Nicklaus's yellow-sweatered, bearlike arm wrapped over Watson's shoulder as they came off that last green after their two-day, head-to-head confrontation.

And I am all admiration for Watson, for having the heart and the skill to play as he did under the stress of that long last hour. Now that he has at length won the championship, I am told by the experts and roving soothsayers that we will see a more majestic Watson. That would be fine. Apart from his superior personal qualities, he is one of the purest shotmakers since Harry Vardon. At the moment, though, the 1982 Open still fills my mind. I can think of only one U.S. Open since the Second World War that can compare with it in dramatic impact—Ken Venturi's triumph eighteen years ago at Congressional, on the outskirts of Washington. The 1982 Open is something to treasure. With the lone exception of that 1977 British Open at Turnberry, when Nicklaus and Watson duelled face to face over thirty-six holes—a rare combination of circumstances—I don't see how a tournament can be any better than the one we were treated to at Pebble Beach. It was just about as good as golf can get.

An Open and Shut Case

Scott Simpson won a U.S. Open shootout with Tom Watson when the long Watson putt above stopped inches short on the final hole at the Olympic Club

by Rick Reilly, *Sports Illustrated*, June 29, 1987

It had been 21 years since the Olympic Club in San Francisco held a U.S. Open golf championship, and with any luck, it will be 121 years before it holds another. Not that the Lake Course at Olympic, hard by the Pacific Ocean, isn't a choice piece of real estate. It's just that an Open at Olympic is about as much fun as having *The Miami Herald* move in across the street. It is the world's only par-70 cemetery, and bulldozed under it are some of golf's greatest players, including Ben Hogan and Arnold Palmer. Olympic hit Hogan with a skinny haystack named Jack Fleck in the 1955 Open, and Hogan was never the same. Then, in the 1966 Open, Olympic tortured Arnie with Billy Casper, who made up seven shots in the last nine holes and saw to it that the army never marched off with another major. And last week came the hat trick. Olympic slipped a Mickey in Tom Watson's comeback cocktail.

Until Watson came to Olympic, golf's Huck Finn had been seated at his own funeral. He had not won a tournament in three years, a major in five. But at Olympic, suddenly he was playing his freckles off, only to come up against a square in a groove named Scott Simpson.

Now Simpson is a decent enough player. But on the thrill scale he ranks just behind Edwin Meese and slightly ahead of a tuna sandwich. Though he had no right to, Simpson ruined Watson's longed-for coming-home soiree, partly because of an ungodly run of putting and partly because of one ungodly piece of luck. Simpson won the 1987 U.S. Open by a single shot over Watson, and so there you had it: Olympic had set up and squashed somebody flat again. How long is it until the British Open?

Do you see a trend here? Look at golf's last *two major*-domos: Bob Tway at the PGA and Larry Mize at the Masters, both quieter than Mafia stenographers. And now comes Simpson, a man who rarely drinks, rarely talks and rarely misses Bible study. If you sat with these three champions—Tway, Mize and Simpson—in one room, you might be able to hear your hair grow. You think that maybe without lot of commercials to do, residuals to cash, golf courses to design and investment meetings to take, they're at the practice range more? Hmmmm.

Simpson, 31, fits the Olympic Wrong Man mold like the golf glove he doesn't wear. He is Fleck/Casper reinvented. He is not just tall and dark and unheard-of, like Fleck and Casper, he became Olympic's predestined party pooper, a cop busting up history's bash, dropping 15-footers down the stretch of what is supposed to be the chokingest tournament in the nation, all with a pulse of about 19. Simpson didn't even know he was in the lead until after the 16th hole.

And once finished, with ABC's cameras riveted on his face as Watson's putt to tie at the 18th missed by inches, Simpson smiled as though he had just scraped off a $10 winning lottery ticket. Later Simpson got *really* emotional.

"This is probably my best year yet," he said. Grape Nehis for everybody.

Like Fleck/Casper, Simpson is not Madison Avenue. Simpson is barely Elm Street. Say, hey, USA: Meet your new Open champion. Simpson, who won the NCAA title in 1976 and '77, says the main reason he's on the Tour is to "make a living for my family," which includes his wife, Cheryl, and their two children. He had "never" fantasized as a kid about winning a U.S. Open. He says he never thought he was "good enough to win a U.S. Open." He says winning an Open "won't mean as much to me as to other guys." He doesn't feel he has gotten the recognition he deserves, "which is fine with me." And before Sunday he had no plans to play in the British Open next month because he would rather stay home and play the Hardee's Golf Classic in Coal Valley, Ill., that week to accrue points toward the $1 million Nabisco Grand Prix bonus pool. Other than that, he's an inspiration to golfers everywhere.

Like Casper, he will tithe 10% of his Open purse ($150,000) to his church. Watson, on the other hand, might consider giving 10% to a psychiatrist. Winless since the 1984 Western Open, Watson quite nearly overcame his own jury-rigged putting stroke, his own fears and, most of all, the unwritten word.

"I've heard everything about me," says Watson. "I'm an alcoholic. I'm on drugs. I'm getting a divorce. I'm moving back to the farm. I'm firing Chuck Rubin [his agent and brother-in-law]. I've heard all the rumors." The only rumor nobody had ever heard—the only one that was true—was that he was making a comeback. And for that he could thank a psychological kick in the rear from his caddie.

Sigh. Can't you just see it? Pretend the Dread Scott Affair never happened. Pretend Simpson forgot to enter. Here's Watson, 37, putting out a two-incher on 18 while 25,000 people at Olympic give him a standing O. It's an even-par round of 70 that has held together despite three bogeys in the first five holes. It's a masterwork of patience and grit and courage, the game of golf grinning from driver to wedge, watching one of its favorite sons come back from a long illness, resplendent and glowing.

Instead, here was Simpson, comparing the U.S. Open with his last victory, the third of his career, this year's Greater Greensboro Open. "This was intense," he admitted. "But so was Greensboro." Greensboro?

Oh, it had all set up so sweetly. Just arriving at Olympic was fresh. Here was a place where the wood came in trees (30,000 of them), not railroad ties; where the rough really was; and where the greens, said a member of the greens crew, Kevin Kelly, "are like Russian newspapers. Very hard to read." So fast and San Franciscan were the greens that occasionally players lined up chips with their backs to the holes.

Mac O'Grady summed up everybody's feelings when he said, "The inclinations and topography of Olympic Club already disturb the vestibular semicircular canals of my inner-ear balancing centers." Does that mean Mac is a little dizzy? It was sort of like putting down Lombard Street. At one point, Jim Thorpe had a two-foot downhill putt, "and I was lagging." He left it short.

Strange occurrences were commonplace. On the 18th on Saturday, Tommy Nakajima, the Japanese star, hit the ball into a tree with bark and bite. If Olympic's greens weren't holding, this tree was. The ball was so stuck that even 18-year-old Kevin Moriarty, a fan, couldn't find it—and he went 40 feet straight up looking for it. Nakajima made a double bogey, taking him from two back of the leader to four. He was last seen seven shots behind and stuffing a chain saw into his bag.

And then there was Senior Open champion Dale Douglass, who wasn't acting his age. At 51, Douglass was the oldest man in the field, but was still only four strokes behind the leaders on Saturday, and this without using a cart the whole week. He finished 31st, which was 15 places better than a younger competitor, Jack Nicklaus, 47, who at 138 actually was within one shot of the second-round lead but who played the weekend in a natty 76-77. "All I want to be is 22 years old again for this one week," Nicklaus said during a practice round, but it was Watson who got younger—and rid himself of burdens—every day at old Olympic.

"You feel like you're climbing up a hill and you're on sand," Watson said in trying to describe the slump. Of course, people didn't want definitions. They want explanations. So they invented some, says his wife, Linda. "Pretty soon it was, 'Hey, did you hear?' Vicious, terrible things. It was rough." Watson said the rumors about him have "hurt my wife and my family," and Linda explained why. "Look," she says. "My job is to be a wife and a mother. And when you start hearing, 'Hey, I know why he's losing. He's got a lousy wife and a lousy marriage,' it doesn't make you feel very good. I had no way to defend myself."

What really happened to Watson during those three years might be that he lost his desire to beat his brains in at the Buick Opens and the Canon–Sammy Davis Jr.–Greater Hartford Classics. "Maybe it was just a matter of me growing up a little bit," said Tom. "Maybe it was a matter of me getting a little more mature. Thinking more about being a father. Not being so one-dimensional. . . . It's not a bad thing. But the fans don't understand it, and the press doesn't understand it, either."

Bored, Watson took five weeks off last year and never picked up a club. The rest refreshed him. "You don't know how nice it is just to change a light bulb," he said. "Usually, if Linda were to say, 'There's a light bulb missing,' I'd be saying, 'Oh well, I'll see ya. I'm going to Westchester.'"

What Watson never stopped pining for, though, were majors championships, so he set out this year with that in mind. And what do you know, if Friday didn't find him leading one, tied at three under par with another redhead, the sartorially slick Mark Wiebe, who became the first person in history to lead the Open in a designer sweatshirt. People may remember Wiebe's sweatshirt more than they remember him, after his horrendous finishing 77-79.

Watson, however, never melted, and he prepared himself for Sunday by laying his fears and hopes buck naked on the table. "I want to win when my guts are on the line," he said. "When it really *means* something." Watson, unlike Simpson, knew that this was something worth losing sleep over.

Maybe almost as much as Greensboro. "Let's face it," Watson said. "I'm nervous. I'm about to play maybe the most important round of golf in my career. I know it. You'll write it. You know it.

That's the game."

Of those who chased him, Watson must have least dreaded seeing Simpson in his rearview mirror, especially with Seve Ballesteros, Bernhard Langer, Ben Crenshaw, Mize, John Mahaffey (all three back), Curtis Strange (four) and Greg Norman (seven) menacing. Even rookie Keith Clearasil, er, Clearwater, the fresh-faced pro from BYU, seemed to own more destiny than Simpson. Clearwater admitted the only things that got him to the Open at all were his wife's feet. It seems that after he won the Colonial in Fort Worth six weeks ago, he stayed out celebrating until 2:30 a.m. Qualifying for the Open meant getting up at 5 a.m. There'll be a U.S. Open next year, he said to himself. "Then I felt these big feet on my back pushing me out of bed. My wife was saying, 'You'll be watching the Open on TV and wishing you were there.'" So he not only qualified but went out Saturday and tied Rives McBee's course record of 64. Then he tripped over his own feet Sunday with a 79.

Anyway, one by one, all of them faded . . . except Simpson. Ballesteros, who came within one shot of the lead, couldn't keep his ball in the short grass and finally flattened under the weight of his own driver. "Someday," said Ballesteros, "they'll play without fairways. Just rough and green. Then I'm sure I will have a very good chance."

And suddenly, Watson and Simpson—history maker and history breaker—were all alone. Then again, maybe Simpson would have faded too, if the poltergeist of Fleck and Casper hadn't intervened on the 11th. It was there that Simpson sailed a bunker shot much too hard and high and, quite probably, off the edge of the green. Only the ball smacked the flag, cuddled down six feet from the hole and begged to be coaxed in for par, when surely bogey or worse had been growling. ("Well," said Watson afterward. "That's the game. I chipped in five years ago.")

Playing in the twosome ahead of Watson, Simpson jabbed first, birdieing the 14th from six feet to tie Watson for the lead at one under par, and then the 15th from 30 feet to take the lead by himself. "I pulled that putt on 15 a little bit," said Simpson, "but then the thing broke right and went dead in the hole. It was lucky." The Ghosts of Olympic be with you.

Simpson led for only a matter of seconds, as Watson, playing behind him in the final twosome, answered with a birdie at 14 to tie it again. Then Simpson holed a 15-foot birdie putt on 16—his third straight piece of putting artistry—to go one up. It was here that Simpson took his first peek at the leader board all day. "I decided not to look at the board until then because last time I did it I think it hurt me more than helped me," he said. Simpson wanted to stay with his style—plodding along, making good pars, "hitting for the middle of the green a lot of times," taking precious few chances. "When I looked, I expected to see myself ahead," Simpson said. Imagine his surprise to see a 37-year-old, washed-up ex-legend loitering one shot in arrears.

Now, admitting to the sticky breath of a six-time PGA Player of the Year on his neck, Simpson promptly hit his approach shot to 17 into a bunker. But this was where Simpson did something unexpected. He drew from history. "I thought about Fleck and Casper," he said. "The one thing I knew I had going for me was that I knew the veterans had lost two times before here. If Jack Fleck could come from behind and win, then I could do it, too."

And so Simpson blasted out to seven feet and, with Watson waiting in the fairway, made the putt. "The best putting day of my life," he said.

And now lay one last hole. From the 8th hole on, Simpson and Watson had both played Olympic in three under par. They were the only players under par for the week.

Somehow, Simpson made a routine two-iron, eight-iron, two-putt par on the short 18th—and stepped aside to watch Watson. On came Watson's pitching wedge from 105 yards, dead uphill, dead on-line . . . but too short.

"I probably should've hit a nine-iron," Watson said. Then the 45-foot putt. Dead on-line. But three inches too short.

Watson wasn't sure whether he should collapse from success or failure. He had missed a few birdie chances—eight feet at the 7th, 10 feet at the 10th and 15 feet at the 16th—but he had persevered. "I have nothing to be ashamed about," he said. "I am disappointed, but it feels good to be in the hunt. I can feel a little of the old magic coming back. I mean, the old magic is right there."

Huck Finn wouldn't say he had returned, but his wife was happy to say it for him. "He's turned the corner. He was in there and he fought, just like the old Tom Watson. It was 1977, 1978, all over again."

For Scott Simpson the year was 1987 and he was looking at the U.S. Open trophy to confirm it. "There sure are some great names on here," he said. "It's kind of hard to believe my name is going to be on there too."

But it will. No bigger than Fleck and Casper, no smaller than Hogan and Palmer.

Come to think of it, maybe that's what Olympic has been trying to teach us all along.

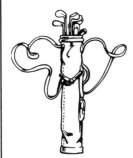

Those Fabulous Four Aces

by Rick Reilly, *Sports Illustrated*, June 26, 1989

At about 10:30 last Friday morning, a car pulled up to the main gate of Oak Hill Country Club in Rochester, N.Y. A man leaned out the window and said to the security guard, "Did I miss anything?"

"Miss anything?" said the guard excitedly. "You missed the four aces."

"Dang," the man said glumly, "and I've got all their albums, too."

Those Four Aces were good, but these four aces were historic. In the first three hours of play in the second round of the U.S. Open, four players had made holes in one on the 167-yard, par-3 6th hole, each using a seven-iron.

"If I hadn't been a part of it," said Nick Price, "I would never have believed it."

8:15 A.M.

Doug Weaver, playing in the first threesome of the day, hits his Spalding number 3 past the hole, 15 feet on the right. The pin is tucked in the front right corner. The ball spins back and straight into the jar. "The crowd sounded like a clap of thunder," says Weaver.

9:25 A.M.

Mark Wiebe, playing seven groups behind Weaver, hits his Titleist number 7 eight feet left of the pin, watches it roll back down into the hole.

Weaver is only 100 yards away, on the 12th tee, when he hears it. "I got to relive that sound again," he says.

9:50 A.M.

Jerry Pate, playing two groups after Wiebe, has heard about the two holes in one. "Well," Pate tells his caddie, "we might as well get us one, too, then." Why not? Miracles are on the clearance table.

Pate hits his Titleist number 3 seven feet past the pin, watches it spin dead back, toward the hole, and dunk. Ace No. 3. "Other than winning one," says Pate, "that's the greatest feeling I've ever had at an Open." Both Wiebe and Weaver hear the screams.

10:05 A.M.

Price, playing in the very next group and only the second player to hit since Pate, lines up his shot as he listens to a thrilled volunteer explain exactly how to make a one here. As soon as Price hits his Spalding number 2, the volunteer screeches, "That's it! That's how you do it!" And sure enough, the ball lands eight feet right of the pin, jumps forward and then rolls backward into what is by now a very exhausted hole.

Of the first 32 players through on Friday, four had made a one. This was either golf by divine intervention or the world's most competitive closest-to-the-pin contest. And you know that somebody sitting at the 6th hole was seeing golf played for the first time. These guys aren't so great. A lot of 'em don't even make it.

According to the experts at *Golf Digest*, the odds of a pro golfer's making a hole in one on a given hole are 3,708 to 1. The odds of four pros in a field of 156 doing it are 332,000 to one. Who knows what the odds are of it happening again?

John Daly Reaches the Unreachable Green

by Dave Anderson, *The New York Times*, June 19, 1993

Lee Trevino likes to joke that, when caught in a thunder-and-lightning storm, a golfer should hold a 1-iron aloft. "Not even God," he says, "can hit a 1-iron."

But John Daly can.

From the time he arrived at Baltusrol on Tuesday for the United States Open, he was aware of the challenge: reach the unreachable green of the 630-yard uphill 17th hole in two shots. For him, that meant a drive and a 1-iron because he doesn't even carry a 3-wood.

"As soon as I walked in here," he recalled, "all the volunteers and members told me, 'We want to see you hit 17 in two.'"

No other golfer had ever done that. And as the Open evolved, it emerged as John Daly's continuing challenge. To have a chance, Daly needed to put his tee shot in the fairway. In the opening round Thursday, he hooked his drive into the left rough, as he had in Tuesday's practice round. Wednesday his drive drifted into the right rough.

But in yesterday's second round, John Daly reached the unreachable green.

After a 325-yard drive into the fairway, he drilled an uphill 305-yard 1-iron shot that landed in the tangled rough between two bunkers, bounced three times, rolled across the green and stopped about 45 feet beyond the cup. He was nearly over the green in two.

"Those were two of the best solid shots that I've ever hit in my life," Daly was saying now outside the scorer's tent after posting a two-under-par 68 for a 36-hole total of 140. "I swung as hard as I could."

As hard as any golfer ever has. When his ball hopped onto the green, a different roar rumbled across Baltusrol's meadows. Golf galleries erupt with a "Nicklaus roar" or a "Palmer roar" or a "Watson roar" when those legendary favorites roll in a birdie putt. But this "Daly roar" around the 17th green sounded like the roars that once responded to a moonshot home run by Mickey Mantle or Reggie Jackson.

This was a roar of awe at how far John Daly hits a golf ball.

Now 27 years old, he's sturdy but not that big at 5 feet 11 inches and 175 pounds. Asked to explain his power, he shrugged.

"I don't know," he said. "I guess the whole body works together."

It works together despite a long corkscrew backswing that would wrench the spine of any other touring pro, and someday probably will wrench his. But he's always swung big clubs in a big way.

As a youngster with Nicklaus clubs, he refused to let anybody cut them down to his size.

As a teen-ager, he was told that he would never play big-time college golf with that big backswing. But he played at the University of Arkansas, and his Ultra Tour golf balls still display a red Razorback logo.

"To hit 17 in two, that's the only goal I had this week," he said. "I told my caddy, Greg Rita, 'We may not play good but at least we'll make history.'"

According to Rita's yardage book, Daly, who was wearing a lime-green shirt, black pants and white shoes, had 282 uphill yards to the front of the

17th green and 287 uphill yards to the pin after his thunderclap tee shot with his Killer Whale driver with a 7-degree loft.

"I swung as hard as I could on both shots," Daly said. "It was just one of those things. Maybe it was meant to be."

As the ball soared toward the green, the gallery watched in silence, then erupted in its Daly roar. In Thursday's opening round, Sandy Lyle of Scotland had been green high in the right rough in two, with a driver and a 3-wood, but not on the green itself. In the 1980, 1967 and 1954 Opens on the Lower Course, no big hitter had ever been close to the green in two. Not even Jack Nicklaus; not even George Bayer or Sam Snead.

In the instant roar and in the whooping applause that greeted him at the green, Daly responded almost bashfully with a quick wave of his white glove. Then the 1991 P.G.A. champion two-putted for birdie 4 as he moved into contention.

"Mentally, the Open drains you," he was saying now. "You've got to have so much patience. You need so much experience to win a tournament like this. The Open is much tougher than the P.G.A. is. The greens at the P.G.A. are soft, the fairways are wider."

Daly has reached a longer par-5 in two shots, the 644-yard first hole at Castle Pines outside Denver, where the International is held.

"I've hit that green with a drive and a 6-iron," he said. "But it's downhill off a high tee and there's the 5,000-feet altitude."

But at Baltusrol yesterday, John Daly reached the uphill 17th, the longest hole in Open history, with a Killer Whale driver and a Wilson Ultra 1-iron that now belongs in a glass case in the Golf House museum in nearby Far Hills, N.J.

No, he couldn't reach Far Hills in two. Or could he?

A Kite Steady in the Wind

by Dave Anderson, *The New York Times*, June 22, 1992

In other moments, Tom Kite had steamed silently and politely when he was reminded that he was the best golfer never to have won a major championship. But now, with the United States Open trophy glistening next to him, he finally acknowledged how much the question about the absence of a major title had annoyed him.

"Bugged the living daylights out of me," he said.

Kite's triumph had been written on the wind that gusted up to 35 miles an hour across the cliffs and coves of Pebble Beach yesterday in the Open's final round. Twenty of the world's best golfers had shot in the 80's, but this Kite had been steady in the wind for a par 72 and a three-under-par total of 285, two strokes better than Jeff Sluman.

No longer would Kite be known merely for having won the most money on the PGA Tour, more than $7 million.

"I always felt good about Tom Kite and his career," he was saying now. "But the only thing most people would say was, 'You've done all these things, but when are you going to win a major?' Like all the other things I've done didn't matter. It was such a narrow focus. There are people who have won majors who I wouldn't trade careers with."

Then he smiled and said, "Surely not now."

All that prize money had never been able to buy the stature that Kite suddenly was smiling about now, the stature that the Open trophy assured. The oldest living Open champion, 90-year-old Gene Sarazen, once mentioned that if an important golfer doesn't win the Open, "there's a gap in his record." But now there's no gap in Kite's record.

"I really feel," he said, "like I perform really well when it counts."

To have won 16 other PGA Tour events and more than $7 million, Kite had to perform well when it counted. But all those millions merely enlarged the monkey on his back when he didn't win the 1989 Open at Oak Hill outside Rochester, after having had a three-stroke lead in the final round going to the 406-yard fifth hole.

He pushed his tee shot into a stream and took a triple-bogey 7. He later double-bogeyed both the 13th and 15th holes en route to a 78, finishing five strokes behind that year's champion, Curtis Strange.

"That was my biggest disappointment," Kite acknowledged. "I still feel like that was my tournament to win or lose and I lost it. This time this was my tournament to win or lose and I won it."

Now 42 years old, Kite speaks with a firm Texas twang. He grew up and still lives in Austin, where he was tutored originally by Harvey Penick, one of golf's legendary gurus. His hands are puffed from having hit thousands and thousands of golf balls. Behind glasses, his eyes narrow when he's surveying a putt from under the brim of his planter's hat.

"But golf isn't an individual game," he said. "You can't beat all these players out here without a great family."

Near the 18th green his wife, Christy, the mother of their three children, joked, "I'm sure now the question will be, 'When will you win your second major?'" His father, Tom Sr., a retired Internal Revenue Service official, also alluded to the question that no longer has to be asked.

"I always thought Tom was a good player and a good man," his father said. "I didn't think it took a major to make him one."

His father handed him a cut-down 3-iron when he was 3 years old and he has been swinging golf clubs ever since. At the University of Texas, he played in Ben Crenshaw's shadow. But he's won much more money than Crenshaw and his Open title now matches Crenshaw's only major: the 1984 Masters green jacket.

"It's not the best golf tournament I've ever had," Kite said. "But for hanging in there on a difficult golf course in difficult conditions, this is the best."

Hanging in there to win is important to any golfer in any tournament, especially in the Open, a tournament that always seemed suited to Kite's game: straight off the tee, consistent irons, good putter on firm greens. But strangely, until yesterday, his highest Open finish had been a tie for eighth in 1974 as a PGA Tour rookie. For all his millions, he had earned only $83,494 in Open prize money.

But the winner's check was for $275,000, lifting his career total to $7,439,440. Now he can put the Open trophy on top of all his bank books.

"It's a cruel game sometimes. It's a cruel game," he said after blowing the Open lead at Oak Hill. "But I'm not going to curl up and die because of one round of golf. I'll come back and contend in some more majors. I promise you."

Yesterday, in a wind that blew apart the world's other best golfers, Tom Kite kept his promise.

Shinnecock Should Be "On Radio"

by Dave Anderson, *The New York Times*, June 13, 1995

When the 100th anniversary United States Open begins Thursday at Shinnecock Hills, he will tee off as the reigning Masters champion, but golf has always meant more to Ben Crenshaw than a green jacket.

Ask most touring pros to identify Horace Rawlins and the answer might be, "I think he made the cut at Quad Cities?" But ask Ben Crenshaw and he would say, "Horace Rawlins won the first Open in 1895 at Newport." He knows golf's history. He knows why the great players of the past were great. He has watched Ben Hogan hit balls. And on a quiet afternoon during the 1981 Westchester Classic, he was sighted reading a book.

"It's about Bobby Jones," he said of the four-time Open champion. "What a wonderful golfer. What a wonderful man."

Two decades ago, Frank Hannigan, then a United States Golf Association executive and now an author and television commentator, mentioned to Crenshaw that the secluded Shinnecock Hills, revered for the quality of its course and for having been the site of the second Open in 1896, was being considered as an Open site.

"If the Open is at Shinnecock," the little Texan said, "it should be on radio, not television."

Virtually all the touring pros would never see Shinnecock Hills until the 1986 Open here, but Hannigan knew that Crenshaw had played it. Not as the host pro at a corporate outing. But on a pilgrimage with two friends in 1973 as a tour rookie because he had heard how wonderful it was. When he shot 65, he was told he had set the course record.

"No, it can't count for the course record," he said. "I hit two balls off the first tee."

On the 14th tee that day, Charlie Thom, the Scottish pro who had been the club pro since 1906, walked down to visit with Crenshaw and his two pals. The old pro held out his left arm.

"He pointed to his elbow," Crenshaw recalled, "and told us, 'This is the name of the hole.'"

At Shinnecock every hole has a name and the 14th hole, with the tee down behind the barn where the old pro lived until he died, is Thom's Elbow, a dogleg right of 447 yards that funnels to a small green protected by bunkers and clumps of small trees and bushes.

"An incredible hole, a sinewy par 4, maybe the best hole on a course where the holes go every which way," Crenshaw said. "You have to bend and shape shots in the wind at Shinnecock."

At 6,942 yards, a natural par 70 with only two par-5 holes, Shinnecock Hills is vulnerable to low scores on a calm day. But when the wind blows, as it usually does, the scores soar. In the 1986 Open, the wind blew in a different direction each day, creating four different courses.

The wind out of the Northeast is the worst. When there's a Northeast wind, the members supposedly stay in the bar and play cards.

In the rain and the Northeast wind of Thursday's opening round in 1986 the touring pros were hitting a driver followed by a 3-wood on the 472-yard

12th hole and not always getting to the green. When the wind roared from the southwest on Friday, they were hitting a driver and an 8-iron on that par-4 hole.

In that 1986 Open, Crenshaw finished with three 69's, but shot a 76 in Thursday's blustery nor'easter. That left him in a tie for sixth, four strokes behind Raymond Floyd's winning 279. Now, only two months after having won his second Masters, the 43-year-old Texan is here in the Hamptons again.

"It's going to be a special Open," he said. "Shinnecock makes your heart beat faster. Everything fits here. It's a marvelous golf course in a unique setting, a touch of golf that emanates from the British Isles. No trees to speak of. Sandy soil. America's first golf clubhouse."

That clubhouse, designed by the celebrated architect Stanford White, has been expanded since 1896, but perched atop the tallest Shinnecock hill, it has the look of a century ago.

The current course, designed in the 1920's to replace the original course that sprawled across what is now Route 27 and the Long Island Railroad tracks, has the look of a British Open with its tall brown rough swaying in the wind that usually comes off the Atlantic, a mile to the south.

"Nowhere in America," Ben Crenshaw said, "is there anything like it."

Unfortunately, the Open at Shinnecock Hills won't be just on radio, but maybe NBC can do the next best thing: put Horace Rawlins's ghost on camera.

Janzen Feels No Payne

by Jim Murray, *The Los Angeles Times*, June 22, 1998

Well, it wasn't a choke exactly. More like a mugging, an unarmed robbery.

Payne Stewart couldn't smuggle a five-shot lead over a competitor safely into the clubhouse here Sunday. Lee Janzen became the U.S. Open champion for the second time this decade. He beat the same opponent he beat at Baltusrol in 1993.

What happened? Well, basically, the golf gods got into Payne Stewart with a vengeance.

Look, when you hit a ball in the middle of a fairway, you have done exactly what the game of golf demands. You can't do it any better.

You shouldn't be penalized. There shouldn't be any moguls to tilt the ball off line or out of bounds, any little glitches not properly a part of the course.

And there probably shouldn't be any divots for your ball to come to rest in.

Payne Stewart hit a near-perfect tee shot on No. 12, a pivotal hole, Sunday. Unfortunately, several other players had done the same thing earlier in the week. The fairway was littered with divots.

Stewart's ball came to rest in one of them. It was a divot filled with sand. We don't replace divots in golf anymore, we pour sand out of a bottle on them.

Unfortunately, unfairly, Stewart's ball, with his near-perfect drive, came to rest on ground that was neither sand trap nor fairway. He couldn't get the club on the ball. He slapped it into a trap. He made bogey from there.

He handed the tournament to Janzen then and there, in a sense.

Stewart thinks you should get a free drop or get to replace the ball no nearer the pin when it lights in a hole in the middle of the fairway. It's hard to disagree with him. You shouldn't lose the Open on a shot in the middle. You should lose it on an O.B., a right-to-right slice, a smother hook, a topped shot, a bladed sand blast. Stewart lost it for doing what the books tell you.

Janzen is a nice enough young man, with this nice, steady golf swing and temperament to match. He's probably good to his mother, pays his bills, goes to church. But let's face it. He's not Tiger Woods, he's not John Daly, he's not even Fred Couples or this baby-faced amateur with a nice smile they had here this week, Matt Kuchar. He's just—well, vanilla ice cream comes to mind. White bread, homemade fudge.

He cries when he wins, which is a nice touch.

Actually, if anyone wept here it should have been Stewart.

He is one of the staples of the tour, recognizable because he chews gum and wears knickers and costumes with it so outlandish a Brit writer once observed that he looked as if he were outfitted for a burial at sea. His garb sometimes looks like three flags sewn together with golden thread.

It is the view here, he also fell prey to a dreaded "Murray's Law." That is the tenet which holds that, in every golf tournament, the golfer, even the successful one, will have one cold round. The good golfer never has a cold last round—the Hogans, the Nicklauses.

The good golfer, too, perceives when he is having this cold round. And the trick is then to steer it in the clubhouse in 72 or 73 instead of 77 or so.

Janzen had already had his cold round as he teed it up for the final round at Olympic on Sunday: two 73's, either of which would qualify.

Stewart hadn't. He went into the final round 66-71-70. He finished with a 74, lost a seven-shot lead over Janzen.

Golf is such a cruel game. A torment. Bobby Jones once said, "Nobody wins an Open. Somebody loses it."

Janzen started out Sunday as if he would be the one who lost it. He bogeyed two of the first three holes.

Meanwhile, back on the tee, Stewart started out as if it were Payne Stewart and 59 of his best friends, out on a Sunday afternoon $2 Nassau with automatic presses. No pressure.

Par golf would have won him the tournament by three strokes.

It appeared as if he wouldn't even need that that. Ahead of him, golfers were leaving the field to him, failing to stop their approaches on greens, leaving 10-foot putts two feet short, hitting tee shots into the rough. When Janzen went to seven shots behind, it looked as if he were toast.

All of a sudden, on the fourth hole, Stewart joined the retreat. He began to rifle approaches through the green, misread putts, hit rough. Oops! Five bogeys.

And Janzen got the wheels back on. He put up four birdies and set sail on his 68. By day's end, he was the only player in the field at par.

The golf gods weren't through with Stewart yet. They had one more cruel trick to play on him.

He came up to the 18th hole, played meticulously and then had this 20-footer that would have tied him for the championship, given him another day.

I don't know about you, but I would hate to have a 20-foot putt decide my future. It was the gods' final bit of torture for him. He missed that putt by inches. He didn't leave it short, it wasn't off line. It was just inches away from $535,000, so to speak.

It just wasn't his day. Bobby Jones would have understood perfectly.

Life is not fair. And neither is golf. That's its charm.

The Greatest Open Ever

from *Payne Stewart: The Authorized Biography*
by Tracey Stewart

CHAPTER 1

This could be it. I leaned forward in my chair, eyes glued to my husband's image on the television screen, anxiously watching and waiting, hanging on the commentators' every word. This could be the critical shot of the 1999 U.S. Open. Payne's caddy, Mike Hicks, handed him his putter as he approached the sixteenth green at Pinehurst No. 2.

The U.S. Open is held each year at one of the most challenging golf courses in America. The mid-June tournament spans a four-day period, beginning on Thursday and ending on Father's Day. Open to both professional golfers and any amateurs who can survive the sieve of sectional qualifying rounds conducted at various locations across the nation, the U.S. Open is truly America's tournament. Nearly seven thousand golfers vie for a spot in the prestigious field each year, hoping to capture the prized silver trophy. Of that number, fewer than 160 men earn the right to tee it up in the Open.

One of the most difficult golf tournaments in the world, separating the good golfer from the truly great, the U.S. Open is "designed to identify the best golfer in the world," according to former United States Golf Association president Sandy Tatum. The players, however, don't always see it that way. Over the years, several have been heard mumbling, both privately and publicly, that the Open is designed more to humiliate them. Indeed, Ben Crenshaw, 1999 Ryder Cup captain, describes the U.S. Open as the "hardest test in golf."

For the 1999 Open, North Carolina's famed Pinehurst No. 2 golf course was configured by the USGA to play as a 7,175-yard par 70. Adding difficulty to an already tough course, USGA officials decided that two of Pinehurst's par-5 holes, number 8 and the hazard-strewn number 16, would be played as long par 4s. The chilly, damp weather that settled over North Carolina that weekend added yet another dimension of difficulty to Pinehurst's treacherous greens.

Payne had taken the lead during Friday's second round, and at the end of play on Saturday, still clung to a one-shot advantage over Phil Mickelson. But as Sunday's final round commenced, Payne's position at the top of the leaderboard was jeopardized as Mickelson, Tiger Woods, Vijay Singh, and David Duval mounted separate charges. Payne started the day playing well and rode a two-shot lead going into the ninth hole. As the round progressed, Duval dropped off, but Tiger Woods and Vijay Singh still lurked just below the top names on the leaderboard. Then, Payne began to struggle. Between holes 9 and 12, Payne missed four greens in a row, settling for bogeys at 10 and 12, which allowed Phil Mickelson to snatch the lead. Fighting back at the thirteenth, Payne sank his putt for birdie, pulling even with Mickelson again.

Meanwhile, Tiger Woods, playing in the group ahead of Payne and Phil, sank a difficult putt at 14 to draw within two strokes. The leaderboard was getting crowded at the top. On 16, Woods drained another sensational putt, dropping him to even par, only one stroke behind the leaders. Making matters worse, Payne narrowly missed his putt for par on 15 and now trailed

Phil Mickelson by one stroke as they approached the sixteenth hole. Payne shut his eyes, shaking off the wayward putt and gathering himself for the final push to the finish.

Mickelson had played flawlessly all day long, sinking difficult putts, hitting incredible shots, and making virtually no mental mistakes. He had not bogeyed a single hole throughout the round. His steady play was especially remarkable considering that on this Father's Day, back home in Scottsdale, Arizona, his wife was due to deliver their first child. Phil knew that at any moment he might receive a phone call telling him that Amy was on her way to the hospital. Given a choice between contending in the Open and being at home for the birth of their baby, Phil had announced in advance that he'd walk away from Pinehurst to be with Amy. It was a decision Payne understood and heartily endorsed.

But the distractions of imminent fatherhood did nothing to diminish Phil's competitive edge. If anything, it inspired him all the more! Thinking about what it might mean to win the U.S. Open on Father's Day, he had mused, "It could be a cool story for my daughter to read about when she gets older."

The weather remained unseasonably cool and wet for June in North Carolina; and though the rain held off, by late Sunday afternoon a fine mist permeated the air. No matter what the weather, the par-4 sixteenth at Pinehurst was treacherous, a hole that only three players had managed to hit in regulation during Sunday's final round. It looked as though 16 might be Payne's waterloo as well. He missed the green on his approach and then made matters even worse by hitting a poor chip shot, leaving himself a monstrous 25-foot putt for par.

Payne chewed his gum pensively as he strode onto the green. Concentration creased his brow, yet he seemed amazingly calm and composed. He leaned over, went through his normal pre-putt routine, then took a smooth, even, pendulum stroke and rolled the putt in as though it were a 3-footer! As the crowd roared its approval, Payne nonchalantly raised his right arm and pointed his index finger skyward in a brief acknowledgment, as though saying, "Thank you very much, but I still have a lot of work to do."

Concerning his performance on 16, Payne later said, "I was kind of disappointed in my chip shot. It was obviously horrible. But then I got myself right back into it and said, 'OK, you gotta stand up here, read the line, and make the putt.' And I did it. It gave me a lot of belief that I still had a chance to win the golf tournament."

When Payne sank that extremely difficult putt, it notched up the pressure on Phil Mickelson, who proceeded to miss a tough 8-footer for par. Suddenly, the two were tied again. Up ahead on the seventeenth green, Tiger Woods's putt spun around the left side of the cup and lipped out. He would have to birdie the last hole to have a chance to win.

At 17, a 191-yard par 3, both Payne and Phil nearly knocked the flag over, sticking their tee shots close enough possibly to make birdie. Payne's ball was about four feet from the cup, and Phil had a 6-footer. Phil missed his putt and had to settle for par. Before Payne lined up his putt on 17, a male voice in the broadcast booth could be heard on the air, saying ever-so-faintly, "Payne's gonna win." Payne made his 4-foot birdie putt and had a one-stroke lead.

After Payne made his birdie, I reluctantly pulled myself away from the television screen in our rented house where I had been watching every shot. I hurried outside to the car. Win or lose, I wanted to be there when Payne finished. Ripping out of the driveway, I roared toward the golf course, trying to locate a radio station that might be carrying the tournament. Fortunately, traffic was light, and I soon raced into the players' parking area near the clubhouse and ran to the eighteenth green.

Thousands of spectators lined the fairways and crowded around the eighteenth green to watch the national championship come to a close. People were sitting on the clubhouse roof, several were perched precariously in nearby trees; everyone strained for any advantage to their view. I quickly made my way out toward the green.

About the same time, in the group up ahead on the eighteenth green, Tiger Woods lined up his putt, a 30-footer that could put him back at even par and possibly keep him in contention. Woods stroked the putt as purely as he had any shot all day. The ball beelined across the green toward the hole but then rolled past, missing the cup by inches. Tiger doubled over in agony as he watched the ball dribble to a stop, possibly dashing his hopes of a championship. He shut his eyes and for a few moments seemed frozen in time, his face grimacing with disappointment. So close, yet so far away.

In the meantime, Payne had teed off on 18. He connected with the shot squarely and thought he had hit it well enough to be safe, though he couldn't see where the ball had landed. He was wrong. His drive had hit the first cut of deep rough, and instead of squirting through and landing in perfect position on the fairway, as so many similar tee shots had done that day, Payne's shot got hung up in the thick, wet grass. The ball bounced first to the left and then jogged back to the right, diving straight into the high grass just six inches off the fairway, in horrible position. After Payne hit his tee shot on 18, the chimes at the nearby Pinehurst chapel began to play. NBC-TV golf analyst Mark Rolfing noticed the sound and exclaimed, "They're playing 'Angels We Have Heard on High!'" The chimes must have struck a soothing chord with Payne.

When Payne trekked down the fairway and found his ball tucked in the rough, he was surprised and a bit disappointed. But Payne loved to hit the tough shots, and this one challenged him.

When Phil's drive landed in the heart of the fairway, Payne's one-stroke lead was once again in jeopardy. As he considered his predicament—178 yards out and in the thick rough—to Payne there was only one option. All week long he had stuck to his game plan whenever he was in trouble. He had learned from experience that when you're in trouble at the U.S. Open, you lay up and try to make par with your short game. He called this "taking your medicine," and he wasn't about to change the game plan that had helped him to lead after more rounds than anyone in the history of the U.S. Open.

Payne took his medicine and hit a 9-iron, landing well short of the bunker. It cost him a stroke, but it gave him a chance—what he knew might well be his last chance—to win the tournament.

"I hit the ball well all week," Payne said later, "and my wedge game had been particularly sharp. So when I drove it in the rough, I took my medicine and got into position to hit a wedge onto the green. Even though I was in the rough, I felt confident I could save par."

From the center of the fairway, Phil Mickelson saw an opportunity. With Payne forced to lay up, Phil felt free to attack the green. He launched an aggressive second shot, which rolled to a stop within twenty feet of the pin.

By now, I had made my way through the clubhouse and outside to an area restricted to players, family, USGA officials, and media; but I was still stuck in a crowd, three or four people deep, behind several taller spectators. I stood on my tiptoes, stretching to see Payne's next shot. "Where's Payne?" I asked a USGA official who was standing nearby. He eyed me curiously, as though he might recognize me, but I didn't give him any further hint concerning my identity.

"He's in the fairway," the official replied matter-of-factly. "He had to lay up."

My heart sank. If the round ended in a tie, that would mean an eighteen-hole play-off on Monday. *Oh, no!* I thought. *Not another play-off!* Payne's track record in play-offs was a lackluster three wins and six losses.

I whispered a quick prayer, "Lord, please be with him and help him to be the best he can be." I didn't pray for Payne to win because he and I had long since learned that there were more important things in life than winning golf tournaments. I did, however, pray, "Help him, Lord, to make the best effort he can and to bring glory to you."

Payne and his caddy, Mike Hicks, surveyed the situation and talked over the next shot. Mike, a thirty-eight-year-old native of North Carolina, had caddied for Payne off and on for more than eleven years; and even though Payne had tremendous confidence in Mike's knowledge of the golf course and in his own ability, he still wasn't satisfied. He paced off the full distance—about seventy-seven yards to the green—and then back, looking over the approach, the formidable bunker in front of the green, and the pin placement. Payne knew he had only one shot. He could not afford to misjudge distance, the speed of the green or anything else. If he didn't get all close enough to live himself with makable putt, the tournament would be up for grabs again.

Lining up over his ball, Payne hit a carefully placed wedge shot onto the green, leaving himself a nasty 15-foot putt for par. It was makable, but by no means a sure thing, especially under these conditions, at the end of the tournament, when one spike mark could send the ball veering off course. Payne knew that possibility only too well because that is exactly what had happened to him on the eighteenth green at the previous year's U.S. Open at the Olympic Club in San Francisco.

CHAPTER 2

AN UNFORGETTABLE FINISH

Payne had led the pack for three days at the 1998 Open. But during the final round, on Father's Day, he had allowed a four-shot lead to slip away. Almost as if it were a replay of the 1993 U.S. Open at Baltusrol, Lee Janzen came from seven shots behind and overtook him. Needing to sink a difficult 25-foot putt on the eighteenth green at Olympic to force a play-off, Payne gave it his best shot but missed the cup by a few inches. Lee Janzen, a tough competitor, especially on difficult courses, returned home with his second U.S. Open trophy.

Such dramatic turnarounds are not unusual during golf's four major tournaments: the Masters, the U.S. Open, the British Open, and the PGA Championship. These four events are known as "majors," even though the field of players competing against one another is basically the same as in other tournaments. Still, the majors have become the standard by which a professional golfer's career is measured. A fabulous player can win a dozen tournaments, and millions of dollars, but if he never wins a "major," he does not attain golf greatness. Thus the most ominous and despised tag in golf, "The Best Player Never to Have Won a Major," has been an albatross around the necks of numerous golf superstars.

Payne had finally removed the albatross from his own neck in 1989, when he won the PGA Championship. He'd won his second major—the U.S. Open—in 1991, but the 1998 Open loss hurt nonetheless. Payne's disappointment, though he handled it well, was very real. After his 1991 U.S. Open triumph, he had won only twice since on the PGA Tour, and by 1999, at forty-two years of age, Payne knew that his opportunities for keeping pace with the young lions on the golf course were growing slimmer. Payne passionately wanted to win at least one more major tournament in his career.

As he approached the 1999 tour season, Payne had only two main golfing goals: to win another major and to make the Ryder Cup team. Both objectives could be accomplished by a victory at Pinehurst. That's why I was surprised when, after he played poorly and missed the cut at the FedEx St. Jude Classic in Memphis the week before the U.S. Open, Payne called home and said, "I'm going to stay here a few days." Payne always looked forward to staying with our friends, Mark and Vicki Hopkins in Memphis. Payne had grown up with Mark and Vicki in Springfield, and we both had developed a close friendship with them, taking numerous vacations together over the years.

Payne's mother had traveled from Springfield, Missouri, to spend time with him while he was in Memphis, so it made sense that he would want to stay in town to visit with her as well. Also, Payne's golf coach, Chuck Cook, and his wife, Lana, were flying in to Memphis so Chuck and Payne could work together before going on to Pinehurst for the U.S. Open. However, from my point of view, remaining in Memphis after missing the cut seemed like a waste of time, and I told Payne so.

"Well, Mom is here, so I'm just gonna stay till Sunday," he said tersely. I could tell that he was still peeved that he had missed the cut.

"I understand," I said, "but I think you'd be better off to get over to Pinehurst and start preparing for the Open. Remember the goals you set. It's a major and one of your goals is to win a major. You really need to think about that."

At first, Payne wasn't overjoyed to hear my opinion on the matter. He insisted on staying in Memphis. A few hours later, though, he called back. "You know, love, you're right. I'm going to go on over to Pinehurst as soon as Chuck and Lana get here."

"Good idea," I replied.

That was so typical of Payne. He adamantly insisted on making up his own mind, but he was always open to advice and quick to take suggestions— once he'd had a chance to think them through. Nobody on earth could tell Payne Stewart what to do, but once he saw the light and took ownership of an idea, he was always willing to change.

Payne, Chuck, and Lana arrived at Pinehurst on Saturday afternoon, June 12, and moved into the house we had rented for the week of the tournament, about five minutes away from the clubhouse. Dr. Richard Coop, a sports psychologist with whom Payne had been working since 1988, had noticed that Payne seemed to play better whenever we stayed in private housing during major tournaments, rather than in hotels. We had rented a home during both of the majors Payne had won previously. Getting away from the crowds allowed him to escape the constant and often frenetic pace of the professional golf circuit. We could relax and talk about anything—anything other than golf—and the brief respite allowed Payne to concentrate better when he returned to the links.

Chuck and Payne began their preparation immediately. On Saturday evening, they walked the course to become familiar with its intricacies. Payne carried his 7-, 8-, and 9-irons, his wedges, and a putter as they played all sorts of shots, chipping to the greens and putting from various locations.

They followed the same routine on Sunday. On Monday and Tuesday, Payne played practice rounds. He took part of Wednesday as a practice day, working on the driving range but not going out on the course. He took the rest of the day off.

By the time I arrived in Pinehurst on Wednesday, Payne was in a good frame of mind. He felt well-prepared to play the Open, and although he had not played Pinehurst No. 2 many times before in actual competition, he genuinely liked the golf course. He was bubbling with confidence.

Aaron, our ten-year-old, was staying with the family of one of his friends back in Orlando, and thirteen-year-old Chelsea was attending a girls' basketball camp in Tallahassee. That allowed Payne and me to relax even more. After Chuck and Lana moved to their hotel room, it was just the two of us at the house. Rather than going out to restaurants, we ate all our meals at the house. Payne enjoyed helping with the cooking, and together we prepared simple, healthy meals of grilled chicken and lots of fruits and vegetables. There'd be no fancy cuisine or newfangled diets at our "training table." For variety, we had spaghetti one night—Payne loved spaghetti—and steak another. Lana and Chuck joined us one night for dinner. Otherwise, we kept to ourselves and tried to maintain a sense of normalcy amidst the hype and hoopla of a major championship.

Many professional athletes become superstitious when something is working well for them. For example, when a baseball team is on a winning streak, some of the guys will wear the same socks or T-shirt every game. Some players establish certain routines and refuse to deviate from them as long as they are winning. They might get up at exactly the same time and eat the same foods at the same time and place. The logic behind these superstitions is: If the wheel is rolling, don't mess it up by doing something different.

Interestingly, perhaps, pro golfers are generally not given to such superstitions. Nevertheless, when Payne got off to a good start by shooting an opening round 68 on Thursday, I remembered that we had enjoyed some mangoes as part of our fruit-and-muffin breakfast that morning. That evening, I made a point of going to the grocery store and stocking up on mangoes for the rest of the week. Mangoes became our signature fruit at breakfast every morning of the tournament.

On Friday, Payne played well again. As I had done on Thursday, I walked the course, keeping about half a hole ahead of Payne so I could watch where his shots landed. Chuck Cook followed Payne on Thursday and Friday as well. Although Payne and I rarely talked during a round unless there was some specific reason to do so, he wanted me to be there as often as possible. He claimed to know exactly where I was on the course at all times. Sometimes friends or fans would distract me from watching him, and Payne always let me know later that he had noticed. "Who was that person you were talking to?" he'd ask with a mischievous grin.

"Aren't you supposed to be concentrating on your golf?" I'd tease in return.

"I am, but I always know where you are on the course," Payne said.

Payne's confidence grew even stronger after he shot another great round on Friday, shooting 69 and leading the tournament after two tough days of competition. By Saturday, the crowds at Pinehurst were so huge I knew I wouldn't even be able to see Payne's shots. I told him, "I think I'm going to watch the round on television today. It's so hard to see out there with so many people. I'll be there, though, when you get done."

Payne understood perfectly.

Because Payne was leading the tournament, NBC focused its cameras on him for almost every one of his shots on the back nine during the third round. I stayed glued to the television most of the afternoon. Payne played well enough to remain atop the leaderboard on Saturday, but something was wrong. He was having trouble sinking his putts. As the afternoon slipped away, so did Payne's lead.

I peered intently at the television screen, following Payne's every move. I rarely played golf—tennis is more my game—but I had watched Payne play week in and week out for twenty years, so I knew his game well. I could usually tell if he needed to make an adjustment. As I watched on television, I noticed that Payne was moving his head ever so slightly on his putts, forward and upward, as though he were trying to watch the ball go into the hole. The slight head motion had already cost him several strokes. I watched helplessly as one putt after another curled around the cup and lipped out. "Oh, Payne!" I cried aloud to the television screen. "Keep your head down!" He ended up shooting a 72, his worst round of the tournament. Though he was still one stroke ahead of Phil Mickelson, and several strokes ahead of the pack, it wasn't a comfortable lead to sleep on.

At the conclusion of his round, I headed to the press tent, where I figured Payne would be answering questions about his round. Sure enough, because he was still leading the tournament, as soon as he had signed his scorecard he'd been whisked straightaway to the media tent. When I arrived, a press conference had already begun, so I slipped in at the back of the tent and waited. When the reporters finally had their fill, I stood at the entrance until Payne saw me and came over. "I'm going to go hit some balls," he said.

"OK, I'll go with you," I said. "You need to spend some time on the putting green too." Payne nodded in agreement. "You need to keep your head down," I continued quietly.

Payne looked surprised. "Really?"

"Yes. When you're putting, you are trying to watch the ball go in, rather than keeping your head down."

Payne and I walked over to the driving range. While most "weekend" golfers take time to hit balls at the range *before* a round, loosening up and establishing their swing routines, many amateur players are surprised to discover how much work the pros put in at the range *after* a round. The golfers whose names are most often seen atop the leaderboard are usually the same players you'll find in the practice areas after they've played their rounds on the course.

Payne often did his best practice work after a round. Rehearsing the good shots, and making minor adjustments to avoid the poor ones, he was committed to practicing after each round of the 1999 U.S. Open. At the Olympic Club in 1998, by the time he'd finished with his media interviews, the sun was usually beginning to set over the Pacific Ocean. Consequently, Payne hadn't been able to get to the practice areas after his rounds, and he later had said on many occasions that he regretted that situation.

He was not about to make the same mistake. So even though it was nearly dusk and a chill swept across "Maniac Hill," as the Pinehurst practice area is known, Payne pulled on his glove and went to work. I watched as he hit one golf ball after another on the driving range, working on his irons for more than half an hour. Then we walked over to the putting green near the clubhouse, and he spent another forty-five minutes working on his putts. He forced himself to keep his head still and not look up until the ball was well away from the putter. He got to the point where he was literally putting with his eyes closed and hitting the center of the cup almost every stroke. I stayed right there with him and watched as he concentrated on keeping his head still during each shot.

"Is that better?" he asked after a while.

"Yes, much better. It looks great."

It was nearly dark by the time we got back to the house. I prepared a simple dinner while Payne showered and then responded to the barrage of phone messages stored in his cellular phone's voice mail. He was always good about returning phone calls, and it seemed that half the world had his "private" cell phone number.

Because Chelsea was at basketball camp, we couldn't talk to her, but Payne made a point of calling Aaron at his friend's home.

"Aaron, I'm leading the U.S. Open again," Payne said enthusiastically to our ten-year-old son.

Aaron was unimpressed. "That's great, Dad," he replied. "Guess what! Conner got a long-board skateboard!"

Payne laughed. Unwittingly, our kids had a marvelous way of keeping Payne's feet on the ground, and he loved them all the more for it. Although they were always encouraging to their father, to them being a professional golfer was no big deal. That's just what their dad did for a living. Some of their friends' parents were doctors, lawyers, dentists, and schoolteachers. It just so happened that their father made his living hitting a small white ball into a 4-inch hole in the ground. They expected him to do it well; after all, he was . . . Dad. That he was one of the greatest players ever to walk the links hadn't yet sunk in to them.

After dinner and his phone calls, Payne settled back to watch the Stanley Cup hockey finals. We stayed up late to make it easier to sleep in a bit on Sunday morning. Because Payne had a late tee time on Sunday, the last thing he wanted to do was wake up at sunrise and pace around impatiently until it was time to get ready.

We slept as late as we could and then enjoyed a leisurely Sunday morning. We had our usual breakfast, including our mangoes, and then Payne got ready to play the final round of the U.S. Open. As part of his normal preround routine, he pressed his own clothes, including his plus fours—the knickers that had become an indelible part of his golf persona. Prior to the birth of our daughter, Chelsea, in 1985, I had always pressed the clothes that Payne would wear on the course. But after our children were born, Payne began doing his own ironing during tournaments. He refused to have his clothes sent out to a dry cleaner or to have anyone else press them. He was fastidious about getting every crease just right. Sometimes, if I was running late, he even pressed my clothes!

With the television blaring and Payne on his cell phone answering calls from friends, family members, and other well-wishers, I went to take a shower. When I came out of the bedroom, I was shocked to see that Payne's eyes were puffy. He looked like he had been crying.

"Luv'ie, what's wrong?" I asked as I crossed the room toward him. Payne wiped his eyes with his knuckle and motioned toward the television. "NBC just ran a Father's Day segment," he replied emotionally.

"So?"

"It was about my dad and me." Payne had been unaware that NBC had planned to broadcast a segment concerning Bill Stewart—Payne's dad, who had died of cancer in 1985—and his influence upon Payne's life and career. Payne had simply been tuning in to watch the early tournament coverage. As he watched the video of himself and his dad, tears flooded his eyes.

Rather than being disconcerted, however, Payne drew strength from the piece. It inspired him to want to play his best Father's Day round ever.

As the time neared to leave for the golf course, Payne dressed in navy blue knickers with a matching tam-o'-shanter hat; white kneesocks and white golf shoes; and a red-and-blue-striped shirt, highlighted by his Payne Stewart clothing line logo. Red, white, and blue. It was, after all, the U.S. Open. Because of the damp, chilly weather, Payne also donned a navy blue rain jacket. On his wrist he wore a dark green wristband, given to him by our son, Aaron, which bore the letters W.W.J.D., for "What Would Jesus Do?"

About two hours before his tee time, I drove Payne to the course. I slowly pulled the white courtesy car to a stop at the base of the circular drive, just past the famed Pinehurst No. 2 clubhouse. I looked across at Payne and tried to encourage him with some words of wisdom before he left to play the final round of the U.S. Open Championship.

"Just go out there and trust yourself," I said to him. "Believe in your heart that you can do it!"

He looked over at me, and with his little mischievous grin he said, "I've got a big heart, love." I laughed, we kissed good-bye and said "I love you" to each other.

The "big heart" that Payne was referring to was a diagnosis he had received in 1994 after a routine EKG in a fitness examination prior to the Los Angeles Open. The doctors discovered that Payne had a bundle-branch block in his heart, an anomaly that meant his heart did not squeeze blood normally and that the beat was not as strong as it should have been. This condition caused Payne's heart to be enlarged.

To keep the situation in check, Payne was advised to take Avapro medication on a daily basis, work out at least five days a week, and limit his consumption of alcohol. The doctors predicted that he would probably need a pacemaker later in life. Rather than worrying about his condition, Payne always made jokes about having a big heart anytime someone mentioned that he had "heart," "courage," or "intestinal fortitude." As he bounded out of the car toward the clubhouse, that big heart was about to be put to the test.

Arriving two hours early was a standard part of Payne's pretournament routine. He was obsessed with being on time. "In my line of work, I can't afford to be late," he reminded me frequently. "If I'm late for work, we don't get paid!"

I, on the other hand, was frequently late. If there was one area in which Payne wished (and prayed!) for my improvement, it was the matter of punctuality. Every year, he asked me to make a New Year's resolution that I would attempt to be on time. I made the resolutions, but my follow-through was less than Payne desired. He never gave up hope though!

After I dropped Payne off at the Pinehurst clubhouse, I returned to our rental home and switched on the television to watch the tournament coverage. Payne, as always, went to the fitness trailer, where he did some stretching exercises to loosen up his neck, back, and shoulders, all of which he had injured at one time or another during his twenty-year career. He usually had a massage at the fitness trailer. Only then, after his body was limber, was he ready to head to the range.

Mike Hicks had Payne's clubs in his designated position on the driving range, but when Payne got ready to hit balls, he felt the sleeves of the rain jacket tugging at his arms. The sleeves were restricting Payne's long, fluid swing, yet because of the weather, he needed the warmth the rain gear provided.

"Get me a pair of scissors, Mike," Payne asked his caddy. Mike found a pair in the pro shop, and Payne proceeded to cut the sleeves off the rain jacket, trimming the garment so that it covered his shoulders and about three inches down his arm, transforming the rain jacket into golf's first "muscle man" look. It didn't look bad! Although Payne was internationally known for his sartorial splendor on the golf course, he was not concerned about appearances today. All that mattered was playing his best. That was Payne though. His attitude was, "If there's a problem, let me fix it." And he usually did.

Coming into the 1999 Open, Phil Mickelson had never won a major, though at twenty-nine years of age, he had already won thirteen times on the PGA Tour. Now, as he approached the green on the final hole of the tournament, he faced a 20-foot birdie putt that could lead to his name being inscribed on the silver championship trophy. Phil's putt was uphill, with a slight right-to-left break. If he made it, Payne would be forced to make his putt just to stay even and send the tournament to a Monday play-off. If Phil missed it, he still had a chance to win because of the difficulty of Payne's putt.

Phil Mickelson is one of the finest putters on the PGA Tour. With his calm demeanor, he rarely gets flustered, regardless of the pressure. To the millions of people watching on television, Phil appeared poised to do what he had done all day—sink another spectacular putt. The thousands of people squeezed around Pinehurst's eighteenth green collectively held their breath as Phil stroked the ball well, then stood expressionless while the ball traversed the twenty feet toward the cup. For a moment, it looked as though the putt was in, but then it rolled off and stopped a few inches to the right of the hole. Payne chewed his gum rhythmically as he watched Phil tap in for par.

Now it was Payne's turn. If he missed the putt yet left the ball close to the hole, he could tap in and live to play another day. But this putt was extremely risky on the notoriously fast U.S. Open greens. Payne would never forget his frustration during the second round of the 1998 U.S. Open, when his 8-foot birdie putt on Olympic's eighteenth green slipped past the cup by inches; and then, because of the outrageous hole location selected by USGA officials, kept rolling . . . and rolling . . . and rolling. By the time Payne's ball had stopped, it was a full twenty-five feet away. His possible birdie had turned into a three-putt bogey. Payne had been leading the tournament by three strokes. He ended up losing by one.

Now, one year later, Payne faced a dicey 15-foot uphill putt with a left-to-right break that would decide the winner of the 1999 U.S. Open. Nobody—least of all, Payne—took the line on the eighteenth green for granted. Many in the crowd were already assuming that we'd be coming back on Monday for a play-off.

Payne slowly went through his usual preputt routine, crouching low, eyeing every undulation in the putting surface, lining up the putt. Finally he stood, pulled the putter back evenly, and brought it forward firmly but smoothly, aiming just to the left inside edge of the cup. The blade connected with the ball momentarily, sending it on a slight banana route toward the hole. Payne did not move his head.

Neither did Phil Mickelson. He watched from the side of the green, knowing that he had done his best and there was nothing further he could do. The tournament was out of his hands.

From my vantage point off the green, I could not see the hole. I saw Payne's ball rolling, as if in slow motion, across the green, bumping over the spike marks, each one a potential land mine that could knock the ball off course; but the ball kept rolling. On line, curving slightly, bending, the ball seemed suspended in time, the Titleist logo turning over and over, still rolling . . . and then, suddenly, the ball disappeared.

The huge crowd at Pinehurst exploded! It was one of the loudest—and best—responses from a gallery that I'd ever heard. Payne had won the 1999 U.S. Open!

In a moment that has since become immortalized in golfing lore, Payne instinctively punched the air with his right arm and fist, his leg extended like a baseball pitcher who had just thrown a game-winning pitch. With that spontaneous gesture, Payne released four days' worth of pent-up emotion as he bellowed from deep within himself. He had shown virtually no emotion throughout the entire day, not even after sinking the incredible putt on 16, but now it all came gushing out.

"You beauty!" Payne shouted, as Mike Hicks ran across the green and leaped into his arms. Payne seemed to catch his caddy in midair with one arm, as Mike patted Payne on the back and congratulated him.

They attempted to smack hands in a high-five . . . but missed. Payne picked his ball out of the cup, kissed it and slid it into his pocket. This was one ball he'd want to keep.

As the crowd continued to cheer, Payne quickly looked for Phil Mickelson. More than anyone, Payne knew the disappointment that Phil felt at that moment, but he also knew the exhilaration that Phil was about to experience. As the two men met, Payne reached out and literally held Phil's face in his hands. The words Payne spoke to his competitor and colleague had little to do with golf championships, winning or losing majors, or silver trophies. Payne had something far more important on his mind.

"You and Amy are going to have a baby, Phil . . . and there's nothing like being a father!"

Phil nodded appreciatively, hardly knowing how to respond. Later, Phil would marvel at Payne's magnanimous comments. "Payne wasn't thinking about himself at the time of his greatest triumph, and that showed a lot of class; that showed the type of individual Payne Stewart was."

On the side of the green, I pushed to the front of the crowd gathered inside the roped-off area where the players exit the green. Roger Maltbie, a green-side announcer for NBC and an old friend of Payne's and mine, spotted me and we hugged. We were both too choked up to speak. The crowd noise was so loud, it's doubtful that we could have heard each other anyhow. But it didn't matter. Words were unnecessary. Tears of happiness flowed freely from Roger's eyes, and I was crying too. Awash in an incredible sense of relief, tears of joy seemed the only appropriate response.

Payne was walking toward me. Because of the throng of people, he didn't see me at first and nearly walked right past.

"Payne!" I called out to him.

He pulled me close and we embraced on the green. With my head buried in his shoulder, I heard him say in my ear, "I did it. I kept my head down. All day . . . all day, I did it. I kept my head down."

Through my tears I said, "I know you did, and I'm so proud of you!"

That's all we had time to say before the USGA officials guided Payne down the stairs to sign his scorecard. Several minutes later, we walked back out on the green for the trophy presentation. Dan Hicks of NBC threw an arm around Payne and steadied a microphone in front of his face.

"You want me to talk?" Payne quipped.

"How do you begin, Payne," Dan said with a smile, "to put this championship—the moment you just realized a few moments ago—into perspective, not only winning the Open for the second time, but in the storybook fashion you just pulled off?"

"Well, first of all, I have to give thanks to the Lord. If it weren't for the faith that I have in him, I wouldn't have been able to have had the faith that I had in myself on the golf course. So, 'Thank you, Lord!'"

The crowd roared its approval in the background.

Dan gulped hard at Payne's response, but it didn't seem to throw him off. He immediately steered the conversation back to golf. "Payne, the resiliency you showed today on the golf course, making all the big, great putts, after last year . . . we know the scars are still there, and to win it coming off that year . . ."

"Well, all I know to say is . . . whooooooo!" Payne let out a yell that would have made his Ozark Mountain childhood friends proud. The crowd loved it and joined with Payne in celebrating.

"You said that experience made you tougher," Dan continued, "and there were numerous times on the golf course today when you had to dig deep."

"Well, I could never give up out there . . . Phil played unbelievably . . ."

Payne turned toward Phil Mickelson and said, "You'll win yours. I know Amy's at home, and I'd like to express to Phil and Amy that being a parent is a special thing. I'm glad that he made the commitment, that whether he got the beep today or not, he was going to be there with his wife . . . and that's very special. There's nothing like being a parent."

When Dan asked him to express his feelings, the ever-gracious Phil Mickelson returned kind words toward Payne. "I had a great time today," he said. "I know the outcome wasn't what I had hoped for, but I thought that the putts Payne made on 16 and 18 showed what a great champion he is, and I think he represents the United States exceptionally well as our champion."

The crowd responded again with an enormous ovation, expressing appreciation for both Payne's and Phil's classy and heartfelt comments. What we didn't know at the time was that Phil's wife, Amy, had spent Saturday night in the hospital and would give birth to their first baby, a darling little girl they named Amanda, on Monday. Had Payne missed his putt on Pinehurst's eighteenth green, the tournament would have gone to a Monday play-off, and Phil might have missed that special time with his family.

Many people were amazed at how Payne handled losing the 1998 U.S. Open and winning the 1999 Open with equal measures of grace. Members of the press, and some of his fellow competitors, were intrigued. Something was different about Payne Stewart. Oh, sure, he was still Payne—spontaneous, outspoken, extremely confident, and always wearing his emotions on his sleeve. He still loved a good party, and he'd still tell you what he thought about a subject if you asked him—or even if you didn't. He still worked hard, played hard, and loved passionately. Yet people who knew Payne well recognized that he had changed somehow for the better, if that were possible. He possessed a deeper, unusual sense of peace . . . a peace that hadn't always been there.

Yellow Jasmine, Par 5, 570 Yards

from *One Magical Sunday: But Winning Isn't Everything*
by Phil Mickelson with Donald T. Phillips

As great as playing in the Ryder Cup was for me, I'll always remember the year 1999 for a much more important event—the birth of our first child, Amanda. In an unusual twist of fate, her birth coincided with a major golf tournament, the United States Open in Pinehurst, North Carolina.

According to Amy's doctors, the delivery date was actually supposed to be a couple of weeks after the Open. But we weren't going to take any chances. I definitely wanted to be there with my wife when Amanda came into the world. So before I flew to Pinehurst, we discussed our options in quite a bit of detail.

> *We figured that the worst possible scenario was that I would go
> into labor on Saturday night while he was leading the tournament.
> Because if that happened, there were no ifs, ands, or buts about
> it—Phil was going to fly straight home. Of course, that would cause*

him to miss an opportunity to win his first major. But he told me over and over again, "If you have this baby without me, I'll never forgive you." And he made me promise to call him the moment I went into labor.

Amy Mickelson

We waited until Wednesday morning and went to the doctor for one final check. He stated that the worst-case scenario was unlikely to happen and that I should go to North Carolina and do my best. Amy agreed to be checked by her doctor every morning at eight o'clock. "Everything will be all right, honey," she said.

Before I left, I kissed her and said: "I'm going to win the U.S. Open, come straight home to you, and we're going to have our first baby together. It'll be the best week of our lives."

Very quickly, I made it clear to both the media and U.S. Open officials that, if my wife went into labor, I was going to leave. "Come on, Phil," one of the reporters said, "this is the U.S. Open—America's national championship of golf. You're not going to walk off the course if you're leading."

"I don't understand that thought process," I replied. "What in life is more important than your children?"

I played very well in the first three rounds of the tournament. Bones carried a pager in case Amy beeped us. We also had a mobile phone in my golf bag, but kept it off so the ringing wouldn't disturb anybody. One beep from Amy, however, and I would be calling her as I prepared to walk off the course.

After Saturday's round, I was trailing the tournament leader, Payne Stewart, by only one shot. We would be playing together in Sunday's final pairing.

I felt my first contraction on Thursday morning. "Oh, my gosh!" said our doctor. "If you had looked like this yesterday, there's no way I would have let Phil go to North Carolina."

By Saturday, the contractions were only four minutes apart. My mom and brother were timing them. "This can't be happening," I cried. "What are the chances? Should I page Phil? What if the baby doesn't come? He has a chance to win the U.S. Open! What are we going to do?"

I got so frantic at one point that my mom just grabbed me. "You need to get hold of yourself, Amy," she said. "If you don't, this baby is going to come."

We headed to the hospital and when the doctor walked in I begged him to give me Tribulatin, a drug that slows the labor process. "I just need twenty-four hours," I said. "Please!" Luckily, after a few hours, my contractions began to taper off. When they released me from the hospital, one of the nurses said: "Honey, I bet we're going to see you again in a few hours. This happens a lot. You're going to have this baby tonight."

I asked my brother to tape my knees together. "Just don't let the baby come for one more day," I said.

I never did call Phil.

Amy Mickelson

Sunday morning broke clear and sunny. It was Father's Day.

The first thing I did before I went to the golf course was call Amy. I asked her how she was feeling and she started to cry. "Why are you crying, sweetheart?" I asked.

"Just because I love you so much," she said. "Have fun today and win Amanda her first trophy."

I really was feeling good that day. I figured if I could just shoot 70, I could probably win. Twice during the round, I had a one-shot lead. But Payne would not back off. On the sixteenth hole, I missed the green on my second shot, made a bogey, and dropped back into a tie. Payne then stepped up and sank a great 40-foot putt to save par.

I was at home lying diagonally on the couch with four pillows under my lower body and a plate of Saltines resting on my belly. I was glued to the golf tournament—even though my doctor suggested I not watch because he thought too much emotion might start the labor contractions again. I was still on Tribulatin and the doctor had also given me a tranquilizer.
    Amy Mickelson

Payne birdied #17 to take a one-shot lead and I missed an easy 8-footer for birdie that would have kept pace with him. So as we went to the final hole, I was a shot back. I played #18 well and made a solid par (for that total of 70 I'd hoped for). But Payne sank a 15-foot putt for par to win the tournament. Of course, he was ecstatic and went over and jumped into his caddy's arms. When I went up to congratulate him, Payne shook my hand and said: "I'm sorry, Phil. Congratulations on playing like a champion."

Then Payne cupped my face in his hands and said: "Phil, you're going to be a father and there's nothing greater in the world. You and Amy are going to make wonderful parents." I was just so impressed that Payne would be thinking about the situation Amy and I were in—let alone mentioning it on the green right after he had just won the U.S. Open.

As soon as I finished my post-round press conference, I flew home. When I arrived at the house, Amy and her mother were fast asleep and I didn't wake them up. It was a difficult night for me. That tournament meant a lot and I couldn't sleep. I kept thinking about the last few holes—reliving every shot. If only I had done this. If only I had done that. I finally fell asleep at 7:30 on Monday morning.

At 9:00 a.m., Amy's water broke and we rushed to the hospital. It's interesting to think about it now, but had Payne missed that 15-foot putt, I would have been teeing off with him in North Carolina for an 18-hole playoff to determine the winner of the 1999 U.S. Open—on that same Monday morning!

Amanda Brynn Mickelson was born on June 21, 1999, at 6:11 p.m.—just about twenty-four hours after the Open concluded. What magical timing. I simply cannot describe how special that feeling was when I saw my wife give birth to my daughter. There are few experiences in life that people always cherish—and those are the events we live for. For me, Amanda's birth was one of them. I never felt so at peace.

My friend Payne Stewart died later that year in a tragic airplane accident. It was Payne's destiny, I now believe, to have won the 1999 U.S. Open. But his passing just reinforces to me how inconsequential golf is in the larger game of life. Payne left behind his wife, Tracey, and their two children, Aaron and Chelsea. He was a very special person and I think of him often.

Pebble

from *In Search of Tiger: A Journey Through Golf with Tiger Woods*
by Tom Callahan

The first leg of the Tiger Slam was the U.S. Open at Pebble Beach, the ultimate U.S. Open course. Although 105 years had blown by since Horace Rawlins beat Willie Dunn by two strokes in Newport, Rhode Island, war cancellations made the centennial and the millennium coincide. For the one hundredth Open in the year 2000, the United States Golf Association was duty-bound to return to Pebble Beach. Just as, later in the summer, the Royal and Ancient Golf Club could reconvene nowhere else but St. Andrews.

Seeing his twin capitals lined up so handsomely before him, sixty-year-old Jack Nicklaus (featuring a new ceramic hip but following the old original heart) took the occasion to announce that this would be his final march on the majors. Twenty-four-year-old Tiger Woods agreed that the stars had seldom been so well aligned. "It doesn't get much better," Tiger said, "than Pebble Beach and St. Andrews."

"This is one of the most gorgeous settings in the United States," said

Nicklaus, who won his second U.S. Amateur and his third U.S. Open at Pebble, "and they put a golf course on it."

"They" were Samuel Finley Brown Morse, the "Duke of Del Monte," and Jack Neville, the architect. Morse, grandnephew of the dots and the dashes, was a young attorney when he first saw, smelled, and tasted the Monterey Peninsula. "It makes you want to shout," he said, "to run rather than walk."

Another lawyer, name of David Jacks, owned the property at the turn of the twentieth century. The City of Monterey had deeded it to him to settle a $1,100 legal bill. This surveyed out to around fifteen cents an acre. For $5 an acre, Jacks shrewdly unloaded it to the Southern Pacific and Central Pacific railroads. They ultimately dispatched Morse to liquidate what was thought to be an unprofitable holding. He bought it himself.

Morse commissioned Neville, the California amateur champion, to collaborate with God on the construction of a golf course true to the jagged coastline. Then, like the old Yale football captain he was, Morse spent the next half century drop-kicking real estate developers off the cliffs. After Morse died, Pebble Beach passed though the cold fingers of Twentieth Century Fox, Denver oilman Marvin Davis, and a couple of different, or indifferent, Japanese concerns before it finally settled into the loving embrace of, among others, Arnold Palmer.

"I first played here when I was thirteen," Tiger said. "I remember thinking how long the course was. Then I came back at seventeen or eighteen to play in the State Amateur, and I couldn't get over how short it had become. Maybe my being six inches taller had something to do with that. The beauty of Pebble Beach still awes me. The mystique of it. It's perfect."

Four months earlier, the AT&T, the old Crosby Clambake, had gone on as usual in its pro-am format, spread liberally over three courses on the piney, deer-laden 17-Mile Drive: Spyglass Hill, Poppy Hills, and Pebble Beach. Were Cypress Point still in the mix, as it had been in Bing's day, one could say "spread conservatively." But because its black membership was holding so steadily at none, Cypress had been tossed over by the PGA Tour.

On the final day of the AT&T, with seven holes left to play at Pebble, Woods was seven strokes behind Matt Gogel but still fervently trying to win his sixth consecutive tour event. Holing out with a thunderclap from the fifteenth fairway, Tiger finished eagle-birdie-par-birdie and, with significant help from Gogel, did it. Woods won his sixth straight tournament. The situation was getting ridiculous.

Speaking of which, Mikhail Baryshnikov was among the amateurs. His presence was hardly ridiculous. Though a beginner at golf, Baryshnikov was either the best or the second-best athlete on the premises. The ridiculous part was that, as Baryshnikov told it, he had fallen under golf's spell while visiting the home of his friend Joe Pesci. It is absurd enough to think of the *Goodfellas* actor and the Russian ballet dancer existing in the same universe, let alone staying in the same house (or having a bite of hog's breath together at Clint Eastwood's Hog's Breath Inn).

"Do you and Tiger Woods know something the rest of us don't?" Baryshnikov was asked.

"All I know at the moment," he said with a sheepish smile, "is that this isn't my stage and this isn't my audience. My audience doesn't walk right up to me and gather around me like this. Tiger is amazing. There are people pressing all around him, standing just off his shoulder, and he can still dance."

By June, Woods seemed to have completely forgotten the AT&T. "It's a different golf course than it was in February," he said. "It's drier, faster. It's the Open."

"At any time of the year," Nicklaus said, "it can be absolutely bluebird weather here, or you can have wind and rain that you can't believe."

In Crosby's time, the most harrowing spectacle in golf could be the sight of Bing climbing the ladder to the TV tower, like a sailor hanging off a mast in the middle of a squall. One year, Jack Murphy of the *San Diego Union* invited me to share an appointment he had with Crosby, who received us in a house adjacent to the thirteenth fairway.

Bing was charming and strange, alternately vain about his vocabulary and monosyllabic. He would laugh about something, and then he would curse about something, and finally he would stare out of the window for long, uncomfortable moments, like the dipsomaniacal actor in *The Country Girl*. Only while discussing the golf course itself was he Father O'Malley.

"This place is the Louvre," he said. "It isn't just the Louvre, it's everything that's in the Louvre, too, with all of the artists gathered round." Bing didn't care for Bob Hope's snappier description—"Alcatraz with grass"—though he nearly smiled when Murphy quoted Johnny Weissmuller, one of the celebrities in the pro-am, saying, "I've never been so wet in all my life."

Crosby, a 2-handicapper who once competed in a British Amateur at St. Andrews, had last participated in his own Clambake in 1956, nearly twenty years earlier. On Saturday that year, he and his pro partner were hopelessly out of contention, sure to miss the fifty-four-hole cut, when, leaning into slanting sheets of chilly rain, they came to the house at the thirteenth hole.

"Ben," Crosby said, "we can pack it in right here and go have a toddy."

"If you don't mind," Hogan replied, "I'd rather play it out." That was Hogan's final round at Pebble Beach. He shot 81.

In absolute bluebird weather, Tiger opened with a six-under-par 65.

It was really a seven-under-par 65, as the long-standing par-5 second hole had been reclassified a par 4 for no compelling reason, other than the fact that Tiger could reach it so effortlessly. He birdied the fourth and seventh holes to go out in 33 and birdied ten, thirteen, fourteen, and eighteen to come home in 32. He didn't drive or strike the ball as well as a bogey-free score implied. A number of times, a woolly lie in the rough forced him to chop out sideways. That produced several eight- or ten-footers for par, and he made them all. Those par putts and the fog rolling in from Baskerville Hall foretold the week.

The Spaniard Miguel Angel Jiménez, whose European Tour nickname is "the Mechanic" (because he looks like he just rolled out from underneath a differential), shot 66. John Huston shot 67. They all went out early, Huston at 6:40 A.M. The next day, they would all go out late.

"Early and late were the winning draws this year," said Colin Montgomerie, who—consistent with his normal fortunes—drew late and early. "Tiger isn't only the best player in the world," grumbled the fuzzy-wigged Scot, "he's also the luckiest."

On both counts, Monty couldn't have been more right.

A series of foggy interruptions made a mess out of that afternoon and the following morning for everyone who wasn't back at the room watching television with his feet up, savoring a 65.

"Look, Jackson," Nicklaus said to his caddie, son Jackie, "we're playing in a cloud."

Not knowing how long the first delay would last, the Nicklauses passed the thickest phase of the pea-souper on the practice green behind the first tee. Absentmindedly Jackie putted, or puttered, with a wedge. "Now all of my golf balls will have smiles on them," Jack complained mildly. "By the way, make sure we have more than three balls."

They laughed uproariously at the inside joke.

Once, before caddieing for his dad in a pro-am, second son Steve (always looking to lighten his load) emptied out all of the balls save one sleeve. During the round, two Nicklaus shots had already found water hazards when, inevitably, Jack stood in the eighteenth fairway considering a final lake.

"I think I can cut a three-wood over it," he said.

"Let's lay up, Dad," Steve said.

"Nah, I can get there."

"Please, Dad."

When finally Steve confessed that they were down to their last bullet, Jack laid up with gritted teeth.

Fijian Vijay Singh enjoyed that. He was on their side of the green, rehearsing putts even before going to the range to hit balls. His tee time was still a couple of hours away.

"Look at my new putting style," Singh said to Loren Roberts, the putting specialist. "[Paul] Azinger touted me on it. This is my second week trying it. I anchor the handle in my belly—Zinger sticks it right into his belly button—and then I just stand up and grip it and stroke it the normal way. For some reason, it doesn't feel like I'm using a longer club. And I'm making more putts."

Men open to putting with their bellies don't usually win the Masters, but Singh did just that two months earlier with a stately display of shot making, including a high, drawn second shot to the par-5 fifteenth green—water short and long—that belongs with the bravest shots ever struck. Els finished second by himself. Tiger was alone in fifth.

Before finally kicking off his forty-fourth Open (a record Tiger can't break before 2039), Nicklaus asked the tee announcer to remind the gallery that this group was to have included the defending champion, Payne Stewart, who died in a plane crash four months after winning the '99 U.S. Open at Pinehurst. Sentimentally, Nicklaus was moved into the defender's slot in the formation.

Once, Jack led the universe in tunnel vision. At his most efficient, he was only faintly aware of other people on the planet, let alone on the course. Every now and then he would remember there were other people on the property and favor them with an incredibly synthetic wink. In those days, when he stood over the ball (interminably), cannon shots couldn't crack his concentration. But now, as the announcer mentioned Stewart, Jack choked up. His drive almost missed Carmel.

Nicklaus shot a two-over-par 73 in the dragged-out first round. Twenty-year-old Sergio Garcia, who wore plus-fours in a lonely tribute to Payne, shot 75. All of the Spaniards had plotted to wear knickers, but at the last minute the others got cold ankles. Singh shot 70. John Daly shot . . . well, himself. Again.

The most unlikely thing that has ever happened in golf, and maybe in sports, was when a monstrously long-hitting stranger from Arkansas won the 1991 PGA Championship. Consider that Daly had to survive a regional playoff just to become the ninth alternate. Then, for a variety of serendipitous reasons, exactly nine players withdrew. The ninth was Nick Price, who would win two of the next three PGAs. Sue Price's water broke that Wednesday. If she had held out (that is, if Gregory Price had held out) for just a few hours more, Daly could not have made it from Memphis to Crooked Stick in Indianapolis. His second-wife-to-be drove the car while he slept in a beery backseat. Though John thought she was twenty-nine and single, she was actually thirty-nine and married. This represented a pretty good capsule of his grasp on things.

Daly made the tee time but had no practice round.

In perhaps the most crucial break of all, John inherited Price's caddie, Jeff (Squeaky) Medlin. Almost any other caddie would have argued for steering some conservative 3-irons into the narrowest fairways. Squeaky, named for the nearly supersonic pitch of his voice, had guts. Hole after hole, Medlin kept handing the driver to the guileless boy with the legionnaire's flap of yellow hair, saying simply, "Kill."

Subsequently, Daly added a British Open victory that was similarly far-fetched. As a result, before Tiger arrived, John seemed to have golf's entire gallery. He also drank most of the beer, smoked most of the cigarettes, and ate most of the M&Ms. He lost a lot of money in casinos, married a lot of women in haste, beat up a lot of furniture in hotel rooms, and made a lot of choices that just missed being right.

For instance, stepping onto a tee box one time at the Bob Hope Chrysler Classic, Daly came upon four blondes in bulging T-shirts. The first T-shirt read "Bob," the second read "Hope," the third read "Chrysler," and the fourth read "Classic." Turning his back on "Hope," he married "Classic." She was his third wife, but not his last.

Coming to the eighteenth hole of the first round at Pebble, Daly was three over par but okay. He blocked his first drive out of bounds to the right. The next two he snap-hooked left into the Pacific Ocean. With his seventh stroke, he finally put an iron shot into play, laid up with his eighth, flew his ninth onto the rocks, took a penalty drop beside the seawall, fluffed his eleventh left-handed, and blasted his twelfth onto the green. He two-putted for a 14 on the hole and an 83 on the round. Saying only "Get me to the airport fast," he withdrew from the tournament. Unlike Hogan, he didn't care to play it out.

At Pinehurst the year before, Daly shot 83 with an 11 that included a two-stroke penalty for swatting a ball that was still moving. As a matter of fact, it was rolling full speed, straight back to him after dripping off one of Pinehurst's inverted-saucer greens. At Congressional in 1997, without a word to playing partners Els and Stewart, Daly walked off after nine holes on Friday. At first they thought he might have gone to the bathroom. Tying and untying their shoelaces, they did everything they could think of to keep from hitting their second shots at ten and automatically disqualifying him. Eventually Els and Stewart got the word from a caddie running over a hill: John was gone. The rest of the day, their twosome poked along maddeningly in a sea of threesomes.

When they came in, I invited Els, the eventual winner, to vent some righteous anger at Daly.

"He's my friend," Ernie said. "I love John. He breaks my heart."

Due to a second morning of fog and a long day of catching up, Tiger didn't resume work until late Friday afternoon.

He was on the practice putting green, five minutes from teeing off, when a giant roar went up at eighteen. "Jack is due to finish any time now," Woods told Butch Harmon, who called out to a headset-wearing TV technician nearby: "Who is it?"

The man shouted back: "It's Jack!"

The best hole at Pebble Beach is the par-4 eighth, which plays a little like two par-3s. First, there's a half-blind tee shot to the edge of a cliff. The drive better not travel more than 240 yards. Then there's a wide-eyed

180- or 190-yard second shot over the cliff, the drop, the surf, the beach, the opposite cliff, a stretch of grass, and a bowl of sand to the green.

A persistent Pebble Beach legend has it that two unobservant Japanese gentlemen drove their cart blissfully down the middle of the eighth fairway and straight off the cliff to their deaths. Even a midair epithet, more Anglo-Saxon than Japanese, has somehow been preserved. But, after researching all of this thoroughly, head pro R. J. Harper found no corpses at the foot of any of the bluffs, just one rather badly barked casualty.

"There was a fellow once at the eighth," Harper said, "who, leaning over the cliff to retrieve his ball, saw another one just a few inches down. Holding on to a twig with one hand, he reached for the second ball and fell a hundred and fifty feet. He only broke an arm and a leg."

Cutting a 3-wood into a breeze, expecting the wind to hold it up, Nicklaus hit the ball a touch too well and rolled it about a yard over the edge. Jack was just getting ready to step down like a flamingo to chip backward onto the fairway when, in an embarrassed voice, Jackie said, "Dad, you're chipping it to a spot where you can drop it anyway for the same stroke penalty."

"Thank you" was all Nicklaus said, clambering back up. But what he was thinking was: *Fried. Your brain is fried.*

Next, Jack hit a lovely 7-iron about twenty feet short of the hole. But, as if it had struck pavement, the ball clicked hard and bounced over the green. "And so I pitch the prettiest little fluff shot you've ever seen," he said later, "and it lands right on the seam between the fringe and the collar and squirts all the way to the front of the green. My favorite hole. I hit three shots as good as I can. And I made double bogey. Somebody was trying to tell me something."

After that, surviving the cut was out of the question. Nicklaus came to the par-5 eighteenth (where Daly used four drives) knowing this was his U.S. Open valedictory.

"When was the last time I even *tried* to knock it on this green in two?" he asked Jackie. "I'll bet it's been twenty years. Let's see if we can do it today."

Instead of the 3-wood he usually elected when playing eighteen as a three-shot hole, Nicklaus took a driver and crashed the ball with all his muscle down the middle. By Jackie's calculations, they had 238 yards left to the front of the green and 261 to the flag. Jack hit a 3-wood. When the ball bounded through the opening in front of the green and rolled up onto the putting surface in two, that was the sound Tiger heard.

Only eleven holes of daylight were left for Woods, who birdied three, bogeyed five, birdied seven, and bogeyed nine, but turned the corner in a hurry and birdied ten and eleven to stand nine under par after twenty-nine holes with only the Mechanic (six under) anywhere in the neighborhood.

The third round resumed at the crack of Saturday, at an hour you might think too early for televised golf, but not when Tiger Woods is involved. When he reached eighteen, Woods wheeled his drive straight left into the ocean and, unaware or at least unmindful of a boom mike on the tee, called out to the Heavenly Father with a blast of self-criticism. The broadcast went still. Admittedly, jerking one's golf ball into the sea isn't all that different from hammering one's thumbnail into plywood. But, as outbursts go, this one went way past spectacular. Texas philosopher Dan Jenkins immediately renamed the tournament "the Goddamn You Fucking Prick Open."

Saturday afternoon, in a major-league wind, sixteen players couldn't break 80, among them Singh and Garcia. Despite a triple bogey at three, Tiger shot an even-par 71, the second-best score of the day. Only Els broke par. For his 68, Ernie was rewarded with a standing-room ticket right beside Woods at Sunday's coronation, a full ten strokes behind. Hugging his wife, Liezl, Els whispered the best news into her ear: "I took fifty bucks off Monty."

"No bogeys today," Tiger informed caddie Steve Williams the following morning. That was their single ambition.

Patiently, surgically, Tiger parred the first nine holes. "All week," he said later, "I made important par putts, those big par putts. You have to make them in the U.S. Open. When you make those eight- or ten-footers for par, they feel better than birdies."

At the second and third holes, he left his birdie putts hanging on the lip and actually smiled. Throughout the opening nine, Tiger hit 4- and 3- and 2-irons off most of the tees. Els nodded. Then, at ten, Tiger slammed a sensational driver, wedged to fifteen feet, and made his first birdie. "If that's not perfect, I don't know what is," Ernie said. "He never got ahead of himself. Just the perfect display of golf. If you want to watch a guy win the U.S. Open playing perfectly, you've just seen it."

The test of the no-bogeys pledge came at the sixteenth hole, a par 4. Tiger hit a 3-iron off the tee into the first cut of rough, caught a flying lie and overshot the green. Being careful with a dangerous pitch, he left himself a fifteen-footer for par and studied it as if it meant the kingdom. ("When I make this putt," Nicklaus used to say.)

Tiger made it. No bogeys today. And no three-putts for the week. A 67.

At eighteen, while Els was playing up, Woods and Williams walked over to the seawall and looked out at the pounding waves. Two days earlier, calculatedly, Nicklaus had taken his own moment with the ocean. Jack knew somebody would snap a picture of him looking out at the sea, and he wanted a photo of the occasion. There are pictures of Woods and Williams, too, but Tiger never thought of that.

"I told Stevie, 'There comes a point in time when you feel tranquil, when you feel calm.' I felt very at ease with myself this week. And for some reason, things just flowed. I'm not going to win every tournament that I play in. But I'm going to try. I'm going to try to get better."

Els, who shared second place with the Mechanic, said, "I really had a good time playing with Tiger today and watching the way he won. I don't know what more there is to be said about him. Anything I say is probably going to be an understatement. It seems like we're not playing in the same ballpark right now." Having also been second to Singh at the Masters, Ernie was halfway to the Bridesmaid Slam. Otherwise, Tiger, Jimenez, and Huston finished in just the order they had started. Els was the only Thursday afternoon and Friday morning survivor left on the front page.

"If I had been luckier with the draw and had played out of my mind," Ernie said, "I probably still would have lost by five, six, or seven. We've been talking about him for the last two years. I guess we'll be talking about him for the next twenty. When he's on, we don't have much of a chance."

Twelve under par, Woods won by fifteen strokes.

"I feel sorry for the younger guys," forty-three-year-old Nick Price said. "Basically, I've had my day."

Willie Anderson (1903) and Long Jim Barnes (1921) were among the older ghosts who had to give up their positions in the U.S. Open record book. Willie Smith's extended run as the champion with the largest winning margin ended at 101 years. But the all-time majors mark that fell with the loudest crash was the one that belonged to Old Tom Morris, golf's first father. For 138 years, a thirteen-stroke margin had been the widest in any major, but no more. Tiger was starting to go after Old Tom Morris.

"I had a wonderful week, a great week, actually," Woods said, "but I can't really tell you, historically, what it means. I'll probably have a better understanding when I'm sixty years old."

Incidentally, the only sixty-year-old in the field three-putted his final U.S. Open hole for par.

"Well, I'll tell you one thing," Els said, "we were playing a different game than I guess Old Tom Morris did back in the 1700s or whatever [1800s]. If you put Old Tom Morris with Tiger Woods, Tiger'd probably beat him by eighty shots right now."

That could be. But what about Young Tom?

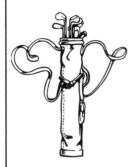

Author, Author: Did Tillinghast Really Design Bethpage Black?

by Charles McGrath, *The New York Times*, June 14, 2009

Who really designed Bethpage Black, the site of this year's United States Open, which begins on Thursday? In most golfing circles, it's practically sacred writ that the course, which opened in 1936, is the last, and possibly greatest, achievement of A. W. Tillinghast, who also designed such New York–area masterpieces as Winged Foot, Baltusrol, Ridgewood and Quaker Ridge. But in 2002, Ron Whitten, a columnist for *Golf Digest*, argued that Bethpage Black was actually the work of Joseph Burbeck, the superintendent of Bethpage State Park during its construction, and in the June issue of *Golf Digest* he repeats the claim.

For Tillinghast fans, who tend to be passionate in their devotion, this is a little like arguing that Shakespeare didn't write *The Tempest*, and the debate, waged on golf blogs and in salvos of essays, has taken on some of the characteristics of the feud between the Stratfordians, who believe in the Bard of Avon, and the Oxfordians, who insist the Earl of Oxford wrote the plays.

In this case, the key evidence for the Oxford side is that Tillinghast's contract called for him to work as a consultant, not an architect, for just 15 days; that the work of laying out three new courses at Bethpage (a fourth was already there) had begun under Burbeck before Tillinghast came on board; and that Tillinghast later credited Burbeck with the idea of creating Bethpage Black as a kind of municipal Mecca, a rival to Pine Valley.

The Stratfordians, of whom the most knowledgeable and eloquent is probably Tillinghast's biographer, Philip Young, believe that Tilly, as he was known, was on the site for longer than the contract stipulated, and that the only reason he wasn't officially in charge of day-to-day operations was that Bethpage was built by an army of W.P.A. workers, and not, as was customary, by his own construction company.

"I don't argue that Tillinghast wasn't involved," Whitten said on Monday. "But I think Burbeck deserves credit as the architect of record, with Tillinghast as a consultant." He added: "I'm basing it on facts. Those who love Tillinghast are arguing from emotion. They don't want their man sharing credit with anyone."

Frank Hannigan, the former head of the United States Golf Association, said that even now it's sometimes hard to tell who's responsible for what on a golf course. "In truth, there are a lot of famous builders, including some professional golfers, who probably don't do as much as Tillinghast did," he said.

Just like Shakespeare scholars, the golf Stratfordians appeal to what might be called textual evidence. Some argue that Bethpage is a masterwork, unlikely to have been created by a novice. Most point to the way many of the holes at Bethpage echo others Tillinghast designed or illustrate his design principles.

This is somewhat subjective ground because everyone agrees that unlike Donald Ross, famous for his domed greens, or C. B. Macdonald, who tended to reproduce his favorite holes on all his courses, Tillinghast had no signature style. He would build deep bunkers on one course, flatter ones on another. His greens were sometimes deeply contoured, as at Winged Foot, and sometimes not. ("A putting green has features just like a human," he wrote. "There are some with rugged profiles which loom head and shoulders above the common herd.")

He let the terrain shape his courses and was one of the first to introduce the principles of landscape architecture into course design. He thought holes should be visually appealing as well as challenging to play, and once wrote: "A round of golf should provide 18 inspirations, not necessarily thrills, because spectacular holes may be sadly overdone. . . . When I speak of a hole being inspiring, it is not intended that the visitor be subject to attacks of hysteria on every teeing ground."

Nevertheless, his fans have identified a number of features at Bethpage that seem to them quintessentially Tillinghast: the oval-shaped greens that often tilt from back to front, the upswept bunkers that flash right up to the greenside and the way the holes tend to be more easily approached from one side of the fairway than the other.

Young, the biographer, contends that the par-5 fourth hole, one of Bethpage's standouts, particularly displays the hand of the master, Tillinghast. "If you stand on the fourth tee and look to the left," he said recently, "you see a long natural valley where 90 percent of architects would have built the next hole. It was Tilly who saw that you could route the hole from one plateau to another plateau and have the green on a cliff edge. It became a memorable work of art."

No one denies that Bethpage is a great course in a league even with Pine Valley, whose landscape it somewhat resembles, and, like most golf courses, it has evolved and been modified over the years. Rees Jones gave the Black, then sadly overgrown, more than a makeover to ready it for the 2002 United States Open, the first time an Open had been played on a public course; he breathed new life into it and probably deserves equal billing.

Who originally designed the course hardly matters except on sentimental grounds, and here the Stratfordians have an edge, because unlike the self-effacing Burbeck, who if he did design Bethpage never claimed credit, Tillinghast was one of the most vivid and flamboyant characters in golf history. He was a sort of mad genius, who along with his friends Hugh Wilson, who designed Merion in Pennsylvania, and the obsessive George Crump, who built Pine Valley in southern New Jersey, belonged to that gilded generation of American course architects who were completely self-taught and yet built courses that have never been equaled.

Most surviving photos of Tillinghast show him with a walruslike soup-strainer of a mustache; in his heyday it was waxed and twirled to a point on each side. He was a rakish high-liver: a drinker, a gambler, a backer of failed Broadway musicals. He arrived at the golf course in a chauffeur-driven limousine and wearing a three-piece suit or even a tuxedo if he had been out too late the night before. He sometimes carried a flask with him, and laborers out on the course used to swear they could smell his "exhaust."

Young said Tillinghast was probably bipolar. There were despondencies, pistol-waving rages and at least one suicide attempt. But when he wasn't disappearing on benders, he was a bundle of brilliance and entrepreneurial energy. When he was down on his luck, he built a miniature golf course and lighted driving range near his home in New Jersey. He also had a short-lived plan for an indoor miniature golf course on West 40th Street in New York that was really a front for a speakeasy. He was a pioneering golf photographer and an even better golf writer, who for years had a column in *Golf Illustrated* and also wrote two collections of golf fiction that in some ways anticipate P. G. Wodehouse.

Until he was in his 30s, though, it didn't look as if Tillinghast would amount to much. Born in Philadelphia in 1875, he was the pampered, rebellious son of Benjamin Collins Tillinghast, who made a fortune in the rubber business. His company sold tires and also rubber suits for ministers who practiced full-immersion baptism. Tillinghast later bragged that he had never graduated from any of the many schools he attended because he either dropped out or was expelled. By the time he was in his late teens, he was a member of a wild, hard-drinking set of young Philadelphia rakes known as the Kelly Street gang, which might have been the model for the upper-class swells in the 1939 novel *Kitty Foyle*.

Golf saved him. He was introduced to the game by his father, and took it up seriously in 1895 during the first of several visits to Scotland, when he befriended Old Tom Morris, the legendary player and course builder. In 1906, a friend, Charles Worthington, asked Tillinghast, then 31 and perpetually unemployed, to build a course on some land he owned in Shawnee, Pa. Except for a little nine-holer he had laid out near his home, using canned-fruit tins for holes, he had no experience, and yet the new course was so successful that other commissions followed and he was soon greatly in demand.

In the late 1910s and the 1920s, he traveled all over, building and remodeling courses as far away as Texas and San Francisco, and leaving his mark at Baltusrol and Winged Foot and more than 60 other tournament-quality courses. During the Depression, though, the golf course business dried up. The Bethpage commission was both a godsend, even though the fee, $50 a day, was far less than he was accustomed to, and a last hurrah. In 1937, after declaring himself disgusted with the golf course business, Tillinghast moved to Beverly Hills, Calif., where he went into the antiques business, probably selling off his own furniture. He died, broke, in 1942.

Joseph Burbeck died in 1987 but remained at Bethpage long enough to oversee the addition of a fifth course in 1958. The architect Alfred Tull was hired as a consultant, but Burbeck's son said his father drew all the plans himself.

Appendix A

The History

1895

The first U.S. Open Championship is held on October 4 in Newport, Rhode Island. In the one-day, thirty-six-hole event, eleven players compete for prize money of $335. Winner Howard Rawlins receives $150 and a gold medal.

1898

The Open becomes a seventy-two-hole tournament, held over three days, with the last thirty-six holes played on the final day. This remains the tournament format until 1965.

1903

Willie Anderson wins the first of three consecutive U.S. Open titles, an achievement that has never since been equaled.

1907

Jack Hobens records the first hole in one at the U.S. Open.

1911

Breaking a sixteen-year winning streak by British golfers, John J. McDermott becomes the first U.S.-born player to win the Open.

1913

In a thrilling playoff performance, unknown twenty-year-old American amateur Francis Ouimet defeats legendary British professionals Harry Vardon and Ted Ray. He is the first amateur player to lift the title.

1922

Spectator tickets are sold for the first time.

1924

Due to a boom in entries, the USGA introduces sectional qualifying rounds.

1933

John Goodman becomes the fifth and final amateur player to win the Open.

1942

Official USGA events are canceled due to World War II. In place of the U.S. Open, top golfers compete in the Hale America National Open, a charity event for the Navy Relief Fund. Ben Hogan emerges as the winner, helped along by a dazzling second-round 62.

1950

When a Greyhound bus collides with Ben Hogan's car in 1949, the golfer's body is so badly shattered that his doctors say he may never walk again, let alone play competitive golf. Proving them wrong, Hogan wins a three-way playoff with Lloyd Mangrum and George Fazio just sixteen months later to capture his second U.S. Open title.

1954

The U.S. Open is covered on national television for the first time.

1960

Starting the day in fifteenth place, seven strokes off the lead, Arnold Palmer records one of the greatest comebacks in golfing history when he scores a thrilling final-round 64 to win the championship by two strokes.

1962

Jack Nicklaus, still in the first season of his professional career, captures the U.S. Open by defeating Arnold Palmer in a playoff. It is Nicklaus's first major title, and he is the youngest champion since Robert T. Jones in 1923.

1965

The U.S. Open moves to a four-day format, with eighteen holes played each day.

1970

Ending a forty-five-year drought for European golfers, Englishman Tony Jacklin leads the Open from start to finish to win by seven strokes.

1977

ABC Sports broadcasts the final two rounds live on television.

1982

ESPN broadcasts the first two rounds live for the first time.

1990

The crowd erupts with delight when Hale Irwin sinks a forty-five-foot birdie on the eighteenth hole to force a playoff with Mike Donald. After a gripping sudden-death finish, the forty-five-year-old becomes the oldest ever U.S. Open champion.

1991

Payne Stewart clinches his second U.S. Open title with a marvelous twenty-foot par putt at the eighteenth. He tragically dies four months later in a plane crash, aged forty-two.

2000

In capturing his first U.S. Open, Tiger Woods becomes the first player in the tournament's history to finish seventy-two holes at double digits under par. His winning margin of fifteen strokes is the largest ever in a major championship.

2004

Challenging the dominance of U.S. golfers, the Southern Hemisphere produces four consecutive winners from 2004 to 2007. South African Retief Goosen wins in 2004; he is followed by New Zealander Michael Campbell in 2005, Australian Geoff Ogilvy in 2006, and Argentinean Ángel Cabrera in 2007.

2005

Bethpage State Park's Black Course in Farmingdale, New York, becomes the first publicly owned course to host the U.S. Open.

2006

Needing just a par to win the tournament, Phil Mickelson makes a disastrous double-bogey on the eighteenth at Winged Foot, handing the title to Geoff Ogilvy. The disappointment is only compounded three years later, when Mickelson becomes tournament runner-up for a record fifth time.

2008

Aiming to become the first European winner since fellow Englishman Tony Jacklin in 1970, Lee Westwood rules himself out of the playoff when he narrowly misses a birdie putt on the final hole. Rocco Mediate takes on Tiger Woods in an epic tussle that culminates in a dramatic sudden-death victory for Woods.

Appendix B

The Champions

Year	Champion	Score	Margin
1895	Horace Rawlins	173	+2
1896	James Foulis	152	+3
1897	Joe Lloyd	162	+1
1898	Fred Herd	328	+7
1899	Willie Smith	315	+11
1900	Harry Vardon	313	+2
1901	Willie Anderson	331	PO
1902	Laurence Auchterlonie	307	+6
1903	Willie Anderson	307	PO
1904	Willie Anderson	303	+5
1905	Willie Anderson	314	+2
1906	Alex Smith	295	+7
1907	Alex Ross	302	+2
1908	Fred McLeod	322	PO
1909	George Sargent	290	+4
1910	Alex Smith	298	PO
1911	John J. McDermott	307	PO
1912	John J. McDermott	294	+2
1913	Francis Ouimet	304	PO
1914	Walter Hagen	290	+1
1915	Jerome D. Travers	297	+1
1916	Charles Evans Jr.	286	+2

1917–18	Tournament canceled due to World War I		
1919	Walter Hagen	301	+1
1920	Edward Ray	295	+1
1921	James M. Barnes	289	+9
1922	Gene Sarazen	288	+1
1923	Robert T. Jones Jr.	296	PO
1924	Cyril Walker	297	+3
1925	William Macfarlane	291	PO
1926	Robert T. Jones Jr.	293	+1
1927	Tommy Armour	301	PO
1928	Johnny Farrell	294	PO
1929	Robert T. Jones Jr.	294	PO
1930	Robert T. Jones Jr.	287	+2
1931	Billy Burke	292	PO
1932	Gene Sarazen	286	+3
1933	John Goodman	287	+1
1934	Olin Dutra	293	+1
1935	Sam Parks Jr.	299	+2
1936	Tony Manero	282	+2
1937	Ralph Guldahl	281	+2
1938	Ralph Guldahl	284	+6
1939	Byron Nelson	284	PO
1940	Lawson Little	287	PO
1941	Craig Wood	284	+3
1942–45	Tournament canceled due to World War II		
1946	Lloyd Mangrum	284	PO
1947	Lew Worsham	282	PO
1948	Ben Hogan	276	+2
1949	Cary Middlecoff	286	+1
1950	Ben Hogan	287	PO
1951	Ben Hogan	287	+2

1952	Julius Boros	281	+4
1953	Ben Hogan	283	+6
1954	Ed Furgal	284	+1
1955	Jack Fleck	287	PO
1956	Cary Middlecoff	281	+1
1957	Dick Mayer	282	PO
1958	Tommy Bolt	283	+4
1959	Bill Casper Jr.	282	+1
1960	Arnold Palmer	280	+2
1961	Gene Littler	281	+1
1962	Jack Nicklaus	283	PO
1963	Julius Boros	293	PO
1964	Ken Venturi	278	+4
1965	Gary Player	282	PO
1966	Bill Casper Jr.	278	PO
1967	Jack Nicklaus	275	+4
1968	Lee Trevino	275	+4
1969	Orville Moody	281	+1
1970	Tony Jacklin	281	+7
1971	Lee Trevino	280	PO
1972	Jack Nicklaus	290	+3
1973	John Miller	279	+1
1974	Hale Irwin	287	+2
1975	Lou Graham	287	PO
1976	Jerry Pate	277	+2
1977	Hubert Green	278	+1
1978	Andy North	285	+1
1979	Hale Irwin	284	+2
1980	Jack Nicklaus	272	+2
1981	David Graham	273	+3
1982	Tom Watson	282	+2

1983	Larry Nelson	280	+1
1984	Fuzzy Zoeller	276	PO
1985	Andy North	279	+1
1986	Raymond Floyd	279	+2
1987	Scott Simpson	277	+1
1988	Curtis Strange	278	PO
1989	Curtis Strange	278	+1
1990	Hale Irwin	280	PO
1991	Payne Stewart	282	PO
1992	Tom Kite	285	+2
1993	Lee Janzen	272	+2
1994	Ernie Els	285	PO
1995	Corey Pavin	280	+2
1996	Steve Jones	278	+1
1997	Ernie Els	276	+1
1998	Lee Janzen	280	+1
1999	Payne Stewart	279	+1
2000	Tiger Woods	272	+15
2001	Retief Goosen	276	PO
2002	Tiger Woods	277	+3
2003	Jim Furyk	272	+3
2004	Retief Goosen	276	+2
2005	Michael Campbell	280	+2
2006	Geoff Ogilvy	285	+1
2007	Ángel Cabrera	285	+1
2008	Tiger Woods	283	PO
2009	Lucas Glover	276	+2

Appendix C

The Records

Most Victories: Willie Anderson, 4 (1901, 1903, 1904, 1905); Robert T. Jones Jr., 4 (1923, 1926, 1929, 1930); Ben Hogan, 4 (1948, 1950, 1951, 1953); Jack Nicklaus, 4 (1962, 1967, 1972, 1980)

Most Victories by an Amateur Player: Robert T. Jones Jr., 4 (1923, 1926, 1929, 1930)

Widest Margin of Victory: Tiger Woods, 15 strokes (2000)

Lowest Winning Score: Jack Nicklaus, 272 (1980); Lee Janzen, 272 (1993); Tiger Woods, 272 (2000); Jim Furyk, 272 (2003)

Highest Winning Score: Willie Anderson, 331 (1901)

Lowest 72-Hole Score by an Amateur Player: Jack Nicklaus, 282 (1960)

Longest Course: Torrey Pines Golf Club, San Diego, CA, 7,643 yards (2008)

Shortest Course (since World War II): Merion Golf Club (East Course), Ardmore, PA, 6,528 yards (1971, 1981)

Youngest Champion: John J. McDermott, 19 years 10 months 14 days (1911)

Oldest Champion: Hale Irwin, 45 years 0 months 15 days (1990)

Fewest Attempts Before First Victory: Horace Rawlins, 1 (1895); Fred Herd, 1 (1898); Harry Vardon, 1 (1900); George Sargent, 1 (1909); Francis Ouimet, 1 (1913)

Longest Span Between Victories: Julius Boros, 11 years, 1952–63; Hale Irwin, 11 years, 1979–90

Most Consecutive Opens Started: Jack Nicklaus, 44 (1957–2000)

Most Consecutive Wins: Willie Anderson, 3 (1903, 1904, 1905)

Most Times Runner-Up: Phil Mickelson, 5 (1999, 2002, 2004, 2006, 2009)

Number of Non–U.S.-Born Winners: 23 players (29 championships)

Number of Playoffs: 32

Number of Holes in One: 39

Credits

Opening the Open

"Open-Minded Geniuses"
Reprinted with the permission of the author,
Frank Hannigan. All rights reserved. Originally
published in *Golf Digest*.

"The Men of the USGA"
From THE MAJORS by JOHN
FEINSTEIN. Copyright © 1999 by John
Feinstein. By permission of LITTLE,
BROWN & COMPANY.

"'Massacre at Winged Foot'
Vivid 32 Years Later"
Reprinted with the permission of the
Oakland Tribune.

The Prewar Era

"Horace Rawlins Champion"
The New York Times, June 6, 1895

"Tie for Golf Honors"
The New York Times, June 28, 1911

"Three Tie in National Golf"
The New York Times, June 25, 1911

"McDermott's Golf Title"
The New York Times, June 27, 1911

"The Open Championship of 1913"
From A GAME OF GOLF by Francis
Ouimet. Reprinted with the permission of the
Francis Ouimet Caddie Scholarship Fund.

"Champion, 1914"
Reprinted with the permission of Simon
and Schuster, Inc. from THE WALTER
HAGEN STORY by Walter Hagen, as
told to Margaret Seaton Heck.
Copyright © 1956 by Walter Hagen.

"Long Thoughts About Inverness and Vardon"
From FOLLOWING THROUGH:
HERBERT WARREN WIND ON GOLF by
Herbert Warren Wind. Published by Ticknor
& Fields, 1985. Reprinted by permission of the
Herbert Warren Wind estate.

"Golf's Greatest Putt"
By Grantland Rice. Reprinted with the
permission of the author's estate. All rights
reserved. Originally published in *Sports
Illustrated*.

"Bobby Jones, Interlachen"
From TRIUMPHANT JOURNEY: THE
SAGA OF BOBBY JONES AND THE
GRAND SLAM OF GOLF by Dick Miller,
published by Holt, Rinehart and Winston,
1980. Reprinted by permission of Dick Miller.

"Bobby Jones—The Gentleman from Georgia"
THE MARVELOUS MANIA: ALISTAIR
COOKE ON GOLF. Reprinted by permission
of the Estate of Alistair Cooke, copyright
reserved.

"Reading and Some Major Wins"
From HOW I PLAYED THE GAME by
Byron Nelson. Reprinted by permission of The
Rowman & Littlefield Publishing Group. All
rights reserved.

Index